Cuba

Cuba

Island of Dreams

by
Antoni Kapcia

BERG

Oxford • New York

First published in 2000 by
Berg
Editorial offices:
150 Cowley Road, Oxford, OX4 1JJ, UK
838 Broadway, Third Floor, New York, NY 10003-4812, USA

Berg is an imprint of Oxford International Publishers Ltd.

Library of Congress Cataloging-in-Publication Data
A catalogue record for this book is available from the Library of Congress.

British Library Cataloguing-in-Publication Data
A catalogue record for this book is available from the British Library.

ISBN 1 85973 326 3 (Cloth)
1 85973 331 X (Paper)

Typeset by JS Typesetting, Wellingborough, Northants.

Contents

Glossary of Abbreviations

(this list refers to those abbreviations that are used more than once in the text, since all abbreviations have been explained and translated on the first occasion)

AIE — *Ala Izquierda Estudiantil* (Student Left Wing)

AJR — *Asociación de Jóvenes Rebeldes* (Association of Rebel Youth)

ANAP — *Asociación Nacional de Agricultores Pequeños* (National Association of Small Farmers)

ARG — *Acción Revolucionaria Guiteras* (Guiteras Revolutionary Action)

CDR — *Comité de Defensa de la Revolución* (Committee for the Defence of the Revolution)

CNOC — *Confederación Nacional de Obreros de Cuba* (National Confederation of Cuban Workers)

CTC — (1939–1961) *Confederación de Trabajadores de Cuba* (Confederation of Cuban Workers)
(1961–) *Central de Trabajadaores de Cuba* (Confederation of Cuban Workers)

DEU — *Directorio Estudiantil Universitario* (University Student Directorate)

DRE (or DR) — *Directorio Revolucionario Estudiantil* (Revolutionary (Student) Directorate)

EIR — *Escuelas de Instrucción Revolucionaria* (Schools of Revolutionary Instruction)

EJT — *Ejército Juvenil de Trabajo* (Youth Labour Army)

FAR — *Fuerzas Armadas Revolucionarias* (Revolutionary Armed Forces)

FEU — (pre-1959) *Federación Estudiantil Universitaria* (University Student Federation)
(post-1959) *Federación de Estudiantes Universitarios* (Federation of University Students)

FMC — *Federación de Mujeres Cubanas* (Federation of Cuban Women)

FOH — *Federación Obrera de La Habana* (Workers, Federation of Havana)

INRA — *Instituto Nacional de Reforma Agraria* (National Institute of Agrarian Reform)

JS — *Juventud Socialista* (Socialist Youth)

MININT — *Ministerio del Interior* (Ministry of the Interior)

MNR	(1952–3) *Movimiento Nacionalista Revolucionario* (Revolutionary Nationalist Movement)
	(1960s) *Milicias Nacionales Revolucionarias* (Revolutionary National Militias)
MSR	*Movimiento Socialista Revolucionario* (Revolutionary Socialist Movement)
MTT	*Milicias de Tropas Territoriales* (Territorial Militias)
OAS	Organization of American States
OCRR	*Organización Celular Radical Revolucionaria* (Revolutionary Radical Cellular Organization)
OPP	*Organos de Poder Popular* (Organs of Popular Power)
ORCA	*Organización Revolucionaria Cubana Antimperialista* (Anti-imperialist Cuban Revolutionary Organization)
ORI	*Organizaciones Revolucionarias Integradas* (Integrated Revolutionary Organizations)
PAC	*Partido Aprista Cubano* (Cuban Aprista Party)
PCC	*Partido Comunista de Cuba* (Cuban Communist Party)
PIC	*Partido Independiente de Color* (Independent Coloured Party)
PPC	*Partido del Pueblo Cubano* (Cuban People's Party) – the *Ortodoxos*
PRC	*Partido Revolucionario Cubano* (Cuban Revolutionary Party)
PRC-A	*Partido Revolucionario Cubano Auténtico* (Authentic Cuban Revolutionary Party)
PSP	*Partido Socialista Popular* (Popular Socialist Party)
PURSC	*Partido Unido de la Revolución Socialista de Cuba* (United Party of the Cuban Socialist Revolution)
SDPE	*Sistema de Dirección y Planificación de la Economía* (Economic Management and Planning System)
UBPC	*Unidades Básicas de Producción y Cooperación* (Basic Units of Production and Cooperation)
UIR	*Unión Insurreccional Revolucionaria* (Revolutionary Insurrectionary Union)
UJC	*Unión de Jóvenes Comunistas* (Union of Communist Youth)
UMAP	*Unidad Militar de Ayuda a la Producción* (Military Units to Aid Production)
UNEAC	*Unión de Escritores y Artistas de Cuba* (Cuban Union of Writers and Artists)

Glossary of Spanish Terms

(the following terms are those important ones used on more than one occasion in the text, whose meaning is not obvious from similarity with English; all Spanish terms used are translated on the first occasion of their use)

ajíaco	– Cuban stew
anexionismo	– annexationism (policy of annexation of Cuba by the United States)
Apóstol	– Apostle (used of José Martí)
auténtico	– member of the PRC-A party
barbudo	– literally 'bearded' (used to describe the 26 July guerrillas)
balsero	– rafter (term for 'boat people' of the August 1994 exodus)
barrio	– (city) district
batistato	– period of Batista's dictatorship
batistazo	– Batista's coup (1952)
bonches	– armed (student) gangs (1930s and 1940s) (also *bonchismo*)
burocratismo	– bureaucratism
campo	– countryside (*campesino*: Peasant)
caso	– affair (e.g. *caso Padilla*)
caudillo	– 'political leader', or 'political boss'
central	– sugar mill (industrial)
choteo	– literally 'ridicule', but used of the tradition of national self-deprecation
cincuentenario	– fiftieth anniversary
colono	– sugar-grower (*colonato*: class of *colonos*)
comandante	– literally 'major', but used as the officer rank among the guerrillas
comercio libre	– literally 'free trade', but used of the limited Bourbon reform
compañero	– colleague or companion, but also in the sense of 'comrade'

costumbrismo	– particular type of realist literature idealizing rural customs
criollo	– colonial-born white person (*criollismo*: belief in *criollo* identity)
criterio	– opinion, belief
cuenta propia	– self-employment (*cuentapropista*: a self-employed person)
dignidad	– dignity
desarrollo	– development (*hacia dentro*: inward; *hacia fuera*: outward)
doce (*los Doce*)	– twelve ('the Twelve')
estado	– state
eticidad	– morality
granja del pueblo	– state farm (literally 'people's farm')
grito	– literally 'shout', but meaning declaration (e.g. *Grito de Yara*)
guajiro	– peasant, countryman
guardia	– (CDR) guard duty
guerrillero	– guerrilla, warrior (*guerrillerismo*: guerrilla ethos)
gusano	– literally 'worm' (used pejoratively of the émigrés)
idiosincracia	– the (unique) national characteristics
independentista	– believing in independence
ingenio	– (traditional) sugar mill
lectura	– reading ('public reading' in the traditional tobacco industry)
libre mercado campesino	– free peasant market
llano	– literally 'the plain', but used to define the urban underground in 1953–8
lucha	– struggle
machadato	– the Machado dictatorship
mambí	– the rebel fighter of the 1868–78 and 1895–8 wars (pl. *mambises*)
mambisado	– term used for the veterans of the wars in post-1902 politics
mestizo	– mixed-race (normally Spanish and indigenous)
microbrigadas	– small volunteer construction brigades
miliciano	– member of the militias
mulato	– mixed-race (normally Spanish and African)
municipio	– local government district
norte	– north (*Norte*: United States)

parlamento obrero	– workers' parliament (workplace consultative assembly)
patria	– homeland (*patria chica*: native region (literally 'little homeland'))
patronato	– the post-abolition arrangement for ensuring slave labour
peninsular	– Spanish-born white in colonial Latin America
pionero	– literally 'pioneer' (referring to youth organization after 1962)
pueblo	– people (*pueblo en armas*: people in arms; . . . *en marcha*: . . . on the march)
rendición de cuentas	– delegate feedback session (literally 'rendering of accounts')
sacarocracia	– sugar-growing oligarchy
santería	– Afro-Cuban religion
sectarismo	– sectarianism
seudorepública	– Pseudo-Republic
soberanía	– sovereignty
solidario	– *(adj.)* with an attitude of solidarity (*solidarismo*: the belief in solidarity)
vega	– tobacco field
zafra	– sugar harvest

Preface

To say that this book is a labour of love may be a cliché but is no exaggeration. It is, or has been, a labour because, from conception to birth, it has taken a great many years to be realized. Even though the actual format and specific theme of the study only emerged clearly in my mind a few years back, it is true to say that it is the culmination of all my study, writings and thinking since I first decided to specialize academically on Cuba, in 1971, when I embarked on my full-study for my Ph.D. in London. From that moment, my focus has followed a logical trajectory, from doctorate, through various new specializations and publications, to the idea of this book, which has been promised to friends and colleagues alike so often that most of them must have despaired of ever seeing it come to fruition. It has therefore been visibly, palpably and painfully a genuine labour.

It has also, however, been a love. For there can be few people who have decided to concentrate their academic or professional attention on Cuba who have not one way or another fallen in love with Cuba and with the Cubans in general. Apart from the evident attractions of the place and the people, it is difficult not to develop at least a degree of affection for the potentially exasperating and always bewildering contradictions of the island and its political process and system. I have observed (so often that they have become personal clichés) that Cuba always manages to surprise you, that no matter how much you may think you understand Cuba you are always likely to discover something unexpected, and that those who claim to understand the Revolution, probably do not, while those who admit to being confused by it, probably do already have some idea of what it is about fundamentally. Certainly, after 28 years of academic specialization in things Cuban, I am all too aware at times of how little I still really know and understand about the process of the Revolution.

Having said that, however, I would like to think that, just as Cuba has got under my skin in one sense over the years, I too have, in another way, got under Cuba's skin, got close to understanding what makes the Revolution tick, what motivates, preoccupies, and annoys Cubans in their daily lives, in their long and painful adaptation to the contradictions, the challenges and the delights of a process that has always demanded as much as it has given. It is therefore that same process that, at risk of being proved very wrong in making any sort of claim to understand it, I am seeking to help explain, whose complexities I am trying to unravel by putting on paper my thoughts about it all. Not that I have not done that already many times, but mostly those publications since 1974 have tended to focus on very specific aspects or on short and general overviews of the present situation or of periods of Cuban history. In a real sense, those publications were steps on the way towards a longer, more detailed and deeper exposition of my views, my thoughts and my understanding of Cuba, which in the end is this book.

What then is its purpose? Basically, it is to challenge, and help people go beyond, the stereotypes that have always abounded in much of the literature on Cuba and, as I observe in the Introduction, have always got in the way of a real understanding of the Revolution. Over the decades, too many casual observers (and not a few specialists) and far too many politicians have approached the Revolution with preconceptions born of the Cold War, of some familiarity with the Soviet Union or eastern Europe, or even of supposed Latin American traditions (of *caudillismo*, of authoritarianism or of personalism). Those preconceptions and stereotypes, while fully understandable and occasionally not without their merit and usefulness, simply do not get to the heart of the unique process of transformation that has existed in Cuba since 1959. I would hope that something of my close familiarity with Cuba, with so many Cubans and with studies of Cuba, would result in my being able to offer a perspective that goes some way towards dispelling that ignorance and revealing something of that 'heart'.

In this task, the book's subtitle – 'Island of Dreams' – suggested itself to me early on. Firstly, all Cuban history since the late eighteenth century can justifiably be seen as the trajectory of the pursuit of a 'dream' – of true independence (political, economic, social, cultural, intellectual or whatever). It has been a dream that, at certain low points, has become more dream-like ('dream' as illusion), as an imagined and even illusory reality, projected on to a possibly unattainable future and stored in a collective folk memory, but that has always remained as a shared vision ('dream' as envisaged future), to inspire, guide and protect. Secondly, the more I investigated the question of ideology (of *cubania* in its specific Cuban context) and the role of that ideology in all the four decades of revolution, including the survival through the 1990s crisis, the clearer it became that one thing that has sustained popular support, cemented unity, fortified collective resolve and rallied flagging commitment over the years has been the shared willingness to go on believing in, striving for and defending that 'dream'. By the 1990s, indeed, that shared dream had become complex, contradictory and many-layered, projecting backwards into a constantly extolled and thus palpable past on which the present had been built, stretching forward into the future, as ever, but also involving a determination to cling to elements of a more recent past, seen as the 'essence' of the Revolution, in the face of pressures, disillusion, collapse, challenge and simple ageing. Cuba was thus, to me, evidently a community in search of, defining itself by, and largely united behind a set of 'dreams' – which the present book seeks to 'interpret'.

I would therefore like to take this opportunity of extending much deserved thanks to a large number of people without whom I could not have made this progress over the years and produced this labour of love. In so doing, I shall inevitably omit, through oversight or through lack of space, a larger number of those whose advice I have sought, who have supported me in one way or another (through invitations to develop my ideas in conferences or lectures, through responses to my seminar papers, through opportunities to publish and so on), or who have simply had to tolerate my little academic obsession with Cuba.

In some sort of chronological order, my first thanks must go to the late Nissa Torrents, my doctoral tutor, who first directed my Cuban specialization and who opened several doors, as well as my eyes, in my academic path; she is still sorely missed by many of her friends and colleagues, but not least by me. Then I owe a great debt to Professor Alistair Hennessy, who, since the early 1980s, has given me such unstinting support, encouragement, opportunity and inspiration with his always perspicacious ideas. Then come the various Cubanists with whom I have worked closely since the mid-1980s – George Lambie, Francisco Domínguez, Jean Stubbs, Chris Abel – and the many other academic colleagues who have helped me in some way or other. Equally, I owe many thanks to the Cubans in the London Embassy who have smoothed many a path and offered many an opportunity to take my studies further, especially Roberto de Armas, formerly First Secretary, and the present Ambassador, Rodney López, and his wife, Lourdes Alicia Díaz.

Then, of course, there are the many Cubans in Cuba who have proved to be so supportive and inspirational in this work, foremost among whom must figure my friends Fernando Martínez Heredia, Rubén Zardoya Loureda and Jorge Ibarra Cuesta, but not forgetting the countless other colleagues from the University of Havana whose friendship, support and advice have at various points been invaluable – Armando Chávez, Emilio Duharte, Arnaldo Silva, Elena Díaz and Beatriz Díaz (of FLACSO-Cuba), the late Carmen Barandela, Carlos Galindo, and many others not from the University, notably Rafael Hernández, Pedro Pablo Rodríguez and Roberto Fernández Retamar. I must also extend my thanks to all those Cubans who allowed me to interview them over the years – Armando Hart Dávalos, the late Antonio Núñez Jiménez, Oscar Guzmán, Manuel Fernández Font, Oscar Pino Santos, Aleida March, Cintio Vitier, Darío Machado, Faure Chomón, Luis Abreu Mejías. In addition acknowledgement and thanks must go to the staff of three invaluable Cuban bibliographic sources: the Biblioteca Nacional José Martí (whose Director Elíades Acosta kindly opened many doors for me, and whose Subdirectora, Teresita Morales, provided constant assistance); the Instituto de Historia de Cuba, whose president, Manuel López Morales, and external relations director, Amparo Hernández Denis, supported me in my work on visits there; and, finally, the researchers based in the Centro de Estudios de Martí, who have supported my efforts over the years with materials and advice.

I also have to extend my thanks to my two universities. Firstly to the University of Wolverhampton – to my colleagues in Spanish and Latin American Studies, who have over the years patiently tolerated my many and repeated absences from work to go on much-envied trips to Cuba, and in more recent years to my fellow researchers who have, through the Research Committee, given me support and money to have time to study and opportunities to travel to and work in Cuba. Secondly to the University of Havana – to the rector, Dr Juan Vela Valdés, who has generously supported my efforts and opened more doors than I could have done on my own, to the department of Relaciones Internacionales (and especially Mayra Rogers Pedroso and Antonio Pozas Ramos) whose support has been so valuable, and to all those who, since the University honoured me with the title of Profesor Invitado in 1998, I am able to call my colleagues, especially in the Faculties of Lenguas Extranjeras, Filosofía e Historia and Artes y Letras, who have generously given me opportunities to visit, work and ply them all with endless questions, not least Hilda Torres (and her husband Carlos).

Finally, of course, pride of place must go to my personal support. Firstly to my family who supported my original interest, and my two sons, Stefan and Jan, who have over the years most patiently of all tolerated my continual absence from home to go to Cuba, my monopoly of the computer and my almost obsessive disappearances upstairs to continue my research. Finally, I have to thank my partner Jean, without whose support, encouragement, advice, help, joint research, and tolerance and patience, this whole project would never have got off the ground, never been continued and never been completed.

Introduction: The Concept of *Cubanía* and the Nature of Myth

As the Cuban Revolution remarkably enters its fifth decade, confounding the predictions of its demise that have characterized its history (especially before 1962, in the late 1960s and following the 1989 collapse of Soviet and eastern European communism), it remains stubbornly enigmatic to outsiders and insiders alike. The Revolution stands out as one of the twentieth century's most challenging phenomena, as a process that, despite endless scholarly, journalistic and polemical study, has persistently defied easy explanation and comprehension.

The questions abound. How has such an apparently chaotic process succeeded in surviving a series of crises that ought to have buried it in economic disaster long ago? How has a system so closely tied to and supported by the Soviet Union survived the fall of the whole Socialist Bloc? How, without losing all credibility with its own citizens, has the process been able to continue re-inventing itself so much that its trajectory since 1959 seems to have zigzagged continually? How did the system, apparently on the point of collapse in 1994 (with media images of desperate refugees on flimsy rafts crossing the sea to Florida), manage to restore public confidence so rapidly as to greet a visiting Pope in January 1998 in what was clearly a popular manifestation of national celebration? Moreover, on that very point, how could a revolution that, in 1961, expelled hundreds of priests and religious, receive the Pope in 1998 without fearing any destabilizing political effect? How, in the 1960s, could the Revolution make its name as an independent actor, challenging orthodoxies of East and West, while still remaining dependent economically on the limited trading relationship with Moscow and Comecon? Finally, how can it be that, after forty years of variable but persistent austerity, a significant part (and probably the majority) of the population appears to remain stubbornly supportive of the leadership and the system?

Beyond these obvious questions, the search for an explanation (if there is, indeed, one single explanation) leads us to two even more fundamental questions that this study will attempt to address. Firstly, what has the revolution actually 'been about' since 1959? Has there been one single, identifiable, 'essence' of the whole confusing process of change, passing through a bewildering series of 'phases', stages, policies and 'rectifications'? Secondly, more fundamentally, why did the Revolution actually happen when and how it did, and did this (and does this still) have any bearing on the later outcomes?

It is this study's contention that the answers to these two basic questions contain the germs of an explanation of the Revolution's survival, and remain rarely satisfactorily answered in the literature. Indeed, while the second question has provided us with an increasingly astute range of answers over the years (after the early crop of occasionally unsatisfactory, wish-fulfilling explanations), the first question has rarely even been addressed outside Cuba, although, inside Cuba, it has never ceased to be addressed, by specialists and also by those thousands of ordinary Cubans who attempt to explain to themselves why, against all the odds, they continue to remain fundamentally loyal to a system with so many errors, weaknesses, failures and contradictions.

Anyone attempting to offer an interpretation of the Cuban Revolution, or, indeed, any aspect of modern Cuban history, immediately comes up against a series of problems. One is the reliability of sources – primary or secondary, inside or outside Cuba; for the reality is that decades of revolutionary change in Cuba have created an uneven distribution of materials, a high level of uncertainty among insular Cubans regarding the motives and trustworthiness of visiting researchers, and an even higher level of partiality among defenders and critics of the revolutionary process alike.

A second problem is the frustrating and continuing inability of the Revolution to fit easily into preconceived models of political or historical analysis, with interpretations often missing the mark if they derive from *a priori* assumptions based on understandings or experiences of, or theories about, eastern European socialism, Latin American authoritarianism or revolution, Western political structures and systems or even theories of revolution in general.

The explanations for this uncomfortable or inadequate fit are easily identifiable. Firstly, the passions aroused by the Revolution from January 1959, and especially by its early radicalization, have been such that a large part of the literature on, journalistic coverage of, and political rhetoric about the Revolution has long been coloured either by bitterness and ideologically-driven opposition, or by blind loyalty or enthusiasm. Secondly, despite Cuba's importance over the centuries – to Spain (historically), to the United States (economically), and to the world (strategically) – the island has always been victim of a relative ignorance. Even when the Revolution aroused outside interest in the 1960s, much that the world learned about the process tended to be based on image, expectation, prejudice or constantly repeated secondary sources. Thirdly, many of the theories applied clumsily to Cuba by historiography and political science have arisen from European and North American experiences, and correspond to European and North American criteria and values. Finally, as the next chapter will endeavour to demonstrate, much of Cuba's historical experience since 1500 has been unusual, even within the ambit of Iberian colonialism, leading to a number of fundamental 'aberrations' from otherwise expected 'norms'. These problems even, or especially, apply to a literature that has, since 1959, been voluminous and often outstanding – I am referring here exclusively to the analyses of the Cuban Revolution offered by observers from the outside (since it is this study's argument that outside judgements of the revolutionary process have often tended to misunderstand fundamental aspects).

Where then does this study fit? What has been the trajectory of this literature? There are many possible ways of outlining a preparatory 'literature survey', but, given the purposes of this study, it is perhaps most useful to avoid attempting a comprehensive and complete survey and instead to focus on purpose and approach, schematically indicating patterns into which one can justifiably categorize almost all of it.

After the initial reaction of either welcome or shock – mostly journalistic (because of the immediacy of the reaction) – the first literature on the new Revolution was one of explanation: of what had happened to bring about the unexpected upheaval and, increasingly, of how and why it had then radicalized so rapidly and so unpredictably. There were three broad types of analysis offered for the first set of explanations – those focusing on the pre-1959 ills of Cuba, such as poverty, inequality and dictatorship (Hart Phillips 1959; Frank 1961); those going deeper into more 'structural' causes, such as dependence and neo-colonialism (Huberman and Sweezy 1961); and those who simply preferred to attribute it largely to American heavy-handedness (Mills 1960).

The explanations of the process's radicalization mostly fell into three categories. The first – including some of the most astute studies of the whole process – was the continuation of the 'structural' analyses, arguing that pre-1959 structures and external relationships had made that radicalization inevitable (Blackburn 1963; Nelson 1972). Secondly, there was a set of analyses seeking to explain it through either nationalism or reactions to American misunderstandings and errors (Williams 1962; Scheer and Zeitlin 1964; Ruiz 1968; Bonsal 1971). Others explained it, often more simply and often polemically, as either the influence of Communism or, intertwined with this, the opportunism, ambition and political skills of Castro – either the Communists used him, or he used them; these analyses tended to be overlaid with Cold War perspectives, either liberal (Casuso 1961; Draper 1962, 1965; Suárez 1967; Thomas 1971) or more overtly anti-communist (James 1961; Weyl 1960; Stein 1962; Urrutia 1964; Goldenberg 1965; Meneses 1966; Halperin 1972; Suchlicki 1972), and included many inspired by often émigré bitterness. Perhaps less ideologically driven, however, was a simultaneous literature fascinated by the figure of Fidel Castro, partly in explanation but mostly in portrayal (Lockwood 1969).

The radicalization also spawned a genre of its own – socialist debate, either inspired by the unusual Revolution or worried by its unorthodoxy, about the origins of the process and, above all, the viability and correctness of its subsequent path

(Dumont 1964; Huberman and Sweezy 1969; Karol 1970; Zeitlin 1970a; Bray and Harding 1974; Fitzgerald 1978; Harnecker 1979; Ruffin 1990).

Simultaneously with the evolving 'literature of explanation' came a number of studies focusing on the post-revolutionary process of change itself (Seers 1964; Cuban Economic Research Project 1965; Dumont 1970; Huberman and Sweezy 1969). That tendency increased noticeably in the 1970s, when, after a decade of confusion and consolidation, it was possible to begin reasoned analyses, based on more careful and specialist fieldwork. These analyses (replacing the earlier explanatory tendency) all stressed process, studying the Revolution's political culture (Fagen 1969), or political system (Gonzalez 1974; Domínguez 1978; LeoGrande 1978, 1979), or its economy (Bernardo 1971; Silverman 1971; Ritter 1974; Roca 1976; Mesa-Lago 1978; MacEwan 1981). The social aspects of the transformation were also starting to be subjected to scholarly attention (Butterworth 1980; Kirk 1989); and many such studies were to be found in a new development, the collections of 'micro' analyses of significant aspects (Mesa-Lago 1971; Bonachea and Valdés 1972; Halebsky and Kirk 1985). This narrower focus continued in longer studies, as the opportunities for sustained fieldwork opened up (Díaz Briquets 1983; Feinsilver 1993; Dalton 1993).

As the Revolution consolidated domestically and began to extend its external profile more significantly on to a world (as opposed to a Latin American) stage, scholarly attention inevitably focused on two new areas – foreign policy and the economy. The former literature now stressed much less the previous concern with Cuba's relationship with either Washington or the Soviet Union, although there were excellent studies of both aspects (Duncan 1985; Smith 1987; Shearman 1987; Morley 1987; Domínguez and Hernández 1989); instead, the new emphasis was on the Third World (Blasier and Mesa-Lago 1979; Weinstein 1979; Fauriol and Loser 1980; LeoGrande 1980; Levine 1983; Erisman 1985; Erisman and Kirk 1991). The economy also now became the subject of a plethora of studies, as a scholarly debate emerged about the measurement and success of Cuba's apparent stablization (Mesa-Lago 1981; Perez-Lopez 1987; Zimbalist 1987; Zimbalist and Brundenius 1989).

As a general rule, the literature on the Revolution was now characterized by less polemical material and more emphasis on processes and subtleties, less on the larger picture and more on narrow aspects, a development confirmed by the birth of the scholarly journal *Cuban Studies*, based in the University of Pittsburgh. The new, more relaxed, attitude also translated into a new focus on pre-1959 history, which, although not about the Revolution as such, was clearly driven by the interest it aroused and attempted in part at least to analyse the roots of the phenomenon. Certainly, this new departure included some of the best works on Cuba (Benjamin 1977; Pérez 1983, 1986a, 1988; Stubbs 1985; Poyo 1989; Schwartz 1989; Scott 1985; Paquette 1988), a tradition continued, especially in North American-based historiography, into the 1990s (Ferrer 1995, 1999; Schmidt-Nowara, 1995a, b).

The crisis of the 1990s, and the collapse of the Cold War, brought an inevitable new crop of studies. In part they were continuations of the old 'collected studies' variety, often timed to coincide with anniversaries, and in this case written before, but now coinciding with, the crisis (Halbesky and Kirk 1990; Gillespie 1990). The reactions to that crisis, however, predictably saw a return of the previous, more polemical, treatment, either critical from the right (Baloyra and Morris 1993; Del Aguila 1994; Cardosa and Helinger 1992), or disenchanted from the left (Habel 1991).

As the crisis evolved and lessened, however, a new tendency was evident – the return of the larger canvas (Pérez-Stable 1993; Mesa-Lago 1993) and the return of a literature of explanation, this time of the actual workings and complexity of the whole process at a time of stress and strain. Some of these new studies stemmed from newer thinking on political structures and participation (Rabkin 1991; Fuller 1992; Bengelsdorf 1994; Eckstein 1994; Stubbs 1989), but others attempted to explain not just the system but the early signs of its unexpected survival (Fitzgerald 1994). In terms of approach, therefore, the wheel had effectively come full circle, with the crisis and the survival bringing a return to the broad-brush approach, the study of process and the literature of explanation.

This survey of the literature, however inadequate, schematic and subjective, allows us to identify where this particular study fits in, for it is not the intention to offer here yet another history of the Revolution, or another detailed account of the Revolution's background. Instead, its purpose is explicitly interpretative, offering a relatively holistic explanation (of the Revolution's roots, evolution and survival) and a perspective of the process, offering also a perspective of that whole experience that might shed new, or different, light on the more confusing, contradictory, but critical aspects of the revolutionary process and its survival into the twenty-first century. That perspective is essentially an analysis of one dimension largely either forgotten or misunderstood in most of the literature on Cuba – namely, ideology, and specifically what Cubans themselves are wont to call *cubania*.

That ideology (*cubania*) should have been relatively neglected by the non-Cuban literature is at first surprising, given the durability of the pre-1959 intellectual elite's concern – or even obsession – with *cubanidad* (Cubanness), and also given the primacy of the term within the Revolution's discourse – although the latter fact already partly explains the neglect, since outside Cuba that concern has tended to be discarded as mere rhetoric or as an appropriation of a pre-revolutionary tradition. More broadly, however, that neglect has arisen from a reluctance to address the whole question of ideology itself.

It is not that ideology was not addressed from the start; indeed, for many early analyses, ideology – in the form of communism – was precisely the problem, an alien import imposed on the system and then, by the 1990s, being clung to stubbornly and conservatively despite its evident failings and the collapse of its credibility worldwide. Indeed, one early study talked of Castroism as 'a leader in search of a movement, a movement in search of power, and power in search of an ideology' (Draper 1965: 48); another referred to a 'revolution without a blueprint' (Zeitlin 1970b). However, rarely have the nature, extent and contradictions of the Revolution's ideological patterns been subjected to deep analysis, going beyond conventional, and often unquestioned, assumptions about the Revolution, communism, Marxism – and, most fundamentally, about 'ideology' itself. There are exceptions, most notably Valdés (Valdés 1975), who led the way with what is still a minor 'classic'; but it was not until the 1990s that the theme was again taken up with more detailed analyses of the mechanisms of ideological 'control' or persuasion (Medin 1990; Bunck 1994).

This reluctance has stemmed from a number of factors. Firstly, among the Revolution's initial supporters, it came from a Western liberal perspective that equated 'ideology' with a rigid, probably extremist, thinking refreshingly absent from the unorthodox Revolution. Secondly, sympathizers were also aware that the whole process had arisen despite, and not because of, any recognizable 'revolutionary situation' and, moreover, that the most ideologically identifiable element at the time, the communist PSP (Partido Socialista Popular – Popular Socialist Party), was noticeably absent from the early power elite. To them, therefore, 'ideology-free' also meant 'communism-free'.

Among those who were more critical observers, however, a similar reluctance on ideology could be seen, arising from two distinct positions. Firstly, it came from the perception of the Revolution as an ideological *tabula rasa* into which an essentially alien ideology – Marxism-Leninism – was imported, and on to which it was then imposed by a conspiracy between a ruthlessly ambitious and even megalomaniac Castro, the Cuban communists and Moscow. Secondly, it arose from the belief that Castro was skilfully able to take early advantage of innate Cuban nationalism and of initial American intransigence to fill an ideological void with a 'natural' ally in the form of communism. Medin later offered a more sophisticated version of this perspective, arguing that Marxism-Leninism was used as a tool to legitimize a pre-existing affinity for radicalism, since 'there had as yet been no projection of a global cognitive-conceptual framework that would theoretically legitimize the socioeconomic and political restructuring' (Medin 1990: 58).

Hence this study's purpose is clear – to trace and explain the trajectory, the evolution of *cubania* (explained here as the teleological belief in *cubanidad*) from a minority (white) intellectual concern, to a broader ideology of dissent (*cubania rebelde*) that underpinned much of Cuban radical dissidence from the late nineteenth century to the 1950s, and finally evolved into the post-Revolutionary *cubania revolucionaria*, a newly hegemonic ideology of dissent that became fundamental in guiding the revolutionary process through the maelstrom of the first decade and the competing orthodoxies of the more recognizably socialist years, to the critical 1990s, where it became a vital element in guaranteeing survival, in balancing the demands for continuity and change, stability and adaptation, and in searching for yet another identity of the *nación*.

What is contended here, however, is that *cubanía* should not be taken at face value. For a start, it has been a deliberately vague concept, malleable and adaptable to all, by all, and for all, and yet has never quite lost the exclusive character of its foundation, as a white, intellectual notion. Therefore, one fundamental factor in the organicity and legitimacy of *cubanía* has been the role of politico-historical myth within the ideology's trajectory, without which *cubanía* would not have been able to evolve and adapt while retaining its core elements and core credibility. This study therefore seeks to identify a working definition of politico-historical myth, and to identify some of the key myths within *cubanía*, before and after 1959.

This discussion, however, immediately raises a number of important theoretical questions, which it is necessary to address at this stage, partly because the study's underlying ideas take issue with existing theories and partly because they themselves necessarily have a theoretical basis. However, it should be stressed from the outset that it is not the intention here to engage in a detailed survey, or critique, of those theories, since not only would that distract from the task in hand, but also because the basic premise of this interpretation is that, since theories have failed to accommodate the Cuban case, the solution may well be to adopt a more empiricist approach, analysing the situation and constructing a theory out of that experience.

For that reason, a brief survey of the theoretical issues is necessary here, the starting-point for which must be the issue of revolution itself, leading immediately to the fundamental question: what actually constitutes a revolution? For simplicity, it is proposed here to make the initial assumption that a revolution can generally be understood as a total transformation (deliberate or accidental) of a given political and economic system and the social structure thereof in a relatively short time. 'Social revolutions are rapid, basic transformations of a society's state and class structures; and they are accomplished and in part carried through by class-based revolts from below' (Skocpol 1988: 4). Such a definition would establish that the Cuba of the 1960s was less controversially recognizable as a revolutionary situation, given that a whole class was effectively eliminated from the social structure (through dispossession and emigration) and that the lives of several groups (notably peasants and black Cubans) were revolutionized rapidly; given also that the expropriation of American property transformed the economic structure and orientation in a matter of months, cutting off historic, and 'natural', trading links; and, finally, given that the old system of competitive politics was replaced by participation, mobilization and single-party rule.

There is therefore a *prima facie* case for the 1960s process in Cuba's being a revolution; what remains to be seen is whether that process continued to be defined as a revolution in any sense. For this purpose, we need now to assess possibly useful paradigms offered by various theories of revolution. In this task, the excellent critique offered by Theda Skocpol (Skocpol 1988: 3–43) can be taken as a useful guide, for she demonstrates the possibility of summarizing the many different theories in three distinct categories: Marxist, 'classical' political science, and 'state-centred revisionist' theories, or what we might call 'revisionist' political science approaches.

Marxism necessarily warrants attention anyway, as it depended from the start on the analysis of revolutionary situations and the prescription of revolution as a solution to identified contradictions. Moreover, Marxism has so influenced our perceptions of sociology and history that we cannot ignore it. Even here, inevitably, there is a 'classical' category and a 'revisionist' approach. The former, based on the writings of Marx and Engels and on the close adherence to these principles of most Marxist thinkers until Lenin, argued that revolutions were essentially class-based movements for change arising out of objective (i.e. structural) conditions in a given society at a given stage of evolution. In particular, it was argued that revolutions grew organically out of societies that were historically evolving and inherently conflictive, meaning that revolutions were, according to classical Marxism, inevitable and part of the process of dialectical evolution, with clear roots in economic processes and with conflict arising over the forces and relations of production.

Later Marxism refined this basic standpoint in several ways. Firstly, greater attention was given to what we might call 'subjective' factors (people and ideas, above all) and to consciousness, rather than simply attributing the incidence of revolution to 'scientific' and objective factors. In particular, writers focused on the role of ideology and a revolutionary vanguard. In the case of the former, the contribution of the innovative Italian Marxist thinker and activist, Antonio Gramsci, was perhaps the most significant, in the challenge he issued to the conventional notion that ideology should be considered as part of the 'superstructure' of society by arguing that it could be an active contributor to the process of revolution, but also in his analysis of the subtleties of hegemonic domination (Gramsci 1986b: 245). The latter revision was also offered by Gramsci, with his discussion of the nature and role of intellectuals, especially 'organic' intellectuals (Gramsci 1986a); but the most significant contribution to the debate was offered by Lenin, who, faced with the practical problem of organizing revolution in an 'objectively' backward Russia, stressed both the role of the vanguard (Lenin 1966a) and the nature of imperialism, which created the space for revolution to happen in countries such as his own, rather than the advanced capitalist societies (Lenin 1966b). However, whatever the differences between these schools of Marxism, they were, and are, all united by their adherence to the notion that revolution is an objective historical process with a high degree of inevitability.

Set against these theories are the explanations offered by traditional and more dissident Western political science. Skocpol has characterized the former as falling into one of three categories – the 'psychological', the 'value consensus' and the 'political conflict' theories (Skocpol 1988: 9). The first tends to focus on revolution as a collective psychological response to deprivation, and as a conflict between preferred values and an intolerable reality. Here the key is the scope of action, with theorists, for example, talking of revolution as a response necessarily within a political core, since reaction from the margins remains a limited rebellion, while a mass reaction from within the core is revolutionary either in intent or by implication. With such reactions, the desired outcome is the displacement of the existing power elite.

The second explanation focuses on revolution as either a violent response of ideologically motivated movements to severe desequilibria in social and value systems, or as an acceptance of violence as a means of altering the system where there is a severe dis-synchronization of values and the real environment, usually as a result of combined internal and external pressures. Thus, for example, a society that was formerly not in a revolutionary situation, i.e. was 'value coordinated' and characterized by consensus, usually based on the socialization of the majority and the legitimacy of authority, can move into a revolutionary situation when the former equilibrium is disrupted. Whatever the case, however, the result is mass alienation and the mass acceptance of an idea of an alternative project, with a de-legitimized government resorting to coercion and the collapse of consensus.

The third such explanation simply sees revolutions as exaggerated conflicts between governments and contending interest groups. All three explanations, however, whatever their differences, agree on one thing: that all political systems contain within themselves the potential for revolution, with the keys being short-term catalysts, the 'revolutionary moment' and the availability and strength of force to challenge the system. In other words, for these theories, revolution is simply an accidental and exaggerated expression of the distortion of normal political processes.

That leads us on to the third school of thought, characterized by its focus less on the process and more on the question of the state, which, according to the previous set of explanations, is simply the milieu or battleground for revolutionary conflict. These theories were stimulated by 1970s debates on the relative autonomy of the state, from which arose the notions, firstly, that a state's rulers can act independently of the dominant class groups in order to implement policies whose long-term purpose is to protect or further the basic interests of the whole ruling class, but also that the state is not merely, as the Marxists would have it, the instrument of class domination alone (giving rise to concepts of the 'relative autonomy of the state'). Of these theorists perhaps the most clear-cut in her analysis is Skocpol herself, contributing to the theory by arguing two things: that revolutions are primarily a matter of the collapse of the old state and the consolidation of the new (which ultimately depends on the ruling class's ability to control and the revolutionary movement's ability to organize) and, secondly, that revolutions are realized on the basis of social conflict. She therefore posits an analysis that focuses on structural issues (based on the premise that revolutions are not necessarily, and indeed are rarely, the 'purposive' phenomena that they can be made out to be), on external structures and development (with effects on the ruling class's ability to control and the availability of an alternative), and, finally, on the state's internal pressures and conflicts.

From this debate it is possible to draw a number of conclusions about common features, especially when pre-1950s principles and theories are measured against the subsequent real Third World revolutions; for many of the 'classical' theories were understandably Eurocentric in their focus. Moreover, the phenomena that developed in Eastern Europe after 1989 have added a whole range of different and unforeseen experiences on which to draw.

On this basis, and given the Cuban case, it is possible to construct something of a 'working model' of analysis of revolution that seems to have some modern validity. This model, above all, sees revolutions as necessarily accidental in their form but structural in their causes, and can be adduced through a series of what we might term empirical 'prerequisites for revolution'.

The first such prerequisite seems to be that they usually occur in a context of change (for the better or for the worse), which may be political, economic or social, and is likely to affect all three areas. It follows that such change must necessarily affect certain key groups, perhaps giving rise to discontent, the frustration of expectations or even increasing confidence. Here what defines 'key' depends on a number of factors, for this status may be determined by their access to, control of, or importance in a critical strategic sector of the economy or the political structure, or their level of education. Whatever the cause of this status, the group must have a collective sense of their identity and be capable of acting collectively.

A further prerequisite would seem to be the existence of a leadership (individual or collective) that is both capable of leading and acceptable in its claim to lead, not least in that this leadership displays an affinity with the values or ideological framework of the key groups; moreover, it follows that this leadership must be organized and politically skilful.

Thirdly, there must be some sort of 'space for action', wherein either the intellectual, political and financial resources for revolution are available, or there is a critical space in the system, a 'disjuncture' created, for example, by partial reform (leading to unfulfillable expectations) or a breakdown in elite unity or strength. In other words, the old system must necessarily be weakened and able to be challenged, either from within (as a result of economic shifts, social change, political conflicts or intra-elite tensions) or from without (by war, economic crisis or climatic disaster). In this sense, all that is necessary is a sufficient weakening for the elite's coercive power and legitimacy to be undermined and for the sense to evolve at popular level that the system is either no longer credible or no longer delivering material benefits, protection or whatever else was expected of it.

A further prerequisite seems to be that there must be an available body of 'alternative' values, however vague and unarticulated; these could be in folk tradition, popular culture, specific manifestos or coherent and public belief-systems; or they could, as in the Cuban case, be political traditions that exist as an 'ideological reservoir'. Certainly, experience would suggest that, if such an alternative is not identifiable and usable, discontent can easily become incoherent protest rather than a genuine revolution.

The starting-point of any ideological analysis of any revolution must necessarily be the axiomatic assumption that, for a revolution to succeed beyond the points of insurrection, victory or initial consolidation, it must be based on a 'blueprint' of some sort, in that there must exist in the minds of enough participants and active supporters a viable, credible and legitimate alternative to the existing system, at the very least to make a challenge to that system seem worth while. Academic opinion varies widely about the essential elements for a 'revolutionary situation' in a given society, but historical evidence would suggest that these ought to include what political science is wont to term an 'alternative project', based on existing beliefs and traditions and proposed by an acceptable leadership.

Equally, there would indeed seem to be a need for a definable 'revolutionary moment', a crisis to weaken the system at a time of pressure or to strengthen or legitimize the alternative at a time of systemic weakness. In other words, revolutionary situations may evolve, but the actual act of revolution itself needs to 'explode'. Finally, one critical prerequisite between the 1950s and 1989 was 'external space', whereby the balance of power allowed a space for a revolution to happen, be it in Algeria in the late 1950s, Cuba in 1959 or Nicaragua in a post-Watergate and post-Vietnam world.

In the case of Cuba in 1959, the existence of an 'alternative' is very much the subject of this study, which leads logically towards a discussion of the question of what constitutes such an alternative and whether it is justifiable to call that an ideology. This, then, is the second theoretical issue to address here; but, once again, we enter into a political and academic minefield, as the debate on ideology – its nature, its definition, its role – has been every bit as intense and dense as that on revolution. There is, moreover, a fundamental problem with discussions of ideology in the Western political tradition, namely that, particularly in North American and British circles and traditions, there has often been an underlying propensity for seeing ideology as necessarily negative, dogmatic and associated with defined ideologies that have seen themselves as such and universally been seen as such.

Moreover, as Eagleton puts it, 'Nobody has yet come up with a single adequate definition of ideology' (Eagleton 1991: 1), and he himself goes on to list no fewer than sixteen different uses of the term and to observe that much debate on ideology is obscured by its tendency to be used pejoratively or in connection for the most part with Marxism, either in debates about Marxism as such or in referring to debates within Marxism.

How then can we summarize the evolving debate on ideology? Broadly speaking, we might say that historically most theories of ideology tend to see it in terms of some sort of 'consciousness' (mostly equated with 'ideas') and in terms of some sort of pattern of domination. In the case of the former, the notion comes logically from essentially Enlightenment concepts of rationality and, later, from nineteenth-century notions of belief, and, finally, from post-Marx concepts of political consciousness. Whatever the root, however, the conventional and long-accepted view of ideology is that it is a set of ideas and beliefs that guide political action and attitudes to the world. Within this, however, mention must be made of the various Marxist tendencies towards a view of ideology as 'false consciousness', not least since this notion has proved so influential in the dismissal of ideology as playing any developmental role, both within the Marxist tradition (over whether ideology is part of the 'superstructure' of an economic and social system) and in the non-Marxist liberal tradition or within the anti-Marxist right. As Eagleton has pointed out, however, such a view takes as its starting-point an essentially mistaken view that 'false' means 'untrue', while the term as originally used by Marx referred not to knowledge but to values (Eagleton 1991: 22–5). It was indeed only very late on, with Gramsci and then the otherwise problematic contributions of 'structuralist' perspectives, together with the development of what is sometimes termed 'social psychology', that the notion began to evolve that ideology might be something other than ideas and beliefs, and might perhaps include unconscious relations between the subject and the environment – marking, in Eagleton's terms, a move from a 'cognitive to an affective theory of ideology' (Eagleton 1991: 19).

As to the question of domination, one consistent feature of Marxist and Marxist-influenced thinking has been the tendency to see ideology as a construct developed by dominant groups, elites or ruling classes to cement their rule and domination. Indeed, one might say that it was only with Gramsci that any more subtle concept began to evolve, focusing more on both the mechanisms of 'domination' (using the broader and more complex concept of 'hegemony') and the possibilities of a 'counter-ideology', dissident and challenging to dominant versions.

Summarizing the debate eloquently, Eagleton offers a series of six, progressively more focused, definitions and uses of the term, which are largely reproduced here. The broadest is the idea of ideology as 'the general material process of production of ideas, beliefs and values in social life' (Eagleton, 1991: 28), which he equates with 'culture', according to which political thought is socially determined. The second, narrower, definition sees ideology as 'ideas and beliefs (whether true or false) which symbolize the conditions and life-experiences of a specific, socially significant, group or class' (Eagleton 1991: 29). Thirdly, ideology is seen as something that 'attends to the promotion and legitimation of the interests of such social groups in the face of opposing interests' (Eagleton 1991: 29), and this is narrowed down further to a set of such ideas and beliefs that are 'confined to the activities of a dominant social power' (Eagleton 1991: 29). Finally, Eagleton offers us the focus of ideology as, firstly, something that 'signifies ideas and beliefs which help to legitimize the interests of a ruling group or class specifically by distortion and dissimulation' (Eagleton 1991: 30), and, then, as something that emphasizes 'false or deceptive beliefs, but regards such beliefs as arising not from the interests of a dominant class but from the material structures of society as a whole' (Eagleton 1991: 30).

Therefore, as with the question of revolution, so too here does it seem apposite to close this discussion with a definition of the empirical view – again, 'working model' – of ideology that underpins this particular study. This definition therefore sees ideology as composed of a variable number of codes, which are, in a sense, the building-blocks of the ideology, defining separately the values, as beliefs, that will collectively form the whole belief-system that constitutes an ideology. What, then, is a 'code'? It is a set of related and cognate beliefs and principles that can be grouped together to make a coherent belief in a single, given, value. Thus, for example, the consensual collective respect for the value of 'action' might be translated into the code of 'activism', with a range of specific principles being understood by that code, and a wide range of explicit and implicit policies and strategies being subsumed in it. Equally, to take a concrete case, it might be argued that British society historically respects the value of hierarchy, leading to a con-sensual code of 'hierarchicalism', which could be said to incorporate beliefs in monarchy, deference, heredity, private schooling, and so on. A code is thus not a myth (since, as will be argued here, a myth must display an internal argument or 'story-line'), but will probably include myths, and many of the constituent beliefs could well become associated with key myths. Nor is it as coherent and all-encompassing as an ideology, since it offers no comprehensive and explanatory 'world-view' and guide for interpretation and action. Taking the British case as an example again, therefore, the code of 'hierarchicalism' could be said to include the beliefs outlined above, some of which have a greater status because of the associated myths. For example, it might be said that a whole myth around the figure of Queen Victoria developed within the belief in monarchy.

In the Cuban case, as we shall see, the code of 'agrarianism' in the 1950s might be said to have expressed the value of 'agrarian-ness', expressing the belief that the essence of the 'real' nation was to be found in its countryside, its rural dwellers, or in certain undefined or general rural 'values', and therefore that its future lay there too. This means that a code can be a myth if it becomes so central to the whole ideology (rather than one facet of it) that it is seen as the distillation of it all. Before that stage, codes are the building-blocks of the belief-system, i.e. the beliefs that individually constitute a 'value', a quality of the group which is extolled, a statement of what is desirable as a quality for all those who belong to that community, which should be put into effect and which is basic to the whole ideology. Codes can thus be of two kinds – 'attribute-oriented' (defining supposedly basic and inherent 'attributes' of the perceived 'group'), or 'means-oriented' (defining the 'means' through which the 'group's' future can be achieved); in the Cuban case, 'moralism' might be said to be an 'attribute-code' and 'agrarianism' a 'means-code'.[1]

Therefore, for a political culture such as Cuba's, which depends heavily on codes, all codes must have several meanings and two functions. The meanings are different aspects of the whole, what we could call 'sub-sets'; thus, to take the British case again, hierarchicalism could be said to have several meanings – the importance of birth and heredity (leading, for example, to a justification of private schooling and the House of Lords), the coexistence of private and public healthcare systems, the belief in an appointed judiciary, and so on.

This explains why the term 'code' is used, for, within this set of theoretical propositions, the term has two distinct but related meanings. On the one hand, an ideological code 'encodes' the 'essential meaning' of one key aspect of the ideology, in a way that is comprehensible more for those whom we might call the ideology's 'initiates' (the people who come to believe in, and who ultimately develop and maintain, the ideology) than for 'outsiders'. This is true not least for the many, complex and perhaps even contradictory ramifications of the code itself. The second reason for using the term 'code' is that it can said to 'codify' the otherwise potentially incoherent and fluid aspects of an evolving ideology.

The two functions are essentially, first, that the code must react to something perceived in the culture's past, and, second, that it must posit a set of policies to achieve, or certain desired features of, the future form of a given society that somehow encapsulates some idealized self-image of that society in its existing form. Hence, to get to grips with what a code means in a given society, it is necessary to identify and understand the problem, real or imagined, against which the code is reacting and the values that it is extolling as the desired components of a future society.

On the basis of these codes, therefore, an ideology forms, recognizable when collectively these have sufficient coherence to be seen by a given social group (usually a national or regional society, or even perhaps a 'clan' or class) as the collective 'world-view' of that group. What is essential here is that the group must

---

1. I am indebted to Rubén Zardoya for his help with this aspect of the theory.

be able to identify itself as really, or potentially, different from others, with a 'world-view' that is therefore both different from others' and unique in itself. The function of this 'world-view', which we can call 'ideology', is that it is accepted by the group (consciously or subconsciously) as expressing the group's preferred and shared view of the 'world' in three key planes – as it has been (i.e. its perceived – real or imagined – collective past, its history), as it is at present (seen either as problematic or as the basis of collective self-confidence), and, most critically perhaps, as it should be in the future.

An ideology thus serves two functions – to explain past and present successes and failures, or dilemmas, and to propose a future that is seen as special to, and appropriate for, the group. The two are, necessarily, linked, as the collective view of a problematic past has to be explained by reference to external factors in order to propose a future that makes sense and is worth while; these external factors may be conquest by another nation or society, cultural domination, and defeat through battles, deceit or internal weakness, and need to be seen as the critical factors that currently prevent the society from attaining its destined future. Equally, the collective view of a successful past will be seen either as the past to which the society, in the case of a problematic present, wishes and expects to return, or, if the present is continuing the 'success', the basis of the even more successful destiny. Thus the question of the future is fundamental, even if not explicit, since it can either posit the continuation of the past and present into the future, or the modification of the present (to rid it of less acceptable and perhaps 'alien' elements and thereby free the path to future 'natural' evolution), or the rejection of the present and its replacement by an alternative that is seen as organic, natural and based on elements of the past, and is codified in the constituent codes.

Discussion of an 'alternative project' introduces a further fundamental issue in any study, and understanding, of ideology – the question of hegemony. For ideologies may be, basically, either hegemonic or 'counter-hegemonic' (or dissident); and what determines which will be the particulars of the case, the society, and the extent of the ruling group's, class's or nation's domination. For the essence of a hegemonic domination (to develop Gramsci) is the unchallenged right of the ruling group to exercise its domination, control or influence over other groups in the society in question, a right that may perhaps be attributable to economic control or leadership (or success), military power, social mores, or religious control, or simply to the weakness of the subordinated – or subaltern – groups. Gramsci's great contribution to the debate on, and understanding of, domination was to look beyond straight economic control or military-political coercion towards systems of persuasion, whereby the subordinated groups accept, or are unable to challenge, the correctness and justice of their subaltern position *vis-à-vis* the ruling and/or dominant group(s).

The means to achieve this hegemony can be many and varied, some more subtle than others. Organized religion is perhaps the most familiar to us, especially where interpretation of the religious codes, dogmas and instructions is left in the hands of a subsidiary and exclusive priesthood. More generally, however, hegemonic domination is exercised through ideology, through the subtle persuasion of the subordinated groups that they have no historic, political, economic or empirical right to exercise any significant authority outside the parameters allowed to them by the hegemonic group, and, furthermore, that the latter's domination is histori- cally just, natural and unchallengeable. Evidently, the process by which such domination is achieved can in each separate case be long, arduous and even bloody, and the subordinated groups' ideological defeat may reflect a more tangible political or military defeat or conquest, or a profound economic or social failure or disaster. A dominant culture tends to divide and rule as a matter of course, setting up a binary division of 'ins' and 'outs', excluding the alternative from acceptability. In other words, domination depends on antagonism. However, in many cases, hege- mony may be exercised by complicity, by incorporation of the alternative, which is portrayed as workable only through the medium of the dominant ideas and structures.

However, just as there is a hegemonic ideology in most societies, so too can there be a 'counter-hegemonic', or dissident, ideology, especially where the former has been imposed on the subordinated groups from outside and where the subordi- nated group possesses a separate history prior to the domination or alternatively some basis – regional, geographical, cultural – for allowing the hegemonic culture and ideology to be seen at some critical stage as unnatural or weak. The ability for a dissident ideology to emerge and even to challenge the hegemonic domination, and thus become truly counter-hegemonic, depends on a vast range of variable factors – the military defeat of the ruling group by outsiders, a dynastic or other crisis of legitimate authority, the collapse of the economic basis for the group's strength, and so on – but, even then, such a dissident ideology must be able to offer, if it is to become truly counter-hegemonic, an 'alternative project'. Before such a project, the dissident ideology might be said to exist at the level of an alternative discourse, offering a defensive mechanism for the subordinated, but hopeful, group; but once that dissidence emerges to take the form of the fully counter-hegemonic ideology, it needs a project.

For such an 'alternative project' to be acceptable and seen as organic to the group, but also integral to the group's whole ideology (for an ideology without a 'project' simply makes no sense), it needs to be based on certain critical elements taken from the dominated group's 'pre-history', which means necessarily taking them from the very context that is now rejected. For there can be no such entity as a totally new ideological project; all projects must take their cue from agreed elements – codes, events, periods and so on – from the otherwise unacceptable past (as opposed to the totally unacceptable present). Since the subordinate group's history belongs to the past, that past (which may possibly share much with the past of the hegemonic group) must provide the basis for the project's and the ideology's 'organicity'. All ideologies base their organicity on the past, and it follows therefore that even supposedly and avowedly revolutionary ideologies must aim both to conserve (agreed critical elements of an acceptable past) and to transform.

One further important aspect of the whole question of ideology as the term is used in this study is the distinction between what we might call the two levels of ideology – the 'popular-empirical' level and the 'intellectual-theoretical' level. The former – which is the sense in which 'ideology' is mostly used throughout this study – refers to the collective 'world-view', based on tradition, collective adaptation to the changing environment, 'folk' culture, the collective experience (especially including perceived 'struggle') and so on. It can be deemed 'popular' in two senses. Firstly, it exists at the more 'unconscious' level of understanding and motivation, not so much unthinking as unthought and largely uncodifed formally, except through the 'codes'. Secondly, it exists as the collective context in which the second level of ideology – the 'intellectual-theoretical' – takes root, develops and adapts. In this sense, the popular ideology can be said to be akin to, but not identical with, what we would mostly call a political culture; it is akin to it, since it is the milieu in which a given collective political life and behaviour operate and evolve, but it differs from it in that it goes beyond the simple role of 'environment', to posit a view of what a social and political system should be. In other words, a popular ideology, like any ideology, offers a goal, a vision of a future.

An 'intellectual' ideology, however, is what we would all most commonly recognize by the term 'ideology', in other words a coherent system of theoretical propositions to posit and explain intellectually a certain 'world-view', usually based on a given, identified philosophy, as well as a given (but not always admitted) historical experience. This level of ideology is the one that catches the political observer's and historian's attention most easily, not least because, once codified in written form, it is identifiable, comprehensible and classifiable. It is, however, referred to here as a 'level' rather than simply a 'type' of ideology, because it is clear that this ideology needs an environment of a given, sympathetic or receptive, popular ideology in which to take root, leading invariably to a dynamic, a dialectical process, in which the intellectual argument of the 'theoretical' ideology informs, directs, focuses and even helps codify the 'popular' ideology, especially in critical circumstances that lead to a close affinity between the two (where both target the same perceived problems and posit largely the same perceived solutions) or in a situation where the adherents of the intellectual ideology are, through their actions, their social identification, their writings and so on, seen by the collectivity to represent an integral part of the 'popular-empirical' tradition that has created the popular ideology.

Indeed, it might be argued that both levels of ideology ultimately need each other to effect this necessary dynamic. However, even without the intellectual codification, the popular ideology does possess its own forms of manifestation, codification and transference, which are the ideological codes. Because it is in the nature of a popular ideology that the integral notions and propositions should remain somewhat unarticulated, and even contradictory, especially if the ideology is to remain organic and flexible, few people in a collectivity are able to adhere to all the beliefs and propositions of the ideology. The component codes can therefore be said to convey a 'message' of the ideology (which gives us the third reason for using the term 'code') to individuals, allowing them to 'customize' the whole 'world-view' to their own situation, preferences and experience.

Moreover, at a certain point in its evolution, an ideological code needs symbols, especially when the ideology is under pressure of some sort, since symbols can preserve, almost 'freeze', the 'core' values and beliefs of the code and allow the individual an even greater personal identification with its propositions.

This brief discussion has also introduced the notion of 'discourse', as separate from 'ideology'. Here it should be said that usage is of little help in distinguishing these, since many writers use the two terms to mean much the same thing, although, once again, Eagleton offers a useful explanation, seeing discourse as concerning 'the actual uses of language between particular human subjects for the production of specific effects' (Eagleton 1991: 9). However, it should be said that the sense in which the term 'discourse' is used in this study owes more to linguistics than to political theory, since what is meant by the term is the form that an ideology takes. Since it is self-evident that an ideology does not exist in a vacuum and must have a form to articulate it, pass it on, and be able to adapt: that form – written, oral, ceremonial, and so on – is discourse. However, to complicate matters perhaps, a given ideology may at certain key stages have separate discourses, separate definable interpretations of the agreed body of values, codes and ideas that constitutes the particular ideology. Such moments may logically be times of crisis, challenge or change, and are likely to affect either the hegemonic ideology or the counter-hegemonic version. At such moments, it is proper to refer to 'competing discourses' within the ideology, until a point when one version gains 'sub-hegemony' over the other. If the process of change – as with a revolution, for example – continues for a long time, then it is logical to expect that this contest may continue, with the competing discourses following parallel trajectories. After all, the very fact of posing an alternative, but as yet untried, project for change, must mean that, entering by definition into the realm of speculation, a radical, revolutionary or left-wing movement, party and ideology can be expected either to split or at least to contain the seeds of an ongoing contest of interpretations.

Here it is important to distinguish this use of the idea of 'competing discourses' from that developed by Gramsci; for him, such 'competition' implied conflict, between a hegemonic discourse and that espoused by an oppressed people, based on their practical experience of social reality (Eagleton 1991: 118). It is, however, equally true that 'competition' may take place between alternative discourses, especially in situations where hegemonic control is weak enough to generate space for such alternatives to develop, but, on the other hand, strong enough (in the sense of being either persuasive enough or well enough established to have developed an inbuilt ability to persuade due to custom and longevity) to ensure that no one alternative discourse develops with a convincing 'counter-hegemony'. It will be argued here that, in nineteenth-century colonial Cuba and, even more contradictorily, in the early twentieth-century neocolonial sequel to that anachronism, such a situation – integral to late colonial societies, especially where the mechanisms of cultural control and persuasion have long been in place and have struck deep roots, creating a 'loyal' constituency among the colonized – prevailed, generating not one but at least three alternatives. As will be seen, these three were gradually reduced to two, both of which survived the victory of the Revolution in 1959 and continued to 'compete' in often complex, contradictory and unseen ways.

Thus, what seems from the outside to be a perpetual state of flux, change and uncertainty in the Revolution may rather be seen as the continuing inevitable competition between discourses over the agreed alternative project that has been offered by a revolutionary ideology that was counter-hegemonic before 1959 and subsequently (after 1959) aspired to be truly hegemonic.

There is in fact a remarkable consistency in the objectives pursued that would seem to indicate the existence of an agreed, shared, 'project', however confused and vague that may be at times. This 'project', for example, seems to include the impulse towards some sort of economic independence, a determination to be guided by Cuban criteria and an awareness of the organic continuity between the Revolution and the preceding historical traditions. That conjecture is based on a study of what, firstly, we might take to be the original manifestation of the coming revolution's 'project', Castro's 1953 defence speech, 'History will absolve me', and, secondly, a comparison with the prevailing debates at all levels in the Cuba of 1999. It becomes clear that one critical element of continuity both between the pre-1959 and post-1959 years, on the one hand, and between the 1960s and the 1990s, on the other, has been this 'project', and, moreover, that the principles and 'world-view' that underlie the 'project' have been a critical factor throughout the whole forty-seven years of change – critical to popular radicalization and support, to vanguard unity and direction, and also to survival.

This discussion necessarily leads on to the final remaining element of this theoretical context, namely nationalism. At one level, the evolution of a Cuban discourse of radical dissent, resulting in, informing, guiding and then complicating the Revolution from 1959, was little more than the evolving expression of a Cuban nationalism. Once again, however, the problem lies in the term itself, and the concept that usually underlies it.

Most of the theories in the literature on nationalism, including many of the 'classical' studies, arise from, and respond to, a particular set of mostly European phenomena, dating from a particular European moment. That moment is the post-1789 'national' awakening that took shape especially between 1815 and 1850, giving rise to the revolutions of 1830 and 1848. There is certainly a whole respectable literature on the evolution of this new nationalism (Gellner 1988; Hobsbawm 1992), locating the phenomenon in social terms (relating it to the confident challenge by the new republican bourgeoisie to essentially aristocratic and monarchical imperial structures), in economic terms (linking it to the rise of industrial capitalism), and also in terms of political theory (identifying it with the rise of the new concept of the 'nation-state', and with 'triumphant bourgeois liberalism' (Hobsbawm 1992: 38). Much of this literature tends to take the view that this new ideology of nationalism, once established as the hegemonic idea of the aspiring new bourgeoisie, then became the orthodoxy of the new nation-state, cementing bourgeois control through a degree of cultural and ideological deception, having created nationalism itself as an essentially fictitious construct. As Gellner says, 'The basic deception and self-deception practiced by nationalism is this: nationalism is, essentially, the general imposition of a high culture on society, where previously low cultures had taken up the lives of the majority, and in some cases the totality, of the population' (Gellner 1988: 57). In this sense, the customary definitions of nationalism reflect closely Marxist notions of 'false consciousness', especially as Marx and others after him tended to see 'the nation' as integral to the evolution of bourgeois capitalism, as part of the nineteenth-century belief in 'history as progress'.

However, when one tries to universalize this approach, to include manifestations of 'nationalism' outside that very restricted context (even if we extend the time-frame to include later nineteenth-century Europe and even what Hobsbawm calls the 'apogee of nationalism' – namely the 1918–1950 period) (Hobsbawm 1992: 130–62), the notion remains essentially frozen in time and space, rationalizing retrospectively from the present use of the term with all its accompanying ideological baggage. Most modern studies of past nationalisms tend to project backwards our notion of the 'nation-state', based on an essentially 'modern' state structure (usually of more or less 'democratic' definition), within essentially modern notions of economic networks and production boundaries. What this means, therefore, is that, once the concept of the 'nation' is established as the intellectual yardstick for theorizing nationalism, all manifestations of nationalism become dependent on this; if a 'nation' is envisaged by the aspiring elites of a given 'national' social group, and certainly if a 'nation' emerges as a result of a political or military challenge, then nationalism *ipso facto* is deemed to have existed. But this approach leaves little intellectual space for similar manifestations of 'identity' either significantly before the so-called 'national' period (for example with the

Catalan revolts of the fifteenth and seventeenth centuries) or in political contexts that do not seem to replicate this standard. Thus, for example, most theories of nationalism treat post-1945 expressions of 'Third World nationalism' either as replicas of earlier European manifestations (with the rise of a 'national' bourgeoisie seen less in terms of its economic objectives than of its desire to lead the new 'nation' politically, echoing the efforts of the liberals of 1830–1850 Europe), or as uncomfortable inclusions within a global, but Eurocentric, theory. Certainly, it would seem that Gellner's observations about 'high culture' have less relevance in nineteenth-century Cuba, where colonialism effectively stunted many Cuban aspirations to create an autochthonous 'high culture', and where, in its absence, the task of defining a 'Cuban culture' then passed to popular forms.

The Eurocentric approach is both problematic and ahistorical. For example, just because a given 'people' did not, in 1600 or 1700, 'dream' of a nineteenth-century nation-state, that cannot mean that something that we might call 'nationalism' did not exist either in their collective minds or as a political expression and objective. It therefore seems more logical – given the evidence of such manifestations, albeit focused less on the idea of a 'state' than on a sense of cultural identity – that we turn to less restricting and more universal concepts of 'nationalism'. Here the work of Benedict Anderson gets us out of our dilemma, with his notion of 'imagined communities' (Anderson 1991).

If we project less the notion of 'nation' than that of 'imagined community' on to thought processes and political phenomena of the past, we perhaps have a more subtle and more usable definition. If a given people did 'imagine' a community to which they already belonged or to which they aspired to belong, a community larger than their locale, in which their 'belonging' was marked by a shared set of common features – speech, cultural traditions, religion, and so on, then this can be taken as some sort of 'nationalism', without having to apply to it *post hoc* rationalizations such as 'proto-nationalism'. As Anderson observes, the task of writing the history of a 'nation' – so fundamental to any nationalism – is selective 'imagined' autobiography (Anderson 1991: 204–5).

The point here is directly relevant to the Cuban case, where orthodox historiography often reflected the view that 'nationalism' either did not exist before the 1750–1820s period, or, alternatively, existed only in embryonic form, as the expression of 'precursors'. However, it can in fact be argued that, if a notion of 'Cuba' existed in the minds of political actors who systematically intellectualized and rationalized the idea in their attitude towards their position within colonial society and their relationship with the metropolis and its local representatives, then an 'imagined community' already existed. Thus, as soon as intellectuals began to coin the phrase *cubanidad* (Cuban-ness), and to develop notions of a specifically Cuban way of doing things, and of specifically Cuban approaches to Cuban problems, or of a 'Cuban culture' (as different from a 'Spanish culture') – in other words, to develop the idea that being born in the colonies in general, and in the Cuban colony in particular, gave the evolving *criollo* community a sense of 'differentness', then we can justifiably talk of 'nationalism'.[2] What few such *criollos* 'imagined' in pre-1750s Cuba (or elsewhere in the Spanish Empire) was the concept of independence, since that was something of a political and intellectual anachronism; once the French Revolution codified and legitimized the idea of 'nation', as an independent representation of a 'community', then the idea of independence – either *of* any such community, or even *from* a larger community (within which the 'nationalist' community felt itself oppressed or estranged, and prevented from expressing its 'natural' 'self') – became logical, acceptable and even desirable. Put simply, one needed a notion of 'nation', rather than that of 'state', for a concept of 'national independence' to exist.

In this sense, the general dislike in modern Cuban historiography for the term *nacionalismo* (it prefers the more acceptable term *patriotismo*) may actually indicate an underlying awareness of these distinctions and of the uncomfortable 'fit' of the Cuban case, in particular, into wider notions of 'nationalism'. This is because, although that preference undoubtedly has its roots in political and ideological positions (wherein 'nationalism' belongs to a particular period in human, economic and political evolution and tends to have negative, if not reactionary, implications), it does offer us something of an intellectual vehicle for rationalizing historical phenomena in Cuba, since the term *patria* (homeland) actually meant more of a 'community' in pre-independence Latin America than *nación* did. As one Cuban historian observes, the very use of the term *criollo* meant a degree of homogenization of the different immigrant Iberian cultures, defining not only the locally-born 'white' communities (as 'different' from the dominant *peninsular* communities), but also a completely new entity, especially as these new communities were more urban and higher up the social ladder than their counterparts in Spain (Torres-Cuevas 1995a: 6–7). It was, indeed, among these *criollos* that a sense of *patria*, or *patria chica* (literally, 'small homeland'), evolved by the early 1700s.

Furthermore, if *patriotismo* offers, through its vagueness, a more usable term to describe the evolution of a Cuban 'nationalism', then, once again, Cuban historiography and political culture come to the rescue, with the development of the term *cubanía* (defined more carefully in Chapter 2), as the political belief in *cubanidad*. While one may find it difficult to identify a clear-cut nationalism, or even a 'proto-nationalism', in pre-1860s Cuba, there is clearly an identifiable tradition of *cubanía*, whose evolution this study intends to explain – in particular tracing its evolution from 'competing discourses' set against the hegemonic, but weakening, ideology of Spanish colonialism, through the emergence of a *cubanía*

---

2. The term *criollo* refers to the locally-born white population of the Spanish American colonies.

rebelde (rebel Cubanness) to an eventual, successful but still problematic, *cubania revolucionaria.*

It is, perhaps, necessary to set this out here, since, not only does the Cuban case not fit conventional definitions of nationalism, but it also does not even fit the usual categorizations of Latin American history, into 'colonial', 'national' and 'modern' periods. This is because Cuba's post-1820s history self-evidently did not share the experience of the other former Spanish or Portuguese American colonies; and this was so in two fundamental respects. Firstly, Cuba was the only society to bridge the experience of the 'old' colonialism (as an essentially imperialist Spanish system that only with the mid-1700s Bourbon reforms[3] began to 'modernize' its relationship with the colonies, seeking to exploit their economic advantages and creating a structure to reflect that) and the 'new' colonialisms of the nineteenth century. Even there, however, the 'new colonialism' exploited vicariously, since Spain was unable to sustain a convincing exploitative colonialism in Cuba in the manner of the developing European powers in Africa. Instead, the effective colonial master in Cuba throughout the nineteenth century (the critical 'bridging' period) was increasingly the United States, which, however, lacked the political and military structures to make that colonialism real until the 1890s. Hence it could be said that Cuba actually suffered from a form of neo-colonialism long before the term was relevant elsewhere. This essential anachronism meant a wealth of complexity and contradiction in Cuban political evolution, complicated by the early existence of both an unusually large proletariat and an unusually weak bourgeoisie, leading to the tendency for a 'popular' pole of dissidence to gain an unusual degree of 'counter-hegemony' within that dissidence. In this sense, Cuban nationalism was less of a middle-class phenomenon than, for example, what one sees in 'classical' European nationalism or in the post-1945 African movements. Thus, as will be argued later, Cuban dissidence tended towards a radicalism not generally reflected elsewhere in the continent, and not least towards one that tended to 'imagine' not simply the 'nation', but also a 'community' that was by definition more radical in its implications than any 'imagined' by nationalists in, say, Mexico or Argentina, and one that was from early on implicitly, rather than explicitly, anti-imperialist. Hence *cubania* belonged neither to the nationalist categories offered by the European experiences, nor even to those of the later anti-colonial manifestations.

The second reason why the Cuban case does not fit easily is that, after 1902, the 'enemy' of 'nationalism' was not an occupying, enslaving power, but rather a suffocating one, dominating Cuba economically, culturally and militarily in ways that would only become more generalized, but rarely to the Cuban extent, in post-

---

3. The Bourbon reforms, from the mid-eighteenth century, were designed by the 'enlightened' Bourbon monarchs in Spain to reassert Spain's colonial hold in the Americas, reversing recent trends towards local autonomy and reforming trade, administration, military structures and education to the benefit of the metropolis.

1919 Latin America or in post-colonial Africa or Asia. That reality made the manifestations of *cubania* most unlike otherwise comparable phenomena in either post-1820s Latin America, or nineteenth-century Europe, or the twentieth-century Third World.

It also led on to one dominant, and overwhelming, feature of Cuban political culture – the obsession with identity, which dominated politics and dissidence from late in the colonial period until the present day. When one examines the nature of Cuban history, such an obsession becomes less 'obsessive' and more logical, because history (as ever, written by the victors) tended until the twentieth century to define Cuba as a culturally dependent, satellite entity, denying it a history of its own. In the words of one Cuban historian, 'en el caso de Cuba, siempre colocada al borde del desarreglo, existe una necesidad vital de autodefinición y autocomprensión' ('in the Cuban case, always perched on the edge of chaos, there is a fundamental need to define and to understand itself') (Torres-Cuevas 1995a: 2). In this sense, therefore, the search for independence, and later 'sovereignty', became naturally a search for a lost 'history' and an attempt to rescue an identity. *Cubania*, therefore, as will be argued henceforth, became less a 'nationalism' than a political expression of a growing collective desire to rescue and define an 'imagined community', with all the contradictions that such a search must necessarily entail.

Hence Cuba became by the 1950s a veritable 'island of "dreams"', mixing illusions with teleological visions, and creating 'real' plans on the basis of long-postponed but still believed 'dreams' of utopia; the following four decades of revolution also, it will be argued, perpetuated that pursuit of 'dreams', and, in so doing, ensured continuity and a vital social, and ideological, cement for an embattled and exhausted population. How, though, was that 'dream' (or those 'dreams') sustained for so long, and even after 1959 (with new pressures and a totally new self-image)? The answer lies, it is argued here, in myth, in politico-historical myth; which is thus necessarily the final theoretical issue to be addressed in this introduction.

The literature on the Revolution has, indeed, partly addressed the question, in two outstanding studies. The first was Judson's path-breaking analysis (Judson 1984), which addressed the importance of myth within the Revolution, stressing the differences between 'mobilizing myth' (before revolution) and 'sustaining myth' (in power). Tending to see myth as equivalent to vision and inspiration, Judson painstakingly identified the mythic elements of the guerrilla struggle, which were used deliberately after 1959 (Judson 1984: 225–64), even tracing mythification during the struggle itself, and highlighted as few had the mythic significance of the post-1959 'militarization' process, with the militia *Manual* analysed in detail (Judson 1984: 232–8), and likewise the role of the early education programmes. The second study, by Valdés, was a discussion of the 'codes' of Cuban political culture – 'patterned categories' (Valdés 1992: 208) – identifying four persistent themes: generations, the 'moralism-idealism syndrome' (Valdés 1992: 209–13), betrayal, and the 'duty–death imperative', the 'politicization of Thanatos' (Valdés 1992: 221). Although this study seeks to go beyond these analyses – taking Judson's definition more broadly and more actively, and seeing Valdés's codes as integral to the *cubanista* myths, they were critical steps in a process of deeper analysis of the Revolution, without which this study's interpretation would not have taken the direction it has.

The concept of myth developed for, and used throughout, this study in particular – politico-historical myth – is close to the anthropological meaning of the term, but has a specifically political reference, building in part on the theories of Georges Sorel (Sorel 1969), who saw myth as integral to radicalism and revolutionary change, but tended to stress more its visionary and inspirational role. It also in part acknowledges the usefulness of the theories of the French anthropologist, Claude Lévi-Strauss (Lévi-Strauss 1972: 186–231), who, for all that they have been rightly criticized and superseded by subsequent studies (usually rejecting his generalizations in favour of more concrete discoveries), long ago suggested ways of looking at myth and symbol that have something to offer to an understanding of political and ideological processes.

The term 'myth' as used here is, therefore, the cohesive set of values seen to be expressed in an accepted symbol or figure, which is perceived by a given collectivity (a class, a society, or indeed, a 'nation' – real or imagined) to articulate the 'essence' of all, or a significant component part, of its accepted ideology, and to articulate it in simple, symbolic or human – and therefore comprehensible – form. It follows, therefore, that a politico-historical myth is the means through which the 'message' of an ideological code is conveyed across time and across a society, to be comprehensible at the individual level, not least because a myth is fundamentally the code expressed as metaphor, converting a symbol normally associated with, and seen as expressing, a code into a more coherent, organic 'message', with a 'story-line'. Myth can thus be seen as the elevation of a symbol into a narrative, and a symbol therefore as the germ of a myth at a stage before organic mythification has set in.

As such, therefore it is essential that such a myth is seen to reflect the collectivity's basic agreed beliefs and self-image. The purpose of politico-historical myth is thus clear: to distil what is a complex, and often necessarily contradictory, system of beliefs in comprehensible form – comprehensible because it is expressed in a single figure, event or symbol with which the collectivity can identify itself readily, since the subject of the myth is seen to express the core value, or values, that constitute the agreed ideology. These values might, for example, be concepts of self-sacrifice, suffering, superiority, or struggle; but what distinguishes a given myth from ideology's values is that the myth is necessarily expressed in personal (human) form, either in a real, a fictitious or a legendary person (for example, an agreed 'national hero', a historic liberator, a patron saint, a Robin Hood-type figure) or in an event (real or imagined) that involved specific and defined human beings (for example, Dunkirk, Custer's 'Last Stand', the storming of the Bastille or any such event seen to be critical to the formation of the 'nation'). In this sense, therefore, it is important to separate the common usage of the word 'myth' from this anthropological-political usage, since, for a myth to be powerful, it does not need to be based on fact; if the collectivity that adheres to the myth perceives it to be true in its essentials or its message, then it exists as a reality.

The key therefore is the extent to which a politico-historical myth is perceived to be organic by those that believe in it. There are three factors that can, together, ensure this. The first is that the myth must have, and convey, a 'story-line', for a myth is essentially a 'sacred tale' (Leach 1974: 54). This must have three qualities. Firstly, the essentials of the 'story-line' must remain unchanged over years, decades or centuries, in order to acquire perceived credibility. Secondly, it must be seen to reflect either the collective perception of all, or part, of the society's or nation's own 'story' or all or part of the 'story' that underlies the accepted ideology. Thirdly, it must be expressed in a form that is changeable and re-interpretable over time, according to the circumstances in which the myth is revived or interpreted. A myth without at least an implicit 'story-line' cannot function in the same way, and becomes a less usable and less re-interpretable symbol; in this sense, a myth becomes distinguishable from a code within an ideology. The former has a 'story-line' and is focused on human figures, while the latter is essentially a microcosm of a belief system, centred around the values that are seen to be encapsulated in a given issue (land, morality, action), or a value expanded to become the subject of a wider programme of political action.

The second prerequisite for a myth's organicity is the agreed perception of the society or nation in which it exists that it is based fundamentally on a given collective experience that, whether real or imagined, is seen to have had, and still have, some sort of lasting relevance for the group. Moreover, the collective context is fundamental, for a given society needs to have a coherence and a collective sense of identity to be able and willing to produce a 'real' (organic) myth. Before it reaches that stage, ideas (which might be concepts, symbols and beliefs) may operate to a large extent in the area of myth, if enough adherents believe in the underlying idea, or if the idea expresses sufficient of the 'essence' of that society's present dilemma, its perceived past or its possible future, for it to take on mythic properties; but it cannot yet function as an organic myth. That needs to be focused on a 'story-line', which pre-organic myths necessarily lack, since the society producing these, or believing in these, still lacks sufficient coherence and sense of identity to have a 'story-line' of its own. If a society has no 'story-line' (no collective consensus on a past, or version of the past, or of a possible organic future), then it cannot produce believable organic myths. Until that point, one should more correctly refer to 'pre-myths', 'pre-organic myths', 'proto-myths', or 'inchoate myths'. Once a society has developed a sense of community and a sense of its identity as different from 'the other' (whatever 'the other' may be – for example, the society that dominates it or in some way denies authority to the oppressed society's 'authentic voice'), then there is a smoother, more natural and more organic consensus on a figure, an event (since that event will be recognized as 'significant' – since there is now a 'history' in which it can be significant), or on a metaphor that is seen to equate to the myth. A pre-organic myth cannot be a metaphor (since there is no consensus on its meaning, and all metaphor needs an 'audience' capable of interpreting its meaning and recognizing its referents). Organic myth, on the other hand, is essentially metaphoric.

The third prerequisite for organicity is the myth's need for a caste of interpreters who are, by definition, accepted by those for whom they interpret, because of either their superior knowledge within the field of the myth, or their perceived organic contribution to the 'story-line' of the myth and the wider ideology, or simply their essentially political prestige. With this prestige, respect and acceptability, these interpreters become the 'high priests' of the myth, in that they are seen to be best placed to interpret the myth legitimately for the rest of the group. The equivalent of the shaman, the priest or the oracle in religious societies and myths, they are, in the context of modern societies and of a given politico-historical myth, more likely to be popular political leaders, writers, artists or even historians (whose 'office' is after all the recording of the society's 'story-line').

What this means is that a myth without an interpreter is incapable of being interpreted and re-interpreted according to certain acceptable patterns – rather than the individualized and therefore atomized versions that would otherwise become the norm. Religious myths are the obvious model here, where a set of codes can be canonified and deemed to be comprehensible only through the mediation of initiated interpreters, whose legitimacy is enshrined in an established set of rules, symbols, incantations and rituals, all then realized collectively at the behest of the interpreter. In the field of politico-historical myth, however, similar patterns are visible, for an ideology also needs its rituals and interpreters to be credible and to survive, and, as in religion, the interpreter of a politico-historical myth must, in order to be acceptable, have an underlying ethos of authority (based on merit, education, or action, for example).

There is another sense too in which the interpreter is critical in politico-historical myth, in that any organic ideology, while it must maintain the perceived essence of its belief-system more or less unchanged (to provide continuity and an underlying 'story-line', which can be reflected in the myth), must be also capable of reinventing itself, and redefining elements beyond the canon (and redefining what the canon is), but never abandoning the concept of the canon itself. In this respect, the only ones capable of directing such a process of redefinition and reinvention (within accepted parameters) are the interpreters.

It is clear from this that the parallels between the anthropological notions of religious myth and the notion of politico-historical myth applied here are necessarily close. This is because, historically, societies have always tended to develop and require two different sorts of myth.

Traditionally, in religious societies (where the hegemonic ideology is essentially a religious belief system, usually involving acceptance of a supernatural entity that controls our existence in some form or other), the essential myth-figures tend to be gods, saints or demons, especially where these are endowed by the society with certain specific values – the god of this, or the patron saint of that. What characterizes religious myth, however, is the essential alienation of its meaning from the common experience and concerns, meaning that the myth survives as a perfect, but unattainable, ideal, whose purpose is to inspire rather than to guide in specific detail.

This brings us necessarily to the concepts of symbol and icon, and of the processes of what we might call 'symbolization' and 'iconization', both of which have a relevance for politico-historical myth too. The difference between myth and either symbol or icon here lies in the 'story-line'; a myth needs one, to remain as a living, adaptable and meaningful guide to real collective action, parallel to the society's self-image, while both a symbol and an icon lack a 'story-line' and thus remain more static, the latter more as a model for perfect being, almost certainly on an individual rather than a collective level.

Thus it can be argued that a politico-historical myth has the potential to revert to the status of symbol – to become 'symbolized'; if that status is maintained for any length of time, without that status's being challenged and without any resistance, or attempt (by accepted interpreters) to rescue the mythic core of the symbol, then the symbol has the potential to become refined to the status of icon. Reversion in this sense is actually more useful, for the evidence is that, when a myth becomes 'frozen' (because of changed circumstances and a changed relevance of the myth), it 'retreats' to the pre-mythic status of symbol, which in a sense puts the myth 'into store', enabling it to be rescued subsequently when either the circumstances change or the old, or new, interpreters gain hegemony and legitimacy and return to the 'message' of the symbol–myth.

However, the process of iconization – which is, thus, not a development of a myth but, rather a development of the previously mythic symbol – requires the sanctification of the mythic subject, with the figure who is the basis of the myth becoming an object for veneration; for an 'icon is also a concrete codification of a truth, a symbol of a myth and an embedding of its basic story-line' (Kapcia 1997b: 90). What, however about the process itself, of what we can call symbolization-iconization? The critical points here are that it can be either the result of accident

– especially when the myth loses its organicity or relevance, because the context has changed – or, even more significantly, can be deliberate, when the hegemonic powers determine that it is in the interests of safety and stability and preserving a status quo that the myth should become more obfuscated so that ideological control can be more effectively exercised through the priesthood.

It should, however, be said that the use of the term 'icon' can be misleading, and even loaded and ambiguous. In Protestant societies, icons are usually seen essentially negatively and as equivalent to idolatry, while Eastern Orthodoxy, for example, sees icons not as objects for an alienated veneration but, rather, as accessible representations of an unfathomable abstract deity. It is clear, therefore, that, just as myth needs to be treated carefully and taken to mean here only what it is defined as, so too should 'icon' either be used sparingly or seen more in its political usage and context.[4]

The fact is that the other kind of myth that societies traditionally develop – the politico-historical myth – uses the same sort of structures, patterns and terminology, at least within the European Christian tradition; but while a secular society and system may seem similar to religious systems, they are actually quite different, and the nature of myth and icon must necessarily differ too.

What then of such politico-historical myths? The most characteristic feature of these is their focus on a real or fictitious figure, whose 'story-line' is seen to represent that of the society at large, reflecting the perceived essence of the social, political, and even moral or spiritual needs of the society. It is precisely the human form of such myths that gives them power, meaning and relevance, enabling the 'faithful' to identify with the figure in a way that an alienated icon cannot. This is especially true because the status of myth has mostly been achieved by that figure's actions at a given moment or period of agreed significance for the society. For a society in need of self-identity, for example, that fact can make the myth a rallying-point for crucial acts of mobilization or simply a basis for a wilful assertion of identity against external attempts to deny it. In this context, the adaptability of the myth is critical to the society's ability to use, re-use and re-interpret it as that society changes, but the underlying sense of loss of identity does not change.

With this in mind, one can thus return to the questions of symbol, and symbolization, and icon and iconization, with reference to politico-historical myth, since the same process whereby mythification can lead potentially to symbolization-iconization can be seen here, but perhaps with some key differences. The first is that, since religious myths focus attention on the 'beyond' while politico-historical myths focus on the past (usually nostalgically, set against the unacceptable present), the potentially positive identification that, as indicated, might well be associated

4. I am indebted here to David Browning, of Cambridge University, for his helpful comments on these points.

with 'icon' seems less applicable. While, in religious myth, the accepted purpose of an icon can be to present an unattainable but still relevant ideal, in politico-historical myth the process of iconization is rarely used to the same effect, since the faithful do not necessarily participate in the ritual with the same conviction as in a religious context. The purpose may well be the same, but the effect may well be different, since organicity depends on the willingness of key groups (defined as 'key' according to the circumstances of the time and place) to accept the myth, even where this might be deliberately created or fostered by an elite wishing to cement its hegemony. For the essence of hegemony is the willingness of the dominated to adopt the hegemonic vision as truly reflective of their situation, their history, their future and their aspirations. Therefore a secular myth must function somewhat differently from a religious myth, since the focus of the latter is neces-sarily on veneration of a deliberately and acceptably alienated supernatural entity and plane, wherein control of the subordinated is enshrined, while a secular myth seeks to be relevant and needs that relevance in order to continue convincing. Thus, when the component parts of the secular myth cease to be convincing, iconization sets in, and may easily become problematic for the myth-making elites.

In this context, therefore, to distinguish the processes of secular and religious myth, it may be as well to talk of one further stage in the iconization process, namely political 'totemization', where a political icon is either a stage in the path towards political totemization (in the context of a lost organicity) or a conscious attempt by the interpreters to make the ideal accessible, or, in the context of ideology, to make the canon comprehensible. However, the very use of the term 'canon' (whether explicit or implicit) means by definition the existence of a necessary aim to objectivize and venerate. Therefore 'icon' in this context is not so much a distortion as a mediation between myth and canon.

There are some further relevant points regarding the usefulness of the concept of an 'icon'. The first is that, as literary criticism discovered long ago, any process of self-definition and self-identification must rely for its coherence and credibility on a parallel definition of 'the other'. Thus, as in personal histories, so too in cultural histories, for it can be argued that a culture can only begin to define itself as different in response to a concept of 'other-ness', which means that any process of cultural self-definition (in a context of historical denial of that identity) must possess an essentially negative dimension – that the culture is only itself because it is not the 'other'.

If we observe this process in the context of theatre, for example, we can see this more clearly, for, if it can be argued that theatre is an appropriate (and indeed almost an 'ideological') way for an author, an actor or an audience to identify naturally with 'the other' (and therefore a valuable way to approach the ideological issues of 'self' and 'other-ness'), it follows that iconization could well be a parallel method to allow an identification with myth (and therefore ideology). In other words, an icon can be the equivalent of the 'other', but the process of identification leads to a sense of 'self', which in turn leads to a strengthening of a group identity. If so, then it must confirm the idea that to talk of 'iconization' as alienation is inappropriate if an icon is seen as static and objectified; on the other hand, if the icon is seen as more active, and more relevant, then iconization is indeed appropriate as a mechanism for defining the collective 'self', for, at one level, the dichotomy between 'self' and 'other' identified here is simply the tension between 'subject' and 'object' in another guise.

This leads on to a further observation, namely that, if all ideology is to do with identity and all ideological battles happen in societies where identity has been denied systematically by some 'other', then notions of schizophrenia may well have much to tell us about the processes of denial and self-definition in the colonial and postcolonial contexts.

The final observation about myth and icon refers to the question of gender, for it seems apparent that figures encapsulated and extolled in myth (and certainly in icon) tend mostly to be male. This is logical, firstly, since secular myths are usually a reflection of male-dominant cultures; but, secondly, because a myth in a dominated society is invariably about concepts such as struggle, conflict and power and, therefore, it follows that the myth's 'story-line' is likely to be couched in essentially and acceptably male terms. It therefore also follows that a society that is more egalitarian in gender terms or more self-confident may well focus less on male figures in myth and icon and more potentially on gender-free issues and female figures (real ones, as opposed to symbolical ones). Thus discussions of 'self' and 'other' that have been developed in studies on feminism may well also have a major part to play in discussions of colonialism and postcolonialism.

This whole discussion has inevitably raised a number of issues that need to be at least partly addressed here. One such is the question of totem, which arose as a possible extension of the process of iconization. What then might be said to be the difference between politico-historical myth and political totem in secular societies? The answer would seem to lie in the distinction between the one – myth – which must have a 'story-line' (with both symbol and icon being understood as a myth whose 'story-line' has become more static or less relevant) and the other – totem – which is a symbol of a myth, a reminder to the adherents of the underlying 'story-line'. Therefore a totem leads to thought, not veneration, and is seen as the symbol of the whole 'clan'. Thus, in political terms, in a given and especially more sophisticated society, a political totem can be a person, an object, or a 'key' word (especially where the underlying myth has a motive power), and can easily be seen as the focus of all good (about the 'clan') or all bad (about the dominant power, set against the 'clan').

The second supplementary issue raised has been that of ritual, vital to the inculcation of myths and beliefs in religious societies. But what of politico-historical myths and secular societies? What sort of ritual does an ideology have? The answer is actually relatively easy and obvious, for it is clear that the ritualization of ideology can be seen most clearly in processions, parades and any sort of 'ritualized' celebration of events, anniversaries, and so on. Furthermore, it may be daily evidenced, but rarely noticed, in the routine manifestations of nationalism, in what Billig calls, 'banal nationalism' (Billig 1995), for 'ritualization' of myth does not have to be ceremonial or special. It may also, however, be manifest in any sort of canonical behaviour, incantation or symbolism that leads to a definition of an 'in' group (with access to the 'meaning' of the signs, the chants and the celebration). What therefore evolves with political 'ritual' is a sense that the group (society, nation) is protected, with responsibility for protection handed over to the accepted 'initiates'.

The observation was also made earlier that myths are necessarily metaphorical, in the sense that metaphors can be either the necessary distillation of the myth, making the myth comprehensible (just as myth makes ideology comprehensible) and allowing people to understand it in their 'authentic voice', or they can exist alongside myth, as another means of internalization. Where this occurs, this must depend on the nature of metaphor and the level of literacy and education.

All of this leads inexorably on to the sphere of language. Firstly, myths imply the use of a common language, since discourse is either ideology or language, and, of course, is frequently both. Secondly, the language of ritual and the language that is the property of the 'priests' of the myth are vital tools in the processes of persuasion, conviction and self-denial or affirmation. One only has to glance at the debates within historiography, autobiography, literature and feminism referring to the question of an 'authentic voice' to see how this operates; but also the outstanding example is the control of religious belief traditionally in pre-Vatican Council Catholic societies through the 'mediators'' exclusive control of Latin. Language is therefore fundamental to the question of ideology, myth and icon.

The sociolinguist Frederick Erickson has begun to unravel this by his arguments about 'utterings' (official discourse) and 'mutterings' (unofficial discourse) in a society.[5] Basically, the conclusion to be drawn from his theories regarding hegemony and discourse is that, if 'mutterers' use the 'voice' of the interpreters to express the ideology, then they are ritualizing their willing acquiescence in the internalization of the hegemonic ideology. If, on the other hand, they use their own 'voice', they are appropriating it, and becoming subjects not objects, while, if they use both, this may indicate either tensions or an awareness of areas of 'competence', meaning the existence of areas reserved for 'authority' (which are too complex or too 'sacred' to be anything other than the property of the interpreters,

---

5. These ideas were outlined in a seminar paper delivered by Erickson at the University of Cardiff in 1997.

who are, by definition, 'the initiated') and other areas that are free for more autonomous grass-roots interpretation. Alternatively, it may reflect the weakness of the ideology. These ideas are given here since they are relevant to the specific research project that was carried out in 1997 and 1998 in Cuba and forms part of the later discussion in this study.

These, then, are the concerns and methodology that have determined the pattern of the study. It is divided into two parts. Part I ('Ideology and Revolution') deals with the relationship between ideology and revolution in Cuba: essentially the evolution of the national 'dream' of *Cuba Libre*, Chapter 1 tracing, in necessary detail and length, the pre-1959 development of *cubania*, locating the emergence of the Revolution in a context of a search for national identity, and Chapter 2 taking that narrative further, into the first decade of the Revolution, as the process sought a definition of a revolutionary identity within that *cubania*, developing existing traditions and currents of dissident nationalism into a coherent strategy for ideological impulse, direction and cohesion. Part II, 'Myth and Ideology', then traces the evolution, within that *cubania*, of the component myths, Chapter 3 tracing the pre-1959 myths and the myth-making process, and Chapter 4 identifying the continued process of myth-making and myth-sustaining after 1959. The Conclusion then addresses the question of contemporary Cuba, explaining adjustment to crisis and the underlying challenges to the Revolution posed by both crisis and adjustment, but also offering a perspective of the system's survival and redefinition within the context of *cubania* and the dynamic role of myth, and offering an overall set of perspectives with which to judge, understand and explain the whole Revolution, not least as it is today in its fifth decade of existence.

One final point of explanation about the study's approach needs to be made here. This is that, since this study is not a an attempt to present a history of either pre-revolutionary Cuba or the Cuban Revolution itself, but rather to interpret it in a particular way, there are necessarily elements that are omitted, at least in more than passing analysis.

One of the most obvious is the question of the role of race in creating a revolutionary alternative or challenge to either imperialism, neo-colonialism, hegemony or the Cuban ruling elites. A proper history would necessarily have to deal with this issue, and this study makes reference to its significant role. This, however, is, if anything, a history of *cubania*, which tended for long periods to remain a relatively narrowly-based 'world-view', although one that, as will be seen, progressively broadened its appeal and relevance, acquired significant social and radical dimensions and so attained a deeper popular legitimacy, with revolutionary implications; a great part of that process was attributable to the growing role of black Cubans and racial issues, especially in the nineteenth century. However, for much of its pre-revolutionary history, *cubania* tended to make assumptions about an eventual *Cuba Libre* that were narrowly defined in racial and class terms.

As this study will make clear, black Cubans were prominent in the developing struggle for radical definitions of Cuba and for social justice, and that contribution was fundamental to the growing strength of a radical discourse in Cuba and a revolutionary alternative, a 'living history of antiracist discourse and mobilization' (Ferrer 1999: 199). However, the fact remains that until 1959, and even beyond, the majority of the 'high priests', the interpreters, of *cubanía* tended to be white (and middle-class and male), who may have been speaking even in a populist way to a wider social audience, but were formed politically and intellectually in a tradition that eventually either excluded race (because of race fears, prejudice or the notion that nationalism superseded racial questions and indeed had solved any racial divisions) or preferred to blur the racial issue for political reasons. As one recent study puts it, 'Revolutionary rhetoric [. . .] made the revolution a mythic project that armed black and white men together to form the world's first raceless nation' (Ferrer 1999: 3). Even in the three wars of independence, the greater the contribution of black Cubans to the evolving struggle, the greater the fear among otherwise radical whites, at all social levels (Ferrer 1999); thus, although there was a general belief that separatism needed to address the question of slavery and racial equality, and that these therefore informed the developing discourse, that often amounted to defining *cubanidad* as against colonial status or 'Spanishness', and did not necessarily mean a consensual view on race and nation.

Therefore a history of a nation's collective and evolving self-perception and self-definition must recognize that, until after the Revolution, these at best implicitly included a black identity in the broader vision, or 'dream', as part of the imagined raceless community, and at times explicitly excluded that identity, that 'other'. The history of black radicalism in Cuba therefore remains to be written, and is indeed partly being rescued by many contemporary scholars; but it generally forms only a part of the picture painted by, and falls outside the remit of, this study.

The second omission, more obvious, is an analysis of the development of a parallel *cubanía* outside Cuba after 1959, not least in the largest émigré community in Florida. Just as, in the nineteenth century, Cuban emigrants preserved their sense of national identity, and indeed developed it radically, with significant effects for the evolution of the eventual ideology of nationalist dissent in Cuba itself, so too one would expect the large and cohesive emigrant community resulting from the revolutionary transformation to preserve a sense of national(ist) identity, especially driven by a belief (at the start) in an eventual return to Cuba to reclaim a supposed inheritance. It is certainly evident that one encounters in Miami many of the same obsessions with *cubanidad*, José Martí and the perceived idiosyncracies of the Cuban character that one finds in Cuba after 1959.

However, it would be inappropriate to include that dimension in this study, since its aim is to explain the Revolution in Cuba, both its origins before 1959 and its evolution after, including, importantly, its survival into and through the 1990s crisis. In that respect, whatever parallels there might be between a Florida-based *cubania* and a Cuban-based one (and there are many, and this is a rich seam for many a research project), the fact is that once a separate *cubania* began to develop outside Cuba after 1959, always for political reasons, its evolution inevitably had less and less effect on the patterns, myths, codes and overall 'world-view' of its counterpart inside Cuba. Only if a significant part of that émigré community were either to return to Cuba or to contribute directly, rather than just financially, to the evolution of the Cuban political system would the two parallel *cubanias* be likely to fuse and would the emigrant version merit inclusion in a specific study of this kind, as having contributed to such a fusion.

Quite simply what this study deals with is the evolution of a specific set of 'dreams' centred around a specific historical experience and, after 1959, a very specific and often isolated collective experience. It is the internal cohesion and inner logic of those collective 'dreams' that is the subject of the analysis here. Other dimensions must necessarily be left for other analyses.

Part I
Ideology and Revolution

The Search for a Cuban National Identity
Until 1958

If modern Cuba's political evolution is, indeed, unique, then the roots of that uniqueness need to be sought in its history, a study of which conventionally begins with the brief British occupation of Havana in 1762 (Thomas 1971). However, that convention was established by a hegemonic sugar 'plantocracy', seeking legitimacy through an identification of Cuba and sugar (Moreno Fraginals 1977: 127).[1] Therefore, the logical place to begin searching is later, with the failure of the Cuban *criollos* in 1810–26 to follow their mainland counterparts in breaking with Spain.

Until then, Cuba's colonial experience was arguably unique only in scale (numbers of slaves, size of garrison and trading importance);[2] indeed, Cuba shared the wider colonial experience in losing embryonic economic autonomy (*desmanufacturación* – 'de-industrialization') (López Segrera 1981: 100) after the Bourbon reforms.

After the 1820s, when colonialism survived, Cuba became (with Puerto Rico) a case apart. Once Cuban *criollos* opted for Spanish imperial protection rather than risk a repetition of the 1791 events in Saint Domingue (Haiti) – where some 500,000 slaves had rebelled – Cuba's unique, and even distorted, destiny was sealed,[3] as a slave-owning, sugar-exporting economy, a destination for largely white immigration, and a system increasingly dominated by an ever more recalcitrant Spanish population and administration.

The most notable deformation, as a reinvigorated colonialism retrenched, was that Cuba seemed to sink into what later Cuban historiography (accepting the

---

1. The case for 1762 as the start of 'modern' Cuba seems overwhelming, given that the occupation exposed the isolated Cuban bourgeoisie to the possibilities of free trade, capitalist production and freethinking, and was when the potential of sugar and slavery was first realized.

2. Havana's role in the colonial fleet system was crucial, as garrison (for protection), supply station, repair-yard, and point where the Americas-bound fleet divided into two or the return fleet gathered.

3. Saint Domingue was critical, haunting an increasingly slave-owning *criollo* class and distorting perspectives long into the next century; the impact of events there was enhanced by the influx of 27,000 French refugees (Thomas 1971: 77, footnote).

version created by American historiography after, and to justify, the 1898 intervention and subsequent occupation) (Perez 1999: 121) would characterize as almost a 'dark age', when *independencia* was not raised seriously outside certain committed intellectual circles. This revisionism was, however, largely attributable to the desire of post-1902 historians to legitimize their own 'generation of 1895', which had 'rescued' the 'real' Cuba begun in the post-1868 independence struggles; one later commentator observed that, until the 1920s, there was a dearth of good historiography,[4] a perspective that was unsurprising, given that, after 1902, with collective disillusion and self-doubt, Cuba's apparent incapacity for independence could be exonerated by the absence of earlier *independentismo*. Also when, after 1902, the idea grew of greater incorporation into the United States' orbit, a similar rationalization of a non-nationalist Cuba was to be expected.

However, although there is evidence of a weaker nationalist constituency in pre-1808 Cuba than in other colonies, Cuban *criollos* were attracted, as elsewhere, by the Enlightenment or the American and French revolutions; indeed, Havana *criollos* gave almost two million pesos to support the North American struggle (Torres-Cuevas 1995a: 14). Equally, there is evidence of the impact of an emancipating freemasonry, especially in 1762, when an Irish regiment was entrusted with spreading the masonic word.[5] These progressive currents were often found in Cuba in the same three main areas of activity as elsewhere in Spanish America – in higher education (the Real y Pontífica Universidad de San Gerónimo, which, after 1842 secularization, became the University of Havana, and the Real Colegio Seminario de San Carlos y San Ambrosio, where the radical priest Félix Varela introduced the study of politics (Simpson 1984: 26)); in the Sociedad Económica de Amigos del País (Economic Society of Friends of the Country), founded in 1792 by Francisco de Arango y Parreño, a young *criollo* sugar planter who argued for a slave-based expansion of the sugar industry;[6] and in magazines, especially the influential *Revista Bimestre Cubana*, which (between 1831 and 1834) became a mouthpiece for enlightened opinion in Havana.[7]

There was even evidence of collective *criollo* self-confidence (similar to that in 1807 in Buenos Aires), in the shape of the 9,000-strong Cuban militia's contribution to the defence of Havana against an earlier British invasion in 1741 (Torres-Cuevas 1995a: 14). Even the use of the term *criollo* indicated a new awareness,

4. Observed by Fernando Portuondo del Prado, in his *Prólogo* (Tabares del Real 1973: 9).

5. I am indebted to Verity Smith; after the British departure, freemasonry was revived by French refugees, the first lodge being founded in 1804.

6. The Sociedades, throughout the empire, manifested Enlightenment thinking on trade, agriculture, education, science and literature, becoming the seedbed for separatism; Cuba was thus part of the intellectual mainstream.

7. The *Revista* (published by Mariano Cubí and José Antonio Saco) was backed by the Sociedad Económica (Liss 1987: 5).

although the process of *acriollamiento* ('becoming *criollo*') reflected more a sense of *patria chica* or *patria local* (Torres-Cuevas 1995a: 12). There were also separatist conspiracies – notably Román de la Luz's masonic conspiracy in 1809 and then, after the continental rebellions had begun, the 1823 attempt by the freemasonry-influenced secret society, Rayos y Soles de Bolívar, which sought an alliance between liberal whites and both free and slave blacks. Certainly, it seems to have been around that time that the slogan *Cuba Libre* (Free Cuba) was coined; and the reforms proposed by the 1820 Liberal Spanish Cortes did stimulate the emergence of a coterie of reformers, liberals, freemasons and radicals.

Cuba was therefore little different from, and may even have been more 'dissident' than, other less prepared colonies; indeed, from 1762, progressive ideas may have been stimulated in Cuba more than elsewhere, for the British occupation set in train developments that would change Cuba irrevocably. Access to non-Spanish shipping (over 700 ships arriving in Havana in those months, compared to fifteen annually earlier) (Thomas 1971: 51), the import of 5,000 slaves, the tantalizing access to North American markets and the impact of new ideas of free trade, freethinking, freemasonry, private property and competition – all broke the stranglehold of a monopolistic and often obscurantist colonialism.

Even after Spain accepted independence on the mainland (although continuing to dream of a possible reconquest),[8] *Cuba Libre* remained in the minds of a minority of Cuban intellectuals, the University becoming 'a source of nationalist sentiment and a distribution point for political polemics with a historical orientation' (Liss 1987: 6). However, such currents were now increasingly overwhelmed and silenced by a combination of factors.

Firstly, Spanish immigration increased, both from Spain – encouraged to 'whiten' the island (Quiroz 1998: 265) – and from the ex-colonies, as thousands of loyalist refugees fled to Cuba, with hopes of a possible return. Secondly, the spectre of Haiti increased, as the slave population rose (to some 150,000 by 1817, with about 100,000 being imported between 1816 and 1820) (Thomas 1971: 65), and as small conspiracies occurred (Morales in 1795 and Aponte, the black freemason, in 1810). Thirdly, sugar now led to prosperity, production rising from 300 tonnes (t) annually in the 1750s to 160,000t in 1836, cane-land increasing from 10,000 acres (1762) to 160,000 in 1792 (Thomas 1971: 61), stimulated by the 1765 *comercio libre* decree, which (unusually in the colonies) allowed Cubans to trade on equal terms (Lynch 1973: 13). Fourthly, colonial retrenchment coincided with the first so-called 'sugar revolution' (stimulated by new technology, capital and expertise) and led to *criollo* recognition that their wealth depended on sugar, and thus on a slavery best guaranteed by Spanish connivance and protection.

---

8. In 1862, Spain returned disastrously to Santo Domingo, invited by the beseiged Dominican government.

The fifth factor was *criollo* awareness that the post-1826 balance of power in the Western hemisphere and the growing understanding between them meant that neither Britain nor the United States (godparents to so many new republics) – nor, it transpired, Bolívar, who, in 1824, specifically ruled out liberation – would insist on Spain's removal from Cuba; and indeed after Canning proposed it in 1823 they defended the status quo,[9] preferring a Spanish Cuba to a weak and vulnerable independent Cuba. Even Jefferson's offer, in 1808, to the Spanish Captain-General in Cuba to purchase Cuba was only a second-best alternative.

Finally, after the restoration of Spanish absolutism in 1823, the sheer weight of colonial administration determined to hold on to its main remaining, and now lucrative, American colony, meant the garrisoning of an average of 25,000–30,000 troops (Thomas 1971: 102).

Nonetheless, some of the exponents of separatism merit mention here, not least because they helped codify the basic elements of the future *cubanía*. The most outstanding was Varela, the first to fully address the question of the Spanish–Cuban political relationship, proposing colonial autonomy in the Cortes, in 1822 (Torres-Cuevas 1997: 311); later, by fleeing Cuba, he began the long tradition of American exile. The other significant 'precursor' was José Antonio Saco, so characteristic of the contradictions of the Cuban intelligentsia, pioneering the proposition of a Cuban nationality (Opatrný 1994: 52), but limiting it to a *criollismo blanco* ('belief in a white *criollo* identity') (Ibarra Cuesta 1967: 25), advocating education to prepare for self-government, Cuban equality within the Empire, and even abolition of slavery and the slave trade, but also increased white immigration as a civilizing counterbalance to the numbers of slaves. In this, Saco foreshadowed the later Cuban positivism.

However, what was evolving was less a 'nationalism' than a sense of *cubanidad*, and, thus, the start of *cubanía* – the belief in *cubanidad*.[10] This, at one level, differed little from the evolving Spanish American concept of the *patria chica* – a proud awareness of the distinctiveness of one's immediate region and its needs. Elsewhere, this 'proto-nationalism' was catapulted into full independence only by Napoleon's 1808 invasion of Spain and the resulting separation of Crown from colony.

---

9. Strategic competition over Cuba largely led President Monroe, in 1823, to declare his 'doctrine', which, opposing any new American colonies and any extension of existing empires, tolerated surviving colonies (including Cuba).

10. The terms *cubanidad* and *cubanía* are well established in Cuban literature and historiography and are thus used here in preference to 'Cubanness'. Elsewhere, the author has used *cubanismo*, which, in Cuba, can confusingly mean peculiarities of Cuban Spanish; equally, *cubanista* (from *cubanía* or *cubanismo*) is used throughout to describe adherents to *cubanía*, since, although the term can also be confusing in Cuba (meaning Cuba specialists or Cubaphiles), there is no easy shorthand alternative.

In Cuba, because of all these obstacles, *criollismo* remained ossified as a relatively limited, mostly cultural, concern with *cubanidad*. However, driven especially by Varela, who advocated Cuban intellectual solutions to Cuban problems, *cubanidad* then gathered momentum, in very unique conditions, going beyond the elementary nationalism just discernible in newly independent Latin America to become a very different and more progressive, and, ultimately, a radical phenomenon.

The reasons may lie in the differences between the republics (often thrust into independence and then beset by internal struggle and economic weakness) and Cuba, where Spanish imperialism, though more intense, racist and oppressive, was nonetheless less efficient than before 1808, opening Cuba to outside ideas, and radicalizing responses, to make *cubanía* into a potentially more radical version of nationalism than any then evolving on the mainland – except perhaps in Mexico.

Meanwhile, Cuban society was changing fast, with the vertiginous development of sugar after 1762 (from 1,500t in 1762 to 26,000t in 1800, 223,000t in 1850 and then 750,000t by 1868), which transformed a once stagnant colony into one of the world's richest, with a dynamic sugar oligarchy – a *sacarocracia* (Moreno Fraginals 1977: 21) – committed to capitalist production and trade, and to technological change. Even slavery, by the early 1800s, was an essentially capitalist enterprise, based on investment decisions and commodity relations that belied the apparent feudalism of plantation production relations.

However, the oligarchy's rise contained the seeds of its own decline, for the relentless logic of 'comparative advantage' and the impulse for limitless growth ensured a monoculture, sugar oligopolistically displacing its potential rivals for economic hegemony, tobacco and coffee.[11] The resulting tendency towards inefficiency was hastened by the oligarchy's fatal lack of capital, which, with technology again about to revolutionize world sugar production, obliged them to cut costs,[12] at precisely the point when slavery was becoming expensive, with British and American abolition of the slave trade (1807–8) and even Spain's formal 1845 prohibition on slave imports. Yet slavery continued as the basis of an essentially extensive production, and oligarchic dynamism began to turn into stagnation and decline, especially for the more slave-dependent Cuban producers in the east, who, by the 1860s, were less able to compete with the Spanish planters elsewhere on the island.

---

11. Tobacco was challenged by the 1817 toleration of landowning, leading to the disappearance of small tobacco growers – *vegueros*. The classic study of tobacco is by Jean Stubbs (Stubbs 1985).

12. The first 'revolution' consisted of mass cane production based on a single mill (*ingenio*) that owned both the cultivation and the processing plant, using new steam technology and railways. See especially Manuel Moreno Fraginals (Moreno Fraginals 1977) and Thomas (Thomas 1971: 109–27, 271–80).

Other significant social changes were also happening. Immigration, and improved conditions saw the overall white population rise from 96,440 in 1774 to 311,051 by 1827, mostly concentrated in the more urban west (Knight 1970: 22), while the slave population grew dramatically, from 38,879 in 1774 to 286,942 in 1827 and, by 1841, to 436,495 (Knight 1970: 22), with further massive importations to follow (387,216 between 1835 and 1864) (Knight 1970: 53).

Socially, Cuban slavery by then was highly complex, varying according to economic activity, size of workforce and nationality of owner.[13] However, one feature of Cuban slave life that was unusual (although not unique) was the evolution of eclectic Afro-Cuban religious expressions, in *santería* and other forms.[14] Arising from the strength of the recent immigration (which made Cuba one of the most African of Caribbean societies) (Benítez Rojo 1996: 68), and from the different cultural African origins of Cuban slaves, fused forcibly in the workplace, this expression served several functions.

At one level, it was a safety-valve, allowing an opportunity for collective self-expression and thus some residual cultural identity in the face of appalling conditions, brutal treatment, collective deculturation and the Spanish preference for formal religious conformity. Thus, while the term 'syncretic' is rightly condemned for implying a non-existent equality of status and power, it nonetheless stresses that, for the oppressed cultures of the Empire (African or indigenous), a tolerated religious hybridity did allow some valuable degree of cultural resistance and defensive self-expression (Benítez Rojo 1996: 160), especially in colonial Cuba, where the Church's institutional and social weakness (with few adherents, neglect from Madrid and no *mulato* priesthood) allowed greater freedom to slaves to preserve their various cultural and religious practices.

Where slave religions were, however, more genuinely syncretic was in the creation, out of different African beliefs, of a unique cultural and religious expression for the new increasingly Afro-Cuban (rather than African) population, with a new cosmology, new beliefs, and new myths and rituals, although these were dominated by the larger groups among the slaves. The effect was doubly significant, ensuring, on the one hand, that the new African population – its majority workforce and, by the 1840s, its majority population, with 43.3 per cent being slave and a further 15.1 per cent being free blacks (Knight 1970: 22) – had an unusual basis for internal cohesion, and, on the other hand, that a unique cultural expression was already evolving in Cuba. While the *criollos* were unsure about their different identity, the evolving Afro-Cuban population was already creating

13. For further discussion of the evolving Cuban institution, see especially Thomas (1971: 28–41, 168–83), Knight (1970: 59–120), and Ferrer (1999).

14. The term *santería* is often misleading; referring to only one of the Afro-Cuban religions, it is often used for all. In fact, it was largely based on the Lucumí (Yoruba) culture, while the more secretive *Abakuá* (whose adepts were *ñáñigos*) was based on the Efik (eastern Nigeria).

the basis for a distinctively Cuban cultural expression. *Santería* can thus rightly be seen as the first mass manifestation of the sentiment that would eventually evolve into *cubanía*.

Hence, Cuba was already, by the mid-nineteenth century, very different from the rest of Latin America, even Brazil (whose continuing slavery bore some resemblance) – a difference now increased by the role of the United States, which, having already been decisive in Cuba's destiny, now began to exercise a critical attraction in the rise of annexationism, an understandably complex and sensitive issue in Cuba. Annexation's roots were to be found in two, almost contradictory, places. On the one hand, it sprang from *criollo* liberalism, which was either inspired by the American experience or believed pragmatically that Cuba needed protection by a larger entity; indeed, the 1823 conspirators sought annexation by Mexico or Colombia (Opatrný 1993: 55). On the other hand, it also arose among sugar planters, who feared liberal Spanish or British abolitionist pressure, with the loyalist Havana *cabildo* (town council) even entering into secret discussions in 1810 with the US consul over possible American annexation and with an annexationist delegation to Washington in 1822.

Annexation was perhaps logical in the first half of the century. By 1861, around 600,000 slaves had been imported into Cuba, leading to a slave population of perhaps 27 per cent of the total 1.4 million, down from its worrying peak of 43 per cent (Thomas 1971: 169).[15] This was the clear majority of the Afro-Cuban population, as there were possibly only about 100,000 *mulatos* and about 30,000 freed ex-slaves (Thomas 1971: 173). In all, slavery (constituting a third of all sugar investment) was an investment to be preserved at all costs and likely to be guaranteed by annexation.

Annexation would also give access to the American market. Frustrated by the brief 1762 access, Cuban sugar had increasingly gone northwards since 1783, when independence cut the American market off from British West Indian sugar, followed by the collapse of Haitian sugar after 1791. Even as early as 1826, 783 of the 964 ships entering Havana were American, and the desire of American traders to increase that relationship was all too evident (Thomas 1971: 194).

Annexation was also attractive, given the weakness of the colonial apparatus that led *criollos* to fear both British abolitionist pressure on Spain (through the zealous Consul, Turnbull) and also the increasing evidence of slave revolt, especially the famous Escalera conspiracy of 1841, which, although largely in the imagination of fearful whites and probably the coincidence of several overlapping conspiracies (Paquette 1988: 263), resulted in 4,000 arrests and the death of the

---

15. Statistics on slave imports are notoriously unreliable and subject to considerable revision. One estimate, for example, has only 467,288 slaves being imported between 1790 and 1865 (Ibarra Cuesta 1967: 12)

black poet, Plácido.[16] Contradictorily, however, Spanish intransigence, welcome against such revolts, also antagonized many *criollos* when, in 1836, Governor Tacón decreed that the new Spanish Constitution was not valid for Cuba.

Thus annexationism took hold, especially in the influential Club de La Habana, becoming significant among liberal and conservative *criollos* alike, with Havana students, for example, enthusiastically supporting Narciso López's 1850 annexationist expedition to liberate Cuba (Pichardo 1983: 42–5). Herein lies the sensitivity around annexationism and the evolution of a Cuban nationalism, with many later preferring to see annexationism either as a desperate aberration from an otherwise consistent trajectory of 'pure' *cubanía* or as simple betrayal of that tradition. Yet, for all its pragmatism (believing in the impracticality of independence), annexationism did nonetheless constitute an argument for Cuban separation from Spain and colonialism, and also for a Cuban identity. For all that self-interest may have motivated some, many genuinely saw annexation as a patriotic solution, and, as one radical 1930s historian argued, it is an error to see annexationism as always and everywhere anti-patriotic (Roig de Leuchsenring 1937; see Opatrný 1993 and Cruz-Taura 1997 for discussion of annexationism).

However, one interesting aspect of annexationism is how and why the idea also took hold within the United States, stimulated by the successful Texan and Mexican wars (1836 and 1845–6), which led to triumphalism, new wealth, a strengthening of the southern slaving states, and the first stirrings of the ethos of 'Manifest Destiny'.[17] A more expansionist United States now returned to the idea of purchase, reiterated by presidents Polk (1848), Pierce (1853–4), and Buchanan (1857–60). By the mid-1850s, the possibility of an annexationist invasion was real enough, with some 50,000 American volunteers, with about $1 million committed and with Britain preoccupied in the Crimea (Thomas 1971: 226). In the event, however, those energies were deployed not in Cuba but in William Walker's bizarre 1854 Nicaraguan expedition, backed by the same Southern interests and by some Cuban annexationists (notably Goicurría),[18] and Cuba's major annexationist invasion (in 1850) came not from Americans but from López, a Venezuelan-born, ex-Spanish army veteran and the husband of a Cuban.

Thus, Cuba's isolation and ossification meant not ideological conservatism, but rather, a basis for three alternative radical visions of *cubanía*, each creating a long tradition of separatist thinking. The first was liberal-inspired annexationism,

16. The full history of Cuban slave revolts has only just begun to be written (Ferrer 1995; Paquette 1988), but it is clear that the rebellions, conspiracies and strikes of the early century frightened the already 'besieged' whites.

17. This concept seems most likely to have been coined in 1845 by the Southern newspaper editor and annexationist, John O'Sullivan.

18. This was Walker's short-lived filibustering expedition to annex Nicaragua and establish an empire.

a *cubanía anexionista*; while the second was an opening to progressive European intellectual and cultural influences, a *cubanía cultural*; the third was the tradition of popular rebellion, both the movement for change through radical ideas, and also the growing slave movement for rebellion and labour protest (such as the 1865 strike on the Aldama plantation), the first stirrings of a *cubanía revolucionaria* (Ibarra Cuesta 1967: 58) – although the lack of consensus on the term 'revolution' and its limitations probably makes *cubanía rebelde* more suitable then than *cubanía revolucionaria*.

Although *criollo* annexationist currents would continue, the realistic possibility of Cuba's annexation as an American state was over by 1861, with the abolitionist northern states opposing the incorporation of another (wealthy) slave-owning state and the South fearful of alienating Europe. Without American interest the idea died, especially as, by the 1840s, there was no further Spanish Liberal abolitionist threat and the costs of the illegal trade continued to spiral (Bergad 1995). In Cuba, therefore, annexation gave way to an interest in an autonomist 'reformism', with the Círculo Reformista being largely composed of previously annexationist planters, recognizing that, with production changes, the end of slave imports after 1865, and with the still worrying incidence of slave unrest, modernization (and not slavery) was the issue, and this could best be achieved through cooperation with a newly tolerant Madrid, which, in 1865, set up a Cuban Constitutional Commission, leading to electoral victory in 1866 for the Reformists. However, in 1867 Madrid suddenly aborted the process, forcing the autonomists (and especially the poorer planters with less to lose) to consider the possibility of a rebellion that would inevitably lead both sides to free their slaves.

Thus was born the rebellion of 1868, a move that resulted, on the one hand, from Spain's intransigence and political incompetence regarding Cuban demands and from the opportunity that was suddenly offered in September 1868 by revolution in Madrid and rebellion in Puerto Rico, but also, on the other, from shifts in sugar production and slavery that were hastening the decline of the traditional Cuban *sacarocracia*, especially in the east.[19] In other words, rebellion grew less out of a consensus on *cubanía* than out of the resigned desperation of a declining oligarchy with nowhere else to turn.

Thus, when Carlos Manuel de Céspedes, a planter from the eastern province of Oriente and a veteran of Spanish insurgency, declared his rebellion at La Demajagua

19. By 1862, the west accounted for 89.9 per cent of foreign trade in Cuba, the east only 10.1 per cent, while the west had 87 per cent of the rail network (López Segrera 1981: 111). The question of 'east' and 'west' is, however, complicated by variations within the east, the western part of Oriente (around Manzanillo) being less slave-based (only 6.5 per cent of the population) than the much more Afro-Cuban eastern part, around Santiago (34 per cent) (Ferrer 1995: 23–6). It was therefore no coincidence that the rebellion of 1868 began around Manzanillo, where emancipation was less threatening, but that the 1879 war was waged mostly around Santiago.

estate on 10 October 1868 (the *Grito de Yara* – 'Declaration of Yara') – a conspiracy with masonic and Reformist connections – it was geographically and socially limited, with support from some ex-slaves, freed by Céspedes and other sympathetic planters.

It was also initially highly confused. Although the *Grito* talked grandly of eventual abolition and equality, and although the rebel Convention in April 1869 at Guámairo declared universal freedom, there was no rebel consensus on independence, slavery or military strategy, and therefore no consensus on *Cuba Libre*. The rebels' attitude to the United States was especially ambiguous, with the Convention actually voting for American annexation (Cepero Bonilla 1963: 209), and with some in the wealthy separatist-Reformist New York-based Junta Central Republicana de Cuba y Puerto Rico entertaining the notion of purchase, briefly reconsidered by Washington.

The slavery issue was, however, more revealing of the divisions. While pragmatism, rather than principle, led to some emancipation, the Convention talked only of eventual abolition, an ambiguity that helped the new Grant Administration in Washington to distance itself from a rebellion seemingly led by ambivalent slave-owners with unclear thoughts on abolition, and to refuse to recognize the rebels' belligerent status or to allow the shipment of arms to the Liberation Army – the *Ejército Libertador*.

Ultimately, it was the Spanish who proceeded towards abolition, when Moret, Prim's Minister of Colonies, decreed, in 1870, conditional and gradual abolition for the nearly 300,000 slaves remaining (with an arrangement – the *patronato* – that guaranteed owners eight more years of labour obligations), and immediate emancipation for slaves over sixty and for those volunteering for the Spanish Army. Indeed, in 1873, slavery was abolished in Cuba's sister colony of Puerto Rico, thereby increasing the pressure. After that, slavery simply withered on the vine or 'disintegrated' (Moreno Fraginals 1983: 55), and, by 1880, when Moret's decree was enacted formally, there were only some 228,000 slaves left (Knight 1970: 176), and, in the end, the *patronato* was ignored by planters aware of the lower cost of free labour. Thus, when the condition was prematurely ended in 1886, there were only 30,000 slaves left in Cuba (Knight 1970: 178; see also Scott 1985).

Disagreements over military strategy reflected these concerns, since one continual problem was the *criollo* elite's permanent fear and mistrust of the increasingly successful *mulato* general, Antonio Maceo, whom some suspected of having designs on the creation of a black republic in Cuba and whose popularity among the rebel guerrillas (the *mambí* troops, as they were called) grew daily. Hence the plans proposed by Maceo, and the Dominican Máximo Gómez, to invade the west and burn plantations were consistently opposed by civilian leaders fearful of both slave rebellion and damage to prosperity and potential western support. By the time that invasion happened, Spanish resistance had been strengthened by the arrival of both the adept General Martínez Campos, in 1876, and increased troops, numbering 100,000 by 1870 (Carr 1966: 309).

Resistance was also bolstered by loyalist and *peninsular* intransigence, which had gained the upper hand, reversing early reform concessions, swelling the ranks of the thousands of volunteers, taking advantage of the political confusion in Spain and capitalizing on the inequality of, and divisions within, the rebel ranks (especially with Céspedes's death in 1874 and the less *independentista* leadership of Tomás Estrada Palma).

Thus, in April 1878, the rebel leadership accepted the Spanish terms, at Zanjón – all, that is, except Maceo, who declared (the *Protesta de Baraguá*) his determination to continue. Finally, in May, he too was forced to surrender, and allowed to leave Cuba – a resistance that was then followed, in August 1879, by a significant ten-month war, the *Guerra Chiquita* (the 'Little War'). Its significance lay in the fact that, although often seen as led by the white Calixto García, it was in fact largely ignored by *criollos*, being a rebellion of intransigent blacks continuing the struggle, under Maceo and the black general Moncada (Ferrer 1995: 128–72).

It had been a curious war, started by a planter who freed his slaves but was no abolitionist, but ending with the eventual surrender of the black leader whose possible success had been constrained by racial prejudices, a war waged by a reluctant leadership alliance between a declining oligarchy and richer, émigré entrepreneurs (unable to agree on goals, vision or strategy); but a war fought increasingly as a social and racial rebellion. It had been a brutal, unforgiving and often disorganized war – 'less a war than a breakdown of order' (Thomas 1971: 254), but was essentially a radicalizing war, fought by *mambises* loyal to a vague vision of Cuba, to emancipation, to each other and to their immediate leaders. Foremost among those representative leaders was Maceo, whose vision of revolution necessarily encompassed racial equality (Foner 1977; Torres-Cuevas 1995b) and who was determined to oust those separatist leaders unwilling to make that connection (Ferrer 1999: 69); for him, Zanjón was merely a truce in the war (Foner 1977: 91).

Defeat now hastened the end of *criollismo* in the Cuban dissident tradition and the change in the character of the rebel, now more *cubanista* (pro-*cubanía*) constituency, since it had been effectively a war 'about the boundaries of Cuban nationality' (Ferrer 1995: 19), and the elitism that the old *criollismo* represented (in which the 'other' was less the *peninsulares* than the masses) (Schmidt-Nowara, 1995b: 445) could no longer be sustained legitimately. Already weakened, the planter class was now terminally wounded by a 'cataclysmic' abolition (Bergad 1990: 262), by the destruction of 1868–78 (with Santiago's mills declining from 100 in 1868 to 39 in 1878 and Camagüey's from 100 to one) (Pérez 1986a: 4), and, after 1878, by the need to mortgage to meet debts. Then came more changes in the sugar economy, especially the rise of European beet (which, by the 1880s, accounted for about 50 per cent of the world's sugar) (Thomas 1971: 270) and the development of the new Bessemer steel (allowing cheaper rail transport and thus the expansion of plantations now able to connect directly with ports other than Havana – Zanetti and García, 1987); these both forced prices down, further impoverishing and marginalizing the capital-starved Cuban growers (Guerra 1970: 267) and increasing the relentless process of concentration in the hands of the new corporate American growers, with half a million tonnes being produced by 1,191 mills in 1877, but over one million from only 450 in 1894 (Pino Santos 1983: 213), and from a mere 207 by 1899 (López Segrera 1981: 126).

This transformed the traditional system – of cultivation on the plantation surrounding, or adjacent to, the mill (*ingenio*), concentrating milling in larger, more industrial *centrales* and leaving cultivation to a network of specialist growers (*colonos*), through contractual quotas, who accounted, by 1887, for possibly 40 per cent of sugar production, with numbers increased by the official encouragement to white immigration (Thomas 1971: 276). It was a virtual 'peasantization' of production in the form of cultivation in the hands of the *colonato*, a class born out of the surviving peasantry in sugar and other staples, white immigrants (attracted by promises of land), the collapse of the *ingenios*, the social fragmentation of the war, landgrants to loyal soldiers (the *realengo*) and the marginalization of the ex-slaves (see Dye 1998 and Scott 1985),[20] largely brought about by the rise of North American and Hawaiian sugar (after 1876 with privileged access to the American market), the new market for white granulated sugar (which removed refining from Cuba) and a drastic price-fall in the 1880s, below viability levels.

Thus, the planter elite disappeared as a class (Pérez 1982: 6), as an economic and political force, so that Cuba, alone in Latin America, would reach independence 'with her social revolution already accomplished' (Thomas 1971: 278). Into the vacuum stepped American corporate interests, facilitated by the McKinley tariff of October 1890 (for which they lobbied), doubling American imports, reviving sugar exports (by 1894, 87 per cent of Cuba's exports went northwards) and bringing in over $30 million of American capital (Thomas 1971: 289–90).

Society was thus even more divided, with existing tensions exacerbated – between masters and the surviving slaves, between the three main crops (sugar, coffee and tobacco) and their underpinning societies, between large landowners and smallholders, owners and tenants, *colonos* and *centrales*, *peninsulares* and *criollos*, landowners and merchants, landowners and financiers, and, most fundamentally, between the capitalist dynamic of sugar and the quasi-feudal social relations in the production system (see especially Pérez 1986a). The recruitment of slaves, as well as ex-slaves, into the Liberation Army had also seriously challenged the social and political order (Ferrer 1995: 68 *et passim*).

20. The *colonos* could be large or small, owners or tenants, black or white; but any cohesion came in their contractual relationship with a single mill.

This all deepened the dilemmas of Cuban dissidence, until the Spanish embarked on a series of triumphalist and punitive response measures (after initial conciliatory promises), obliging the Cubans to pay for several things – Spain's American debt, the cost of Spanish wars (including those in Cuba), the Spanish garrison in Cuba, and the new colonial administration (Pino Santos 1983: 215). These payments absorbed the whole colonial budget, humiliating the Cubans into paying for their own enslavement, and making an average Cuban pay some sixteen times more tax than an average Spanish taxpayer.

Spanish retribution had two distinct social effects. On the one hand, it drove the final nail into the coffin of the 'doomed class' (Pérez 1982: 19), for the colonial authorities specifically targeted white *criollos* for retribution and expropriation (Quiroz 1998: 295–305), weakening any elite ideology among a Cuban bourgeoisie that 'would remain an estranged elite, artificial in some ways, superfluous in others, and always subservient to interests from abroad and vulnerable to forces at home. What was imposed on Cuba was not an ideology that justified elite rule as much as an elite rationale that underwrote United States' hegemony' (Pérez 1982: 21).

However, it also hit the fortunes (and political attitudes) of the small middle class, whose rise had been stimulated by educational change, who had mostly remained loyal or neutral during the war – except for some student political activism, from an isolated, but famous, protest by the Havana medical students in 1871 to the first Havana student strike of 1892 (Simpson 1984: 283) – and on whose skills, efficiency and tolerance colonialism increasingly rested.

Other social changes were now under way. Firstly, slavery's decline and abolition (although with no single social outcome, its effects depending on a range of variables within each region) did tend to push the ex-slaves either into the depressed east or towards Havana (Bergad 1990: 265), towards either the lower levels of the *colonato*, the emerging sugar and tobacco proletariats, or, for most, a marginal, immiserized and often transient existence, disaggregating Afro-Cuban culture and destabilizing in effect a still unsettled countryside (Scott 1985). The banditry that resulted was for many of them both a means of survival and an essentially political resistance, a continuation of the struggle (Schwartz 1989: 178–81).

Secondly, immigration was encouraged, not least by the rising labour costs after abolition (Schmidt-Nowara 1995b: 419), swelling the more prosperous ranks of the *colonato*, the skilled trades of the new proletariat, the tobacco *vegas* of Pinar del Río and, above all, stable urban employment in petty trading, artisan activity or small-scale industry in Havana. Some 250,000 Spanish immigrants entered Cuba between 1878 and 1895, most choosing to stay (Pérez 1986a: 10).

There was a third, new, phenomenon – emigration, which by the end of the century saw 100,000 Cubans leave (Pérez 1986a: 11). On the one hand, this simply continued the traditional northward emigration of the marginalized intellectual and professional class, further weakening any cohesion of a progressive domestic middle class. By the 1850s, there were 1,000 Cubans in the United States (Olson and Olson 1995: 17). However, a significant proportion of the tobacco workforce now migrated to Florida, fleeing the war and the transfer of cigar and cigarette processing from Cuba to the United States, to gain access to the increasingly protected American market. For the imposition of a new American tariff in 1857 (against refined tobacco) meant the wholesale shift of relatively new cigar manufacturing to the mainland United States and, with it, the emigration of a significant proportion of the skilled workforce, so that, by 1880, there were 7,000 Cubans in the United States, 2,000 of them in Key West, the latter figure rising to 5,000 by 1885, working mostly in over 100 cigar factories (Olson and Olson 1995: 20; Poyo 1991: 25); by the 1890s there were almost 20,000 in the country (Olson and Olson 1995: 24).

There were, thus, four new social groupings by the 1890s. There was a small but growing middle class, in the professions and also in a small commercial middle class, stimulated especially by tobacco (Ruffin 1990: 61). Secondly, there was the *colonato* – as yet far too variegated in size, status, legal rights and prospects to be considered, or to consider itself, as a separate class, but increasingly important, producing by now about 80 per cent of Cuban sugar. Thirdly, there was the small but growing proletariat, found mostly in the *centrales* (although more of a semi-proletariat, given its relations of production and its lack of education) (Ibarra Cuesta 1992: 174), in tobacco manufacturing and processing (probably the one Cuban industry then with a class of large-scale industrial wage labour) (Stubbs 1985: 67), in Havana transport and construction, and in Florida. Finally, there was an unprecedented large-scale 'marginal' population, increasingly urban and thus exacerbating unemployment (an estimated 20,000 in Havana alone) and swelling the ranks of a new 'underclass' (Pérez 1986a: 9).

With this came political changes. Firstly, the Spanish authorities, despite promises of electoral equality and incorporation, instituted a political exclusion such that, by the 1890s, some 1.4 million Cubans accounted for only 10,000 voters in the political system (only 24 per cent of the eligible population), while some 140,000 *peninsulares* (80 per cent of their total) wielded 42,000 votes (Pino Santos 1983: 218; Pérez 1986a: 17). This guaranteed power to the loyalist, intransigent Unión Constitucional – the 'Orangemen of Cuba' (Carr, 1966: 380), bent on even greater colonialization of Cuba, rendering futile the accommodationism of those Cubans of the new Liberal Party who, after 1878, threw in their lot with the Spanish, believing that 'reforms were the best guarantee of empire and empire was the best guarantee against revolution' (Pérez 1986a: 16), and that the fulfillment of *cubanidad* 'could best be guaranteed within existing albeit modified structures of empire' (Pérez 1982: 8). Eventually, even they began to withdraw from the Cortes.

Meanwhile, in the middle class, the influence of new currents of thinking from Spain, France and other parts of the Americas could be detected. Socialism was one of those, with few middle-class adherents but with a longer-term importance. Mostly a Fourierist mutualism in the 1840s and 1850s, with the new craft unions, the idea gained ground especially among the specialist trades of the tobacco and printing industries, manifesting itself in the press – the bourgeois *El Siglo* (which, in the 1860s, was openly debating socialist ideas) (Casanovas Codina 1995: 86), and the more proletarian *La Aurora* (1865), edited by the Asturian cigar-workers' leader, Saturnino Martínez (who, though a gradualist ex-Reformist, founded the influential Asociación de Tabaqueros de La Habana) – and in people such as Diego Vicente Tejera, who, though believing in conciliation and class harmony (Abreu and Cabrera 1988: 43), founded the Partido Socialista Cubano.

Positivism was another, appealing as elsewhere in Latin America to the ambitions of the rising elite, given its commitment to progress as an ethos that expressed, on the one hand, the aspiration of the Cuban 'technocratic' elite to hegemony, and perhaps some autonomy from unprogressive colonial authorities and oligarchy, and, on the other hand, a determination to avoid the spectre of chaos and racial and social upheaval that still haunted the white population. This commitment to technological development, in turn, meant a greater neo-annexationist attraction towards the 'new' United States – vibrant, dynamic, technically adventurous and with its own racist imperatives – as well as the expansion of education for the Cuban bourgeoisie. The most outstanding Cuban positivist was undoubtedly Enrique José Varona, whose stance was as expressive of his class's contradictions as Saco's had been before, mixing frankly elitist political and social views and cooperative attitudes towards the United States with arguments for reform, education and a more socially tolerant Cuba.

The third influence was liberalism, which, where not imbued with positivism, was influenced by European Radicalism, arguing for social reform, social harmony and a powerful, socially benevolent state. This current was relatively weak in a Cuban bourgeoisie which, unlike others in contemporary Latin America, lacked political cohesion and progressive dynamism; however, it merits attention because it influenced the evolving perspectives of one thinker who was to play the greatest role in the transformation of the *cubanista* tradition – José Martí.

It was, therefore, elsewhere where the significant political developments were taking place, in a new working class with a propensity for radicalism stimulated by demobilization and a new collective working environment. It was also stimulated by a Spanish immigration that included hundreds of politically committed and active anarchists, anarchosyndicalists and socialists (more militant than their Cuban counterparts), whose cultural centres (Centro Gallego, Centro Asturiano, Centro Catalán, Centro Canario and Centro Vasco) also became seedbeds of radicalism and bases for trade union activity, for these migrants formed, fostered, led and radicalized the existing trade unions. This was especially true in tobacco, responding partly to the changes in production methods and conditions, partly to the traditional guild rights and community, and most visibly through the institution of the *lectura* ('reading'), the practice – set up by Martínez in 1866, banned and then reintroduced in 1878 – whereby a worker was employed to read to the workforce, normally and increasingly political material (Stubbs 1985: 98). This unionism tended to be directed either towards a 'revolutionary romanticism' (Stubbs 1985: 89), leading eventually to Martí's rebellion, or anarchosyndicalism – represented by Enrique Roig San Martín, and the black leader Carlos Baliño, or towards the more docile, disciplined reformism of Martínez, the inheritor of the largely white, male, urban guilds.

This radicalization was paralleled in the Florida Cuban workforce, where, freed of the constraints of a repressive colonialism and based in a cohesive and agglomerated immigrant community – with some 80 per cent of the Cubans in Tampa being working-class and some 20 per cent being black (Olson and Olson 1995: 24) – they responded rapidly to new ideas and to the emerging *cubanista* radicalization in Cuba. As early as 1871, the Sociedad El Ateneo was set up to foment revolutionary nationalist activity (Alvarez Estévez 1986: 41), and in 1870, the Club Patriótico Cubano existed in Key West (Poyo 1989: 43), with the following decades seeing more patriotic clubs founded throughout the Cuban émigré community (Poyo 1991), and with radical nationalism hegemonic in the community by the 1880s (Poyo 1989: 55). Thus, in 1892, the significant anarchist-led Congreso Obrero Regional was founded in Havana, followed, in 1896, by the powerful anarcho-syndicalist Unión de Fabricantes de Tabacos y Cigarrillos.

The separatist unity of 1868 was thus split three ways – apart from the few *criollos* clinging unrealistically to the idea of autonomy. The most vociferous activists were those elite dissidents based in New York, setting up separatist clubs and lobbying American politicians, but now with a pragmatic preference for some sort of dependence on the United States, a 'neo-annexationism'. The reality was, by now, that exile had become such an integral part of the tradition of dissidence that a base in the United States was seen as unproblematic and possibly even patriotic; indeed, one irony of Cuban nationalist history is that American exile was fundamental to the formation of a Cuban national identity, and even the taking of American citizenship by patriotic Cubans was not seen as a contradiction, since 'naturalization was also a way to create space inside Cuba, a way to defend nationality by affirming what Cubans were not – they were not Spaniards' (Perez 1999: 39).

Secondly, there were the former rebel leaders of 1868–80, whose distrust of civilians had made them more 'militarist' in their visions of liberation and a free Cuba, and who still engaged in small-scale uprisings and invasions (1883, 1885, 1892 and 1893). Finally, there was the growing dissidence, in both Florida and Cuba, with either an internationalist ideology of political struggle against imperialism or a class-conscious antagonism towards the class structures that had ensured defeat in 1878.

However, the rise of the new middle class had created an intellectual generation that, rather than gravitating towards the traditional elite, was now attracted by the new proletarian radicalism, which, in turn, tended not to exclude them, valuing the contribution of ideas and of intellectuals, in both a socialist and a traditional Cuban respect for their political importance. Thus, Cuban socialism (on balance including more intellectuals than the more class-conscious anarchist or anarcho-syndicalist movements) saw significant contributions from, among others, Tejera, Roig and Marx's son-in-law, Paul Lafargue.

This, ultimately, was where Martí's real contribution came. It is impossible to summarize the political significance or ideas of the thinker and activist who, firstly, has so dominated modern Cuban political culture, and has been the subject of so much critical and even hagiographic attention, so much admiration, and so much rhetoric, and who, secondly, left a body of writings that fills many a library shelf. In this context, his immediate importance in the 1890s was political, seizing the moment, recognizing the changed character of Cuban dissidence and sensing the nature of the new United States and the internationalist implications of the Cuban struggle.

Although long committed to *Cuba Libre*, being imprisoned and exiled early on, and with an evident sensitivity to Cuba's dilemma and to the poor, Martí showed few signs of going beyond his class's conventional perspectives until exile exposed him to new ideas and opportunities, in particular leading him towards Krausism, whose concept of social harmony and historical progress appealed to an essentially moral outlook that had led him instinctively to oppose both colonialism and slavery (see especially Ibarra 1980; Turton 1986, on Krausism; Kirk 1983; Abel and Torrents 1985). Exile also allowed him, as a journalist and diplomat, to travel and broaden his experience and his perspectives, leading finally to the decisive experience of the 1880s United States, bringing him into contact with the various Cuban communities and developing his awareness of the evolving country.

That experience led him to three decisive perspectives, all fundamental to eventual Cuban liberation and the evolution of a *cubania*, which – disoriented, demoralized and divided – was in crisis after 1878. Firstly, he recognized the importance of the coherent new radicalism, commitment and unified strength of the Florida proletariat (not least in their 1893 strike, which he supported actively). He thus became aware that a popular *cubania* was Cuba's future and that, ultimately, *nación* (the nation) would be equated with *pueblo* (the people) – a significant development in his thinking and in the coherence of the evolving *cubania*, less folkloric and more popular, radical and based on the real experiences and aspirations of an entirely new social class (Poyo 1985; Poyo 1989: 59–62).

Secondly, Martí developed a growing sense of internationalism, leading to a clearer view of imperialism, in both the declining and unjust Spanish Empire and the vibrant expansionism of a United States that, though still admirable for its liberalism, had threatening implications for Latin America. This perspective then became a 'continentalism', extolling the distinctiveness, unity and cultural strength of 'our America' (*Nuestra América*), a vision less racist and exclusivist than Rodó's idiosyncratic concept of a morally superior 'Latin' America (as opposed to a supposedly grasping materialist 'Anglo-Saxon' North).[21] Martí's America, instead, saw indigenous cultures as forgotten and the poor as the basis of the future. This internationalism, coupled with his belief in liberation through social revolution, placed him – as Retamar observed later – closer to later Third World perspectives than to the generation of Bolívar (Fernández Retamar 1967b: 20).

Thirdly, Martí recognized the importance of a single, unifying party – created in 1892 as the Partido Revolucionario Cubano (PRC – Cuban Revolutionary Party), which, cutting across classes, ideological and political differences, would create a focused strategy for national liberation and also a basis for a stable and united political system (Poyo 1989: 97–111; Ibarra 1980). The party successfully united thirty-four American-based separatist clubs and organizations, a tribute both to the Florida workers, whose decisive commitment to the Cuban cause saw them contribute 10 per cent of their wages to it, and to Martí, who, alone, saw the potential for the Cuban liberation movement of an inherently internationalist but patriotic working class, if it were convinced of the party's commitment to social revolution after liberation.

As a result, by the 1890s, the two levels of ideology – popular and intellectual (or 'empirical' and 'theoretical') – had clearly begun to interact in a dynamic dialectical process. Socialism and anarchosyndicalism, at one level, and other philosophies at the intellectual level had helped shift *cubanía* more coherently to a radical, leftist position, after which it retained a tendency towards socialistic, revolutionary propositions, solutions and strategies for change.

The PRC, however, still bore the traces of the old splits, since its other external base was the increasingly bourgeois, émigré 'pole' of the the eastern American seaboard, with a less convincing ideological commitment to full liberation, a suspicion of the Florida radicalism and an uncertainty about the practicality of full independence that suggested intervention and some form of 'annexation' by the United States.

Within Cuba, elite opinion was, however, also shifting, with a fall in the sugar price (1893–4) and the 1894 Wilson tariff (imposing 40 per cent duties on Cuban sugar, reversing the 1890 tariff). With the moment right, the signal was given in March 1895 by the *Manifiesto de Montecristi,* Martí's and Gómez's declaration of the Second War of Independence, and, in April, the invasion of Oriente.

---

21. This refers to the 'classical' view of the continent's 'Latinness' in Enrique Rodó's influential 1900 essay, *Ariel*.

This struggle was partly a re-run of 1868–78: Spanish resistance was fierce, sizeable and brutal, with numbers rising from 16,000 to 52,000 (Thomas 1971: 319), with loyalists again enlisted as volunteers, and with General Weyler enacting a policy of concentration of civilians and 'scorched earth'. Once again the war became a bitter and uncompromising struggle between largely black *mambí* guerrillas – perhaps 30,000 by December 1895 (Thomas 1971: 324) – and equally intransigent and ruthless troops – perhaps over 200,000 by the end, plus 80,000 volunteers (Thomas 1971: 353).[22]

This war, was, however, quite different. Firstly, rebel divisions did not simply replicate those in 1868–78; instead, the growing cleavage between a 'civilianist' political leadership and the more 'militarist' perspective of the 1868 veterans increased after Martí's death in battle on 19 May 1895. Martí had been the one leader with authority and popularity to bridge that divide, yet even he differed with the military leaders, and some speculate that his decision to lead his troops into battle, on a conspicuous white horse, was a self-immolatory gesture to prove his military contribution (Cabrera Infante 1994: 146–7).

The second difference was that fewer Cubans were prepared to support Spain, whatever their doubts about Martí's more radical vision, and even some Spanish entrepreneurs and landowners began to contemplate a 'neo-annexationism', preferring American dependence to a visibly decrepit colonial system. Thirdly, there were no rebel hesitations about advancing westward, the Liberation Army reaching the Havana area in January 1896, with the predicted destruction. Fourthly, Weyler's policies – if anything, even more brutal and hard-line than in 1876, with 'counter-insurgency' strikes, martial law and so effective a concentration that thousands died of disease – aroused the attention of the new American 'yellow press', which now launched a circulation war and a successful anti-Spanish and pro-intervention campaign. Even Madrid began to doubt, worried by escalating costs, the American threat and the appalling death rate among the Spanish troops.[23] Therefore, with Cánovas's assassination in June 1897, Sagasta's new Liberal government made moves towards a settlement, proposing constitutional reform and autonomy – to the horror of the loyalists, whose resulting street riots (organized by the Constitutional Union) led to the American dispatch of the battleship *Maine* to Havana to protect American citizens and property.

By then, however, Spain had lost any claim to authority or legitimacy for continuing colonialism, and the two armies had reached a stalemate. Now, in the

---

22. The war saw over 600,000 Spanish troops committed in Cuba (Segré *et al.* 1997: 51).

23. One estimate (Thomas 1971: 444) is that, of over 200,000 troops, over 53,000 were killed by disease, only about 9,000 dying in action or of their wounds; another, however, gives 32,500 Spanish dead, of whom 14,500 died of diphtheria or typhoid, 6,000 of yellow fever and 7,000 of malaria (Carr 1966: 384).

United States, with a more colonialist attitude, more evident expansionism in policy-making circles, and corporations beginning to counsel intervention to prevent further damage to their interests, McKinley's election in 1896 spelled the end for Spain.

With the still mysterious explosion of the *Maine* in Havana harbour on 15 February 1898 fuelling the press and the ambitions of the imperialist Theodore Roosevelt,[24] the United States declared war on Spain in April, landing 6,000 troops in the east and easily defeating the demoralized and sickening Spanish forces in two sea battles (Santiago and Manila) and one brief land battle, at San Juan Hill in Santiago.[25] The Cuban War of Independence had, at a stroke, become the Spanish–American War. In August, Madrid sued for peace and, in December, Spain and the United States (but, significantly, not Cuba) signed the Treaty of Paris, giving the United States the remaining colonies of Cuba, Puerto Rico, the Philippines and Guam from 1 January 1899, and erasing the Cubans from the accepted narrative of the fighting; for, having intervened to liberate the oppressed Cubans, the Americans had then proceeded to reject rebel claims for recognition, to marginalize the Cubans during the fighting, and to exclude them from the Paris discussions, and now refused the Liberation Army access to the ceremony of the Spanish withdrawal. The message was clear enough; Martí's dire warnings about a new imperialism were being realized, and the exhausted rebels, after three wars, were now deprived of the fruits of their efforts and of the Spanish defeat. Moreover, Cuba was in severe distress, with a population collapse – a decrease of 58,890 since 1887 (Pichardo 1986: 60) – widespread deprivation (even in the middle class) and an economy in ruins, with most mills either closed or operating well under capacity, and with 52 per cent of the land now being held by non-resident landlords (Thomas 1971: 425).

Finally, the fragile nationalist unity was split even more between the two familiar poles: between the pragmatic, neo-annexationist, western urban, white, bourgeois Cuba (represented by the Asamblea de Representantes) and the ideologically committed, radical, rural or émigré Cuba, largely eastern, black or *mulato* and class-conscious (represented by the 48,000-strong Liberation Army). The old divisions may even have deepened, with economic and social changes concentrating land and wealth in fewer hands and radicalizing a more proletarian working class. Furthermore, within weeks of the victory, the Cuban leader, Estrada Palma, disbanded the PRC, weakening the *cubanía rebelde* pole and strengthening the reborn *cubanía neoanexionista*.

24. Roosevelt was still then Assistant Secretary to the Navy, a post he resigned immediately to campaign for intervention and form his Rough Rider volunteers.

25. Although American sea-power was overwhelming (with only two American non-combat deaths in the two sea battles), in Santiago some 700 Spanish troops held out against the 6,000 Americans, inflicting heavy casualties.

The following 1898–1902 American military occupation (under Generals Brooke and then Wood, and six provincial governments) was unquestionably a turning-point, setting patterns of structure, production, trade and thinking that would determine subsequent history, being deliberately designed, by both Wood and Roosevelt (with a characteristic contempt for Cubans and all 'Latins'), to modernize and 'Americanize' Cuba rapidly, encouraging an efficient and smooth incorporation into the American system, as colony or protectorate, with Cuban acquiescence.

The decision was therefore taken to maintain a system that had ensured Cuban subservience. The Spanish civil service and legal structure were retained (leading *peninsulares* being coopted into the government); the Church was left under a largely Spanish clergy (by 1907, there were 202 Spanish priests but only 106 Cubans) and was still administered from Madrid (Pérez 1986a: 61); commerce was, likewise, still Spanish-controlled – Spaniards representing over half the merchant class, overwhelmingly so in retailing (Pérez 1986a: 60–1) – although there were only 130,000 Spanish residents after 1898 (out of the total population of over one and a half million); and finally, pre-war property rights, already weighted against Cubans, were guaranteed, and continuing Spanish immigration was encouraged – 55,000 more arriving between 1898 and 1901 (Pérez 1986a: 77), and 17,000 arriving in 1901 alone (Pérez 1988: 202). These moves further demoralized the *cubanista* camp and ensured the loyalty of the Spanish and conservative Cubans. The message was clear: the war had served American purposes, and the *mambises'* goal of social revolution was opposed vigorously by a more powerful, efficient and determined neocolonialism.

The double pressures of modernization and 'Americanization' transformed Cuba. Sweeping health and sanitation reforms reduced disease, especially yellow fever (which had killed so many Spaniards and Americans), although the Cuban Carlos Finlay's contribution to the cure was largely ignored by subsequent non-Cuban historiography.[26] Education was reformed along American lines (Pérez 1995: 35–52), 1,500 Cuban teachers being trained in the United States, with the English language and the United States' history being taught in schools, and thousands of schools being opened, with rolls rising by one-third (Paulston 1971: 378). Varona was given funds to remodel the University of Havana into a large-scale, modern, and Americanized structure. Rural peace was guaranteed by a *Guardia Rural* that, constructed out of the Spanish Army and, selectively, the Liberation Army, was trained and led by American officers and staffed by an officer corps whose racial composition was guaranteed by property and literacy qualifications.

Even the economy recovered, damaged Cuban interests being officially protected: the March 1899 Foraker Law prohibited new American interests; a two-

---

26. More Americans (about 5,500) died from disease in 1898–1902 than from the fighting (698) (Thomas 1971: 405).

year debt moratorium was announced; export tariffs were abolished; and duties on much-needed machine parts were reduced. However, the military authorities allowed this official protection to be flouted systematically, and American capital flooded in, taking advantage of the vacuum and Cuban weakness, doubling during the occupation from $50m to $100m (Thomas 1971: 466), and dominating critical areas – especially tobacco exports (90 per cent) and the transport system. Land too was eaten up, with colonization schemes, some 13,000 American citizens purchasing $50m. of land by 1905, and American citizens or corporations owning 15 per cent of Cuba by 1906 – helped by Civil Order No 62, which opened up 'common land' to purchase (Pérez 1986a: 72). Cuban recovery was also hampered by the authorities' preference for Spanish and American enterprises' having privileged access to Spanish and American credit.

Finally, the occupation attempted to Americanize Cuba culturally, through sport and religion, with a concerted effort by American Protestant churches to proselytize (in the east) and colonize (see Deere 1998; Pérez 1995: 53–72; Pérez 1999: 109–25), and with the impact of those southern, pro-annexation, Americans who remained of the 5,000 migrants after 1868 (Olson and Olson 1995: 18).

The Americans' political objective was clear: the elimination of the nationalist threat and the creation of a loyal Cuban elite. The Assembly was pressed to dissolve the Liberation Army (March 1899) and replace itself by the Asamblea Nacional, and established an electoral system that, through literacy and property qualifications ($250), ensured the exclusion of almost two-thirds of the adult male population, especially Afro-Cubans and the rural working class (Pérez 1986a: 38).[27]

That system created three separate parties, two recognizably 'nationalist' (the Partido Republicano de La Habana – led by the 1895 veteran, José Miguel Gómez – and the Partido Nacional Cubano – later called 'Nacional' or 'Liberal', and led by Máximo Gómez till his death in 1905) and the third being the conservative Partido Unión Democrática (largely accommodating the old Unión Constitucional). With three of the four main leaders of the 1895–8 struggle dead – Martí (1895), Maceo (1896), García (1898) – and only Máximo Gómez left (and even he collaborated with the occupation, thereby legitimizing it) (Pérez 1995: 20), there was little resistance to this development.

The final nail driven into the nationalist coffin was the notorious Platt Amendment. Based on recommendations by the US Secretary of State, Elihu Root, and backed by Wood, it was introduced in the US Senate by Orville Platt as an amendment to the US Army Appropriations Bill; approved in February 1901, it was incorporated at the insistence of the McKinley administration into the Constitution of the future Republic.[28] Resistance was weakened by the nationalist dilemma:

27. The 1900 electorate consisted of 200,631 Cubans, 70 per cent white (Thomas 1971: 461).

28. After voting 16–15 in favour in February 1901, delegates to the Constituent Assembly were persuaded to vote again in June, with a more convincing 15–11.

without the Amendment, there would be no Republic, and patriots such as Manuel Sanguily and Varona thus voted reluctantly to accept it.

The new Republic thus came into being obliged to include in its Constitution clauses severely restricting Cuba's freedom of action and undermining claims to genuine independence. Under the Amendment Cuba would be unable to sign treaties that 'reduced independence' or ceded territory for military purposes, or to borrow more than its income; would be obliged to ratify all 1898–1902 decrees, to sell or lease territory to the United States for use as coaling stations or military bases (determined by the US president), to sign a permanent treaty with the United States, and, lastly, most ominously, to give the United States the unilateral right to intervene to 'preserve independence and adequate government, to protect life, property and liberty' and to uphold the Treaty of Paris obligations (Pichardo 1986: 119–20). The Isle of Pines – later renamed the 'Isla de la Juventud' (see Chapter 4) – was also ceded to the United States, although this was never enacted.[29] The implications were that external loans could only be contracted from the United States, whose unilateral right to intervene in effect made Cuba a protectorate.

While the Platt Amendment legalized the Americans' neocolonial hold, economic neocolonialism was established by the 1903 Reciprocity Treaty between Havana and Washington, against which Sanguily voted, given that, while Cuba was granted the security of 20 per cent preferences in the American market, American exports to Cuba were, reciprocally, granted a range of preferences between 25 and 40 per cent (Pichardo 1986: 220–36).

Cuba was thus tied into a double dependence on American consumers and manufacturers, with a dual role, exporting raw sugar and importing finished goods (López Segrera 1981: 126; Benjamin 1977: 180),[30] and the Treaty encouraged further economic penetration: by 1909, Cuban mills produced only 31 per cent of Cuba's sugar, while, by 1928, American capital (only $98 million in 1909, 23 per cent of that in sugar) had reached $1,505 million, 53 per cent in sugar (Pino Santos 1973: 31).[31]

The Treaty also meant short-term prosperity, sugar production rising from one million tonnes (1903) to four million in 1919; but the dangers of monoculture soon became evident, with Cuba's entrepreneurs and government unable to control the key economic decisions and with the economy's 'poles of command' clearly in the United States (government, investors and market), allowing Cuba a reflexive

29. American residents of the island attempted to incorporate it into the United States in 1904, the US Senate refusing to ratify that.

30. Between 1902 and 1906, 45 per cent of Cuban imports were American, rising worryingly to 74 per cent by 1921 (López Segrera 1981: 126). Benjamin cites a 54 per cent dependence on American goods in 1932, rising to 71 per cent by 1938 (Benjamin 1977: 180).

31. Additionally, by the 1920s, 13,000 Americans owned land in Cuba, and a quarter of all American capital in Latin America was in Cuba (Benjamin 1977: 19).

development at best. This increased vulnerability was demonstrated by a price-fall in 1910 and the sudden post-1914 boom, while the still relatively inefficient production process depended increasingly on cheap labour from Jamaica and Haiti (accounting for over 95 per cent of immigrant labour) (Alvarez Estevez 1988: 35).[32]

However, the implicit lack of manufacturing base precluded an economically and politically strong industrial bourgeoisie, and the new elite became effectively a dependent, *comprador*, neocolonial elite, at best 'managerial' or 'bureaucratic' (Ruffin 1990: 61), and at worst spineless, venal and conservative. In many respects, the 1895 war had interrupted and destroyed the process of social consolidation then under way (Bergad 1990: 341).

Therefore, post-1903 Cuba had three distinct levels of politics. At the top was the American relationship, with the political agenda increasingly determined by Washington and especially by the American Ambassador, the real ruler of a state administered by a bureaucratic caste that had been revitalized by the occupation and now rebuilt with the support of a neocolonial 'corps' of Spanish administrators, former loyalists and 'neo-annexationists'.[33] This level of politics also controlled law and order through the use of American troops as and when justified by the Amendment or determined by the Ambassador; the first two decades saw troops intervene on three occasions – 1906–9 (5,000 soldiers under Charles Magoon), in 1912 (with the revolt of the Partido Independiente de Color), and in 1917–23 (when 17,000 troops quelled another rebellion).

Within the framework of neocolonialism came the second level, formal national politics, which, weakened by the Amendment and the 'protectorate', lacked legitimacy and stability and became a permanent struggle whose goal was not the exercise of power (denied by Platt) but the spoils of office. The violence of the war was thus resurrected as rural instability, with a persistent recourse to arms. The formal inheritors of the PRC mantle were the anti-Platt National Liberals and the more conservative and pro-American Republicans, but differences were formal, based on personality and region – although some *independentistas* continued to work within the Liberal Party, hoping to rescue something from the disaster. Two new parties were also formed to further personal ambitions – Estrada Palma's Partido Moderado (from old Republicans and dissident Liberals), which later became the Partido Conservador, and Zayas's Partido Popular.

This was the level where pre-1898 rivalries and ambitions were played out by the *monopolio político del mambisado* ('political monopoly of the ex-*mambises*')

32. Between 1907 and 1929, 120,972 Jamaicans entered Cuba, and, between 1912 and 1929, 183,183 Haitians (Ruffin 1990: 75). By the 1930s, between 150,000 and 200,000 Caribbean workers had entered (Carr 1998: 83).

33. Even the first (unopposed) president, Tomás Estrada Palma, was both an annexationist and an American citizen.

(Figarola 1974: 203) – leading 1895–8 veterans, who invoked the shared legitimacy of the war, often to justify recourse to arms, leaving others to depend as 'clients' on their patrimonialism (Domínguez 1978a: 35), with the *caudillos* ('political strongmen, or bosses'), appropriating to themselves the title of *mambí* (despite being almost always white ex-officers). Indeed, the new politics was ambiguous, presented as *cubanía* yet proposing a politically safe discourse, reflecting the old divisions. Thus the Republic revived the concern with (a mostly folkloric) *cubanidad*, but also a history rewritten to prove the essential shallowness of *independentismo*.

In such instability, violence was inevitable. Protesting against a fraudulent electoral defeat in 1905 (by Estrada Palma), the Liberals immediately rebelled, to be vindicated when Magoon subsequently handed them the government; they rebelled again, in 1917, against Menocal's unconstitutional re-election. With Máximo Gómez dead, no one remained from the 'heroic' leaders to provide any consensual stability; instead, the '1895 generation' confirmed American expectations of incompetent and unstable politics.

At the bottom was the residual popular *cubanía*, demoralized after three struggles and threatened constantly by the attractions of prosperity and, in the patrimonial structure, by the legitimacy of a *neoanexionismo*, as was inevitable in the new 'empire', even more efficient, dynamic and determined. *Cubanía* seemed seriously undermined, and the old ideals were remembered only in people like Sanguily and in a defiant popular culture (see Ibarra Cuesta 1994: 194–234).

Furthermore, a renewed Spanish immigration now followed independence, constituting 60 per cent of the half million permanent immigrants by the 1930s – one-third to Havana (Segré, Coyula and Scarpaci 1997: 52; Pino Santos 1973: 126),[34] 400,000 arriving in 1902–16 (Pérez 1988: 202). By 1931, some 613,790 Spanish migrants lived in Cuba, 484,730 more than in 1899 (Ibarra Cuesta 1992: 164). This time, the new migrants did not necessarily share the politics of the more radicalized Cubans; indeed the Spanish workers in Cuba may have been more anarchist or anarchosyndicalist than the predominantly socialist Cubans (Ibarra Cuesta 1992: 174).

There were now rural changes too, furthering the decline of the traditional elite and peasantry (by 1934, 40 per cent of those with land in 1899 had lost it), but also the rise of a petty bourgeoisie now dependent on professions and the state. New cleavages now began to appear, in society and in the collective psyche.

The most worrying, and tragic, cleavage was that between black and white. Having profoundly affected 'both the discourse and practice of nationalism' (Ferrer 1999: 10), having fought loyally for *Cuba Libre* in three wars (see Helg 1995),

---

34. Immigration statistics sometimes confusingly include seasonal workers; for example, in 1902–25 one million migrants arrived, but only 600,000 stayed (Pino Santos 1983: 126).

and having campaigned actively for black rights in a growing black press (Ferrer 1995: 246), Afro-Cubans now found themselves deliberately excluded from power, politics, employment and wealth. Disaffection led, in 1907, to the Agrupación Independiente de Color and then the Partido Independiente de Color (PIC – Independent Coloured Party), under Pedro Ivonet and Evaristo Estenoz (see especially Helg 1991).[35] After the Morúa law (1910) banned racial parties, the PIC was repressed, and rebellion broke out in Oriente in 1912, lasting several months and resulting in 3,000 dead (and American intervention to reassure American entrepreneurs and residents), after which white Cuba sought to expunge the Afro-Cuban element from official Cuban history, classifying it at best as picturesque folklore. Henceforth, the 'official' *nación* would mostly exclude the Afro-Cuban, although blacks continued to struggle for rights and reform, and for a *cubanía* that would include them.

Cubanía thus began to change, in particular explaining the separatist failure through a peculiar focus on the supposed *decadencia* ('decadence') of the Cuban, based on a 1924 lecture by the respected anthropologist Fernando Ortiz. Highly moralistic (talking of 'betrayal' and moral weakness) and ahistorical (ignoring earlier elite dynamism), this analysis illustrated the disorientation of intellectual dissidence, especially in the new cultural magazine, *Cuba Contemporánea* (Wright 1988), and owed much to the remnants of positivism (Ubieta Gómez 1993: 117), especially the importance accorded to Varona (see Guadarrama and Tussel 1987). It was also reflected in the rebelliousness surviving in groups such as the Asociación de Veteranos de la Guerra de Independencia (Independence War Veterans' Association), almost as a nostalgic lament for lost innocence,[36] and in the general ennui, self-deprecation and collective self-doubt now taking root, seemingly accepting American prejudices about Cuban indolence, disorganization, degeneracy and inferiority. It seemed that even the popular *cubanía* was resigned to the accommodationist perspective of weak national roots.

In the first two decades, there were in fact three separate *cubanías*, two of them more visible, determining the debates about *cubanidad*. The hegemonic *cubanía* was that associated with formal politics, with neo-annexationism dressed as 'accommodationism' in a *cubanía neoanexionista* – either a resigned realism (arguing for Cuba's 'natural' satellite status and economic dependence) or a sort of 'comparative advantage' in which Cuba's people and sugar were its 'essential' resources.

35. Tabares del Real (Tabares del Real 1973: 51) refers to the Partido de los Independientes de Color.

36. Historiography on this period seemingly confuses the Asociación de Veteranos and the later Movimiento de Veteranos y Patriotas. The former, founded in 1902 and led by the more prominent war leaders, became part of the political establishment and patrimonial system, but included aggrieved veterans hoping to use it to rescue the 1895 ideals. The latter, founded in 1923, was a more radical movement, led by some veterans (such as Federico Laredo Brú) but also by leading young radicals (especially the poet Rubén Martínez Villena, Julio Antonio Mella and Juan Marinello).

The second, also visible, was a *cubanía cultural*, continuing the old Eurocentric cultural and intellectual currents, but in a new concern with *lo cubano* ('things Cuban'), part in protest (at the lost dream) and part nostalgic (to rescue a cultural *nación*). Its most notable expression was *Cuba Contemporánea*, who, preoccupied with *la problemática de Cuba* ('the problem of Cuba') and with rescuing *lo cubano*, advocated the regeneration of national values, through a network of nationalist publishing houses and newspapers. Yet their nationalism was limited to a cultural crusade, lacking an economic or political context (Wright 1988: 111–12), and was largely white in conception and expression.

Beyond these two *cubanías* lay the hidden remnants of a stubbornly resistant, if demoralized, popular *cubanía*, a *cubanía rebelde*, existing more in potential than in visible reality. However, radicalism survived in three areas. It survived in the Cuban (rather than Spanish) trade unions, doubtless increased by American pressure on the Cubans to put their labour house in order or risk intervention under the Amendment, egged on by entrepreneurs fearful of labour militancy (Pérez 1986b: 55). The second area of radicalism was, implicitly, the various Afro-Cuban religions that flourished in urban Cuba, offering a collectivizing solace and context to the demoralized *mambises*; the increasingly popular imported congregational and evangelical Protestantism, especially in Oriente, were also a forum for a residual collective identity. The third radicalism was found among those – in the Liberal Party, the PIC or the 1909 Liga Antiplatista, for example – who hoped to realize a truly independent Cuba (now extolling *soberanía* (sovereignty) rather than *independencia*) through formal politics.

What united these distinct but often mutually antagonistic visions of *nación*, these three competing discourses within *cubanía*, was the emergence of the 'raw material' for an eventual consensual ideology of *cubanidad*, as a new, and more radical, *cubanía*, found in the beginnings of several shared values that would evolve into the ideological codes of the revolutionary *cubanía*. In a sense, a Cuban identity had for long been a negative, since 'Cubans defined themselves through denial' – of Spain, of Catholicism, and so on (Pérez 1999: 89); now there was the start of a more positive definition in these emerging values, which were, as yet, simply an evolving belief in the values on which a 'real' *Cuba Libre* would be based, arising coherently from the rather inchoate thoughts, ideas and traditions of the preceding decades, and from Martí's writings above all.

In 1902, there were seven such beliefs (which, still putative codes, we might term 'value-beliefs'). The first was the belief in an agrarian *cubanidad* – a recognition that Cuba's past and destiny lay in sugar, partly accounting for the consensus behind Sanguily's proposed 1903 law against Americanization (Pichardo 1986: 261–3). Secondly, *nación* was seen as based on a collective ethos, recalling 1895's brief unity and lamenting the subsequent disintegration, which echoed colonial cleavages; this expressed itself through the many contemporary mechanisms of collective action and 'belonging' – religions, unions, clubs, parties and associations. Although Afro-Cuba was not explicit, the experience of recent shared struggles probably still implied for most Cubans an adherence to the vision of a racially unified community; however the anti-black sentiments of many insurgents, elite and popular, made that somewhat fragile (Ferrer 1995).

Thirdly, *Cuba Libre* would be based on *eticidad* (morality), the theme of 'moralism-idealism' (Valdés 1992: 213), recalling campaigns against the immorality of colonialism and slavery, and now rejecting 'betrayals', but above all symbolized by the life and death of Martí, the embodiment of that *eticidad*. That was linked to the fourth belief, in a *Cuba Libre* based on a history of *lucha* (struggle), whose best, and most quintessentially Cuban, moments had come in struggles for ideals (especially Maceo's *Protesta de Baraguá*) and whose worst periods had seen quiescence, submission and accommodation. The fifth 'value-belief' was in a *nación* based on culture, education and the intellectual – recalling the tradition of intellectual leadership, but also the former positivist and Krausist faiths in fulfilment, liberation and progress through education. The final 'value-beliefs' were in a benevolent state (set against a decrepit and malevolent colonialism) and in the idea of revolution, as purification and renewal.

These values (collectively an embryonic vision of *nación*) were not shared equally by all three *cubanías*. *Neoanexionismo*, for example, extolled activism (to legitimize the ex-combatants) and patronized culture, paying lip-service to morality and a strong state, but avoided the dangers of collectivism. *Cubanía cultural*, equally, downplayed activism, rejecting it for a belief in 'culture for culture's sake', but remained loyal to other values. Only the *rebelde* alternative adhered to all the values, largely unnoticed.

For two decades this was the sorry picture of the so-called *seudorepública* (in nationalist demonology), the 1895 hopes now in ruins, political and economic realism determining *neoanexionismo* and nationalist divisions. Then came a sugar crisis to remove even that, as, with the end of the European war in 1918, expectations of the inevitable price-fall were confounded as the boom continued into 1919 (with demand rising but beet production weak), the price rising to a spectacular twenty cents a pound (from an average of between four and seven cents), with talk of a possible forty or fifty cents. This encouraged Cuban producers to borrow heavily to increase production – the *Danza de los Millones* (Dance of the Millions) – until, in 1920, came the inevitable crash, as European production revived and new suppliers met the demand; the price collapsed to six cents in October and a calamitous three cents in January 1921.

The crisis had four immediate effects. Firstly, it accelerated a process of 'dependentization', as over-stretched Cuban sugar holdings and banking interests collapsed, bought out by American interests, notably corporations and banks, so that, while in 1916 there had been 122 Cuban banks (and only 26 non-Cuban), the figures rocketed to 320 and 74 in 1920, and by 1925 the figures were 67 and 93 (Pichardo 1986: 459).[37] Cuba's dual role in the neocolonial relationship was thus reinforced with a vengeance, eliminating the chance of autonomous development, and thus of any real political independence.

Secondly, the crisis undermined economic confidence and the carefully constructed neocolonial relationship. The 1906 military intervention had, by confirming the problems of instability and conflict, and the enduring popularity of the supposedly nationalist Liberals, effectively forced the Americans to abandon their goal of a natural majority for acquisition through 'Americanization', obliging them towards a new aim of a natural majority for neocolonialism through prosperity. Now even that seemed unlikely, lacking the legitimacy of a 'critical mass' of politically significant Cubans to believe in its benefits; after 1921, the consensus was that the relationship brought suffering, vulnerability and dependence.[38]

Thirdly, the crisis breathed new life into radicalism, with new hope, a new focus, and a new direction. Firstly, in April 1924, the newly-formed Movimiento de Veteranos y Patriotas, already the focus of much nationalist militancy against the Republic's ills and the Zayas government, organized an abortive rising in Las Villas province, which, with talk of 'revolutionary intentions', threatened the system's stability, aroused government fears, and promised a new, unifying, political movement (Pérez 1986a: 242–8). Another pole of protest was the unexpected re-emergence of the intellectuals, with a radical perspective and a cultural critique of the Republic (López Civeira, Loyola Vega and Silva León 1998: 150). The cue was given by Ortiz (founding his Junta de Renovación Nacional Cívica, for 'regeneration' by the intellectual vanguard), by Varona (now scathing about the Republic's immorality) and, above all, by the *Protesta de los Trece* ('Protest of the Thirteen') – the anti-corruption protest by Rubén Martínez Villena and fourteen other intellectuals, with thirteen then signing a manifesto, creating a short-lived Falange de Acción Cubana and, eventually, forming the *Grupo Minorista*,[39] and the equally influential *avant-garde* magazine *Revista de Avance* (1927–1930). The

37. Accounting for 28 per cent of loans in Cuba and 20 per cent of deposits in 1920, American banks owned 81 per cent and 69 per cent respectively a year later, the National City bank alone purchasing 60 of the 150 Cuban mills (Pérez 1986a: 188). Benjamin cites Cuban banks accounting for 70 per cent of loans and 80 per cent of deposits in 1920, but only 18 per cent and 31 per cent a year later, after which foreign banks controlled 80 per cent of Cuba's sugar, US-owned mills producing only 35 per cent of the crop in 1914, but 62 per cent in 1927 (Benjamin 1977: 16–17); this latter figure rose again, by 1928 to 75 per cent (Perez 1986a: 188). American capital also dominated rail, electricity, telephones, ports, mining and manufacturing (Benjamin 1977: 16–18).

38. In 1913–28, American capital in Cuba rose by an astonishing 536%, to one and a half billion (American) dollars (Pérez 1986a: 188).

39. The thirteen were those of the fifteen protesters (against the government's corrupt sale of the Santa Clara convent) who signed the subsequent manifesto; they included Martínez Villena, Jorge Mañach, Juan Marinello and José Z. Tallet.

protest stimulated a whole *enragé* generation, as other intellectuals used their position more polemically. A new historiography was especially significant, led by Ramiro Guerra y Sánchez – with his path-breaking critique of the *latifundio* (the large landholding), *Azúcar y Población en las Antillas* in 1927 (Guerra 1970) and his *En el Camino de la Independencia* in 1930 (Guerra 1974) – and, with Emilio Roig de Leuchsenring, boosting the new generation's confidence, legitimizing radicalism through the prestige of scholarship and engendering a whole tradition of critical historiography. Now, however, the focus was not on Platt (symbolic of Cuba's humiliation) but corruption and dependency, perfect targets for the moralistic impulses of the old *cubanía* and the new *decadencia*.

The focus was apposite because of the roots of corruption, in the colonial past (given Spanish colonialism's 'culture of corruption') (MacFarlane 1996: 55) and in specific patterns of rule, patronage and trade after 1806, colonial inefficiency meaning that, after the 1850s, a combination of inadequate pay and a relative administrative autonomy generated an inevitable recourse to peculation, while the slave trade itself (fundamental to the economic system) meant official collusion in illegality, blurring the lines between the permissible and the impermissible. The American occupation had then generated a widespread pursuit of office and employment in a context of immiseration, unemployment and patronage.[40] Finally, after 1902, it became clear that wealth came from access to office, and that, as the economic structure excluded many Cubans, security came through political activity, administrative patronage and corruption, especially as electoral fraud was widespread and open. The presidencies of the 1895 veterans José Miguel Gómez (1909–1913) and Mario García Menocal (1913–1921) were especially corrupt, with patronage, fraud, nepotism and, above all, the control of the revived lottery.[41]

The 1920–21 crisis now revived radicalism through two groups – Havana students (numbers swelled by post-1900 expansion) and a reinvigorated working class. The former first espoused the issue of corruption, inspired by the *Protesta*, but then created a political force in the Federación Estudiantil Universitaria (FEU), which, under Julio Antonio Mella, published a manifesto in January 1923, adopting the Argentinian ideas of university reform, and arguing for anti-imperialism (against American aggression elsewhere and American control through Platt, including the Isle of Pines) and an educational revolution. It mobilized demonstrations, a strike (till 15 February), and the First National Student Congress of October 1923 (attended by Guerra, Roig and Martínez Villena) (Soto 1985a: 126), and created, in November 1923, the Universidad Popular José Martí, to link students and

40. One study sees corruption as endemic in both colonialism and the 'national' period (Miller 1996: 65–96), leading one to expect an even greater problem in Cuba, given both prolonged colonialism and subsequent neocolonialism.

41. Outstanding examples of corruption were the 1905 elections (with an estimated 150,000 fictitious voters) (Pérez 1986a: 93) and the lottery, generating from 1909 about eleven million dollars annually (Pérez 1986b: 216).

workers. Mella then went on to found the Liga Anticlerical and the Liga Antimperialista in 1924.

Cuban student radicalism was not unique, and the 1918 Córdoba reform movement – which had an impact in Havana in 1920 (Roa 1964: 235) – spawned similar movements and demands all over Latin America. It also coincided with Haya de la Torre's 1924 Peruvian APRA movement (Alianza Popular Revolucionaria Americana); although a Partido Aprista Cubano was not founded until 1933 – then influencing other movements, notably Joven Cuba (Young Cuba) and the *Auténticos* (see later) (Anderle 1975: 37) – Aprista ideas were an integral part of the atmosphere (Anderle 1975).

At a time of intellectual ferment, coinciding with the Russian and Mexican revolutions, anticolonial struggles, Fascism and corporatism, these ideas found fertile ground in a Cuban bourgeoisie frustrated by exclusion from American interests and patronage, and disenchanted by economic collapse. Mella now added a Cuban dimension; after a two-decade neglect (Wright 1988: 111), he now engendered through his 1924 pamphlet, *Glosando los Pensamientos de José Martí* (Comments on Martí's Thought) (Mella 1941) a rediscovery of Martí not so much as a symbol of purity and unity, but rather as a profound radical thinker on class, nationality and anti-imperialism. In this, the new student radicalism echoed the old *cubanista* belief in the role of 'culture' (see Kapcia 1985 and Raby 1975).

Proletarian radicalism was also nothing new, the first two decades being characterized by labour unrest and militancy, especially in sugar, with a 1902 general strike (with five killed), a 1906 strike wave and a 1907 rail strike broken by imported American labour (Tabares del Real 1973: 51). Now, after dislocation, came a new strike wave, the Congreso Obrero Nacional de Cuba (Cuban National Workers' Congress) – representing 90,000 workers, from which evolved the anarchosyndicalist Federación Obrera de La Habana (FOH – Havana Workers' Federation), under Alfredo López, sponsoring a three-week rail strike and a long sugar strike in 1924–5; and, in 1925, the third Congreso Nacional Obrero set up the first national confederation, the Confederación Nacional de Obreros de Cuba (CNOC – National Confederation of Cuban Workers), the moderate socialists being replaced by the anarchosyndicalists' militant and class-conscious challenge to capitalism, the state and imperialism.

That ferment also, however, created in 1925 the Cuban Communist Party, whose founding members included Mella, Carlos Baliño (Martí's socialist PRC colleague) and José Pérez Vilaball and Alejandro Barreiro (the secretary-general and treasurer of the FOH).[42] Although unable to challenge the anarchosyndicalists' ascendancy

---

42. The party emerged from the Agrupación Socialista de La Habana of 1918, becoming the Agrupación Comunista de La Habana in March 1923 (with *agrupaciones* in five other locations); in August 1925, at the Congreso de Agrupaciones Comunistas, the Partido Comunista de Cuba was founded.

for a few years, the new party rapidly proved to be more disciplined and more ideologically coherent than any previous leftist grouping, attracting radicals and progressives from both working and middle classes, with 3,000 members by 1933 (Anderle 1975: 31).[43]

The crisis now also produced the 1924 election of Gerardo Machado, Liberal 1895 veteran and ex-Guardia Rural, on a platform of morality and regeneration, populist nationalism and populist reform (including diversification and public works) and *cooperativismo* (unity of classes, races and parties). This campaign (backed by Ortiz, Guerra, the FEU and the Movimiento de Veteranos) responded to the new grievances and the climate of resurgent *cubanía* (see Berenguer 1926: 169), represented by the evolution of the 'value-beliefs' of 1902 into more complete and complex, recognizable ideological codes, each with an implicit argument and 'programme'.

Thus, the concern with the agrarian essence of *cubanidad* had evolved into an 'agrarianism' – a belief that *Cuba Libre* should have a consensus on land ownership, sugar protection and rural labour, based on equality and autonomy; the idea that sugar might be 'curse' and 'blessing' now entered the political culture. The belief in a 'collective' identity had become a programme for defensive collective action, welfare and equality, to which Machado's *cooperativismo* responded explicitly. The *República Plattista* had made *eticidad* into an ideological issue – 'moralism' – whose watchwords were *dignidad* (dignity), *honestidad* (honesty) and *cubanidad* – confirmed by the plethora of manifestos, declarations and movements for 're-generation', renewal, morality and honesty. Equally, the idea of 'action' had become a code of 'activism', extolling action for liberation as quintessentially Cuban and heroic, and rejecting as unpatriotic inaction or collaboration. The rise of the students, the influx of new ideas and the rediscovery of Martí all created a code of 'culturalism', seen as essential to *cubanidad*. 'Statism', of course, had developed in opposition to the *seudorepública*'s essential weakness and corruption, reinforced by a contemporary radicalism seeing the state as vital for progress; as anarcho-syndicalism declined, 'statism' grew in importance in the *cubanista* vision, with its own implicit programme. Finally, renewed radicalism and activism now made 'revolutionism' a code, implying the inevitable realization of Martí's challenge to transform neocolonialism to fulfil Cuba's destiny.

However unformed the underlying ideas, these codes were clearly being shaped at several levels of society, in different interpretations of *cubanía,* and in every action, manifestation and crisis. That the codes were now shared by more Cubans was clear from the strength of oppositionist and radical groupings, union militancy, and the blossoming literature of dissent; what those codes specifically proposed,

---

43. The party's youth movement counted 3,500 members and the women's organization 5,500 (Anderle, 1975: 31).

other than a link between present battles and forgotten traditions, was, however, less clear, and almost certainly mostly implied a white Cuba, for the marginalization of Afro-Cuba even extended to radicals, despite black activists' prominence in union and political struggles. Nonetheless, the new crisis had reversed the old dilemma of a loss of collective self-confidence's being tempered by a comforting economic confidence; now the crisis, interestingly, saw economic confidence fall but political confidence rise – a development vital to a new sense of identity-building.

At that stage, however, the new *cubanía*'s embryonic nature made different versions acceptable, with Machado's project seeming both *cubanista* enough to be believable and concrete enough to be practical. However, he proved as self-serving and conservative as his predecessors, and the difference between the confidence of 1922–4 and the brutal reality of the *machadato* (Machado's dictatorship) – especially when renewed economic crisis undid his plans, showing *cooperativismo* as simply a modified patrimonial cooperation between 'patron' parties (López Civeira *et al.* 1998: 168) – gave decisive force, direction and shape to the evolving *cubanía*. Indeed, the *machadato* was when the inchoate values of a '*pre-cubanía*' were converted into the definable codes of the eventual ideology (Benjamin 1975).

For Machado posed a triple crisis. Firstly, authoritarianism then proved politically explosive, undermining the delicate balance and challenging his repression, his patronage (based on the army, congress and a supposed affinity with Afro-Cubans), and his accommodationism with the United States. That repression had three main targets – the Left (the Communist Party being outlawed within a month, and leading activists, including Mella, being arrested or deported); the students, who had helped his ascendancy and backed his election, but who now threatened destabilization (the FEU also being outlawed in 1925 and its leaders arrested); and the trade unions. Here, his onslaught (which, by early 1927, had killed 150 leaders: Pérez 1986a: 264) accidentally furthered the communists' advance by targeting the anarchosyndicalists (Tabares del Real 1973: 119). He then galvanized opposition in 1928 by extending his term of office by two years (the *prorroga*), an abuse of the constitution that unleashed more unrest, with a general strike in 1930 (of 200,000 workers) and renewed student militancy, resulting in 1930 in the re-formed Directorio Estudiantil Universitario (DEU), out of the ashes of the original DEU, successor to the old FEU.

The second crisis was more structural, for Machado's attempt to capitalize on dissidence through a quasi-populism was flawed. Elsewhere in Latin America populism's short-term success, in rapid modernization and incorporation of dissent, depended on the rising new 'national bourgeoisie'; before 1929, many such movements had successfully mobilized, challenged, awakened expectations, and channelled incipient radicalism, but, after 1929, the tactical alliance between some of the old oligarchy, prepared to avoid annihilation through nationalism, and the aspiring elite proved to be the *sine qua non* for the next stage, integrating dissent into a controlled system or movement. Yet Cuba lacked both a traditional oligarchy and a modernizing 'national bourgeoisie' capable of controlling, enacting and developing a reform project.

There is, however, no historiographical consensus about the Cuban bourgeoisie's strength. Some see it as weak (Boorstein 1969: 13; Ruffin 1990: 63–77; Bray and Harding 1974: 599), or assert the lack of a national bourgeoisie (Ibarra Cuesta 1979: 155), seeing its potential in 1895 but its absence, division and lack of self-identification in the 1920s, unable to defend its own interests or challenge the external relationship (Ibarra Cuesta 1992: 102–8). Instead, the Cuban bourgeoisie until 1933 seemed a loose and contradictory fusion of the larger *colonos* and ranchers with tobacco manufacturers, the remainder being Spanish (Ibarra Cuesta 1992: 65–83). O'Connor challenges that view, but argues that the class 'lacked a progressive optimism, creative ideology of its own making and, in fact, assumed a dependent status' (O'Connor 1970: 23). It seems, therefore, that the bourgeoisie was too weak to provide the basis for a successful populist project, for 'there were not enough of them to make up for their individual weakness, to make them in the aggregate into a force that could worry imperialism and its local partners' (Boorstein 1969: 13). Even after 1921, the disaggregated elite was unable to unite around a nationalist programme, and lacked a consensus on nationalism in 1933–4 (Pollitt 1984: 113).

The third crisis was the project's economic vulnerability, demonstrated dramatically in 1929, when sugar prices fell even below the 1921 level, the American market suddenly disappeared and production plummeted.[44] Now elite resistance to change dissipated, especially after a failed 1931 coup by the Asociación Unión Nacionalista – a rebellion of the *viejos* (old) *caudillos* (Cabrera 1977: 19) – despite the army's debilitation through corruption and authoritarianism (Chang 1981: 145–88).[45] Now sectors of that elite moved towards the evolving dissidence to salvage what they could.

One result was a new, enigmatic terrorist group, Sociedad Revolucionaria ABC (ABC Revolutionary Society),[46] including some intellectual and political activists

44. Prices, already low (4.19 cents in 1924 and 2.5 cents in 1926), now collapsed to 1.72 cents (Pérez 1986a: 279), and 0.93 cents in 1930 (Brundenius 1984: 10). Cuba's market share fell from 49.4% (1930) to 25.3% (1933), production falling by 60 per cent, exports by 80 per cent (Pérez 1986a: 279–80).

45. The rebellion, occurring simultaneously in several places – especially Río Verde (Pinar del Río) and Gibara (Oriente), was engineered by the 1895 veterans Carlos Mendieta and (ex-president) Mario García Menocal, but attracted others, including Antonio Guiteras.

46. The initials ABC meant nothing, referring to the independent operation of the organization's secret cells.

drawn from the ranks of oligarchic youth (such as Joaquín Martínez Saenz and Carlos Saladrigas, and the *Protesta* veterans Francisco Ichaso and Jorge Mañach). ABC was never Fascist, as some claim (Tabares del Real 1973: 59), although it advocated a totalitarian state and boasted its 'Green Shirts'; its vision was more corporatist and moderately nationalist, proposing a programme of realistic modification of the Cuban–American relationship (Farber 1976: 55), sugar protection, state control and elitist hierarchy. Adopting some of the emerging *cubanista* values, ABC even espoused 'revolution', but also argued for class collaboration and was vehemently anticommunist.

The new disjuncture now produced violence and unrest. The former was perpetrated by the police and army, and by ABC and other similar 'action groups', such as the Organización Celular Radical Revolucionaria (OCRR – Revolutionary Radical Cellular Organization) and Pro Ley y Justicia ('For Law and Justice'). Unrest amounted increasingly to a full-blown working-class rebellion, in collaboration with the more politicized sectors of the middle class, especially the DEU, renewing the dissident alliance of 1923–5.

The DEU was now more radical, stimulated by its 1931 offshoot, the Marxist Ala Izquierda Estudiantil (AIE – Student Left Wing), challenging the DEU's call for a multi-class uprising.[47] The AIE was increasingly spearheaded by communists, already leading the Left, although the catalyst for Machado's fall – the January 1933 sugar strike – happened against communist advice. Within weeks, the spreading labour unrest led the American Ambassador, Sumner Welles, to mediate between the opposition and Machado, supported by an opportunistic ABC (leading to a splinter group, ABC Radical). By then, however, the movement was uncompromising, and, in August 1933, Machado was toppled by demonstrations and a general strike, reflecting the wider revolution in the factories and cane-fields. This was followed by an attempted restoration, under the oligarchic Carlos Manuel de Céspedes and the 'young Turks' of ABC, doomed as the violence led, on 4 September, to a mutiny by disgruntled non-commissioned officers (NCOs) at Havana's Campamento Columbia.

The result was a widespread rebellion, with three distinct, simultaneous poles. The NCOs were the first pole, because they acted first and remained the most significant, represented by the Unión Militar Revolucionaria, under Pablo Rodríguez and a stenographer, Fulgencio Batista.[48] This was no 'junior officers' rebellion, as some claim (Raby 1975: 17), but a more significant mutiny by NCOs who, given a special role in the Republican Army (by the 1923 *Ley de Sargentos*

47. This group included many later members of either the Communist Party or dissident leftist groups: Ladislao González Carbajal, Aureliano Sánchez Arango, Raúl Roa, Piro Pendés, Manolo Guillot, Carlos Martínez, Gabriel Barcelo, Pablo de la Torriente Brau and Rafael García Bárcena.

48. Raby refers to Batista's past associations with ABC (Raby 1975: 18), although, given their elitism, that seems unlikely and there is no other evidence to support that.

(Sergeants' Law) to allow promotion to the officer corps), were frustrated and excluded from advancement by an army that was only partly modernized and 'pseudo-professional' (Chang 1981: 37), lacked an officer school, was highly politicized (and used by Machado in rural education) and had been ridden with corruption since 1918. The mutineers therefore responded to the vacuum and the wider rebelliousness by rebelling themselves, and competed for control of the streets with other 'armies' – notably the student militias (the *Ejército del Caribe* (Caribbean Army), ABC Radical (and ABC itself) and Pro Ley y Justicia) (Soto 1985b: 127).

They also competed, however, with the old officer corps, which resisted the mutiny. On 6 September, possibly around 400 of them took refuge in the prestigious new Hotel Nacional, resolving to resist until the advent of American intervention under the Amendment, and doing so until they were subjected to a ferocious siege and bombardment on 2 October, when they negotiated a surrender. On leaving, however, several were killed or wounded, and others were arrested.[49] In all, the affair constituted a turning-point, being one of the rebellion's most revolutionary acts, eliminating the NCOs' most serious rivals, but frightening many wavering moderates into seeking more stability.

The other turning-point was a second officers' rebellion on 9 November, supported by ABC, OCRR and elements of the Unión Nacionalista. This too was suppressed (at the students' request) by Batista, now largely unchallenged, increasingly aware of his student allies' essential weakness and of his own power, but fearful also of the labour threat.

The second pole was the DEU, which, on 5 September, took power, setting up the *Pentarquía*, a junta of five 'intellectuals' (1920s veterans and members of the Movimiento de Veteranos), the DEU acting as the 'assembly' and government.[50] Five days later, one of the Pentarchy – Ramón Grau San Martín – took personal control, with the 'assembly' – the Junta Revolucionaria – based firmly at Columbia.[51] The most vociferous pole, but certainly the weakest and least coherent, the students were trapped between Batista's ambitions (and a worried Washington) and the forces to their left.

This 'left' included the socialist Minister of the Interior, War and the Navy (*Gobernación, Guerra y Marina*), Antonio Guiteras. A veteran of the 1928 DE U and

49. There is no historiographical consensus on the cause of the shooting (possibly on Batista's orders or through accidental firing by students or soldiers) or the numbers involved, estimates varying widely between 250 and 409 for those besieged, and, for those killed, between 9 and 50 (Tabares del Real 1998: 315) or even 100 (Mazarr 1988: 201), The most likely figure seems to be eleven officers killed (plus two in the preceding battle) of the seventy shot at while awaiting transport (Soto 1985a: 134).

50. The five were a banker, two lawyers, an editor and a doctor.

51. The *Pentarquia* collapsed at the unilateral nomination of Batista, as colonel, to lead the new army, leading Irisarri to resign, and later, after 1934, to join Joven Cuba (Cabrera 1977: 38).

of the 1931 Gibara rising, he proposed economic independence from 'imperialism', a workers' and peasants' revolution and land reform (Cabrera 1977: 70–1). In government, he was instrumental in many popular radical measures: the abrogation of the Amendment, the refusal to repay the Chase National Bank, intervention in American properties (two *centrales* and the Cuban Electricity Company), labour reforms (including an eight-hour day and a minimum wage, and a controversial 50 per cent quota of Cuban employees in all enterprises), protection of sugar and the *colonos*, and other social and political reforms (including female suffrage).

Right-wing pressure continued: from ABC, which, largely excluded by the rebels as dangerously elitist and even fascist, remained marginal, armed and critical, increasingly expressing oligarchic conservatism and fear of social disintegration; and increasingly from Batista (now a colonel, as the mutineers replaced some 400 removed officers).

The third pole – labour – was therefore critical to the outcome. Building on the 1930–33 rebellion, and growing (claiming 400,000 members by 1934: Stubbs 1985: 91), the increasingly communist-led CNOC undertook further revolutionary action in the cane-fields, declaring 'soviets' in Oriente and seizing some forty mills. This was the pole feared most by Washington, whose refusal to accord it diplomatic recognition ensured the Grau government's isolation and downfall, and who, through Welles and then Caffrey, persuaded Batista to fill the vacuum (Morley 1987: 32–3) in a coup in January 1934, to the relief of many Cubans, tiring of chaos and seeing Batista as the strongest of the revolution's participants.

Thus ended the 'government of the hundred days', so pivotal to Cuba's political and ideological evolution. Firstly, the reform programme enacted (but never enforced) became the platform for subsequent 'revolutionaries'; secondly, 1921–31 had unravelled the carefully constructed neocolonial system, ending the hopes of both a 'natural' annexationism and Cuban autonomy, and had seen the emergence of a coherent dissidence; thirdly, the revolution began a new era, replacing the 1895–8 war as the legitimator of political activism and of all the main protagonists until 1953. Fourthly, it showed the potential for, but the limits of, genuine popular unrest; 1930–33 saw a real 'labour uprising' (Pérez Sarduy and Stubbs 1993: 7), recognized and remembered by Grau and the DEU activists, who feared its radicalism, and by those who resisted it – fears that had ensured the marginalization and bloody repression of worker radicalism. The revolutionary challenge came not from the visible 1933–4 events, which represented the climax of bourgeois rebellion and a moment of truth for dissident sectors of the elite, but, instead, from the 1930–33 rebellion, which Washington attempted to end through mediation and support for Batista.

Finally, 1921–34 confirmed what the 1890s had signalled – *cubanía*'s inherent propensity for radical solutions. For the combination of social unrest, political dissidence and intellectual ferment further fused the two levels of ideology – the popular and the intellectual – and, with the disappearance of an anarchosyndicalist alternative, Marxism had begun to exercise a subsequently unchallenged hegemony within the evolving dissidence, as an explanation of Cuba's situation (based on Leninist theories of imperialism). Henceforth, Marxism became the most coherent, consensual 'intellectual-theoretical' level of ideology in the dissident *cubania*, leading most radical dissidence to be expressed as 'anti-imperialism', 'class struggle' and 'historical progress', positing a future based on egalitarianism and a benevolent state.

Therefore, 1921–31 was also a watershed in the evolution of *cubania*. The *machadato* had proved that, while the pre-1921 coexistence of three separate *cubanias* was possible and even necessary – since prosperity justified one (*cubania neoanexionista*) and allowed the second (*cubania cultural*), while 1895–8 provided a folk-memory for the third (*cubania rebelde*), after 1931 a tripartite ideology was unsustainable. This was because the 1929 crisis delegitimized the notion of satellite status, and thus any remnant, resurgence or modification of *cubania neoanexionista*, while the *rebelde* challenge forced waverers to choose, and, increasingly, became the only version proposing real change, to which the indecisive *cubania cultural* would have to adapt.

However, if the old system was deteriorating, a new 'alternative project' was still not in place. Whatever the consensus about Machado or neocolonialism, and however much the three *cubanias* were becoming one, that process was delayed by the rebellion's effects. Hence, the new dissent was still fragmented, reflecting the new social and economic cleavages, for the 'official' revolution of 1933 was less a revolutionary challenge than disintegration into revolt, producing a vacuum where individuals had an inordinate role and judgements were flawed. Some – notably Guiteras – shared labour's goals of deep transformation; but the government's programme was less a radical project for change than a populist project for modernization, echoing post-1929 measures elsewhere in Latin America – although, in Cuba, even the most innocuous measure had revolutionary implications for the basic Cuban–American relationship.

The revolution's inglorious end – a coup by the least ideologically motivated of its protagonists, encouraged by a Washington that (though scrupulously non-interventionist) was ever watchful – left *cubania* in crisis. The consensus of September 1933 had collapsed, and the hopes for this latest *lucha* had again proved illusory against new 'betrayal' and external pressure.

Now corrosive disillusionment was exacerbated by new divisions, partly echoing those of 1921–31, between those nostalgic for and seeking to resume the latest 'heroism', in the embattled tradition of *cubania rebelde*, and those who (with the Platt Amendment abrogated in 1934 with Washington's approval) were led by resignation or enthusiasm towards a familiar 'accommodationism', a new *cubania neoanexionista*, believing that, after 1929–34, Cuba was best served by the new, if still dependent, relationship with the apparently less imperialist United States. Alongside bourgeois and business pro-American aspirations, these accommodationists included those who, persuaded of nationalism after 1929, had been alarmed by the subsequent radicalization or simply judged that Batista's new relationship with Washington was desirable.

The residual *cubanía rebelde* generally reacted to the coup by seeking self-protection in new groupings, most notably Guiteras's brief-lived TNT and Joven Cuba, Pablo de la Torriente Brau's Organización Revolucionaria Cubana Antimperialista (ORCA – Cuban Anti-imperialist Revolutionary Organization) and Izquierda Revolucionaria (Revolutionary Left), a new home for many AIE activists. Some of these merged in the Bloque Septembrista and the Coalición Nacional Revolucionaria, which then, under Grau, created (on 8 February 1934 in Miami) the Partido Revolucionario Cubano-Autentico (PRC-A – Authentic Cuban Revolutionary Party), thereafter simply known as the *Auténticos*, with an armed wing in Organización Auténtica (under Carlos Prío Socarrás and Aureliano Sánchez Arango). These all united in a challenge to Batista, the general strike of March 1935, to which Batista reacted bloodily.[52]

The ensuing repression (resulting in Guiteras's death and a weakening of the unions)[53] led to inevitable recriminations and soul-searching on the Left, but also forced some into other commitments, especially the Spanish Civil War, in which the Republicans attracted a significantly high level of Cuban support, with two effects after 1939 – strengthening the leftist, and often communist, beliefs of both returning volunteers and Spanish Republican refugees, but also disenchanting some of those same volunteers, and pushing them in alternative political directions in Cuba (see especially Kapcia 1993: 81–2).[54]

After 1935, however, those choosing neither Spain nor the *Auténticos* tended to divide between a withdrawal from open commitment (the intellectuals retreating into artistic vanguardism and labour activists limiting themselves to economism) and an increasing search for meaning in, or alongside, the growing Communist Party, which shared a Latin American characteristic of a quasi-monopoly of intellectual political commitment.[55] The intellectuals' gradual preference for either

52. The strike was largely engineered by DEU and *Auténtico* elements around Grau, against the advice of Guiteras and the communists; ultimately, however, all opposition elements supported it.

53. The CNOC numbers fell to 220,666 in 1938 (Chang Pon 1998: 373).

54. On his return from Spain, the ex-Joven Cuba Rolando Masferrer founded the MSR (Movimento Socialista Revolucionario) in 1944, eventually supporting the *Auténticos'* anti-communist drive in the unions and the University, and then Batista.

55. The artists and intellectuals joining, or supporting, the Communist Party included the painter Wilfredo Lam, the poet Nicolás Guillén, and the novelist and music critic Alejo Carpentier, as well as Marinello, Raúl Roa, Emilio Roig, Pablo de la Torriente Brau and Raúl Cepero Bonilla. Some later parted company with the party, Roa, for example (with Tallet), founding Partido Izquierda Revolucionaria in 1937 (Pérez Rojas 1975: 211).

'retreat' or communism recognized the reality of 1930–33, that *cubanía cultural* was no longer an option.

A further complication was the communists' unclear position. Often deliberately marginalized by the 'official' 1933 revolution, the party had rejected the DEU as petty-bourgeois nationalism and was suspicious of the mutineers' radicalism, opposing, with the CNOC, the implicit racism of the '50 per cent law' (Carr 1998: 107). Nonetheless, despite reservations about the general strikes (1930, 1933) and even the 1933 'soviets', the party responded to popular demands, leading and organizing the discontent and popular radicalism. However, although prestigious, growing – to 6,000 (Suárez 1967: 2) – and admired for its discipline,[56] it was neither part of *cubanía rebelde* (although often close, sharing many of its precepts) nor supportive of *cubanía neoanexionista*.

Ironically, however, it was the latter current that offered them their next role, when Batista, having supressed the Left in 1935 and with Guiteras dead, realized its potential and proceeded to develop his own *cubanía neoanexionista*, cleverly dressing it as *rebelde*, a manouevre made possible by his legitimacy from his role in 1933.

Ruling through puppets between 1934 and 1937,[57] he decided to recognize the Left's continuing strength and the legitimacy of 1933 by responding to an offer of a tactical alliance from the communists – also ready to compromise. Guided by the Comintern's strategy of 'Popular Frontism' and the hegemony within Latin American communism of 'Browderist' gradualism, the party possibly approached Batista in 1936 (Karol 1970: 81), then Grau in 1938, but, being rebuffed, turned again to Batista.[58]

The deal was simple and astute. Batista would legalize the party (in 1937 as the Unión Revolucionaria Comunista – URC), tolerate their activity (the paper,

56. After the deaths of Martínez Villena, Baliño and Mella, and under the more working-class activist, Francisco Calderío (thereafter known by his *nom de guerre* Blas Roca), the party was reorganized in 1934 (or 'purged' – A. Suárez 1967: 3), so that no member of the 1933 Central Committee was still in the party in 1952 (A. Suárez 1967: 3); that was when 'Trotskyists' were expelled, although few were probably real Trotskyists, being simply dissidents, especially in the Oposición Comunista de Izquierda (many of whom went on to found a small Partido Bolchevique Leninista in September 1933) (Anderle 1975: 33). One writer argues that the black Sandalio Junco was expelled in 1932 for his colour (Moore 1988: 47), although this is unconfirmed and the party's record in defending black workers was exemplary (see Carr 1998).

57. The 'puppets' were Carlos Hevia (1934) for two days, Carlos Mendieta (1934–5), and José Barnet (1935), again for a few weeks; only the veteran politician and 1931 rebel, Miguel Mariano Gómez, dissented (1935–6), until Batista popularly engineered his impeachment, to be succeeded by another 'puppet' in Laredo Brú.

58. Earl Browder, leader of the American Communist Party, was confirmed by the 1935 Comintern as the theoretical authority of 'American communism'; he argued that, Latin America being still feudal or semi-feudal and thus unready for socialist revolution, the communists' best strategy was gradualism, alliance with the 'progressive bourgeoisie', and a trade union focus.

Noticias de Hoy, began in 1938), and allow them hegemony in the unions – after 1939, reorganized as the Confederación de Trabajadores de Cuba (CTC – Cuban Workers' Confederation), with a black communist, Lázaro Peña, as their first secretary-general.[59] In exchange, the party would support Batista's populism, largely built on the feasible aspects of the 1933 mandate. This ensured Batista's lasting popularity and the quiescence of the communists who, in 1944, confirmed this by renaming themselves the Partido Socialista Popular (PSP) – a title that persisted until 1961.[60]

This strategy succeeded, leading to the communist front (Partido URC, known as PUR) for the 1938 congressional elections and, in 1939, to a formal alliance with Batista for the Assembly designed to rewrite the Constitution[61] – the CSD (Coalición Socialista Democrática – Democratic Socialist Coalition), which gained the communists 97,944 votes (8.9 per cent) and six seats.[62] Under the *Auténtico*-based coalition, the Constituent Assembly produced a radical constitution in 1940, enshrining the basic demands of the whole 1933 revolution. Finally, seen as responsible for all the post-1934 reforms and the new constitution, Batista was overwhelmingly elected in 1940 over Grau,[63] presiding, until his departure in 1944, over a swathe of nationalist and social reforms, assuaging popular demands and creating an image of modernization (see Kapcia 1996a). The benefits were obvious for both Batista and the communists, whose support continued to rise,[64] and whose membership to grow,[65] and whose popularity remained, especially among the unionized workers (Zeitlin 1970a: 57–63).

The basis for this populist strategy of 'regulation and redistribution' (Domínguez 1978a: 54) was the space offered by the new Cuban–American relationship, based partly on the new American isolationism and Roosevelt's 'Good Neighbor' policy,

59. That hegemony lasted well into the 1940s (until challenged by Grau); in 1940, 37 per cent of the CTC Executive Committee were communist (Dana Sims 1991: 126).

60. One source gives the date as 1940 (Suchlicki 1988: 212), but there is no other evidence of this.

61. The 1938 elections were contested mainly by the PUR, the right-wing Frente Democrático de la Oposición (uniting ABC, Gómez's Acción Republicana and Menocal's Demócratas Republicanos), and the Bloque Revolucionario Popular (consisting of the newly formed PRC-A – and the Organización Auténtica, together with the Partido Agrario Nacional and the Unión Revolucionaria) (Le Riverend 1971: 314).

62. The CSD won 36 seats, to the 45 for the new alliance between PRC-A, Menocal's PDR and ABC (the latter winning four seats) (Le Riverend 1971: 316).

63. Most of Batista's 1933-inspired reforms were, ironically, passed by the Mendieta government, proving their fundamental lack of radicalism (Domínguez 1978a: 78).

64. Although their vote fell to 81,200 in 1940, it rose again to 120,000 in 1944, and 176,000 in 1946, falling to 143,000 in 1948 (Domínguez 1978a: 107), the latter figure still only representing 7 per cent.

65. By 1946, the party claimed 37,000 members, although one leader claimed only 20,000 and even the CIA only cited 10,000 (A. Suárez 1967: 6); in 1952, it claimed 61,000 'supporters' (1967: 5).

and American capital's retreat from certain sectors, especially sugar (halving between 1929 and the 1950s),[66] although its investment increased in oil, manufacturing, commerce, mining and utilities. It was also based on two key 1934 measures – the Jones–Costigan Act, establishing the system of annual sugar quotas for the American market's traditional suppliers and allocating a guaranteed, if reduced, Cuban share of 34.7 per cent (1957) (Ibarra Cuesta 1995a: 47), and the new Reciprocity Treaty, reinforcing, on a reduced scale, the effects of the 1903 Treaty.[67]

This allowed a partial 're-Cubanization' in those sectors where American capital had less interest (especially utilities, land and sugar-growing) and a defence of the symbolically important 68,000 *colonos* (1958) (O'Connor 1970: 56), accounting for about 80 per cent of sugar production (Dye 1998: 13).[68] The quota also guaranteed security, welcomed especially by the unions, with rising income, sugar sales and economic activity (Farber 1976: 102).

Those same guarantees, however, had disadvantages that, ultimately, undermined the new arrangement and weakened both Batista's and then the *Auténticos'* populism. Firstly, the quota (determined annually by the US Department of Agriculture) made Cuban sugar stagnate, deterring long-term planning and increased production, but ensuring greater dependence and fewer opportunities than before 1929. Hence, although periodically the price would rise or competitors' production decline, the 1934–58 period overall represented an unprecedented plateau in the otherwise upward trajectory of the modern Cuban sugar economy, though with recession at a critical time politically (1952–4). Secondly, the Treaty, though ensuring security, ensured also two more decades of the old dual role: primary producer for a single market and captive market for American manufactured goods (rising from 54 per cent of the Cuban market in 1932 to 71 per cent in 1938: Benjamin 1977: 180), and food ($465m in 1956: Ibarra Cuesta 1995a: 79).[69] While other Latin American economies were developing import-substituting industrialization strategies as a base for later manufacturing, the Cuban economy was apparently volunteering for a continued dependency. This meant that Batista's 're-Cubanization' occurred more by default than design, and was only ever partial and misleading .[70]

66. The 1929 figure was $575m, falling to $227m in 1946, and rising slightly to $265m in 1958 (Brundenius 1984: 17). By 1939, 55 per cent of Cuban sugar came from American-owned mills, falling to 43 per cent in 1951 and 37 per cent in 1958 (O'Connor 1970: 27). For the whole economy the comparable figures were $919m in 1929 but $657m in 1950 (MacEwan 1981: 13).

67. This Treaty allowed import preferences of between 20 and 60 per cent for 480 different American manufactured goods (Pino Santos 1973: 48).

68. These were protected by the 1937 Verdeja Act, later the Sugar Coordination Law.

69. These changes are highlighted by the figures for import domination for 1902–6 (45 per cent) and 1921 (74 per cent) (López-Segrera 1981: 142).

70. American capital's retreat from sugar disguised the fact that its remaining mills were more productive; sixty-six American mills in 1939 produced 55 per cent of Cuba's crop, with the thirty-six Cuban mills accounting for only 22.4 per cent and the thirty-three Spanish mills, 14.32 per cent (Ibarra Cuesta 1995a: 69).

Thus Batista's populism, lacking a long-term economic basis and also without an indigenous industrial base (Boorstein 1969: 4), lacked a powerful 'national bourgeoisie' capable of using a project of populist restructuring to build a powerful state and political stability.[71] The post-1934 Cuban state simply lacked that cohesive social and political strength, and Batista's populism depended on a divided opposition and the fragile economic success of the 1939–45 war years (with demand and world prices high). Post-1934 populism therefore repeated, albeit more impressively, the essential weakness of Machado's, and depended on maintaining neopatrimonial structures, not developing them – an inertia that increasingly marginalized groups and politicians.

Compounding the divisions between the sugar-linked sectors and classes (rural and urban) and the residual sectors, stagnation now reduced the beneficiaries and increased both rural unemployment and rural–urban migration. With a weak state, an illusory economic security, an over-large and sugar-dependent or state-dependent middle class (possibly 33 per cent of the population, with nearly 200,000 state employees in 1949: Farber 1976: 104–5), a growing urban poor, and the proletarianization of sectors of the middle class, Cuba displayed the more extreme features of dependency (Ibarra Cuesta 1995a: 94).

The political effects became clear. Firstly, with the Left defeated, its agenda appropriated, and the communists seemingly abandoning a revolutionary position, the radical pole of dissent, whether socialist or *cubanista* (it now being increasingly difficult to distinguish the two) disappeared from public view, intellectual radicals choosing to follow the PSP or to retreat into individualistic dissidence (like Roa) or artistic rebellion.[72] Secondly, the *cubanista* argument became confused, between an apparently moribund radicalism and a flawed and limited *neoanexionismo*, seemingly removing the United States from the nationalist agenda (Domínguez 1978a: 115). Superficially it echoed the pre-1924 disillusion, confusion and ambiguity; but 1940s Cuba had changed fundamentally, Batista proving critical in a 'double-thread' of post-1934 Cuban politics – continuing the legitimacy of 1933 and deepening the political vacuum (Kapcia 1996a: 89).

In particular, the infusion of leftist perspectives and discourse into the *cubanista* codes gave them a latent optimism, a long-term vision and a fundamental rejectionism that meant a greater likelihood of political non-conformity. Furthermore, 1933–5 had been an indelible experience, a moment of collective power remaining in individual and group memories.

71. This weakness was illustrated by the size of Cuban industry – by the 1950s, 80.6 per cent of industrial enterprises had fewer than twenty-five workers, and 45 per cent had under five (Pino Santos 1983: 104) – and by the *colonos'* continuing domination of sugar cultivation.

72. Roa's biography particularly reflected the intellectual left's trajectory. A veteran of the Universidad Popular, the Liga Antimperialista, the DEU and the AIE, he was exiled in 1935, founded ORCA and then, returning, founded an independent radical magazine, *Baraguá*. The artistic rebellion came especially from *Ciclón*.

Finally, corruption now came to the fore, an issue that, being a constant of Cuban politics, had the potential for deep, highly moralistic cleavages, acquiring a new, and significant, importance – reflected by the section in the PRC-A programme on the *psicología y moral de los cubanos* (Cuban Psychology and Morale) (Grau San Martín 1936: 66–71). The problem now was its sheer scale, scope and shamelessness. Before 1921, peculation and electoral fraud had dominated, and still remained as a problem, with Batista's personal enrichment by some $40m. by 1944 and with impeachment proceedings issued against the post-1948 president, Prío; now, however, it also included institutional patronage, a vast, visible and blatant degeneration of political life and an explosion of large-scale crime. All of this corroded the political fabric and public confidence.

No aspect was perhaps more damaging than the emergence of *bonchismo*. At one level, this was simple gangsterism, uncontrolled warfare between 1937 and 1947 between armed groups – based in and around the University of Havana, but also in some Havana secondary schools (Pérez Rojas 1975: 201), ostensibly with political motivation (their names testifying to their ideological roots), but in practice settling personal scores, indulging in robberies, and competing for power in the grey area between formal politics and the ever murkier underworld, into which American crime syndicates had been allowed to enter since Prohibition.

The term *bonchismo* came from the original group, *El Bonche Universitario* (literally, 'the University Gang'), which partly responded to a contemporary political agenda. From that several groups evolved, three dominating – Masferrer's MSR (Movimiento Socialista Revolucionario – Revolutionary Socialist Movement), with about 300 members,[73] the Spain-veteran Emilio Tró's UIR (Unión Insurreccional Revolucionaria – Revolutionary Insurrectional Union), and, with as many as 800 members, ARG (Acción Revolucionaria Guiteras – Guiteras Revolutionary Action), under Eufemio Fernández Ortega and Jesús González Cartas (Suchlicki 1988: 194; Pérez Rojas 1975: 201–20). Although the three often collaborated, they most frequently engaged in open warfare, with the MSR's Manolo Castro and Tró himself being killed.

Deep down, however, *bonchismo* reflected the degeneration of the once 'heroic' student 'action groups' of 1931–3, many of whom, with Batista's rise, refused to disarm and, with no definable and unpopular enemy (such as Machado), turned their activism on each other, their numbers swelled by disillusioned Spain veterans, and also by former members of Joven Cuba and the Communist Party (disillusioned by the expulsion of 'Trotskyists' and the deal with Batista) and equally disillusioned *Auténticos* (after Grau's acceptance of Batista's electoral legitimacy in 1938).[74]

73. MSR members included the ex-communists Carlos Montenegro and Roberto Pérez Santisteban (a former Trotskyist), and also Mario Salabarría, Boris Goldenberg and Faure Chomón (later of the DR and, after 1959, an ally of Castro).

74. One notable 'action group' that did not disband or turn to gangsterism was De La Torriente Brau's ORCA, founded in 1936.

Once the habits of armed group action had become permanent, the political elites then decided to capitalize on them, the PRC-A especially using the UIR to expel communists from the University and the CTC in the late 1940s. Then, in 1949, to purge the problem, Prío (by then president) struck a deal with three leading *bonchistas*, exchanging peace for their nomination as police chief in Marianao (near Havana) and head of the National Police Academy (Tró), Havana police chief (the ARG's Fabio Ruiz) and chief of the secret police (Salabarría) (Szulc 1986: 89–90; Thomas 1971: 741–3), with 1,220 government jobs going to group members and to an MSR offshoot, *El Colorado*. Thus, the PRC-A, its moral credibility already in question, both legitimized the *bonches* and discredited formal politics.

Therefore, by 1949, the possibility of rescuing honour from a corrupt polity had disappeared, which, given the hopes of 1933, had seriously demoralized that dwindling number of Cubans still prepared to believe in the political system.

Corruption was also significant because of the *Autenticos'* record in office (1944–52). Rooted in the DEU rebellion and the Grau circle of 1933–4 and attracting others from the PAC (in 1937) (Anderle 1975: 71), they had hoped to capitalize on their radical nationalist legitimacy with the name of Martí's PRC, reinforced with *Auténtico*. After opposing Batista (and the communists) in 1938 and 1940, Grau was elected in 1944 on a platform of three *cubanista* issues – revolution, nationalism and morality (with the slogan *cubanidad y honestidad* raising great hopes) (Llerena 1978: 35).

However, both Grau (1944–8) and Prío (1948–52) governed Cuba in ways that contradicted that platform, proving to be unrevolutionary, accommodationist and corrupt. The *Auténticos* were unrevolutionary in their growing anti-communism (following Washington's wishes after 1948), their assault on the Left inside the party and beyond (see Dana Sims 1991) and their refusal to challenge the new rich.[75] This was not surprising, as their claim to 'revolution' referred more to their 'authentic' 1933 past than to intentions. Thus, although they claimed to be 'essentially nationalist, socialist and anti-imperialist' (Grau 1936: 100), by 1939 they were silent on imperialism and spoke of the 'coexistence of classes', advocating a 'civilian and democratic version of reform rather than a militarist and authoritarian one' (Farber 1976: 89). They were un-nationalist in their loyalty to Washington in the emerging Cold War, and their refusal to challenge the American relationship or the new international financial orthodoxy; with Batista stealing their nationalist clothes, there was little space left for a convincing limited nationalist programme. Thus, morality was the one field where they might have left their mark; but here

75. In their assault on the communists in the CTC (in which the prominent and popular black sugar workers' leader, Jesús Menéndez, was killed) the PRC-A were supported by Washington and the Havana-based anticommunist union organization, ORIT (Organización Regional Interamericana de Trabajadores – Inter-American Regional Workers' Organization).

they failed spectacularly, tolerating and participating in greater peculation, fraud, patronage, degeneration and crime (see Valdés 1975: 23–7; Vignier and Alonso 1973).

This latter failure was ultimately more damaging than the other two, for it could be argued that accommodationism and moderation had previously brought benefits and security. Firstly, if morality becomes a political issue it tends towards absolutism in its rejection of partial correctives and its Manichaean dichotomy of indivisible right and irremediable wrong. Thus, by promising to end the problem and then surpassing their predecessors' corruption, the *Auténticos* condemned themselves, and made morality into an even more powerful and less subtle issue, especially as this development coincided with the eclipse of several earlier *cubanista* codes. By 1952, moralism was probably the dominant code, encapsulating all the hopes invested in *cubanía*, distilling so many of its principles. Thus, when dissidents invoked *eticidad*, they were often seeing corruption as a visible manifestation of the crumbling system and the 'betrayal'.

Secondly, the *Auténticos'* failure on morality was damaging, since they had explicitly appropriated the *martiano* mantle, with their formulaic exaltation of a statuesque, anodyne, apolitical version of the *Apóstol*, converting the 1920s 'radical' image into the safe *héroe nacional* (national hero).[76] However, by failing so dismally to realize the appropriated project, they furthered a process whereby their discourse became inherently more powerful and more usable. With the moderation, disappearance or failure of the leading 1933 protagonists, and with increasing collective disillusion, the codes of *cubanía* remained available with an increased motivating power in the vacuum, although still lacking a context, a movement and a leader.

Briefly, an opportunity seemed to arise, in 1947, with Eduardo (Eddy) Chibás's PPC (Partido del Pueblo Cubano – Cuban People's Party) – the *Ortodoxos*, born out of the dissidence, disillusion and frustration of *Auténtico* youth and the Oriente base, and also Chibás's personal frustrations (he had expected to inherit the party's 1948 candidature from Grau).[77] The *Ortodoxos* reflected the *cubanista* mood (with their timely symbol of a broom) and also, in their name, the shift within *cubanía* towards a more *rebelde* discourse, recognizing *nación* as *pueblo*.[78] Their rise was rapid and destabilizing for the establishment, making inroads into the PRC-A's

---

76. In particular, the public busts of Martí, appearing after a decade of independence, now became ubiquitous, and a hagiographic literature was encouraged, especially Jorge Mañach's 1940 *Martí, Apóstol*.

77. Although Chibás had been 'nominated' in 1946 by a PRC-A Holguín assembly, a rigged party meeting in March 1948 selected Prío.

78. Leading members included Emilio Ochoa, Manuel Bisbé, Luis Orlando Rodríguez, the ex-AIE García Bárcena, the historian Hermino Portell Vilá, the ex-*Protesta* and ex-ABC Jorge Mañach and Luis Conte Agüero; the party had a high proportion of university lecturers and lawyers.

base, the middle class (Farber 1976: 126); and, even after Chibás's accidental suicide (on radio in 1951) in an anti-corruption protest, the momentum carried his successor, Roberto Agramonte, towards certain victory in the 1952 elections. The year 1948 was thus more of a turning-point than it seemed, confirming the end of *Auténtico* radicalism and manifesting a demand for a clean and radical alternative (see Stokes 1951).[79]

At one level, the *Ortodoxos* were simply the latest move by the political elite to rescue the failing populist project; deep down, however, they represented more. Firstly, they signalled a social shift, in the shape of the growth of the middle class, with about one-tenth of the active population being classified as professional, managerial or executive (Pérez-Stable 1953: 27). Secondly, they indicated a political shift, within *cubanía rebelde*, from an ambiguous 'nationalism' (implicitly radical) to a more identifiable radicalism, reflected in renewed labour militancy, with a record 120 strikes in 1951 (Farber 1976: 130). A 'nationalist' definition had simply become discredited by Batista and the PRC-A, while the *Ortodoxos* – identified with youth and Oriente (both at the heart of the *cubanista* tradition) and emphasizing the talismanic issue of corruption – focused the otherwise inchoate dissent. Even more than before – without other clear targets – corruption had become so central to Cuban politics that there was now a significant political space for anyone demonstrably capable of holding the moral high ground, untainted and within the *rebelde* tradition.

This shift reflected deeper movements within *cubanía*. Firstly, for all their hegemony on the Left, the communists' increasing moderation and public identification with Stalinism led younger Cubans to seek more dynamic revolutionary alternatives, more responsive to their generation. For the experience and 'betrayals' since 1923 had gradually added 'youth' as a new, powerful, theme in *cubanía*, a belief in the redemptive, renovative potential, duty and destiny, of the young, representing the 'next' generation to take up the fallen banner of Martí and the *mambises*.

On the basis of a perceived, shared tradition, legitimized by the 1940 constitution, it was therefore possible, in the early 1950s, to identify more clearly the codes that individually articulated the cubanista values and collectively constituted the overall ideology of cubanía. The early Republican 'value-beliefs' had evolved, through the 1920s 'proto-codes', into the identifiable codes of a more holistic ideology, strengthened by the lack of alternatives and the increasing negativity

---

79. The results of those elections were: PRC-A (again with the Republicans) 45.83 per cent, Coalición Liberal-Democrática 30.42 per cent, PPC 16.42 per cent, PSP 7.33 per cent. This gave the PRC-Republican Alliance seventy-eight seats in the Lower House and thirty-six in the Senate, to the combined opposition's fifty-eight and eighteen. Significantly, the PRC-Republicans and the PSP lost votes from their pre-election registrations, while the PPC gained, presumably at the others' expense (Stokes 1951: 74).

and confusion. These in turn represented both the tradition that the next dissident generation would inherit and a possible platform for them to mount their dissidence, just as the '1930 generation' had referred back to pre-existing codes, using them as the material for their programme.

Agrarianism still remained; while confidence in sugar had been repeatedly undermined by dependency, to which, some argued, a reliance on a raw material with a limited market and growing competition had condemned Cuba, most Cubans tended to accept the 'natural' equation of Cuba with sugar and, thus, of *cubanidad* with the countryside and its character. This agrarianism saw the radicalism of the independence struggles manifested in the (rural) *mambises*, emphasizing that they had been fought by peasants, slaves and ex-slaves and the much-valued (if neglected) *guajiro*.[80] Even Batista had identified with the *colono*, as the bulwark of an independent Cuba. By the 1950s, therefore, a generally shared belief of many (mostly urban) Cubans was that the *campo* (countryside) held an almost sanctified connection with the past heroism and the future glory of the 'real' Cuba, as opposed to the 'unreal', often corrupt, distorted urbanism in which most Cubans lived and worked.

The second code was still the underlying collectivism, implicit in the traditions and 'dreams' of *Cuba Libre*, although this had partly evolved into a less explicit *solidarismo* (belief in solidarity), underpinned by complex values and often contradicted by the much-vaunted uniqueness of the Cuban character (its *idiosincracia*), since popular culture tended to sustain the image of the self-respecting Cuban male as an untameable, incorrigible, sexually predatory 'character', with a self-deprecating cynicism – the *choteo* – that, presumably, undermined any collectivist ethos.[81] However true this self-image, pre-1950s Cuba abounded with references to, expressions of, and the search for various forms of collectivism.

This was partly rooted in the earlier seminal philosophies – Krausism, Marxism, and Martí's vision of a Cuban 'community', without racial or social distinctions, a belief that was never formally questioned. At other levels, it reflected the highly unionized culture (especially in sugar, railways, print, transport and tobacco)[82] and the Cuban penchant for clubs and groupings – the various *centros culturales*, societies and sporting gatherings. As before, it still survived in religion; while this

---

80. The *guajiro* was the (largely white) peasant who was much romanticized in *costumbrista* literature and art, popularly endowed with 'typical' Cuban attributes, especially simplicity, guile and stubbornness. The butt of much popular urban humour, the term *guajiro* was more sympathetic than *campesino*.

81. The discussion of the *choteo* grew after Mañach's 1928 *Indagación del Choteo*.

82. After 1947, any residual ideological militancy gave way to 'economism' and the CTC was incorporated, being first *Auténtico*-dominated (till 1952) and then Batista-dominated (Pérez-Stable 1993: 49). In the 1950s, of 900,000 rural workers, few were unionized, but one-third of millworkers were and one-quarter of the industrial labour force (O'Connor 1970: 183–4).

applied less to a Catholic Church that had become more urban and middle-class, and that was still Spanish-dominated (only 556 of the 1,167 religious being Cuban: Kirk 1989: 97),[83] it was more evident in Protestantism (long seen during the colonial years as a rejection of Spanish Catholicism and a natural community for independence: Pérez 1999: 55–60) or the Afro-Cuban religions, which were increasingly referred to as *santería*.

Certainly, given the extent of these formations in modern Cuba, it is remarkable that the hegemonic individualistic self-image denied it; Cubans were wont to work, play, pray and fight in groupings, and expected the 'real' Cuba to emerge through that medium. One could thus talk, in the 1950s, of an unrealized propensity for communal solidarity, in which many believed, but against which the individualizing and atomizing system acted.

What this code reacted against was clearer than ever: the history of division, disunity, inequality and acquisition; what it proposed was a *Cuba Libre* socially, racially and politically united, equal and collectively defined. Therefore an understandable sub-belief of this code was egalitarianism, which responded to the shameful inequalities of slavery, the countryside, the urban slums and racism. However, despite this formal anti-racism, this *cubanía* was still implicitly white-defined; a multiracial community probably meant, for most bourgeois *cubanistas*, a populist vision at best.

The third code – moralism – was now even more powerful, with many aspects that went to the heart of Cuba's situation and had three related meanings. The first was the usual moral dimension of Cuban politics, whether in anti-corruption or in the tendency for all discourse to be essentially moralistic, invoking dignity, sovereignty, sacrifice and honour. The second meaning was an underlying millenarianism, corresponding to a shared sense of a stolen destiny and a belief in an essentially nineteenth-century view of history as progress towards an inevitably better future, repeatedly denied. The third meaning was the continuing theme of 'renewal' characterizing all discourse, with its concomitant themes, and myths, of history and generations. This drive for renewal saw the present negatively, with a dual view of history – as betrayal or denial, and as heroism. It is interesting that this moralism exercised such motive power in the one Latin American society with a weak Catholic Church, perhaps responding to a moral vacuum and to deep-seated moral needs neglected by organized religion.

Moralism's targets were, most obviously, an increasing perception of a history characterized by immoral episodes, actions and attitudes, challenged by the parallel history of moral resistance. This perspective saw a corrupt and illegitimate colonialism, dependent on slavery, followed by humiliating betrayal in 1898–1903, and

83. By 1955, some 212 private schools were Church-run (Kirk 1989: 97), but there were only 200 Catholic parishes, with 700 priests (30,000 people per parish or 8,500 per priest, compared to Ireland's 3,000 and 450 respectively) (Olson and Olson 1995: 45).

then by the next fifty years of endemic corruption, ever deeper despite promises and heroic resistance, culminating in Batista's coup (the *batistazo*) in 1952, seen as the ultimate humiliation, coming at a moment of particular shame for many Cubans at the image that the North American world had of Cuba, as an island of prostitution, gambling and crime (Pérez 1999: 470). It was also a history whose tone was set by the example and writings of essentially 'pure' figures, especially the *Apóstol* Martí, epitomizing pure, honourable nationalism. The mythification of Martí, indeed, grew as corruption became more endemic. What this code proposed was an imperative for honesty, a system that would work structurally against corruption and defend moral values of commitment, honour, selflessness and purity, valuing youth, education and culture.

Equally present in the canon was activism, whose critical concept was, even more, *lucha*, repeated throughout the Republican campaigns, disputes and rebellions, and seeking legitimacy in a perceived tradition of political behaviour. 'Action' had become synonymous with 'real' *cubanidad*, and activism meant – explicitly or implicitly – respect for action (set against theory), and, therefore, for men of action in Cuba's past, including many dissident intellectuals respected as *homo faber* and *homo poeta* – Martí, Mella, Guiteras and even Chibás (whose 'action' had been his self-immolation against corruption). There was in this respect a sense that such 'heroes' (the term itself being part of this code) were quintessentially Cuban in fusing action and intellect.

Fundamentally, activism opposed two Cuban realities: the experience of subordination and the sense of *choteo*. Subordination had been an undeniable reality since 1492, a history of domination occasionally challenged by unsuccessful but heroic struggles. In this perspective, Cuba's failure to share the wider movement for independence in the 1820s was attributable to its leaders' unwillingness to act, a complaisance continuing for the next fifty years, autonomism being preferred to independence. Even after the heroic *lucha* of 1868–78, the elite that should have provided the new moral leaders preferred humiliating surrender to Maceo's heroic resistance at Baraguá. That domination was followed by American neocolonialism, with a humiliating accommodationism and the ambiguities of a love–hate relationship with the metropolis, the effects of a quota-based dependency and the benefits enabling many Cubans to accept their satellite status. However, codes imply greater simplicity of vision for their effect; hence, 'action' was the necessary antidote to a perceived ambivalence that continued to condemn Cuba to dependent status.

The *choteo* – although including a tendency to disparage the establishment and extol the virtues of the common man – reflected this ambivalence, for in few Latin American nations was nationalism so deeply ingrained and radical, or was radicalism so integral to the political culture, yet in few was this national self-deprecation so visible. Reacting to previous inaction and the frustrations of 1898, it implied – as many believed in 1902 – that Cubans were unready for independence and that a Cuban identity was a fiction. Thus activism challenged this resignation, implying that to act was 'Cuban' and to be cynical was an essentially 'un-Cuban' response to failure.

The values that activism extolled were, therefore, visible political commitment and a willingness to act boldly, to continue an apparently doomed but principled struggle – a stance supposedly manifested by slaves, by *mambises* and by Martí, whose prophetic words expressed it eloquently – 'Otros lamentan la muerte necesaria: yo creo en ella como la almohada, y la levadura, y el triunfo de la vida' ('Others lament the inevitability of death, but I believe in it as the pillow, the leaven and the triumph of life': Martí 1975: 327). The national anthem's words reinforced that regularly – 'morir por la patria es vivir' ('to die for one's country is to live').

Set alongside this was, however, culturalism, which, by the 1950s, meant four things. Firstly, it implied a faith in education *per se* and as an empowering and liberating experience, again expressed in Martí's repeated phrase – *ser culto es el único modo de ser libre* ('being educated is the only way of being free': Martí 1991a: 289) – a belief rooted in the Enlightenment, positivism and socialism, and in Martí's beliefs and actions.[84] Secondly, it posited a faith in the intellectual's political role – born of Cuba's specific experience and self-justification by those intellectuals who articulated the *cubanista* canon. Thirdly, therefore, it gave students an organic role, as the supreme manifestation of the intellectual (and as the coming generation, in a culture extolling renewal through generations) – a reflection of both wider Latin American traditions and the Cuban reality, of Havana students' being accepted as the vanguard of radical patriotic *lucha*. Finally, culturalism meant a growing pride in *cultura cubana*, referring either to 'high' culture (whose most famous exponent was Martí) or to popular culture – normally, by then, meaning artistic expressions of the African heritage in dance, crafts, and song. Here, Fernando Ortiz's much-admired writings contributed much to the evolution of a perceived Cuban identity; his much-quoted image of the Cuban 'melting-pot' as the *ajiaco* (the stew) responded to a deep-seated *cubanista* desire for 'community' and unity, culturally legitimizing a particular political position.[85] If *cubanía* was the ideology of Cuban nationalism, then Ortiz was one of its prophets, and practitioners of 'Cuban' culture were its 'high priests'. Culturalism thus saw culture, broadly or narrowly, as essential to the 'struggle', expecting patriotic Cubans to be proud of their identity through culture; reading Martí was as patriotic a duty as dancing the *son*.

84. The words are from *Maestros Ambulantes*, in *La América* (New York, May 1884). This quotation has developed a life of its own, usually repeated as *ser culto es ser libre*.

85. This image was introduced in Ortiz's lecture *Los Factores Humanos de la Cubanidad*, on 28 November 1939, then published in *Revista Bimestre Cubana* (March–April 1940, Vol. XX, No. 2). (N. Suárez 1996: 9).

This code reacted against three realities: a history of 'philistinism', of denial of Cuban culture and intellectual activity, and of a pursuit of wealth, with its implications of dependence and corruption; the widespread image of contemporary Cuba as an island of brothels and gambling, a means of survival but a source of shame; and the 'other' history of educationalism, in the 1901 expansion, the 1920s Universidad Popular José Martí and student movement, and even Batista's programme of rural soldier-teachers. This history was significant precisely because, by then, many students were either seen as *bonchistas* or marginalized politically.

In this litany of codes, it is worth noting that two that were only emergent in the 1920s had now grown in importance. The first was statism, a belief not unique to Cuba but, given the unusual relationship with the United States, one with radical implications, for, although the establishment of post-1945 Britain, for example, might tolerate nationalization and a welfare state without threatening a revolution to modernize outdated social and economic structures, in Cuba that proposal would immediately threaten the system, inviting American hostility.

In fact, statism in 1950s Cuba meant nothing more radical than welfarism, the belief in the duty of a benevolent state to protect weakened entrepreneurs and workers, enact *solidarismo* for the poor, and build a strong independence. This was simply contemporary orthodoxy, building on traditional Catholic social thought, the ideas of many previous reformers (such as Martí and Grau), and Cuban leftist traditions. There was also a specifically Cuban motive, for a powerful state might help achieve community and unity.

Statism's targets were easy to identify – most evidently the ravages of *laissez-faire* economics, corporate exploitation, the inefficient and unequal *colono* system, and the earlier weak state structures – under Spain, and then under a neocolonialism in which Plattism and the quota had created a weak civil society and a weak satellite state. What it proposed was equally identifiable – policies borrowed from the 1933 'government of the hundred days', Roosevelt's much-admired New Deal, post-1945 Britain, post-1930s populist Latin America, Batista's 1938–44 progressive legislation and the 'developmentalist' or structuralist strategies proposed by the new United Nations Economic Commission for Latin America, under Raul Prebisch.

The second newly developed code was revolutionism, the belief in the idea of 'revolution', which, necessarily, was never defined precisely, remaining 'cloudy' (Llerena 1978: 40), but which had long been integral to the *cubanista* canon: 'very probably the majority of voters, still longed for fundamental reorganization of various institutions and still thought of the "revolution" as the embodiment of those aspirations' (Stokes 1951: 76). Although undefinable, 'revolution' focused on traditions 'associated in the public mind with heroic rebellion against illegitimate or excessively authoritarian power' (Llerena 1978: 38), and on *eticidad*, for 'the Cuban political opposition desperately desired the 'revolution' to mean, at least, fundamental departure from the venality, corruption and fraud so characteristic of Cuban colonial and republican politics' (Stokes 1951: 77). By the 1950s, this idea was sufficiently detailed, sophisticated and powerful to be a code (rather than a rhetorical aspiration), set against perceived historical problems and implying a clear set of values identified with *Cuba Libre*.

By the 1950s, Cuba was an extreme example of a political culture characterized by the invariable frustration of radical rebellions, meaning that the code reacted against a lack of revolutionary change at key moments. Such a history of frustration might easily have produced an institutionalized apathy (which the *choteo* and accommodationism partly reflected); in Cuba, however, failure strengthened 'revolution's' appeal, because of the enduring strength of radical perspectives. Revolutionism also reacted against an exceptionally suffocating history of colonialism and neocolonialism, highlighting the absence of the 'real' *Cuba Libre* (which, increasingly, was what 'revolution' meant) and making every reform implicitly revolutionary; equally, however, every 'revolution' threatened to become mere 'reformism', given the weight of dependency. Finally, revolutionism had a clear and increasing moral dimension, creating a Manichaean view of Cuba's history as a dichotomy between good and evil, morality and immorality, the 'real' and the distorted, demanding uncompromising responses to the immoral and false reality that many Cubans sensed was Cuba's dilemma.

Revolutionism's explicit and implicit propositions fitted comfortably with the rest of *cubanía* – the awareness that *soberanía* could only come by breaking with dependency, and the need for Cuban political discourse to focus on 'renewal' and a refusal to compromise – an imperative leading Grau to take Martí's party's name, and to Chibás's 'orthodox' challenge to their claim to 'authenticity'. Therefore, however unrevolutionary, no new political force in 1950s Cuba could progress without acknowledging this tradition, rejecting the consensual projects of social or Christian democracy. All politicians knew the requirement to stress *revolución*, *pueblo* or *nación* or risk loss of public credibility.

Finally, there was evidence of an emerging potential code – 'internationalism' – confirming that *cubanía rebelde* had abandoned narrow nationalism. Rooted in the Cuban rebellions of late colonialism, this code had evolved through the eclectic, cosmopolitan influences of the 1920s, the growing hegemony of an internationalist Communist Party/PSP, and experiences such as 1936–9 Spain, to be reinforced by the discrediting of *Auténtico* nationalism. Thus, it was a new departure – reflecting a less introspective radicalism – when, in 1947, 1,200 Havana students and *bonchistas* allied in an abortive expedition from Cayo Confites to overthrow the Dominican dictator, Rafael Trujillo, and when, in 1948, a small Cuban student delegation joined the international anti-imperialist Bogotá youth conference called by Perón and the communists against the new OAS (Organization of American

States)[86] – both episodes involving the student activist Fidel Castro (then in Acción Radical Ortodoxa) (Szulc 1986: 97).

However, 'internationalism' did not then mean anti-imperialism, for there was (by contrast with the situation in the 1920s) no consensus on a concept that was too explicit. The essence of a successful code is its imprecision; an explicit code risks an inability to be universally appropriated. Moreover, in Cuba, anti-imperialism could only target the United States, about which there were fears and no consensus. However, in time, this code began to change into a potential anti-imperialism.

These codes therefore now provided a ready-made set of rhetorical targets and policies, a framework for all political movements to seek credibility, all of which had to reflect one or more of the codes in their name, platform or public *raison d'être*. The codes also, *de facto*, made Cuban political discourse revolutionary, nationalist, moralistic and collectivist (or *solidario* – 'in favour of *solidarismo*'), with implicit roles for the *campo*, the student, the intellectual and the *pueblo*. The existence of this cumulative ideology therefore meant that Cuba's essentially negative, self-doubting, demoralizing and resigned self-image was countered by a set of essentially positive shared beliefs, with a view of *nación* that contradicted the established *cubanía neoanexionista*. There was therefore a clear enough 'alternative project', which, given opportunity, context and direction, could emerge, its legitimacy unchallenged.

Socio-economically Cuba had also evolved significantly. The tendency to stagnation had become more evident in industrial employment and the discernible shift from primary to tertiary sector (Collazo Pérez 1989: 161), the balance of the rural workforce actually changing little between 1907 and the 1950s (O'Connor 1970: 22). Cubans were therefore poorer, more unemployed and more urban than ten years earlier; per capita income fell over the decade (Brundenius 1984: 8), while unemployment levels of over 16 per cent were recorded for 1956–7 (Pino Santos 1973: 123) – apart from the annual curse of the *tiempo muerto* (dead time) outside the *zafra* (sugar harvest), when unemployment could double from the harvest norm of between 8 and 10 per cent (Zeitlin 1970a: 49).[87] Simultaneously, there were population shifts, rural Cuba losing some 345,000 migrants to Havana (Pino Santos 1973: 129), where work was less reliable, where some 300,00 inhabitants (possibly a third) were 'destitute', and where 6 per cent lived in shanty towns (Segré *et al.* 1997: 77). This was all underpinned by economic instability and consequent income instability (Núñez Jiménez 1959: 91) and a dramatic rise in

---

86. The delegation consisted of Castro, the FEU's Enrique Ovares, the PSP's Alfredo Guevara and Rafael del Pino.

87. One estimate has the 424,000 agricultural labourers working an annual average of only 123 days (O'Connor 1970: 58).

public debt (from 80 million pesos in 1948 to 582 million in 1955 and 788 million in 1959 (Collazo Pérez 1989: 35)), with implications for confidence and long-term prospects.

At that moment the whole system reached its turning-point, between March 1952 and July 1953, opening on 10 March 1952, when Batista, having returned to contest the 1952 election, anticipated an Agramonte victory with his coup. It now seems most likely that, apart from personal ambitions and fears, he was encouraged to intervene by Cuban and American interests worried by labour unrest and by a possible *Ortodoxo* anti-corruption drive, or by military concerns about unrest (García-Pérez 1998: 1–12).

Whatever the causes, the unexpected coup traumatized Cuba, few politicians or political groups being able or willing to react, the *Ortodoxos* being split between insurrection, peaceful resistance and electoralism (Ibarra Cuesta 1979: 171). In part this was shock, many Cubans believing that Agramonte would bring real change and end the humiliations of corruption – a hope partly driven by the historical significance of the year, 1952 being the fiftieth anniversary (*Cincuentenario*) of formal (if questionable) independence, which, in a political culture attuned to anniversaries, was imbued with wider significance. Would Cuban youth (as the *Ortodoxos*) achieve what the 1895 generation had failed to achieve – a real *soberanía* – and return to the standards of honesty, integrity and purity absent since 1902?

This idea, with its generationalist tone, was strengthened by the approach of 1953, the *Centenario* of the birth of Martí (the leader most embodying those lost qualities, whose death had seemed to destroy the destiny of *Cuba Libre*), which saw a plethora of publications on and by Martí (Corbitt 1954) – over 500 in 1953 alone (Hennessy 1963: 354) – focusing again on his ideas as well as his symbolism. Thus the ground was being prepared for a new generation imbued with an assumed destiny – the *Generación del Centenario*, a term that carried more prestige than the alternative *Generación del Cincuentenario* (of Independence) (Ibarra Cuesta 1979). Indeed, resistance now came from precisely those quarters, small groups beginning to protest – Acción Católica (in the University of Havana), Acción Libertadora (1953–4, led by a former leftist activist, Justo Carillo), a strange group called AAA (Triple A), led by a DEU veteran, Aureliano Sánchez Arango,[88] and even *Auténtico* plans for a non-existent 'action group'.

---

88. Carillo was a veteran of both ORCA and the small and short-lived MIR (Movimiento de Izquierda Revolucionaria). The name AAA, with no apparent meaning, was jokingly assumed to mean *Amigos de Aureliano Arango* – (Aureliano (Sánchez) Arango's Friends). There is no evidence for one claim that it was formed by the PRC-A (Bourne 1986: 71), and it most probably reflected the ambitions and maverick politics of its founder, who had moved through the DEU, the Liga Antimperialista and the communists (Mencía 1986: 201), to be a 1952 *Auténtico* congressional candidate.

Yet three groups were, ultimately most significant. The first was the Movimiento Nacionalista Revolucionario (MNR), under the *Ortodoxo* García Bárcena, eclectically including leftist radicals and Acción Católica corporatists (Llerena 1978: 47), but significant because of its size and its members' subsequent migration to other groups – notably Carrillo and Enrique de la Osa (to found Acción Libertadora) (Mencía 1986: 217), and several future members of Castro's group – Armando Hart, Faustino Pérez, Frank País, Marcelo Fernández Font and Vilma Espín.[89] The second, in 1955, was the DRE (Directorio Revolucionario Estudiantil), a small arm of the FEU inaugurated semi-formally in the University's *Aula Magna* under the charismatic FEU leader, Catholic activist José Antonio Echevarría (García Olivares 1988: 138).

The third appeared dramatically on 26 July 1953, with the attack on two Oriente barracks – Moncada (Santiago) and Bayamo. The group's origins had, however, been laid before, possibly on the day of the *batistazo* (Szulc 1986: 151) – although the talk of *el movimiento* may have reflected enthusiasm and a collective will rather than a firm organization. Certainly, by 27 January 1953 (the eve of Martí's birthday), the nucleus was formed when Castro and others led a torchlit march from the University steps, leading to the adoption of the title *generación del centenario* (see Rojas 1973).

Moncada now challenged Batista and the establishment's quiescence, and galvanized the underlying, putative dissidence so far manifested only incoherently. The action was significant in three respects. Firstly, in conception it was no mere gesture, being carried out by 165 young Cubans on two heavily fortified army strongholds.[90] As a known student leader (see Szulc 1986: 84–133) and *Ortodoxo* election candidate, Castro already stood within the *cubanía rebelde* tradition, and the attack, designed more to rally opposition, struck a *cubanista* chord, echoing Guiteras's 1931 plans to assault Moncada and actual attack on the San Luis barracks.

Secondly, the action was seen as more immediately heroic, determined and quintessentially Cuban than the traditional politicians' procrastination or accommodation; that so many were killed as a result and so many tortured by the police reinforced that *cubanista* image. Moreoever, Oriente had always been seen as the cradle of *cubanía* and the most patriotic region, and it had all coincided with the *centenario*, its sacrifices echoing Martí's death at Dos Ríos.

Finally, the episode allowed Castro (a lawyer) to outline the rebellion's *cubanista* programme and beliefs in his two-hour defence speech, which was a *tour de force*

89. Acción Libertadora also included some who later gravitated towards Castro – País, Pepito Tey, Rufo López Fresquet.

90. Once again, accounts differ considerably over the numbers involved, the lowest figure being 148 (Mencía 1986: 188) and another being 151 (Szulc 1986: 188).

of rhetoric, argument and political acumen later to become characteristic. The speech was later elaborated and disseminated as the manifesto of MR-26, the Movimiento Revolucionario 26 de Julio (26 July Movement), which Castro from prison on the Isla de Pinos organized in Havana and Santiago.[91] The manifesto, taking the speech's quintessentially *cubanista* final words – *La historia me absolverá* ('History will absolve me'), evoked the whole *cubanista* tradition, and included a detailed account of Cuba's underlying dilemmas and social situation and both an implicit programme for the future (based on the inherited *cubanista* codes, the 1940 constitution and the *Ortodoxo* challenge). It also clearly identified with the example, ideas and emblematic role of Martí, for speech and document were explicitly *martiano* at a critically *martiano* time, repeatedly invoking Martí as the action's *autor intelectual*, and the final words – *condenadme; la historia me absolverá* ('condemn me; history will absolve me') echoed Martí's well-known essay, *El Presidio Político en Cuba,* – *decidlo, sancionadlo, aprobadlo, si podéis* ('say it, sanction it, approve it, if you can') (Centro de Estudios Martianos 1991: 57). It was effectively the first clear elaboration of the 1950s *cubanista* codes; just as Martí's writings had earlier codified the bases of the later *cubanía*, so too did this now crucially codify the more coherent ideology of *cubanía*.

The manifesto spoke of agrarianism, analysing the dilemma of sugar and the evils of rural poverty and marginalization. It extolled communal action and identity, setting a united, integrated nation against the present fragmented reality. The moral dimension was evident – in Moncada, in the underlying self-sacrifice and idealism, and in the final words, evoking a particularly Cuban sense of history (as both heroic and shameful past, and, with the final word's future tense, as destiny) and the sense of 'absolution', justice, duty and purity. Activism was implicit in the document's genesis, but explicitly placed in a tradition of *lucha*, heroism and commitment, on which *Cuba Libre* would be based. Culturalism was explicit in the repeated commitment to education's liberating role and the *cubanidad* of Cuba's cultural heritage – 'a culture of its own' later defined as an 'essential aim' (Program Manifesto of the 26th of July Movement, 1972: 127) – while the newer codes of statism and revolutionism were also explicit in the plans for a benevolent redistributive state and the commitment to revolutionize society and also the external relationship, indicating the greater evolution of internationalism – the speech-manifesto referring to a wider Latin American context (of struggle, suffering and heritage) to which Cuba now belonged.

91. In 1952, the nucleus of the Movement was probably Fidel and Raúl Castro, Abel Santamaría, Jesús Montané, Melba Hernández, Haydee Santamaría and Nico López. By 1953, it had attracted some members from the MNR (Hart, Pérez, País, Espin and Pedro Miret) and others such as Ramiro Valdés and Juan Almeida. Szulc's estimate of 1,500 by December 1952 (Szulc 1986: 170) almost certainly exaggerates the size and the level of organization.

Two significant developments now came in the following five years: the continuity with Moncada and *cubanía* was reiterated in successive manifestos, declarations and agreements,[92] and the military and political challenge successfully evolved. Aspects of that challenge were vital in reinforcing the rebellion and the cohesiveness of its *cubanía*. The first was Castro's 1955 decision, on release under an American-induced and self-confident amnesty, to go to Mexico and not Miami; in Florida, he might have followed tradition, but would also have identified with the United States, which, though absent from the public agenda of radical politics, was still seen as fundamental to the 'problem', and would also have risked being seen as yet another exiled politician, politicking and hatching futile plots. Instead, setting himself apart in 'revolutionary' Mexico, Castro identified with broader traditions of Latin American radicalism, and then met, and enlisted, the Argentine Ernesto Che Guevara – a critical juncture in the subsequent revolution.

The second reinforcement came from the discrediting of alternatives. Those few who participated in Batista's staged 1954 elections discounted themselves, and the PRC-A contemplated, through the 'Varona plan', possible elections with Batista still in power (Ameringuer 1985: 346). Also, most resistance groups had either collapsed or lost members to MR-26 – except the DRE, which, on 13 March 1957, launched a bold attack on the Presidential Palace (resulting in Echevarría's death) and set up the DR 13 de Marzo (13 March Revolutionary Directorate), a guerrilla group in the southern Sierra de Escambray. Then, when moderate politicians around the Sociedad de Amigos de la República (including the respected 1898 veteran Cosme de la Torriente) launched a 'civic dialogue' with Batista, they seriously misjudged a polarized popular mood represented by large demonstrations in Havana in October and November 1955 and the low electoral registration.

The third critical factor was Castro's dogged survival against all odds. Surviving Moncada, he experienced bloody disaster in December 1956, with the abortive Oriente invasion by 83 rebels on the tiny yacht *Granma*, to coincide with insurrection in Santiago. The survivors' regrouping in the nearby Sierra Maestra served several political (as well as military) purposes – strengthening a lasting image of invincibility (which, given the general demoralization, easily became hope after the guerrillas' subsequent victories), and, in the Oriente mountains, recalling past struggles, and increasingly coming to be seen as the new *mambises*, especially when the *Ejercito Rebelde* (Rebel Army) began its westward advance in 1958, recalling Maceo but, this time, unstoppably.

As the *batistato* deteriorated into corruption and repression (against youth and the Sierra peasantry), and as the army's morale and effectiveness were undermined,

92. Those manifestos were especially the Programme-Manifesto of November 1956, the Sierra Manifesto of July 1957, and *Nuestra Razón* (Our Cause) of July 1957.

the image of an Oriente-based, young, successful, rural, 'natural' rebellion increasingly contrasted with Batista's ageing, decrepit, gangsterish 'pseudo-Cuba'. Finally, with Castro's political skill ensuring astute pacts with the credible opposition (especially with the DR in Mexico in 1956), there was only one alternative to Batista – Fidel Castro and the MR26; even the failure of the April 1958 general strike, organized by the Movement's Frente Obrero Nacional Unido, did not prevent the growing image of success.

When Guevara entered Havana, on a symbolically apt New Year's Day 1959, it was the culmination of a rebellion that represented to many Cubans an opportunity to realize the aims of past struggles and the whole *cubanista* project. Although the military dimension was critical to the rebellion's success, the ideological, political and symbolic dimensions evidently played a part that would survive beyond the victory. For many Cubans, the 'dream' implicit in *Cuba Libre* was about to be realized; the next forty years would show how far expectations would be met and how the 'dream' would itself evolve.

–2–

The Search for a Cuban Revolutionary
Identity After 1959

While there was an understandable confusion about the nature, origins and intentions of the new Revolution – inside Cuba but also outside, not least in Washington (Scheer and Zeitlin 1964; Paterson 1994) and Moscow (Shearman 1990), what was immediately clear was its broad popularity. However much the 26 July Movement had acted alone and however thin its ranks until late 1958, by the time Castro entered Havana on 8 January 1959 (after a triumphal progress through Cuba), the Revolution enjoyed a visibly broad base of active and passive support that crossed traditional political, regional and social boundaries – the Havana elite (apart from the most *batistiano*) sharing in the early euphoria as much as the poorest Sierra peasants (Pérez-Stable 1993: 63–4). Contemporary accounts (recalling 1944 Paris) confirm that all Cubans had their own reasons for seeing in Castro and the young *barbudos* ('bearded ones') – who most clearly represented the rebellion – and in the 'Revolution', a moment to be welcomed (see Lockwood 1969). For a population that had seemingly remained apathetic to corruption, the *batistazo*, Moncada and the apparently futile *Granma* invasion, it seemed to herald the end of an age that had left many Cubans with an unpleasant taste and much resigned cynicism about a Cuba where corruption was so endemic and accepted, where divisions were so great and where authoritarianism seemed to reign with impunity. The chord that the Movement had struck in 1953 and 1956–8 still rang true for most Cubans, unaware as yet of the rebels' ideological motivation. It was indeed fitting that the 1960s should be ushered in by an event that not only went on to contribute to later global radicalism but also foretold, in its early euphoria, the rebelliousness of that decade.

Even politically, there was no challenge to, or doubt about, the Revolution, for all potential alternatives had either collapsed in 1952, withered away subsequently or allied with the impending victory – as with the PSP and DR, the former unconditionally (to their lasting political credit among the rebels), the latter more cautiously but, ultimately, self-effacingly.[1] Even the outside world seemed to give the Revolution an unprecedented moment of uncritical tolerance and space.

However, if there was uncertainty about the first cabinet's political intentions (although it contained enough solidly liberal politicians and technocrats to give some (false) clues to a likely direction), the ideological credentials of the underlying 'revolution' and the rebels were seemingly impeccable;[2] although a discredited Congress was immediately replaced by a Council of Ministers, there were few fears of authoritarianism, with Constitutional Reforms published by 14 January. For this rebellion, in most Cubans' eyes, had challenged Batista with a clearly defined *martianismo*, with public manifestos reiterating slogans, policies and ideas inherited from previous expressions of *cubanía*, and now seemed to reaffirm its continuing adherence to that tradition, being still led by the young Castro who had invoked Martí in 1953, had been an *Ortodoxo* and had (like so many before him) begun his rebellion in Oriente. Thus, even with few policies outlined clearly, most Cubans were aware of the likely *cubanista* ideological flavour, inclination and direction of their new Revolution.

If that was the picture in 1959, however, things had become much clearer by the end of 1962, the intervening years seeing fundamental changes. Firstly the period had seen the rapid deterioration in relations with Washington, the final break in January 1961, and the defining moment of the April 1961 Bay of Pigs (*Playa Girón*) invasion, when 1,200 émigrés, trained and financed by the CIA, had invaded in an attempt to galvanize a reputedly massive opposition that American intelligence and quixotic émigrés had believed to exist.[3] Simultaneously, the social revolution was accelerating, the Revolution was becoming politically ever more radical, and the early attempts at a conventional developmentalist economic strategy had failed, succeeded by a Soviet-backed drive to industrialize, diversify and socialize. Then, in October 1962, came the second defining moment of the early years, the Cuban Missile Crisis (*Crisis del Caribe*).[4] All these traumas, surrounded by other turbulent

1. The DR had remained small but effective and prestigious, led, after Echevarría's death, by the ex-MNR rebel, Faure Chomón; it remained separate from the 26 July Movement, with some 2,000 members (Suchlicki 1988: 15), until Guevara's column reached that region, after which an uneasy cooperation was agreed. However, a splinter group, under the anticommunist Eloy Gutiérrez Menoyo, had set up separately as the Second Revolutionary Front of Escambray, which never cooperated.

2. The first cabinet included Manuel Urrutia (one of the liberal Moncada judges) as President, José Miró Cardona (a respected lawyer) as Prime Minister, the 1952 *Ortodoxo* candidate Agramonte as Foreign Minister, several veterans of the different 'action groups' – including Rufo López Fresquet (Treasury) and Felipe Pazos (National Bank), and a handful of 26 July people or activists close to them, notably Hart (Education), Augusto Martínez Sánchez (Defence), Raúl Cepero Bonilla (Commerce), Manuel Ray (Public Works), Osvaldo Dorticós (Revolutionary Laws) and Lluis Buch (Minister to the Presidency).

3. The invasion, directed from Florida and Central America and long expected by the Cubans and long denied by the Americans, was an unmitigated disaster, most invaders being either taken prisoner or killed and the Cuban defence forces successfully isolating potential and real allies of the invasion.

4. This was the famous stand-off between Washington and Moscow over the placing of offensive nuclear missiles in Cuba; although the outcome was superpower *détente*, the effects for Cuba were mixed, with Moscow's public climb-down and the Russians' refusal to realize their pledges to defend the Cubans, but also with a clear American undertaking not to invade Cuba thereafter.

events and processes, meant that there could be no doubt about the political direction and ideological colour of the newly radicalized Revolution. The direction was clearer because the political sensitivities of early 1959 – to ensure a broad internal coalition and a liberal external face – had been replaced by a radicalized, and radicalizing, environment. Liberals had either been swept away, marginalized or outflanked, or had chosen to oppose the new direction, many marginalizing themselves publicly by siding with the Bay of Pigs invasion; the ever-loyal PSP had moved in, replacing them both in the vanguard and, critically, at the grass roots, providing the revolutionary process with a hitherto absent guiding base. The conventionally social democratic, liberal or developmentalist ideas of the first government had thus either become irrelevant to the new needs and environment, or been overtaken by a new set of radicalized demands and imperatives that were, in fact, rarely new, but often seemed so.

In this context, the underlying ideology was also clearer, both explicitly (in Castro's public declarations of, firstly, the Revolution's 'socialist character' and then his Marxism-Leninism) and also implicitly.[5] For, after the challenges of October 1962 (and Moscow's behaviour towards its new ally), it had become clearer that, whatever the newly defined 'socialism' and Marxism meant, the Revolution was also being driven forward by a radicalized definition of the old *cubania*, which had long proposed such reforms as agricultural rationalization, planning, national control, redistribution and industrialization.

This clarity, and greater radicalism, came from five factors above all. The first was the increasing sense of siege for those Cubans who remained after the 1961–2 crises and emigrations. This 'siege' was real enough, at one level, created by Washington's 1960 imposition of a progressively tighter trade and credit embargo and the marshalling of regional allies behind the 'quarantine' strategy, through Cuba's expulsion from the OAS in 1962 and pressure on Latin American countries to break diplomatic relations with the Castro government.[6] It was also real because of American attempts after 1961 to avenge their embarassment (especially in the case of Robert Kennedy) (Heymann 1998: 253–77) by replacing overt warfare by covert support for subversion, in Operation Mongoose (Blight and Kornbluh 1998: 107–32); for, although that threat had mostly been eliminated before and during the 1961 crisis, small insurgent groups still survived, replenished and supplied from Florida.[7] The 'siege' was also, however, wider than that, since the relationship

5. The 'socialist character' was publicly declared on 16 April 1961, at the funeral of Cubans killed in the pre-Playa Girón aerial bombings. In December 1961, Castro announced his undying commitment to Marxism-Leninism.

6. In 1962, all except Mexico had broken relations.

7. In 1960–1 there were some 179 insurgent groups in Cuba and possibly as many as 3,000 deaths resulting from their campaign; even in 1961, there were still possibly 100,000 suspects able to be arrested by the CDRs before the invasion (Blight and Kornbluh 1998: 10–20).

with Moscow (having shown, to many Cubans, how unwilling it was to defend Cuba) was now damaged; while the world breathed a sigh of relief that the crisis had passed without nuclear war, many Cubans (leaders and led) felt genuinely betrayed and alone.

The 'siege mentality' that resulted pervaded all aspects of Cuban life, partly making a virtue out of necessity. Cuba, in a sense, now turned in on itself, consciously deciding to reject reliance on outside aid, models and advice, and to build its future on a more empirical and indigenous 'model'. This political introversion had a clear ideological parallel, as the shutters went up and external criteria and ideas tended to be filtered through caution and reserve to protect the infant Revolution from further damage. In this environment, the strength of the process's indigenous radical and nationalist traditions became an evident source of both pride and inspiration.

Therein lies the second factor, in the inherent radicalism of the *cubanista* discourse, which now, after the early sympathy for, and influence of, Socialist-Bloc thinking, began to regain its hegemony within the revolutionary vanguard. For the whole period of 1961–3 had been characterized by a steady movement towards Soviet and Soviet-backed economic models of industrialization and collectivization, and a willingness to let the PSP take an ideological lead at grassroots level; from March 1962, with the 'Escalante affair' (see below) that ended. The lack of a viable alternative to the radical thrust of the inherent *cubanía* now meant that, in an environment of rapid change, *cubanía*'s underlying tendencies emerged as more powerful. This is where the concept of an 'ideological reservoir' becomes especially important, for, in the absence of any convincing alternatives to *cubanía* in the 1950s and after 1959, the underlying principles and codes of that discourse were not only unchallenged but also acted as a means of socialization.

The third factor was the sense of exclusiveness engendered by siege and isolation, and strengthened by the mass emigration of those unable to adapt to or accept the new radicalism. That emigration came in three stages: between January 1959 and October 1962, it was mostly political (ex-*batistianos*) and ideological (anticommunism), with some 250,000 leaving (Olson and Olson 1995: 59); by December 1965, it had become more economic, the residual middle class leaving (some 35,000), in fear of expropriation (1995: 60); after that came the 1965–72 'air-lift', organized by Washington with Havana's agreement, leading to 3,000–4,000 leaving annually, a further 230,000 emigrants by 1969 (1995: 61) and a total of some 613,000 Cubans in the United States by 1970 (Casal 1979: 109). It subsequently tailed off, with only 38,000 leaving in 1973–9 (Olson and Olson 1995: 76). This all inevitably strengthened the resolve and sense of righteousness of those who remained, especially as the economic and social damage caused by the exodus was all too clear, with, for example, one-third of all practising doctors leaving Cuba during this period (Huberman and Sweezy 1969: 56).[8]

This linked into the fourth radicalizing factor, the effect of the rapid politicization of many of the working class and peasantry, evidently driven by the experience of the early years to intensify their demands for their just deserts through strikes, protests and land seizures (Zeitlin 1970a).

Finally, there was the evident process of radicalization undergone since 1956 by the small nucleus of rebels who constituted the original *guerrilla* and remained the core group of the expanded Rebel Army. This was a larger group than the twelve, fifteen or eighteen survivors of the *Granma*, but considerably smaller than the few hundred who could be considered the long-serving guerrilla fighters by December 1958;[9] but, whatever its composition, the evidence is that, between 1956 and 1959, the political perspectives, vision and aims of the Sierra rebels (the *sierra*) had shifted noticeably to the left of their initial position.

This has been attributed commonly to three basic factors. The first is the contact with the Sierra peasantry, certainly the poorest, most neglected and most marginalized of the few definable peasants still to be found in Cuba. For many guerrillas – many middle-class and urban – that contact was a culture shock of deep personal and long-term significance. The *campesino* to whom they had theoretically committed themselves after 1953 was now a flesh-and-blood reality far different from the perhaps idealized picture painted by political propaganda and *costumbrista* literature – living in brutalizing conditions that belied the sophisticated image of Cuba that Havana represented, even to many Cubans. If Havana could (not unjustifiably) claim statistically to be on the edge of the First World, then the 1950s Sierra belonged firmly to the Third. As contact evolved, and as more peasants – initially suspicious of well-spoken urban white youths, whose presence threatened their

8. In addition, the authors give a figure of 141 out of 158 senior professors of the University of Havana Medical School leaving (Huberman and Sweezy 1969: 56)

9. There is no consensus on the numbers, not least because of the fluidity of the situation. Nonetheless it does seem (from various accounts and the author's own interviews) that, by January 1957, there were about 30 to 40 guerrillas, rising to about 90 by March (as Frank País's volunteers joined), and 200 by the time Herbert Matthews visited the Sierra in the summer. By the May 1958 offensive, there seem to have been still only about 500 at the most (Castro's own figure), including Raúl Castro's 200-man column in the north of Oriente. From that point onwards, the numbers grew rapidly, with about 1,000 being trained in the Rebel Army's 'training school'. By 31 December 1958 (conventionally taken in Cuba as the point to define combatants as *rebeldes*) there were probably about 3,000 (Castro's figure again), although some put the figures as high at 12,000 and others as low as 1,500 (A. Suárez 1967: 33; LeoGrande 1978: 279). The discrepancy is almost certainly because, by the end of the insurrection, many young Cubans would support it in some form or other, describing themselves as *rebeldes*, while the real figures should probably be based on those who, armed with proper weapons, constituted the recognized guerrillas of the Sierra (under Castro) and the columns of Raúl Castro, Juan Almeida and Che Guevara.

safety, and even hostile to the point of betrayal – rallied to the revolution, providing men, materials, information and support, the guerrillas' awareness of peasant values grew accordingly, and, with it, their own ideas about the importance of the land, the peasantry and the countryside. Their evolving awareness thus enabled them to adjust comfortably to the ideological framework offered by the code of agrarianism, and to take that code further still, strengthening it and making it implicitly more radical.

The second factor in the guerrillas' radicalization was the group's cohesive unity and developing camaraderie, which created a supportive collective environment for the process of radicalization that political struggle can often bring. That unity remained, and grew, as the rebellion evolved, creating an internal dynamic, group loyalty and defensiveness (especially within the twenty or so 'core' survivors of Moncada and the *Granma*), which, in the circumstances of January 1959, led easily to a greater propensity to adopt more radical solutions. In a sense, they felt that they alone, or more than anyone (including the urban rebels who had supported them), had been hardened by the fire of struggle, giving them the right to speak on behalf of 'their' Revolution, and to challenge previously unchallenged truths.

This growing dynamic led to the third factor in the guerrillas' radicalization: Castro's role and close affinity with, and susceptibility to the influence of, Che Guevara. Whatever the truth about the nature of charisma and the historical significance of 'great men', the evidence is compelling for a high level of admiration for, and reliance on, Castro within his immediate circle of *compañeros* (comrades) and within the 'core' group generally. That he seemed bolder, more commanding, more eloquent and more decisive than others is clear, and his record for turning apparent defeat into victory and for inspiring loyalty led many to follow his lead. Moreover, the evidence is equally compelling that, if anyone, then and immediately afterwards, exercised a political influence over Castro, it was Guevara, whose own process of radicalization (differing substantially from that of his Cuban comrades, who had, after all, grown up in an essentially ambiguous political culture) was equally important. He had become politicized first in Argentina and then through his experience of Latin America, and especially Guatemala in 1954;[10] furthermore, his willingness to tackle, and understanding of, political texts, especially Marxist ones, had already made his ideological position more radical than the others' still confused positions. Equally, not only did he partially influence Castro – perhaps on the need for a decisive anti-imperialism against inevitable American reaction, but he also commanded much respect in the group as the struggle progressed (see Anderson 1997).[11]

10. Guevara had been in Guatemala in the latter days of the reforming Arbenz government (1951–4) and during its overthrow by General Castillo's US-backed invasion, an experience leaving a deep impression, especially about the possibilities of popular revolution, the need for discipline and organization, and what he saw as the United States' essentially imperialist instincts.

11. A series of interviews carried out in 1996 and 1997 by this author also confirms this fact.

Thus, from a variety of sources (the *cubanista* tradition, popular pressure, the nationalist reaction now fostered by American opposition, and the *sierra*'s intellectual radicalization), there was already, in 1959, a considerable and inevitable pressure pushing the rebel forces to the left and a growing distance between the Sierra rebels and others.[12]

Therefore, as the initially fragile unity began to fragment, the most coherent, united and organically popular pole of the revolution – based on Castro, the Sierra group and certain other favoured protagonists – began to dominate ideologically and, with that, ensure that its inherently more radical definition became the most visible, legitimate and durable of those available. That early fragmentation was perhaps predictable in the stresses of revolutionary upheaval, for the January 1959 unity was fragile, ephemeral and – despite the visible enthusiasm and even ideological consensus on *cubania* – essentially negative, defined more by what it opposed than by what it proposed. For what united the armed rebels (already composed of at least two differently motivated groups – the 26 July Movement and the DR) and the other forces that initially supported the Revolution was not a rejection of the whole fabric, ethos and orientation of the pre-1959 system (probably only sectors of the 26 July Movement and the PSP agreed on that root-and-branch rejection) but, rather, the narrower consensus on the need to reject the *batistato* and to replace it with a 'cleaner' version of pre-1952 Cuba, perhaps the one proposed by the *Ortodoxos* until 1952.

Even within the 26 July Movement, that narrow consensus prevailed, since it was becoming clear to many rebel leaders in early 1959 that the guerrillas' political radicalization had not been shared by the rest of the urban movement, the *llano*. A necessarily more inclusive, amorphous and ideologically mixed grouping than the relatively small *sierra*, the *llano* included pre-1952 politicians and activists, political novices, Moncada and *Granma* veterans, new supporters, PSP sympathizers and so on – all of them more affected than the isolated guerrillas by pressures from the media, politicians and neighbours. The *llano* therefore lacked not only the *sierra*'s collective impulse to radicalization, but also a cohesive political or ideological unity around which to offer a coherent and viable 'alternative project' for the Revolution. Moreover the *llano* was much more likely than the *sierra* to attract opportunists, who, seeing the direction of the political and military wind and bringing pre-1952 habits of patronage and clientelism to a supposedly revolutionary commitment, nailed their colours to the revolutionary mast. It was, therefore,

---

12. In the early days, there was probably already an effective hierarchy within 'the Revolution': (in descending order) the Sierra group, the urban wing (Resistencia Cívica – often also called the *clandestinidad* (clandestinity), the *lucha clandestina* (clandestine struggle) or the *llano* ('the plain'), to distinguish them from the *sierra*), the DR, the PSP and the various 'liberals'; by 1961, a different hierarchy was evident, with some of the *llano* having been either marginalized or having left to oppose, and with the PSP now closer to the guerrillas.

unsurprising that the guerrillas' natural tendency to see themselves as the *illuminati*, the battle-hardened veterans of the 'real' struggle, increased with their daily contact with their much more politically and ideologically heterogeneous urban counterparts, many of whom still shared the political discourse, objectives and programmes of the 'old' politics, rather than their own, palpably 'new', version.

It is probably true, however, that the differences between the *sierra* and the *llano* are often exaggerated. At one level they were mostly strategic arguments, the latter believing that the guerrillas should bring the war to the west earlier than they did (not least to relieve pressure); at another, they simply confirmed that the *llano*, larger and more amorphous, inevitably had less internal cohesion than the *sierra*. The differences are therefore perhaps no greater than those in the Escambray between the Rebel Army and the DR, which preferred spectacular actions directed at key figures to grass-roots activism.

However, throughout this process of ideological divergence, there was a significant organic convergence between the *sierra*'s increasingly precise radicalism and the wider population. For, while vanguard consensus on the *cubanista* codes was based on generalities and principles (rather than precise policies), the popular adherence to *cubania* was instinctively less concerned with precise programmes and more focused on deeply held convictions; for the pre-1952 politicians, the *cubanista* codes were guides for public policy-making, while for the average Cuban they were basic convictions and articles of faith. Thus, while a *llano* activist might differ vociferously, for example, with an ex-guerrilla over what agrarianism might need to produce a precise policy formulation on sugar, land reform or peasant involvement, the relatively non-participant inhabitant of Havana, Cienfuegos, the Sierra de Escambray or Oriente was more interested simply that agrarianism was being addressed. That organic consensus was vital to the *sierra*'s ideological legitimacy, especially as that group daily became the nucleus of the real power behind the political process.

With radicalization thus practically predetermined, many other factors now came into play to accelerate that. Externally, the most significant was American opposition to the still relatively modest reform proposals. That Washington should have set its face so firmly against the fledgling revolution is now unsurprising, given the mutual 'legacy of mistrust' (Domínguez 1989a: 20) and the depth of ignorance and suspicion in Washington political and intelligence circles when it came to judging Castro. That reaction partly reflected poor intelligence-gathering and a surviving tendency, in a Cold War-driven Pentagon and State Department, to view all radicalism as tantamount to 'communism' and to oppose any nationalization of American property in the Third World and, certainly, in the 'backyard'.

More fundamentally, however, it reflected the traditional ignorance, neglect and general lack of *sui generis* interest characterizing American attitudes and policies towards Cuba. For it is now entirely possible to construct a view of the modern United States–Cuban relationship as one blighted by the former's historical 'blind spot' about the latter, with repeated American attempts to act in, or on, Cuba determined by a pathological inability to understand the aspirations, feelings or motivations of Cubans (see especially Mazarr 1988; Paterson 1994). Perhaps this simply reflected the general post-1845 American attitude towards Latin America, which emerged most visibly in 'Manifest Destiny' and in various activities in the region; however, in Cuba, that attitude ran perhaps even more deeply, fostered by decades of purchase attempts, Cuban failures and the whole post-1898 experience.

Now, on top of these ingrained pressures, that incomprehension was exacerbated by each Cuban step towards radicalism made by a government that was operating increasingly within a context where definitions seemed ever simpler and options ever narrower (increasingly matched by a Cuban unwillingness to compromise with a government that seemed uninterested in understanding).[13] Moreover, as that government and the political apparatus moved leftwards, those more prepared (ideologically, socially, culturally or simply opportunistically) to adopt postures closer to Washington's found themselves marginalized, and then, by 1961, removed from power. This was especially true as the measures most opposed by Washington – land reform, nationalization, and the public trials of known *batistianos* – proved to be among the most popular in Cuba. By the end of 1960, indeed, there were few influential Cuban politicians left who were prepared to support, tolerate, understand or even listen to Washington's public position; they were either out of power (and often out of Cuba), unpopular and therefore silent, or persuaded of the need for intransigence.

Alongside this rapid deterioration, which accelerated the process of radicalization, there developed an alternative, countervailing, external relationship that further intensified that same process – that with the Soviet Union. There were a number of reasons why, in 1960, Moscow should not have lent its support to the revolution in Cuba. Firstly, it is now evident that Moscow did not really understand the phenomenon any more than anyone in Washington (Shearman 1990). Furthermore, already accepting the principle of 'peaceful coexistence', and with an ideological position that saw Latin America as unready for socialist revolution, the Soviet Union had no reason to suppose that Castro was any different from any other *caudillo* in a region notorious for its instability and personalism. Moreover, its always loyal PSP allies had been arguing until as recently as 1958 that the revolution was not to be supported formally.

13. The countdown to rupture from mid-1959 has been amply documented by many a narrative; basically, from the first expressions of Washington's disapproval (of the May 1959 land reform) to the final diplomatic break in January 1961, the relationship deteriorated through a series of moves and counter-moves that saw the quota steadily reduced by Washington, and finally removed in July 1960, American interests reduced and then finally nationalized by the rebel government, and hostility become all too apparent by the end of 1960.

However, there were other compelling reasons that made Moscow's eventual support likely. The first was that a relatively new Soviet leadership, anxious to prove itself, was seeking to gain advantage over the United States; having successfully withstood the 1956 eastern European revolts with no American counter-move and seeing the apparently drifting Eisenhower administration coming to an end, that leadership gambled that it had little to lose by identifying itself with an apparently popular and different rebellion in the heart of the 'backyard'. As the Revolution radicalized, world events also shifted to make Soviet support both more logical and more problematic. One such shift was rising tension in Berlin, but also the Vienna meetings between Khrushchev and the new, apparently inexperienced, American president, Kennedy, all of which seems to have convinced Khrushchev (under domestic pressure for policy failures) that his counterpart could be challenged (Shearman 1990). The Cuban success in 1961, where Kennedy's hand was seemingly less than decisive, served to convince Krushchev further that more active, and even military, support was advisable. By that stage the Revolution was already moving inexorably towards a radical internal configuration, with official identifications with 'socialism' and Marxism-Leninism, and with the PSP being given authority and some leadership within the vanguard and its organizations.

What really made the Soviet link into a force for radicalization was Moscow's policy of supporting the Revolution unconditionally, just as the PSP had done from 1959. That decision, set against American opposition, made many nationalistically inspired rebels sympathize more readily, and even uncritically, with Soviet positions than they might have done before. Guevara, certainly, tended to hold the early view that the Soviet Union was a fundamentally progressive ally for the Third World, with a propensity and a duty to support revolutionary struggles like Cuba's.

Therefore, when the Soviet Union offered aid and advantageous trade links in 1960 – at a time when the American links and quota were being punitively cut – most Cubans were eager to accept that help and the accompanying advice.[14] As the Cuban middle class left in droves, taking out valuable expertise, through Moscow's offer to replace these people by their own advisers and technicians, to train a new generation of Cubans to run their Revolution, to replace now defunct American machinery with their own, and, most vitally, to underwrite the social revolution and the drive for economic development many Cubans (especially the more radicalized) found themselves sympathizing naturally with the Soviet system, principles and policies.[15]

14. In February 1960, the Soviet Union agreed to purchase 575,000 tonnes of Cuban sugar for 1960, rising eventually to one million tonnes annually for 1961–4, all at guaranteed prices that ensured stability in an otherwise unstable world market (see Pérez-López 1986: 124–36).

15. In 1960–65, for example, 3,000 agricultural workers, 200 shipping officials and 500 students were sent from Cuba to the Soviet Union to be educated, and by 1968, 2,600 Cubans had studied in Soviet universities (Gouré and Weinkle 1972: 78).

Matching these substantial, but very specific, pressures for radicalization, both external to Cuba and within the revolutionary leadership, was a wider, deeper, and ultimately more significant, process that was being daily experienced by the whole Cuban population and that propelled the Revolution's grass roots towards a more radical definition. Much of the literature on Cuba has tended to accept, implicitly if not explicitly, the early view of the Revolution as an essentially top-down process of radicalization, in which an ambitious, uncompromising, committed vanguard either imposed its will, its goals and its definition on a bewildered and eventually trapped populace (according to one version) or seized the initiative to direct, focus and shape the inherent but unformed sympathies of a loyal population (according to another). Either way, the Cuban population has usually been seen as more or less passive, either acted upon or mobilized. However, the evidence now points less to a slavish following of the vanguard and more to an enthusiastic (if not always clear) and dynamic willingness to be involved, on the part of a significant proportion of the population (Free 1960; Zeitlin 1970a). If this is true, it offers an important further fundamental element in the explanation of an otherwise puzzling process of deep, rather than superficial or vanguard, radicalization.

Overall, the general Cuban population seems to have experienced a process of political radicalization that mirrored – and expanded – that experienced by the guerrillas, driven by the actual experience of social revolution, which changed perspectives fundamentally and built on the pre-existing propensity for a revolutionary definition of change (Zeitlin 1970a). In many senses, this simply paralleled other recorded examples of processes of the collective radicalization of groups whose shared experience of struggle, sacrifice and even 'siege' have found expression in a fundamental reformulation of their political definitions, goals and self-image.[16]

What, then, provided the ammunition for this process in Cuba? Firstly, the whole experience of collective mobilization itself fundamentally and irrevocably changed the political perspectives of those who participated in it, for it was a profoundly empowering, as well as involving, experience that affected many aspects and much of the waking time of the lives of most Cubans. The simple reality of 1960s Cuba was that it was extremely difficult for most Cubans to avoid being mobilized in some organization or other, or in one of the many campaigns of the revolutionary process.

There were, for example, the political parties or movements: the original three allied groups (26 July Movement, the DR and the PSP) each kept their own organizations, memberships, and insignia well into 1960, when the first of the

16. Such cases would include the British population at war (1940–45), whose shared struggle led finally to the Labour landslide victory of 1945, and the politicization of the British coalfields during the various miners' strikes of 1972–85.

three unifying successor parties (ORI, PURSC and PCC) was begun. Then there were the many bodies that organized Cubans in their daily lives, both politically and socially, the most important of which were the CDRs (Comités para la Defensa de la Revolución – Committees for the Defence of the Revolution), the neighbourhood groups set up in October 1960 to maintain counter-subversion vigilance and prepare 'civil defence' against the coming invasion; by 1961, the CDRs included some 800,000 Cubans (Pérez-Stable 1993: 99). Secondly there were the various surviving unions, still grouped in the CTC, which, until November 1961, was still the Confederación de Trabajadores de Cuba – although the organization had effectively been replaced by a short-lived 26 July Movement-backed 'front', but then became the Central de Trabajadores de Cuba).[17] In agriculture, there were two main organizations, the most important being the National Institute for Agrarian Reform (INRA – Instituto Nacional de Reforma Agraria), the all-encompassing body that (directed by Castro himself, Guevara and the geographer and ex-PSP activist Antonio Núñez Jiménez) became the main medium for rural radicalization, collectivization, reform and education. In addition, for the 30,000 small farmers who survived the 1959 and 1963 land reforms there was the National Association of Small Farmers (ANAP – Asociación Nacional de Agricultores Pequeños.[18] The last major national mass organization was the Federation of Cuban Women (FMC – Federación de Mujeres Cubanas), set up in August 1960 and, thereafter, instrumental in the many mobilizations, not least the seminal 1961 Literacy Campaign.[19] Then there were the military-oriented organizations, the Rebel Army – which soon became the Revolutionary Armed Forces (FAR – Fuerzas Armadas Revolucionarias) – and the emblematic militias, numbering between 200,00 and 300,000 Cubans by 1961 (Matthews 1970: 218; Pérez-Stable 1993: 99). Finally, there were the many cultural organizations, from the post-1961 National Cuban Writers' and Artists' Union (UNEAC – Unión Nacional de Escritores y Artistas de Cuba) down to the most local manifestations.

As for the campaigns, the first decade saw innumerable examples – the Literacy Campaign, the 1962 and 1968 campaigns against bureaucracy and 'sectarianism',[20]

---

17. The CTC was purged of its *batistiano* elements after 1959 and briefly led by activists from the 26 July Movement (notably David Salvador, organizer of the April 1958 general strike); by 1962, however, more radical cadres had assumed power, mostly close to, or members of, the PSP.

18. ANAP was set up in January 1961 to unite the thousands of remaining private farmers, largely left alone by the 1959–63 reforms; it thereafter acted on their collective behalf in dealings with the government, and also as a channel for communication, training, credit and cooperation.

19. In 1961, about 17,000 Cuban women were members, but, by 1962, this had risen to 376,571. By the end of the decade, 1,324,751 women were members (Domínguez 1978a: 268).

20. The anti-bureaucracy campaign was principally following the 'Escalante affair' (explained later), while anti-sectarianism followed the resurgence of that affair in 1968 (also explained later).

the 'Revolutionary Offensive' of 1968,[21] the various and repeated alerts (especially April 1961, October 1962 and the whole *lucha contra bandidos* ('struggle against the bandits') until about 1966.[22] Finally, there was each year's call to arms for the *zafra*.

Of all these mechanisms, three stand out as especially significant, for their depth, impact and symbolic role – the Literacy Campaign, the CDRs and the FAR–militia complex. It is impossible to overestimate the long-term political impact of the first, the process that did more to transform political life, commitment and definitions in Cuba than any other (see especially Fagen 1969). In conception it aimed to both address the most glaring of Cuba's ills – the lack of education, especially rural, and the 23 per cent illiteracy rate[23] – and, acting on the Movement's countless declarations since 1953, realize the quintessential *cubanista* aim of universal education. Involving 271,000 Cubans as teachers (Fagen 1969: 47) or as pupils, it created a credible, exciting and empowering image of a society mobilizing and uniting to defeat one of the more shameful effects of underdevelopment and also achieve a long-overdue integration and a practical solidarity. Whatever the educational successes of the campaign (which, with characteristic ambition, aimed to eliminate illiteracy between 1 January and 22 December), through its slogan of 'If you do not know, learn; if you know, teach' and through the dispatch throughout Cuba (especially the rural areas) of mostly young urban volunteers to live with their 'pupils', and teach them to read and write, it was an experience from which everyone emerged with their views fundamentally changed. The urban volunteers had their eyes opened to poverty and were inculcated early with the values of public service, self-sacrifice and solidarity, while the illiterate (mostly the rural poor) were made rapidly aware of the real practical, as well as political, benefits that the Revolution would bring to them personally, with some 707,000 Cubans benefiting from the campaign (Fagen 1969: 50). It was the first, but most heroic and massive, of the many mobilizations that created and confirmed a collective self-image of the Revolution as a *pueblo en marcha* ('people on the march'), overcoming with subjective commitment the objective obstacles that underdevelopment and poverty had erected against full social integration and against educational

21. The Revolutionary Offensive (March 1968) was the decision to accelerate the drive towards communism by taking over all remaining non-agricultural enterprises (some 55,600 in all).

22. The *Lucha contra Bandidos* campaign was the 1962–6 conflict, mostly in the Sierra de Escambray, between government forces (often local militias) and the various counter-revolutionary groups who were infiltrated into Cuba from the United States, mostly as part of the CIA's Operation Mongoose. The Sierra was Cuba's most conservative and Catholic rural region, where many farmers opposed the agrarian reform.

23. Educational standards, once high, had fallen by 1959, so that, compared to the 63 per cent enrolment in public schools in 1925–6, by 1942–3 there was a figure of only 35 per cent (Paulston 1971: 379).

progress – a significant moment in a revolution whose major contribution to socialist and revolutionary theory would be the belief that subjective conditions for revolution (in the action of committed and politically conscious individuals) could overcome the lack of objective conditions.

The second mechanism was the CDR, a vital link in the political communications network that characterized the early revolution. As has been seen, their original purpose was to combat invasion and subversion, a role that they performed to great effect in April 1961, with their contribution to a well-prepared defensive operation in rounding up thousands of identified potential 'fifth columnists'. Thereafter their importance to the Revolution simply could not be ignored. On the one hand, they continued their vigilante role, becoming both the eyes and ears of the Revolution but also the main means by which the average non-combatant Cuban could contribute to the Revolution's defence. On the other hand, they broadened their role well beyond their purely defensive function, becoming the grass roots of the whole mobilization process (although they continued to organize the nightly *guardia* rota for all CDR members, a duty that is still evident) and the main mechanism for other mobilizations – educational, sanitary, social or economic. By 1963, they included one-third of the adult population, rising to 80 per cent by 1972 (Domínguez 1978a: 264).[24] As the role of a 'leading Party' became either uncertain, or actually downgraded, the CDR became in effect the principal mechanism through which most Cubans were informed, involved, consulted and mobilized, and in which many Cubans cut their political teeth in debates, responsibility and campaigning (see especially Fagen 1969; LeoGrande 1979).

The FAR were formed in mid-1959 from the somewhat *ad hoc* structures of the Rebel Army, which continued for some months with some separation between the 26 July Movement cadres and the DR people, each of them jealously guarding their own collective identity – not least through distinct armbands, until these were abolished (to coincide with the decision that all Army members, except the Castro brothers, should shave off the beards that were still largely being worn almost as a badge of office or proof of past service).[25] By then, most of the Army were Cubans who had belonged to none of the insurrectionary or pre-1959 radical organizations, so the time was felt to be appropriate to formalize the system through the FAR, with a separate Ministry (MinFAR) in October 1959. After this FAR became the most significant structure and mobilizing organization in Cuba, involved in education, economic activities and even the grass-roots administration of INRA, but

24. The 1961 figure of 798,703 (in 107,000 different CDRs) had risen to 4,800,000 by 1976, despite an intervening decline during 1966–7, when membership fell by some half million and the number of CDRs fell from 103,000 to 72,000 (Domínguez 1978a: 262–4). Suchlicki cites four and a half to five million for the early 1980s, in 30,000 CDRs (Suchlicki 1988: 68).

25. I am indebted here to several of those interviewed in Cuba between 1996 and 1999 for this detail.

always with its revolutionary legitimacy and core veterans (the Rebel Army, after all, being formally the Ejército Rebelde del Movimiento 26 de Julio). The introduction of compulsory military service in November 1963 obviously helped this process.

The Revolutionary National Militias (MNR – Milicias Nacionales Revolucionarias) were created in October 1959 against the impending invasion – although it is claimed that they were to counterbalance the FAR after the Matos affair (see later) (LeoGrande 1978: 280). They soon included thousands of those who, though they were not serving soldiers because of their necessary productive, educational or service work, could at least feel that they were valuable 'civic soldiers' (Domínguez 1978a: 341), alert in Cuba's defence. Boosted especially by the atmosphere of vigilance, siege and threat around the *Crisis del Caribe*, the militias realized the self-image of the *pueblo en armas* (people in arms), recalling the *mambises*, the 1930s 'action groups' and, naturally, the 1953–8 rebels, empowering average Cubans by entrusting them with arms and the responsibility for defending Cuba and the Revolution. They thus echoed the political importance of the British Home Guard in 1939–45 or the armed citizens of an Israeli kibbutz after 1949, in being an organization contributing little militarily to the collective effort but involving thousands politically. Moreover, militia members were educated politically with materials that explicitly emphasized both the *cubanista* codes and the newly evolving socialist orientation (Departamento de Instrucción, MinFAR 1960); needless to say, this experience, in such a collectively empowering environment of siege and mobilization, profoundly affected those involved, increasing the sense of defensive unity in isolation – a sentiment expressed eloquently in the final pages of Edmundo Desnoes's telling novel, *Memorias del Subdesarrollo* (Memories of Underdevelopment), as the *Crisis del Caribe* unfolds and the sense of defiant isolation grows: 'We're on the summit of the world and not in the depths of underdevelopment' (Desnoes 1971: 119) and 'we're no longer an insignificant colony, we've already rushed into history' (1971: 122).

Beyond mobilization, many reforms similarly radicalized their beneficiaries – a phenomenon that said much about the context of those reforms and their long-term implications. For example, the most significant early social reform, the agrarian laws of May 1959 and October 1963, went deeper in meaning and impact than their relatively moderate content might have suggested objectively (O'Connor 1970: 90–134, 319–27; Gutelman 1972: 238–60; Dumont 1970: 27–103; Aranda 1968). The pre-1959 agrarian patterns in Cuba had exhibited many of the worst Latin American excesses of inequity and inefficiency, almost two-thirds of those working the land being tenants on only 42 per cent of the cultivated land (Pino Santos 1973: 90); the laws therefore aimed to correct that, creating the conditions for both a full integration and a rationalization of agriculture, the realization of a basic goal of *cubanía*.

The 1959 law simply confirmed the unremarkable 1958 declarations of intent, following the well-worn Latin American principle of 'land to the tiller' and legislating against both the *latifundio* (permitting a maximum holding of 402.3 hectares) and the *minifundio* (with a minimum entitlement of 27 hectares).[26] The 1963 law, following the intervening radicalization, simply reduced the maximum to 67 hectares, eliminating the potential problem of a comfortable 'rich' peasantry, but, significantly, not prohibiting private holdings as such, which continued to account for some 30 per cent of the cultivated land until the 1970s. The laws' radicalism lay in the fact of state intervention and the steady shifts towards cooperativization and then collectivization, all directly affecting American-owned property, and, secondly, in the accompanying INRA-led social revolution, which dramatically changed all peasants' lives and put agriculture at the centre of the political stage.[27] The whole process and its effects irreversibly put the rural population on the Revolution's side, and the rapid drift from cooperatives to collectives (*granjas del pueblo* – people's farms) was in part a response to the workers' search for job security.

The second radicalizing reform was the Urban Reform Law of March 1959 (and the October 1960 elaborations), which, by halving rents and then abolishing renting, created a new class of owner-occupiers who – again, given the law's radicalizing context – became staunch supporters of the Revolution rather than the self-focused 'house-owners' that might have resulted in a more capitalist-oriented system. Moreover, as much bourgeois and petty-bourgeois housing was now converted into multi-occupation dwellings, the law was seen as immediately redistributive, a realization of the Revolution's declared egalitarianism.

All the other early reforms confirmed this trend. There was an immediate and sustained campaign against the deficiencies of health-care provision, establishing a free and universal system with a politically effective mass involvement in preventive care (Leyva 1972: 456–96; Feinsilver 1993). Beyond the 1961 Campaign, education reform was widened and deepened (Paulston 1971: 385–95; Valdés 1972), converting comfortable residential properties into schools, making education free from June 1961, increasing the budget dramatically – from 90 million pesos in 1959 to 290 million in 1969 (Valdés 1972: 439) – and more than doubling primary school enrolments (Fitzgerald 1994: 42).[28] These reforms not only immediately and tangibly affected the well-being, abilities and economic opportunities

26. The reform allowed exemptions from the maximum (up to 1,342 hectares) if productivity exceeded the national average by 50 per cent; all farmers cultivating up to 67 hectares became owners.

27. Although the 1959 law stressed cooperatives as the basis of the new social landholding system, it also allowed for Soviet-style 'state farms' for those sectors, such as cattle-rearing, where subdivision and redistribution made little economic sense. By 1963, policy shifts, economic momentum and labour drift meant that cooperatives were in decline and state farms were becoming the norm.

28. The actual figures were 625,729 in 1958–8, rising to 1,427,607 in 1969–70 (Fitzgerald 1994: 42).

of the thousands of beneficiaries – the lowest 40 per cent of income earners increasing their share of income from 6.5 per cent in 1958 to 17.2 per cent in 1962 (Brundenius 1984: 108) – but also profoundly altered the collective self-image, confirming universally the leadership's determination to realize its many promises.

The longer-term effects should not be underestimated, either, for, by prioritizing attention on, and investment in, an expensive but politically desirable social revolution, the Revolution ensured enduring political support from a population that was to experience decades of hardship and pressure. Because most Cubans benefited early on, the Revolution thereafter won a commitment and a sense of belonging to a collective process that was to prove valuable in later years.

That leads naturally to a further structural factor contributing to the general radicalization – the overall sense of collective solidarity increasingly created. This solidarity began – naturally enough – in the collective euphoria of January 1959, but then evolved through the collective experiences of reform, participation and mobilization, emerging most clearly from 1961–2 as the sense of collective defensiveness began to grow. To the self-images of *pueblo en marcha* and *pueblo en armas* were now added that of the embattled enclave, heroically resisting the might of imperialism and struggling for emancipation alone and through its own efforts – a self-image that, often explicitly, recalled Sparta, the British wartime 'Dunkirk spirit', the North Vietnamese struggle (with which many Cubans felt an increasing affinity) and even pre-1967 Israel.

Moreover, this solidarity was based on a double exclusion. It excluded, firstly, the thousands who had left Cuba since 1959, who, whatever their motivations and however much their emigration to Miami might eventually be welcomed as a source of dollars, were initially rejected in a Cuba that closed ranks against those who were seen to have preferred a search for material security and the all-powerful dollar in the 'bowels' of the *monstruo* or, at worst, had explicitly taken sides with the country that was now determinedly blocking the popular changes and had participated in the 1961 invasion and other activities.[29]

There were many different, and often contradictory, reasons for this rejection, ranging from simple envy, through a sense that the emigrants were unpatriotic (by not sharing the necessary hardships of the process of change and by seeking exile in the very power that was now seen as the cause of so many woes and the target of the renewed patriotism), to a revolutionary commitment against the émigrés' profoundly counter-revolutionary position. Whatever the motive, the effects were

---

29. The *monstruo* reference recalls Martí's often quoted final letter in 1895 about the United States – *Viví en el monstruo, y le conozco las entrañas* ('I have lived in the bowels of the monster and know him well': author's translation from the letter to Manuel Mercado) (Martí 1975: 311).

similar, increasing the sense of communal, patriotic solidarity and collective self-righteousness of the embattled David against the philistine Goliath.[30] As the Revolution's press began, routinely, to refer to all émigrés as *gusanos* (worms), many Cubans began to agree emotionally with the sentiment inspiring that rejection.

This sense of exclusiveness also had other effects, especially the growing tendency to demand revolutionary conformity, considering deviations from the 'norm' to be inherently unrevolutionary and even counter-revolutionary. 'Deviation' could, of course, easily be translated into a rejection of 'deviancy', of 'abnormal' dress, hairstyles, sexual orientation or behaviour; certainly, by the end of the first decade, there was considerable pressure on young people to follow the new dress, style and orientation codes and considerable suspicion of those who still challenged the 'norm' – not least homosexuals (Lumsden 1996), Black Power activists (Moore 1988), and those who imitated the American 'beat' generation in art or behaviour (Yglesias 1970). The episode of the UMAP camps (Unidades Militares de Ayuda a la Producción – Military Units to Aid Production) – explained later – was one outcome of the conformism arising from the sense of exclusivity.

This solidarity also increasingly, and logically, excluded the United States itself, as the long-standing Cuban ambivalence towards its northern neighbour – the always challenging love–hate relationship, the dichotomy of attraction-rejection (Pérez 1999) – became a more one-dimensional opposition – unsurprisingly, since that ambivalence had long meant that it took only a marginal shift in the whole, finely-balanced, Cuban–American relationship to bring to the surface either an intensified nationalism, against either some slight or the cost of dependency, or, alternatively, an admiration for the often envied American way of life or for American actions. However much the breakdown in United States–Cuban relations during 1959–61 was a collision of perspectives and interests that was waiting to happen, a more understanding willingness by Washington to cooperate with the early Revolution might have generated a stronger constituency within Cuba for a less radical, nationalist or socialist definition of revolution, and, certainly, one more sympathetic to prevailing American thinking.[31] It is not difficult, indeed, to see a greater propensity among less radical Cubans for a more liberal, reformist programme, perhaps along Kennedyite lines. Such a development would immediately have complicated the radicalizing impulse of those rebels already committed to a deeper, if not yet socialist, revolution, and would have deepened internal divisions;

30. This too was a reference to that same final Martí letter, with the second half of the familiar quotation being *y mi honda es la de David* ('My sling is the sling of David') (1975: 311).

31. There is, inevitably, much debate about a hypothetically more understanding American policy. Early commentators, recognizing the Revolution's nationalist impulse and regretting American attitudes, tended to believe that a less antagonistic policy might have kept Cuba away from the Soviet Union (notably Mills 1960: Bonsal 1971); later scholarship, however, has tended to see the conflict as more deep-seated and structural and less likely to be affected by nuances of policy from Washington.

however, the fact was that the strong American opposition early on meant that the antagonism latent in the old ambivalence re-emerged to consolidate nationalist support for both the leadership and radicalization.

Any explanation of the 1959–62 radicalization must also necessarily focus on the PSP's role. Overall – until the PSP overplayed its hand in 1962 – the party's approach to the evolving insurrection and revolution was, from late 1958, a model of good political judgement. Before 1958, the party had viewed Castro's rebellion with suspicious distance, at best, and, at worst, outright hostility. Having already condemned Castro's 1948 Bogotá activity as 'adventurist' (Szulc 1986: 126), the PSP leaders then condemned the Moncada attack as 'putschism' and 'adventurism' (Pérez-Stable 1993: 69), following this with tactical criticism of the apparently futile and costly *Granma* invasion (Anderson 1997: 296), and then, as late as April 1958, criticizing the Movement-led general strike as 'adventurist' (Anderson 1997: 314). The party was seemingly endeavouring to keep its options open until very late, still talking of the *vía pacífica* as late as October 1958.

This caution was easy to explain. Firstly, Castro's actions did indeed seem not only pointless but positively dangerous, pointless because they had visibly and bloodily failed and ran counter to the party's Browderist moderation and the specific theoretical positions for Cuba and Latin America (which implicitly rejected armed struggle) and dangerous because they threatened to provoke a repressive reaction by Batista, which could easily include the visible communists. In a Latin America where the Cold War had seen Washington persuade governments to outlaw their own national Communist Parties, the PSP's relative freedom was a luxury to be preserved, and the party was thus understandably wary of anything that might upset effective coexistence – not least because the PRC-A's assault after 1948 had weakened communist influence in the CTC. Moreover, although there is no evidence of this, some PSP members may have harboured thoughts about an arrangement with Batista once the dust had died down, given their previous fruitful collaboration.

However, by late 1958, the PSP's position had changed, having become untenable in the face of both an increasing polarization in Cuba (between an ever more repressive dictator and an ever more popular and apparently invulnerable Castro) and growing pressure from the party's youth wing, the JS (Juventud Socialista – Socialist Youth), which now saw increasing numbers of its members and would-be members cooperating with, and even joining, the Sierra rebels, one of whom was, of course, the ex-JS Raúl Castro. Within the leadership, too, the voices for cooperation – notably the subtle Carlos Rafael Rodríguez, Jorge Risquet, Ursino Rojas (the sugar union leader) and Lionel Soto – were becoming louder daily, with 'discreet' contacts by October 1957 (Anderson 1997: 297).

Thus, in February 1958, the party announced its support for the rebellion, sending some of its leaders, including Rodríguez, to the Sierra. This meant that, in January 1959, the PSP was the only pre-1952 political organization to emerge from the *batistato* and the insurrection with its national structure intact and united, as a recognized part of the rebel alliance. Moreover, the party then took the further intelligent step of irrevocably cementing its relationship with the rebels, declaring unconditional support for the new Revolution and offering itself in whatever capacity might be necessary. When other pre-1952 parties, some new groups and Washington were all tempering their attitudes with conditions for support, the PSP gesture won considerable sympathy among the 26 July rebels, especially with the Soviet Union's equal willingness to help unconditionally. This was when public reaction to the PSP's presence at the side of, and even within, the leadership was more positive than it might have been in early 1958, not least as (given that the first two years were a period of complex developments and reactions, but often simple, and even simplistic, definitions) there was a greater popular tendency to accept the simple but effective equation that the Revolution's enemy's enemy was, *ipso facto*, the Revolution's friend – an attitude undoubtedly helped by memories of the PSP as a successful union force and a pragmatic influence on progressive legislation and social reform after 1938.

There were many rebels – especially the more politically aware anticommunists – who, not sharing this developing sympathy or tolerance, chose to make an issue out of what they saw as a threat to their revolution. These included Castro's first choice as president, Manuel Urrutia, who resigned in May 1959 alleging communist influence in the new land reform – leading to Castro's characteristically defiant nomination as his successor of the ex-JS Osvaldo Dorticós and his own assumption of the mantle of Prime Minister – and the ex-*comandante* (rebel commander) Huber Matos, who resigned as military commander of Camagüey province, trying to rally resistance to the communists' influence (leading to his arrest and a thirty-year sentence for treason). Moreover, most of those – often liberals in the American mould – who resigned from the government during 1959–60 did so on the same grounds (of a creeping 'communization'), and many of the thousands of early emigrants cited the same fears. That fact only made their prophecies more self-fulfilling, furthering the radicalization process by removing from the political equation any definition that might have argued for a less socialist orientation. Thus, the PSP presence proved doubly radicalizing – as a radical input to vanguard debates and perspectives, and scaring off those who would have resisted radicalization. However, it is significant that the daily newspapers of the two main revolutionary groups – the 26 July Movement's *Revolución* and the PSP's *Noticias de Hoy* (Today's News) – remained separate until 1965 (when they merged as *Granma*), often differing in their perspectives, interpretations and focus, and thus maintaining the coexistence of two different identities within a (then) formally unified party.

The PSP's proximity to the rebel leadership was evident in more concrete terms, not least in their advice which, although there is still no consensus on its extent, nature or importance, was apparently significant in at least three areas – in the Soviet link, in the move towards a planned economy, and in the formulation of the land reform. This collaboration was often sealed in the 1959 regular late-night meetings in Tarará, east of Havana, between the 'inner group' of the new revolutionary leadership (notably Fidel and Raúl Castro, Guevara, Ramiro Valdés and, until his death, Camilo Cienfuegos) and PSP representatives, especially Roca, Rodríguez and Escalante (Anderson 1997: 384). These sessions were enhanced notably when the land reform discussions (involving contributions from the Movement's Miret and Espín and the PSP's Oscar Pino Santos, Alfredo Guevara and Antonio Núñez Jiménez) demonstrated a closer affinity between the rebels' radicalism and the perspectives of like-minded elements in the PSP.[32] In this respect, the leading PSP activists, theorists or cadres did indeed contribute substantially to the process of radicalization, not least because all three policy areas had longer-term revolutionary implications, striking at the heart of the American–Cuban relationship.

The second practical PSP contribution to the process was the use of its cadres, bureaucratically or directively at grass-roots level. For Castro was well aware that, with a need for a human infrastructure to enact the revolutionary programme and with the 26 July Movement lacking a nationally coordinated membership, the PSP was the only reliable body capable of providing that. Hence, from early on, PSP members were enlisted – and volunteered, at party encouragement – in the local administration of the land reform, the militias, the Army and the nationalized industries. They were also influential in the new Escuelas de Instrucción Revolucionaria (EIR – Schools of Revolutionary Instruction) that were set up in January 1961 to provide political education and 'ideological formation' (Fagen 1969: 105) for the less coherently politicized Movement rebels, especially with the move towards socialism.[33] Between 1961 and 1967, there were twelve Schools (plus the main party school, the Ñico López academy), through which some 700 students passed, roughly half from the 26 July Movement and half from the PSP (Fagen 1969: 107). Although the 26 July Movement set up the EIR, they were, inevitably, often staffed by PSP members; however, the lack of Soviet textbooks in Spanish meant a reliance on Roca's classic text, *Fundamentos del Socialismo* (Basics of Socialism), Castro's *La Historia Me Absolverá* and other lesser-known Latin American texts – all of which meant a far from orthodox education for the students, but a growing affinity with the PSP position. This tendency was increased by the

32 Once again this is all borne out by many of the author's own interviews, in 1996–7, with leading protagonists from the 1960s.

33. Szulc claims that the first EIR was established in late 1959 (Szulc 1986: 379), but there is no other evidence of this. Medin, while confirming the January 1961 date (Medin 1990: 11), then later refers to the EIR being founded on 2 December 1960 (Medin 1990: 74); in fact the latter date was when they were announced.

move towards ideological education elsewhere; for example, by 1962, the University of Havana required the universal study of dialectical materialism (Zeitlin 1970a: 21).

This influence might not have been as great had it not operated in something of a political (but, as will be seen, not an ideological) vacuum, arising from the fact that at that stage, for all the popular consensus for radical reform, the leaders' determination to effect that programme, and the unifying effects of American opposition, there was no national political structure, no 'party of the revolution', no 26 July Movement congress, no formal link between vanguard and grass roots. Before 1959, rebel 'membership' was achieved only through a swearing-in ceremony; after 1959, it still remained somewhat loose, although there were *Casas del 26 de Julio*. Instead, there was a critical gap early on between the formal power, the cabinet (exercising government but not power), and the real power, the Rebel Army (exercising power but not government), and, throughout, a fierce debate about what kind of revolution the process might become, its direction and its political orientation.[34] Those gaps, debates and uncertainties created a sufficient vacuum – at intermediate and base level – for a determined, disciplined and ideologically coherent organization to operate with disproportionate influence.

Finally, in this catalogue of the factors contributing to the post-1959 radicalization, one has to consider the role played by Castro himself. Apart from the issue of his overall influence either in Cuba generally or among the guerrillas in particular, it is evident from all accounts that Castro was fully aware that, if the Revolution's aims were to be compromised to meet American demands or to keep liberal support, the rebellion would be condemned to the same historical fate as so many preceding nationalist or radical movements (which he was not prepared to contemplate) and that the population's expectations were unusually high and probably more solid than others perceived them to be. Thus the force of his personality worked not only on his 'inner circle' and the guerrillas but also on the wider population, through a skilled use of television and radio, public meetings and rallies, and extensive direct contact with ordinary Cubans – the so-called *democracia directa* (direct democracy). The greater his public determination not to compromise, the greater the population's faith in him and willingness to follow his lead and definition.

Discussing Castro's supposed or real role, one must also necessarily consider the question of Che Guevara, for many the *éminence grise* of the radicalization and the subject of countless myths, inside and outside Cuba, from 1959. Many later critics, for example, saw him as responsible for the late 1960s 'utopian'

---

34. For the first month, Castro remained outside the government, as head of the Rebel Army, yet evidently continued to be treated as the real leader, advising the government in no uncertain terms and carrying out the important negotiations on future policies and laws.

economic policies, or for the shift towards Marxism and collaboration with the PSP. Others have presented him as the non-Cuban outsider (Bourne 1986: 259), ideologically hard-line and humourless, within a coterie of less ideologically clear and more relaxed Cubans. There is a further leftist myth of Guevara as the last remaining hope of a genuinely revolutionary Cuban socialism, resisting the PSP's 'Stalinism' or Castro's growing 'authoritarianism' (Habel 1991: xviii).

Such myths arose largely from Guevara's prominence by Castro's side and their evident mutual trust, but also from Guevara's significant roles in his six-year association with the revolutionary government – responsible for political security in the first weeks (with a firm and punitive control from the Cabaña fortress), involved in the secret land-reform discussions, head of the seminal Industrial Department of INRA (in late 1959), Director of the Banco Nacional (1959–61) and, from 1961, Minister of Industry – apart from his apparent role in shaping Cuba's foreign policy, especially in supporting revolution in Latin America and the Moscow alliance.

On examination, however, the truth is somewhat different. Firstly, the evidence points to a simultaneous radicalization process in Guevara himself and in the Revolution as a whole, with Guevara being more influenced by the process than influencing it in a supposedly radical direction.[35] Certainly, there is ample evidence of his shift to a more revolutionary Marxism after, and not before, 1959, in a characteristically rigorous programme of political self-education, often late into the night alone or through special classes, through an extensive and eclectic reading programme from a range of Marxist sources, including *Capital*, the young Marx, Gramsci, Carlos Mariátegui (the heterodox Peruvian Marxist intellectual and leader), and the seminal Argentine philosopher Aníbal Ponce, but also through his careful empirical analysis of the Cuban experience (Kapcia 1997a: 30).

Beyond that, however, an examination of the areas of his supposed influence produces a rather different picture. In the economy, for all his leadership of the 'radical' arguments in the 1962–5 'Great Debate' (see below), Castro's eventual selection, in 1965, of the subsequent strategy was actually a compromise between Guevara's belief in central planning and voluntarism, and Rodríguez's belief in a sugar-based future.[36] Moreover, the post-1966 commitment to the 'moral economy' (see below), actually came after Guevara had left Cuba and especially after his death. On balance, decisions were probably motivated as much by the rebels' growing radicalization, an economic crisis demanding fundamental solutions, the decline in consumer goods, the need for capital accumulation, the growth of a black economy and the need to prevent a bureaucratizing institutionalism.

35. Again, the author's interviews bear this out strongly.

36. The 'Great Debate' was both seminal and symptomatic of the early tensions and debates within the Revolution and the political and intellectual elite. The details are covered later in this chapter.

Equally, in foreign policy, the picture testifies more to a coincidence between Guevara's preferences and the preferred direction of the whole vanguard. His visits to the Third World and Moscow, for instance, seem in the event to be less significant than the role played in Moscow by Raúl Castro and Rodríguez; the reality was that Cuba was unable to do more than support Algeria and other radical African forces with a few men and weapons. Moreover, Guevara's domestic responsibilities allowed him little opportunity to play a decisive role in the Revolution's external framework and, even with such an opportunity, there is evidence that he argued consistently for better relations with Washington (Anderson 1997: 518–20) and that he was somewhat lukewarm about Soviet socialism, however much he believed in their duty to support Cuba. In Latin America, furthermore, given the later pre-1959 manifestations of *cubanía*, a defiantly insurrectionary policy might have been expected, with or without Guevara's more strategic arguments (which anyway came later in the 1960s).

Focusing on internal political developments, however, Guevara was almost certainly less suspicious in late 1958 than some of his Cuban colleagues about grass-roots cooperation with the PSP, and more willing, after 1959, to use the PSP to exercise control and execute policies. He also had no problem with defining himself early on as Marxist and communist; even that, however, is hardly conclusive proof of his influence, since, again, there is every reason to suppose that the inherent *cubanista* tendencies towards radicalism, the general familiarity with the PSP (and some rebels' previous association with the JS), the PSP's willingness to support unconditionally and Washington's inevitable anticommunist suspicions and hostility would all have conspired to push the rebels in that same direction, with or without Guevara.

Ultimately, therefore, the picture of Guevara is less one of influence by a radical ideologue on a largely untutored, unsuspecting, gullible group than one of coincidence, with Guevara being the rebel leader best able and most willing to articulate the new positions being adopted and place them within a clear ideological and theoretical context, legitimizing the new positions in revolutionary Marxist terms. Seen in this context, then, his role is not only less seminal but also less problematic than some have argued, particularly regarding his abrupt departure from Cuba in 1965. For one story immediately disseminated then outside Cuba was of a major disagreement between Guevara and Castro (A. Suárez 1967: 221–3), or the ideas that Guevara was disillusioned by the Revolution's direction, was marginalized by Castro or realized that he had no place in the new structure.[37] In the light of the

37. Anderson's biography of Guevara partly concurs with this latter judgement, suggesting that Castro preferred him to continue the struggle in Africa after Guevara's public criticisms of the Soviet Union's lukewarm support for the Third World (J.L. Anderson 1997: 627–8). Generally, however, he confirms that Che's own frustration and integrity led him to prefer to lead the struggle on the ground rather than from a desk, and that he felt that he had contributed as much as he was able by then.

evidence, however, and given the close coincidence between the two leaders (attested by all) and between Guevara's and the Revolution's separate but associated evolutions, none of these explanations seem so likely. Moreover, with the Revolution seeming to follow a more 'Guevarist' direction after 1965, a bitter break seems improbable. Overall, the most likely explanation is to be found in a combination of three motives: his initial 1956 undertaking to Castro to move on once the revolution was established (which, by 1965, he believed it to be), a characteristic restlessness at being desk-bound in roles that suited his talents least, and Castro's awareness that an insurrectionary strategy enacted by none other than his closest *compañero* would testify fully to the Revolution's Third World and revolutionary commitment, perhaps enabling the isolation to be broken.

This then is the obvious array of explanations of the unexpected process of rapid, and popular, radicalization. However, there is one further factor that always underlay them all, more organically, as Castro made clear in his 1953 defence speech and in his determination to set himself apart from the tradition of betrayal and compromise. This was the past, present and future role of ideology, and specifically the potential of that manifestation of *cubania* that had become counter-hegemonic in the Cuban dissidence, *cubania rebelde*.

Cubania in 1959 may have been somewhat inchoate, given the contemporary confusions, but its components, expressed in codes that had survived intact and fortified, were still present in the political culture and, in the combination of circumstances that had conspired to make the 1952–8 period so volatile, were even more powerful and organic. Thus, *cubania* was, in the circumstance, an 'ideological reservoir' especially usable by any force perceived as *cubanista* in its ethos, image and adherence to the codes, behind a clearly popular leader. With Chibás gone, and the alternatives collapsed, the 26 July Movement had proved to be that force.

We have already seen how *cubania*, and especially *cubania rebelde*, had developed, become radicalized and popular, and begun to constitute a coherent 'alternative project' in the pre-revolutionary years, so that there was little doubt that, whether represented explicitly by *History will absolve me* or the various 26 July Movement manifestos, or implicitly by the myths and the rebellion, many Cubans were conscious of that 'project' for *Cuba Libre*. This meant that, immediately after the victory, there was little doubt of *cubania rebelde*'s counter-hegemony within the rebellion and its popular acceptance, although the first months saw several different options posited by political groups, movements or documents. Only one – the rebellion's – really held any sway, credibly and with a high degree of historical legitimacy.

Such a scenario was perhaps to be expected in the first flush of revolutionary zeal, where victory in itself gave an understandable immediacy to the rebels' popularity and thus to a popular identification with their ideas, programmes and principles. What, however, made the Cuban situation unusual was that this identification survived the early months intact, then characterizing the continuing popular support and mobilization for the Revolution, despite severe social shocks (such as the exodus of much of the middle class and the division of many Cuban families), economic crises, political stresses and a frightening external environment of invasion and nuclear threat. Each of these alone might have been expected to dent, if not undermine, such popular identification, based as it was on a discourse that was scarcely articulated. If anything, however, each one seems to have reinforced that identification.

The principal reason for this continuing attraction probably lies in the peculiar nature of the early political configurations, for one can argue that a revolution that addresses the problems that are, by popular consensus, most in need of correction, but that also, simultaneously, succeeds in erecting a political structure that, although reflecting that demand, leads to institutionalization, risks a loss of flexibility and improvisation that is vital to the spontaneity of popular support. Indeed, that was an outcome that the Sierra rebels initially feared, when resisting the PSP's attempts to lead, direct and take over 'their' Revolution.

However, until at least 1961 the Revolution was characterized by a lack of political structure and system, the 26 July Movement remaining largely a loose organization (except for the creation of the FAR) and the leadership steadfastly resisting American and liberal pressure for elections. Even when the ORI was founded, the two ex-guerrilla movements (26 July and Directorio) never formally dissolved themselves, although the PSP did. Even after the 1962 'Escalante affair', the same held true, with the ORI's successor – the PURS – being largely a 'pre-party' in transition towards the envisaged single-party structure, and with that eventual single party, the PCC, remaining until 1975 as a low-membership, vanguard-run body that met nationally only as the Central Committee and *Buró Político* (Politbureau) and lacked a national congress to formulate policy (and create a possibly inertia-producing bureaucracy).[38] This meant, therefore, that, throughout the years of crisis and change, the system actually lacked a force for conscious national control, coordination and socialization, which, in post-1945 eastern Europe, for example, the various Communist Parties had provided. Instead, such forces as existed either lacked national coordination (the CDRs) or had a specific focus that limited them (INRA).

The only national organizations with a politicizing potential were the FAR and the militias. Indeed, FAR's role in the whole process should not be underestimated,

---

38. The PURS did exist formally, especially at the grass roots, becoming a valuable mechanism for political involvement and education for the diverse cadres; but pressure of mobilization and activism distracted most members from routine party work, a problem persisting in the successor PCC (evidence from the author's interviews).

especially as, with its leadership and initial 'core' membership being the reconstituted Rebel Army, it represented less an orthodox military structure than a partial institutionalization, or legitimization, of the *sierra*. For the Rebel Army was clearly generally seen as the most legitimate organization for political socialization, mobilization, education and ideological training, as well as civil and military defence.

What characterized all these organizations, which were in a sense realizing the mobilization, socialization and control aims of a 'leading party', was their evident adherence to, leadership by, and identification with not just a socialist definition of revolution, but also a recognizably *cubanista* one. Therefore, at a time of bewildering and exciting change and empowerment, the main mechanisms and forums that existed in which Cubans could be educated, debate, share their common concerns and exchange their individual experiences in the collective struggle, were unmistakably imbued with, and committed to, a new, *revolucionaria*, version of *cubanía rebelde*, giving them a direction and legitimacy that might have eluded a less *cubanista* structure. Within the CDRs, the militia and INRA, for example, the loudest discourse was usually *cubanista*, and the political or historical education textbooks often focused on Castro's speeches, Martí or Cuban history, alongside the gradual insertion of more orthodox socialist models.

After 1961, with the growing influence of the PSP and Moscow, and the radicalization of perspectives among the leaders, more socialist and Marxist elements were introduced, especially in the EIR (where the cadres were trained politically) and in the press and the education system (see Medin 1990). Even this, however, did not contradict the underlying thrust of *cubanía*. For the whole discourse of *cubanía* had increasingly included elements of Marxism, and the privileged position in the *cubanista* tradition of prominent Marxists, and even of the Communist Party/PSP, meant than there was little dissonance between the evolving *cubanía revolucionaria* and the growing influence of Marxism and communism. Therefore, when Castro's First Declaration of Havana (1959) implied a more radical vision of Cuba and the world than that evident in the Movement's previous pronouncements, few Cubans saw this as a political break with the past, such was the affinity between the rebels and the radicalized populace, and such, too, was the pace of change and of the evolution of political perspectives.

It might thus be argued that, by the mid-1960s, the two levels of ideology – popular-empirical and intellectual-theoretical – had again furthered the process of dynamic, dialectical fusion. The already unchallenged hegemony of Marxist perspectives within the evolving *cubanista* dissidence had meant that, after 1959, this process would organically evolve further. The only complication was provided by the existence of at least two, competing, versions of Marxism at the intellectual level – one offering a clear, coherent and easy set of explanations and propositions, the other less coherent but, ultimately, closer in purpose, meaning and impulse to the thrust of the existing and evolving (popular) *cubanía revolucionaria*. The explanation and vision offered by the latter version in the early 1960s was never comfortable, proposing austerity, struggle and isolation; but it was more ideologically comforting than a version that was often seen as more relevant to European circumstances.

All of this is indeed borne out by early surveys of Cuban popular views, not least the revealing 1963 survey of youth opinions under UNESCO auspices (Toroella 1963), which demonstrated that questions about the 'purpose of life' and the 'most important things in life' elicited responses that stressed social well-being (19 per cent in the sixteen-to-eighteen age bracket and 26.4 per cent of the nineteen-to-twenty-three group, in answer to the first, and 20.82 per cent and 24.17 per cent, respectively, to the second – Torroella 1963: 73–4), while patriotic sentiments were somewhat confused and varied (18 per cent of the younger group seeing the most important thing as usefulness to the *Patria*, but, puzzlingly, only 9.39 per cent of their elders – Toroella 1963: 74). Those same respondents, however, confirmed clearly – 30.31 per cent and 29.48 per cent respectively – that 'progress' was defined by the 'advance to socialism' (Toroella 1963: 83).

Hence the younger generation seemed already to have been influenced by the new experience and atmosphere of a fused *cubanista*-socialist politicization; for Cubans formed educationally and politically in the pre-revolutionary Cuba, but now steeled in recent struggles, continuity was fundamentally achieved through the legitimacy of *cubanía*. The consistent thread of the process, together with the language of texts, the press, the leaders and above all the media, was still identifiably *cubanista*, with the *rebelde* version having now evolved steadfastly into a *cubanía revolucionaria*.

It is therefore, contrary to some leftist expectations, possible to argue that it was the lack, rather than the existence, of a nationally controlled and directed political structure and organization that guaranteed the survival of an inherently revolutionary discourse as the guiding ideology of a revolutionary process that gathered pace in a particular context, ensuring greater radicalization. Moreover, as the 1960s progressed, the actual shared experience of social change and political involvement proceeded to strengthen that identification, as the collective struggle either reinforced the existing *cubanista* codes or added new ones. Had a politically powerful and legitimate alternative existed to provide a convincing project to challenge a *cubanista* interpretation of this experience, then the process and direction of politicization might well have been different; the fact is, however, that, with liberal, pro-American and pro-Moscow 'projects' all either discredited or marginalized, there was no such challenge.

For example, as the agrarian reform experience progressed (evolving and radicalizing as much empirically as deliberately) more and more Cubans, rural and urban, saw the traditional agrarianism enhanced, while the essential moralism of *cubanía* was strengthened, echoed and deepened by all the early moves – Playa Girón, the educational reforms and Campaign, the 'cleansing' of corrupt Havana, and so on. Similarly, the codes of collectivism, revolutionism, statism and culturalism were all enhanced, rather than weakened, by the early experiences, while the newer code of internationalism was boosted by the post-1962 commitment to the Third World and Latin America and by the new alliance with the 'progressive' Socialist Bloc.[39] Most clearly, though, the code of activism was strengthened and reiterated throughout, as everything was continually expressed in epic combative terms – *defensa*, *movilización* (mobilization), *lucha*, *ejército* (and, within that, much talk of literacy *brigadas* and construction *contingentes*), *campañas* (campaigns) and so on – while 'confrontation and heroism' were presented as the essential content of the messages to shape a revolutionary consciousness (Medin 1990: 29).

The essential codes of pre-1959 *cubanía* therefore not only remained intact but were seen to be even more relevant to the daily lives of the ordinary Cuban and to the destiny of the Revolution. Always imbued with a revolutionary potential in the particular context of the Cuba of the 1950s and 1960s – by implying both a break with existing patterns of economic orientation and control and a context in which compromises would be unacceptable – these codes now gained in radical significance in the environment of change, collectivization, social improvement and, above all, popular empowerment. Thus, the ordinary Cuban who, by participating in the CDR or the militia, was becoming more aware of his or her worth, role and potential, was more likely to respond positively to those aspects of the hegemonic discourse reflecting a new environment that had given them such an opportunity and restored a much-lamented sense of national identity and pride.

Needless to say, this was no simple environment, even though the changes meant an inevitable simplification of issues and choices. *Cubanía*'s ascendancy and new legitimacy did not mean that it reigned unchallenged, for the lack of organizational cohesion meant a vacuum as well as an opportunity, in which it was challenged repeatedly, at certain critical points and throughout the process, especially as the early momentum shifted the Revolution leftwards, towards organic definitions of socialism and, eventually, a more Soviet-oriented communism.

That challenge came from two directions principally. The first was from what we might call liberalism, although the term, at that time, covered several different groups and perspectives. At one level, it included those who favoured populist projects like those of either the *Auténticos* or the *Ortodoxos*; yet initially they represented a minimal challenge, since few took them seriously or saw their project

39. Although Cuba had links with the FLN in Algeria from 1960 and, with the Declarations of Havana, had committed itself to supporting 'national liberation' struggles, it was really only after 1962 (with Moscow's limited commitment clearer and with Cuban security ensured) that Cuba's significant role in the new Third World developed. Moreover, 1962 saw Cuba expelled from the OAS, after which the Revolution had little to lose by fomenting insurrection in the region.

as much more than a less objectionable version of the old politics. It was only after the traditional politicians had left that such perspectives, most notably from Prío Socarrás and Raúl Chibás, really began to make the running in opposition to the rebel leadership.

More characteristic of the liberal alternative were those 'technocrats' represented in the first government, such as Pazos and López Fresquet, whose vision largely reflected perspectives offered by American liberal opinion (as represented by Nelson Rockefeller or the Kennedys) or by European social democracy – a belief in a socially responsible mixed economy within a pluralist polity. They were, however, in a clear minority within, or outside, the vanguard and, often owing their position to their American or European experiences, tended to strike few chords among a Cuban population that demanded different, and more immediate, action, and was prepared to put its faith in a different project. Thus, when Miró Cardona resigned as Prime Minister in February 1959 over alleged 'extremism' and was replaced by Castro, there were few public protests, most Cubans seeing the move as reflecting the former's marginalization and the 'natural' accession of the genuinely popular Castro.

For both liberalisms, April 1961 proved to be a watershed, since liberal support for the invasion tended to paint them all with the same brush and, thereafter, condemn all declared liberals to political oblivion within Cuba.

Liberalism might also include those churchmen who, especially around the Catholic Church, protested against the Revolution's leftward shift, especially after the middle class (largely that church's base) had begun to leave and after the start of the Soviet economic relationship in 1960. However, to qualify the 1960s Cuban Catholic Church as liberal is a misnomer, since it had long been identified with right-wing positions, as a result of recent immigration by Spanish clergy and the Church's association with the Havana elite. However, the hierarchy's posture can justifiably be included within the broadest sense of the term 'liberal', in that it took sides against Batista at the end of the dictatorship but then expressed doubts about, and then opposition to, the Revolution in the language of liberal-democratic anticommunism, stressing freedom of worship and freedom of education among the other political and civil freedoms that it increasingly claimed were being eroded. The term 'liberal democracy' is not simply a broad term, either, for the Church's definition of democracy was 'liberal' (in the North American sense) rather than 'social' or even 'Christian' (in the Western European sense), although some of the more progressive groups (such as the MNR and the DR) that initially sided with the Revolution and from which several activists emerged could be clustered within that latter category. In other words, what the Church advocated by its liberalism was *laissez-faire* freedom to maintain its traditional educational and welfare role, as the state took control over areas in which that freedom had allowed it to operate significantly and prestigiously. Hence some churchmen sided with the 1961 invasion, to the long-term detriment of the Church's position in Cuba and the expulsion of approximately half Cuba's priests (some 130) in September 1961 (Azicri 1988: 189; see also Crahan 1989; Kirk 1989a; Jover Marimón 1971).

The final group who might be classified as liberal within this context were those intellectuals who – such as Guillermo Cabrera Infante – welcomed the revolution in January 1959, only to find themselves either marginalized by it, or drifting away from its cultural policies and precepts, eventually choosing to leave. These people were liberal in one of two senses. On the one hand, they reacted artistically to the Revolution in a spirit of *por la libre* ('anything goes') (Boorstein 1969: 135), responding enthusiastically through cultural exuberance largely without structure, direction or definition. It was a natural explosion of pent-up expression from intellectuals who had either spent the 1950s in self-imposed European or American exile (rejecting the philistinism of a materialistically-oriented and crime-ridden Cuba and pursuing the artistic Holy Grail in the usual directions for Cuban cultural emigration) or had retreated from an environment that no longer valued their contribution into a hermetic, almost cabbalistic, literary elitism. The result was an effervescence of poetry, narrative and visual arts that put Cuba back on the cultural map, stimulated by the new freedom, new publishing opportunities,[40] a new readership and the knowledge that the rebel leaders were from their same intellectual and social milieu.[41] The principal outlet and stimulus was, indeed, the Monday supplement of the Movement's paper, *Lunes de Revolución*, which, under a small, dynamic group of young intellectuals (especially Guillermo Cabrera Infante, Carlos Franqui, Pablo Armando Fernández and Herberto Padilla), made it the standard-bearer of the new literature (see Casal 1971).

It was, however, this magazine that, in 1961, came into conflict with the new political direction, in an affair over the censorship of a film (*PM*) made by Cabrera Infante's brother that indicated the new limits of artistic freedom and resulted in the supplement's closure, the group's dispersal and Castro's somewhat ambiguous address to a July 1961 gathering of worried intellectuals (*Palabras a los Intelectuales* – 'Words to the Intellectuals'), in which he defined the limits as *dentro de la Revolución, todo; contra la Revolución, nada* ('within the Revolution everything; against the Revolution nothing') (Castro Ruz 1961: 20).

Their position was related to the other prevailing intellectually liberal belief in the artist's role as critical conscience of the Revolution. Responding to two contradictory impulses and events – on the one hand, the hopes for the restoration of the

40. In 1959, the Imprenta Nacional was created, followed by many smaller, specialist, presses – La Tertulia, El Puente, Ediciones Revolución (later Ediciones R), Ediciones Granma, Ediciones Unión, Verde Olivo and others. These were all subsumed into the Instituto del Libro in 1967.

41. In 1967 alone, eight million books were printed, rising to thirteen million the next year, with 600–700 titles (Casal 1971: 456).

intellectual's traditional importance and, on the other, the reality of the gradual marginalization of a group whose standpoints had been developed outside Cuba, within a Western intellectual tradition, influenced by French and central European precepts, this position came increasingly into conflict with a political and social process that had different objectives and priorities and that, through the educational and political revolution, was challenging traditional definitions of the intellectual. For alongside those who sought a role as a 'critical insider', there were a number who revelled in the new emphasis on 'decolonization', seeing their, and the Revolution's, cultural task as the *descolonización de los valores sin perder rigor ni complejidad* ('decolonization of values, without losing rigour or compexity') (Desnoes 1967a: 104). However, as the pre-1959 writers struggled for a role within a process that was radicalizing faster than they could comprehend and in unfamiliar directions, leaving them either behind or on the sidelines (Fernández Retamar 1967a: 170), many had recourse to pre-1959 criteria in their work. The result was, once again, conflict between the new pressures of the 'siege' and a viewpoint that made little sense to many activists. One outcome was the UMAP episode, when, after 1965, a number of younger, more rebellious and unorthodox, writers were detained and sent to UMAP camps for 're-education', until UNEAC intervened to persuade Castro to close the camps; another was further emigration and, eventually in 1971, 'the Padilla affair' (Kapcia 1983; Index on Censorship 1972).[42]

Nonetheless, whatever the definition of liberalism, all those people, groups or postures that identified themselves, or were identified by others, as such, found themselves marginalized by the mid-1960s, not only by the political vanguard, but also by the average Cuban, who was increasingly unable to understand the positions that they posited.

The second challenge to the rebel discourse came, more significantly, from the Left, from the PSP, although this did not constitute a challenge until it was itself challenged. Any inherent mutual suspicion and antagonism between some PSP cadres and some guerrilla rebels had been largely smoothed out by 1961, when Castro's recognition of the need for a reliable political structure to effect the revolutionary transformation gave the PSP's high-ranking Aníbal Escalante the responsibility of uniting the three rebel forces into a single body, as the basis of the future PURSC (announced on 26 July 1961). The date of that new body (16 April 1961) – and not 1925 – is, indeed, still recorded as the founding date of the

---

42. The affair was triggered when Herberto Padilla, winner of the 1968 UNEAC poetry prize, praised the work of the émigré novelist Cabrera Infante and criticized that of Lisandro Otero, a more politically acceptable writer and cultural diplomat; Padilla's work had already been criticized by UNEAC, along with that of the winner of the theatre prize, Antón Arrufat. Now Padilla was detained and then issued an *autocrítica* (self-criticism), resulting in a hostile reaction abroad, especially in France, where previous sympathizers condemned 'Stalinism' and 'censorship', in turn generating a fierce polemic against them from Cuba.

eventual PCC (Partido Comunista de Cuba – Cuban Communist Party), and the youth wings had already been fused in October 1960, merging the Movement's AJR (Asociación de Jóvenes Rebeldes – Association of Rebel Youth) – founded in 1960, significantly on Martí's birthday, 28 January – and the pre-1959 JS, but still under the name of the AJR.

The new body was the ORI (Organizaciones Revolucionarias Integradas – Integrated Revolutionary Organizations), with some 15,000 members (Domínguez 1978a: 321). In March 1962, however, Escalante announced the ORI National Directorate of twenty-five, fourteen from the July 26 Movement, one from the Directorio, and no fewer than ten from the PSP. It then rapidly became clear that Escalante, following either advice from Moscow or his own political nose, had assigned too much power to the PSP, which, for all its usefulness, did not, in many rebels' opinion, deserve to share power equally with the Sierra group. Moreover, it transpired that there was a well of grass-roots Movement resentment in the *ad hoc* workplace-based *núcleos de revolucionarios activos* (NRA – 'nuclei of active revolutionaries'); that most had appointed secretaries from the PSP (with Escalante reserving the right to approve all party posts); that PSP cadres had even tried to undermine the 26 July people in the FAR (by dispatching them to the EIR and replacing them with their own members); and that, overall, the new party was not so much 'integrated' as 'organized' (by the PSP).

Betraying deeper tensions, and growing Cuban dissatisfaction with Soviet economic advice and heavy-handedness, the crisis exploded when, on 13 March 1962, Escalante made a speech on the anniversary of the death of the DRE's Echevarría without mentioning his Catholicism. On 26 March Castro, taking that as his cue, denounced *sectarismo* (sectarianism) in general and Escalante in particular, who was ignominiously sent into a diplomatic semi-exile in eastern Europe, and the ORI was suspended, half the members being expelled (Domínguez 1978a: 213).[43] In its place, the PURSC (Partido Unido de la Revolución Socialista de Cuba – United Party of the Cuban Socialist Revolution) was formally set up in a February 1963 congress, with a much more selective membership procedure,[44] which meant that, by 1963, over half the members were new (Domínguez 1978a: 214), a membership rising to 32,537 by 1964 (Domínguez 1978a: 321). This whole episode effectively began a steady downgrading of the PSP within the structures, so that, even after the PCC was established in 1965, based on the PURSC statutes, there were only twenty-three PSP members on the 100-strong Central Committee and none at all on the Buró Político (Domínguez 1978a: 310). Moreover, the party itself remained small, with only about 50,000 members in 1965 and 200,000 in

---

43. Interestingly, the youth organization, renamed in April 1962 the Unión de Jóvenes Comunistas (Union of Communist Youth – UJC) kept its new name, but had no further congresses until 1972.

44. Members were selected by their workplace colleagues as 'exemplary workers'.

1972 (Suchlicki 1988: 11). In the end, therefore, the carefully constructed PSP influence within the new structures was substantially weakened, and even the new, merged, newspaper – *Granma* – carried a name more redolent of the 26 July Movement's past than the PSP's.

However, for all its specific significance, the affair revealed a deeper tension between the 'orthodox' radicalism (represented by the PSP – and therefore Moscow) and the decidedly unorthodox radicalism of the young rebels, whether of Castro's movement or the DR. This was already evident in tensions between individuals and groups, and would be echoed later over the Missile Crisis, the 'Great Debate', Third World policies, the second 'Escalante affair' of 1968 (see later), and all the subsequent debates.

At one level, this tension was a complex ideological debate about 'subjective conditions' and 'objective conditions' for revolution, reflecting a wider instinctive argument between 'scientific' and 'voluntaristic' approaches to Cuba's problems. The 'scientific' label referred to the orthodox position adopted, as we have seen, by the Browderist PSP and Moscow about the structural inability of a country to move towards revolution and socialism in advance of the objective conditions for it, which, in the context of Latin America, meant once feudalism had disappeared and capitalism had created its own internal contradictions. The communists' role was, therefore, to work patiently with 'progressive' forces, concentrating on elections, alliances and the small industrial working-class – precisely the Cuban party's policy from the 1930s. Therefore, no matter how popular or radical the Revolution might be, the PSP argued that it was still not ready to advance to socialism, which implied the need for strategic internal and external alliances, the postponement of ambitions and economic caution.

The alternative view, represented instinctively by the Movement and, increasingly, more intellectually by Guevara, was that the 'objective conditions' for revolution could actually be created by the 'subjective conditions' (meaning the actions of dedicated revolutionaries), precisely as had happened in Cuba, where the unfavourable conditions of 1953 had been converted into the victory of 1959 by dedication, political skill and struggle, not by waiting but by acting. While it would be some years before Guevara, above all, articulated this posture in Marxist terms, it was already implicit in the tenor, attitude and actions of the *sierra,* who all, like Guevara, tended to theorize from empirical positions.

Later on, this was precisely the conflict of perspectives manifested in the mid-1960s 'Great Debate', for many either the epitome of the early internal battles or the last fling of the 'pragmatists' within the Revolution before the Guevara-influenced 'idealists' began to have their way, with disastrous economic consequences. It is by no means easy to summarize the complexities of the motives, discussions and outcomes of the 'Debate', nor, indeed, to define when it actually took place. Certainly, by 1963 it had begun and by 1966 it had apparently been resolved.[45] In between, it involved the remarkable phenomenon of an officially encouraged intellectual debate, in the pages of the contemporary academic and political journals, between at least two schools of socialist economic thought in Cuba, a debate encouraged by a vanguard anxious for practical solutions to the questions posed by succeeding post-1959 economic failures engendered by following conventional economic models (see especially Mesa-Lago 1978; Martínez Heredia 1989; Tsokhas 1980; Bernardo 1971; Brundenius 1984: 49–53). The first model had been the Keynesian and New Deal-inspired ideas associated with the UN Economic Commission for Latin America (ECLA) under Raúl Prebisch – structuralist reform to escape from the development trap that Prebisch had identified for Latin America. These ideas implied export and agricultural diversification, land reform, protectionism, import-substituting industrialization, welfare and a state economic role, and had been broadly applied in Cuba until 1961, when capital shortage, the private sector's weakness, the embargo and the political shifts made them untenable. That model had then been followed, until about 1963, by an intensification of these ideas based on the 1930s Soviet experience – of a growing state role leading to centralization, command planning (through JUCEPLAN – the Junta Central de Planificación – Central Planning Board), agricultural collectivization, heavy industrialization, an accelerated shift away from sugar and an expensive social revolution, all underwritten by Soviet support. This model (which, without the political connotations, might be termed 'Stalinist') had collapsed by late 1962, in the face of plummeting sugar production, inefficiency and tensions between Cuban ambitions and Soviet advice.

There was a further complication in that, even with the second strategy, there was no consistency or coherence in the policies followed, since economic decision-making was split between one set of policies in the industrial area (managed by Guevara and his supporters), and another in the agricultural and foreign trade sectors (run by Carlos Rafael Rodríguez, Alberto Mora and the post-1961 Director of the National Bank, Marcelo Fernández Font). Such incoherence could not continue, whatever the overall strategy.

Thus, especially after March and October 1962, the way was open for a new economic path; the only problem was identifying it, and choosing between those (most notably around Guevara) who argued for a radical break with existing models, and those (around the old PSP, supported by foreign advisers, such as René Dumont and Charles Bettelheim) who still argued for a less ambitious version of the second strategy. Castro, unable to decide, therefore called for the 'Debate', which continued until 1965, when Castro declared the strategy to be followed thenceforth.

The two sides were, however, never clear-cut, and did not break down easily into ideological categories. On the one side, the 'orthodox' argument was that

45. Most commentators suggest that it lasted between 1962 and 1965 (Fitzgerald 1994: 49).

Cuban underdevelopment imposed objective constraints on the Revolution's ability to accelerate and spread the social, political and economic transformation process, all of which meant the *a priori* need for a pattern of economic change based on the retention of certain key mechanisms of the pre-existing capitalist system in Cuba, most notably efficiency criteria, market mechanisms, decentralization, indicative planning, bank credit and investment decisions, material incentives and a concept of enterprise profitability. The underlying socialist principle was that enterprises would be autonomous, trading with each other in 'commodities' on the basis of the Marxist 'law of value'. While this position was seen as a realistic or pragmatic strategy in the light of the distorting social and economic effects of Cuba's previously dependent relationship with the United States, it also claimed legitimacy from Lenin's New Economic Policy, which had also addressed the need to correct the economy by conventional means before the political revolution could be enacted.

Set against this was what is often called the 'radical' or 'idealist' camp, seen as radical both through its strictures and its leading exponents, who were, besides Guevara, the emerging 'dependency' analysis around the American journal *Monthly Review* and the Belgian Trotskyist Ernest Mandel (Lowy 1973: 35–74). This position differed fundamentally from the 'orthodox' view in that it argued that political consciousness (supposedly created by the right economic conditions) did not in fact depend on economic change but, rather, could actually help contribute towards that change, since the law of value had little relevance for what was an essentially underdeveloped and dependent economy in the process of revolution, a situation that created its own rules and that made need, and not value, the priority. The economic argument here was that planning and any degree of socialization of the means of production (implicit in a socialist revolution) would distort the capitalist market, meaning that market mechanisms could not be relied upon to function properly, while the retention of capitalist mechanisms of any kind would simply exacerbate capitalism's inherent inequalities and perpetuate capitalist thinking. Thus, set against the idea of autonomous enterprises trading in 'value', they posited the idea of the national economy as one single enterprise, controlled by central planning and a budgetary system of finance that would allocate resources to enterprises according to social need, which, rather than efficiency, would be the principal guide to decisions, with traditional incentives and accounting having a role, but a much reduced one.

The detail of the 'Debate' is given here simply to demonstrate that it really did not reflect conventional criteria of 'hard-line' and 'soft-line', 'reformist' and 'radical' or even 'idealist' and 'pragmatic'. For the supposedly idealist arguments were actually partly driven by the practical realities that Cuba then faced – increasing political demands by a more radicalized population, capital shortage, a suffocating embargo, a new trading relationship that hardly obeyed market rules, and a shortage of material goods to soak up the surplus money that social reform had generated. The supposedly pragmatic argument, on the other hand, assumed a number of factors that simply did not, and could not, exist then in Cuba. Moreover, there was an underlying motivation to both positions, namely that, while Comecon's idea of the 'socialist division of labour' had apparently given Cuba a role as provider of raw materials to the more developed eastern European countries, to the 'radicals' socialism meant equality between trading partners as well as within a socialist society.[46] The argument that Cuba's future should be industrial thus reflected a determination to go beyond this new 'socialist dependency', while the counter-argument that Cuba's 'comparative advantage' lay in sugar reflected both realism and the needs of the new trading partners.

At one level, therefore, the 'Great Debate' reflected the other early political tensions between 'orthodox' (or 'old') communists – guided by Moscow in their views about Cuba's role, future, direction and orientation – and the less orthodox and more empirical rebels. It was, however, not that simple, not least because the apparent settlement of the 'Debate' was actually a compromise – with a sugar-based future based on central planning – that reflected economic realities as well as political balance. Moreover, even when the 'moral economy' took off in the late 1960s (see Mesa-Lago 1978; Kahl 1970), apparently following the 'radical' arguments, the supposed 'losers' were never marginalized and, indeed, re-emerged after 1970 to take their place again in the new economic direction.

How, then, can we interpret these tensions, arguments and differences in ways that help us to understand what was actually going on? The answer, once again, lies in the realm of ideology, but, rather than in the conventional sense of either 'ideological versus pragmatic' or 'hard-line Marxism' versus 'unorthodox idealism', in an understanding of the ideological effects of Cuba's previous and surviving experience of dependence, neocolonialism and underdevelopment.

For what this analysis of Cuban history has revealed is the constant tension, since at least the late eighteenth century, between two essentially different perspectives of Cuba (its past, its present, its nature and its future): between, on the one hand, what we might call an 'externally-oriented' (or 'externally-focused') perspective, seeking inspiration, guidance and legitimacy in essentially exogenous criteria and models, and, on the other, an 'internally-oriented' or 'internally-focused' perspective, seeking the same things in endogenous criteria and models. These perspectives are, in a sense, a philosophical version of the familiar economic models of *desarrollo hacia fuera* (outward development) and *desarrollo hacia dentro* (inward development), with which students of nineteenth- and twentieth-century Latin American economic history are familiar. The division was inevitable, as

46. Although Cuba did not join Comecon (the Council for Mutual Economic Assistance – CMEA) until 1972, it was still affected by its guidelines, as most trade was with Comecon members.

Spanish colonialism, followed by American neocolonialism, proceeded to set up externally-derived models (of thinking, economic orientation and political structure and action) and, in the process, necessarily to degrade, denigrate, subordinate and weaken any internal alternative to this pattern. While this experience of what Freire has called 'cultural invasion' (Freire 1972: 121) was little different to that of any other dependent Third World society, the circumstances of Cuba's experience in the two centuries before 1959 made the pattern of hegemonic control even sharper, and even more firmly embedded, to the extent that, by 1959, one can talk of discourses rather than perspectives, and even therefore of discourses within the emerging ideology.

We have, indeed, already seen how even *cubanía* itself encompassed perspectives that were either *anexionista* (or *neoanexionista*), *cultural*, or *rebelde*; it was therefore logical that, even after 1959, there should be no clear-cut consensus about what the new revolutionary perspective actually meant. After all, one of the essential problems with seeking guidance from internal models and criteria in a situation of dependency, 'cultural invasion' or hegemonic control, is that those in the dependent, 'invaded' or controlled society often lack the confidence and the intellectual tools to identify such criteria and models, and must either invent or imagine them, or identify them only when the systems of control and hegemony have been weakened through external factors, thus temporarily creating 'spaces' within the fabric of dependence. By definition, therefore, a dependent society that embarks on a revolution must be in a situation where control has not just been weakened, but has broken down, for the dissidents among the 'invaded' to contemplate and enact their rebellion and to identify alternatives within themselves. However, the fact of rebellion, while it creates a new confidence, does not, and cannot, immediately destroy old patterns of thinking, which must lead to the situation of 'competing discourses' within the new and evolving revolutionary ideology as the processes of economic, social and political change create a new context for that ideology to either cohere, adapt or evolve further.

In this respect, therefore, the tradition of an 'externally-oriented' discourse in Cuba can be seen to be reacting to the endemic lack of collective self-confidence and also, before 1959, to the complication of rising prosperity on the surface, creating a tension between a subliminal awareness that the underlying lack of self-belief is being countered by the attractions of security and material advancement arising from the dependent relationship. In this context, the exogenous models and criteria were naturally accepted as either inherently better, or more appropriate, for Cuba and the Cubans, and psychological stability depended on the elimination of thoughts of a 'dangerous' alternative discourse; Cubans were obliged to believe patriotically in the rightness, appropriateness and inevitability of such exogenous models, since endogenous solutions were, by definition, impossible, unstable and even unnatural. It was this thinking that had allowed no fewer than four incarnations of annexationism to survive, all of them perceiving themselves, and often perceived by others, as patriotic and as *cubanista*.[47]

On the other hand, the 'internally-oriented' discourse sought answers, solutions and models – as well as a definition of *nación* and the 'essence' of *Cuba Libre* – at times of stress, crisis and external pressure (when the walls of dependence had been breached or undermined, and therefore when the legitimacy of the exogenous models had been undermined and the self-confidence of their adherents had been weakened) or, alternatively, at times of heightened politicization.

In this light, therefore, the early and later debates of the Revolution, and the tensions, 'factional' disputes, political 'battles' and apparent confusion of the whole trajectory can be seen as not only the reaction of a Third World country to the pressures and changes in a world over which Cuba exercised no control, but also as the manifestations of these 'competing discourses'. Thus the early 'liberal-radical' tensions were essentially a competition between the two discourses, in which those who adhered, consciously or subconsciously, to the externally-oriented discourse sought definition (as well as security) in exogenous models and criteria of economic, political, intellectual and cultural behaviour and thinking, while the alternative discourse sought the answers in 'Cuban' criteria and empirical models. Equally, whatever the specifics of the circumstances, motivations and arguments of the PSP–*sierra* tensions, all these differences can be seen in terms of an inevitable competition between exogenous and endogenous models and criteria. In this sense, Rodríguez, Escalante, Pazos and Padilla were simply following a long tradition of *cubanía* that understandably sought its answers outside Cuba.

This pattern becomes clearer when one considers the process of transformation after the 'Debate', which, coinciding with the creation of the PCC, saw the leadership embark on a campaign of radicalization that took to their logical conclusions the directions hinted at early on.

After the 'Debate', for example, came the 'moral economy' – so called because the strategy, taking Guevara's concepts of subjective conditions and the ideas of voluntarism and revolutionary consciousness, set out to construct a communist society as soon as possible. The most visible mechanism for achieving this was the application of 'moral', rather than material, incentives, on the grounds that the use of the latter would ensure the survival of a capitalist mentality and mechanisms. Moreover, Cuba's parlous economic state and the embargo meant that material incentives threatened instability, as the economy lacked the basis for them, in either wages or goods (Silverman 1971; Bernardo 1971; Mesa-Lago 1978).

Moral incentives thus took several forms – emulation, entry to the party, workplace recognition, and so on; but the ethos was also reflected in the general emphasis

---

47. The four 'incarnations' are: pre-1860s (the real and explicit 'annexationism'); between the two wars of independence; under the Platt republic; and, finally, after 1934.

on wage equality, the move away from money transactions, voluntarism, and, above all, the concept of the 'new man'. Superficially, this latter concept simply seemed to be a translation to the Cuban context of earlier Soviet ideas, filtered through the writings and promptings of Che Guevara, who outlined the need for a new conciousuness, to be embodied in a 'new man'. As we shall see in Chapter 5, however, the idea had a definite *cubanista* pedigree, prefigured in the Movement's manifestos, and in the thrust of much of *cubania*'s moralism.

Increasingly, this economic moralism was linked to the public commitment (made in 1963) to produce, in 1970, a record 10-million tonne *zafra*, compared to the previous record of over 7 million and the norm of between 5 and 6 million. The process, whose political objective was clearly to galvanize the population to a goal with both political and economic benefits and, potentially, leading to greater economic independence, would involve even greater mobilizations, sacrifice and collective identity, and would distract attention from short-term austerity and failures (by 1963 the Soviet-backed industrialization drive had faltered, and rationing had become a daily fact) by focusing on a future aspiration. The social objective was linked to the economic – 10 million tonnes of sugar would, it was hoped, be enough to meet trading obligations and sell the surplus on the world market, thus helping to liquidate the debts to Moscow and begin investing capital in longer-term social improvements and economic diversification.

By 1968, the drive was faltering, with growing political tensions, evident, for example, in an increasing absenteeism, a disenchantment with the trade unions (which, by then, had tended to become mechanisms for mobilization and labour discipline, rather than for effective representation), and a tendency towards disorganization and bureaucratic inertia – what Dumont called the 'bureaucratization of anarchy' (Dumont 1970).

The stresses were addressed in two specific ways. Firstly, in February 1968, the 'Escalante affair' reared its head again. Having returned from eastern Europe in 1966, Escalante had proceeded to form within the party a group of like-minded members whose goal was both to deflect the Revolution from its 'chaotic' and heretical path, especially in the economy and abroad, and to redress the imbalance between the 'new communists' (now clearly dominant and defining socialism in their unorthodox way) and the orthodox arguments of the 'old communists', which had been defeated in 1962 and in the 'Debate'. It thus represented both a personal and a political campaign, partly encouraged by a Moscow that looked askance at Castro's heresies and feared for the stability of 'peaceful coexistence' with the United States if Cuba's continental insurrectionary campaign continued. The result was, however, predictable: Escalante was again detained, his *microfacción* was uncovered, and he was sentenced to thirty years' imprisonment. The fact that this resurgence of *sectarismo* coincided with a campaign being waged against *burocratismo* (bureaucratism) in the system enabled the vanguard to present them both in the same light, as the same problem; indeed, one purpose of the rebels' general resistance to institutionalization after 1962 was their recognition that it might easily allow PSP elements to re-emerge and renew their attempt to take over the Revolution. Therefore, although bureaucratization resulted from general administrative inefficiency and inexperience, the prioritization of political over economic goals, and the centralization of economic control, it symbolized the dangers of orthodoxy, inertia and perspectives that looked outwards rather than inwards.

The problems were also addressed in the March Revolutionary Offensive, which meant the state takeover of all remaining small enterprises, such as 11,878 grocery stores, 6,653 laundries and eight electrical stores (Huberman and Sweezy 1969: 134–5). Designed to reactivate the flagging morale of the workforce (and perhaps redress the demoralization following Guevara's death in October 1967), the move actually worsened the situation, exaggerating disorganization as an already inefficient state structure now grappled with the administration of the smallest enterprise at street level, as morale sank even lower and absenteeism increased, reaching 29 per cent in 1970 (Fitzgerald 1978: 11). So great was the problem, indeed, that an anti-loafing law was introduced in 1971.

Meanwhile, the political system was now characterized more by movement and mobilization than by consolidation and representation. The party existed, but never met in a national congress, and tended to consist of the *sierra*-dominated Central Committee at the top and, at the grass roots, cells acting without national coordination and with few ways to channel their views. The CDRs were, as we have seen, in some decline, and the attempt to set up a local government system, Poder Local (which involved assemblies at work and elected some 10,887 delegates in 1966) (LeoGrande 1979: 46), had stagnated by 1968.

Cuba's external image, and the internal feeling, were still however characterized by revolutionary zeal, commitment and change, an image exemplified by the Revolution's external projection. From 1961, but especially once the Missile Crisis gave the Cuban leadership the reason and the space to embark on a more ambitious policy, the insurrectionary foreign policy of the two Declarations of Havana (1959 and 1962) took shape as a sustained strategy to support revolution throughout the Third World, by funding, training and arming a plethora of Latin American guerrilla groups, and with contacts with, and support for, African liberation groups (notably the Algerian FLN and the Angolan MPLA) (see Domínguez 1989c; Aguilar 1983). It was this manifestation of radicalism that took Guevara first to the Congo (to support an anti-Tshombe rebellion, in 1965), and then, in 1966, to attempt to establish the continental *foco* in Bolivia, leading in October 1967 to his death.[48]

---

48. The *foco* was the name given by Guevara to the free-standing guerrilla group that would operate in the countryside, among the peasantry, acting as the vanguard (the 'subjective conditions') of the revolution. The whole approach was given the term *foquismo*.

For all this new radicalism's internationalist focus and character, its underlying *foquismo* can actually be seen as an external dimension of the strategies and postures being adopted by an increasingly 'inwardly focused' Revolution. Further manifestations reinforce that view – the commitment to the 'moral economy' and to the 1970 *zafra*, the 'Revolutionary Offensive', and the tendency towards a defensive exclusivism that increased towards the end of the decade as the economy failed, Guevara was killed, internationalism seemed defeated and the internal political pressure grew.

The discourse of *cubanía rebelde* – the version most associated with the young rebels – thus evidently continued to gain gradual hegemony within the Revolution and within popular support, but never totally eliminated the challenges from alternative interpretations. That fact alone also guaranteed that the thrust of the competition between the two discourses would further the process of radicalization. For a truly hegemonic ideology, by definition, allows no challenge, and, thus, no movement for flexibility, reinterpretation and adaptation, and is thus inherently static and conservative, and must necessarily lead to the adoption of inherently conservative perspectives among its adherents. On the other hand, when, as in the Cuban case, an already explicitly revolutionary ideology is unable to dominate completely, the tension and the dialectical relationship between it and its alternative – especially when the latter is also self-consciously radical – must lead to a structural process of debate, reinterpretation, self-criticism and revision that necessarily sustains the momentum of radicalism. In an already destabilizing situation of revolutionary transformation, when the certainties of daily life are either disappearing or being revised radically, the fact that the competing discourses of the Revolution were both in their way radical in intention (with more conservative alternatives gradually becoming either marginalized or discredited) created an ideological environment that could only enhance the revolutionary thrust of the popular process. In this sense, therefore, the 'competition' between the two discourses merely reinforced the already identified affinity and fusion between the two levels of ideology – popular and intellectual – since, by the late 1960s, *cubanía revolucionaria* could be said to be explicitly Marxist in inspiration and direction, and thus capable of accepting both interpretations of the hegemonic intellectual ideology, unconsciously gravitating towards the 'inwardly oriented' perspective, but more consciously attracted by the 'outwardly oriented' discourse, which offered protection, security and stability. Thus, as we shall see, when circumstances in Cuba changed to make stability seem even more attractive, as an alternative to exhausting radicalism, there was a natural willingness to shift towards the alternative pole of Marxist discourse.

Thus, the image and reality that the Revolution presented both to the outside world and to its participants was by then one of a largely 'inwardly oriented' radicalism, which, as such, tended to look in two ideological directions simultaneously. On the one hand, there was an evident and explicit commitment, in the vanguard and, increasingly, throughout the population, to an overtly revolutionary definition of socialism and communism, based on empirical criteria, the uniqueness of the Cuban case and the commitment to a subjectivist version of Marxism. The organic connection between this manifestation of Cuban socialism and the pre-existing traditions was not always clear to many outsiders at the time, who often tended to compare the Cuban case to Mao's China, the Vietnamese struggle or the 'pure' radicalism of the early Soviet revolution. There was, however, a connection, for the other ideological direction in which the Revolution of that period looked was towards indigenous Cuban experiences, traditions, models and beliefs. Indeed, once again, the affinity between *cubania rebelde* and the ideas and policies being followed in the name of a particular definition of Marxism was close and intuitively identified by most adult Cubans, to the extent that, by the late 1960s, the *cubania revolucionaria* that had emerged was a fusion of the two radical Cuban ideological traditions – *cubania* and Marxist socialism – both intertwined so frequently since the 1890s that it was more and more difficult to talk of two traditions, of two separate currents. For by then *cubania* organically included an ever stronger Marxist strand, and 'revolution' was being driven by existing nationalist traditions and a renewed commitment to both indigenous and externally-generated definitions of socialism, communism and Marxism.

If we therefore again examine the ideological codes of *cubania* in the late 1960s, this becomes clearer. For example, the agrarianism of the early Revolution was now perceived as something both more organically Cuban and necessarily revolutionary, reflecting the Revolution's roots (in the Sierra), its base (in the *campesino*) and its public commitment abroad (in the support for *foquismo* and the new theory of a revolutionary peasantry). Thus, what was occasionally mistaken for Maoist-influenced policies was actually rooted in the empirical (a reliance on Cuba's two 'natural' resources, its land and people), the traditional (the belief that *Cuba Libre* was to be found in the *campo* and an agrarian future) and the theoretical (with the new thrust of unorthodox challenges to the Marxist canon).

Similarly, activism now meant a revolutionary commitment to an ever more demanding process of transformation, to Latin American and Third World revolution, to a 'guerrilla' definition of economy and society, to mobilization as a way of revolutionizing and a way of being, to the challenges to both Washington and Moscow, and to militant conformism. The 1968 theme of the Revolution as *cien años de lucha* ('one hundred years of struggle') was an explicit identification of the internationalist and socialist transformation that the Revolution then represented with the particularities of a Cuban tradition of struggle.

Equally, the contemporary moralism – so apparently indicative of the process's definition, with the 'moral economy', the 'new man', and Guevara's selfless commitment to the Third World struggle from 1965 – could be seen within a clear Cuban and *cubanista* tradition of *eticidad*. The 'moral economy' came therefore not just from Marx, but also from Martí, the two roots being perhaps more fused in this one code than in any other. Collectivism too, was logically the underlying code of the whole mobilizing system, while culturalism was explicit in the cultural radicalization, not only taking its cue from external definitions of socialism, but consciously building on *cubanista* traditions and the experience and model of the Sierra.

All of this meant that the two most recent pre-1952 codes – statism and revolutionism – were implicit in everything that now happened, to the extent that it is increasingly possible to talk of their fusion into the others. There was no need, in 1968, to talk of statism, since there was no other definition acceptable, with few private farmers, no private enterprise, no private education, and an overwhelming belief among most Cubans that the state had an inevitable duty and ability to provide, protect and unify. Equally, revolutionism hardly needed to be specified, since practically everything that the process did at that time was explicitly or implicitly revolutionary, or seen to be so. Once *cubanía rebelde* became a coherent vision of, and commitment to, *cubanía revolucionaria*, there was no need for a separate code of revolutionism, since every *cubanista* code, which had always had the potential to be revolutionary, had now become revolutionized. Agrarianism, collectivism, moralism, activism and culturalism were now all revolutionary in nature and purpose.

The final code – internationalism, which had begun to evolve so late before the Revolution and had been enhanced in the early days, had also become so revolutionary in its explicit nature and purpose, and so expressive of the process, that it too had a clear identification with the new ethos. Indeed, the Revolution of 1968 was so internationalist in its projection – with the sacrifice of one of its most significant leaders in Bolivia, with its David-like challenge to both superpowers – that it was easy then to forget the code's *cubanista* roots and to see this manifestation as exclusively the result of the 'new' Marxism. In fact, as we have seen, this code was *cubanista* to the core, and its popularity reflected not just a commitment to revolution abroad, but an enhanced sense of *solidarismo* and a fierce collective – national – pride in Cuba's achievements, struggle, defiance and isolation. In a sense it was *cubanía hacia fuera* (outward-projecting *cubanía*), the necessary concomitant, rather than the opposite, of a *cubanía hacia dentro* (inward-projecting).

However, talk of a radicalizing and directing role of ideology in Cuba immediately brings into focus the critical question of ideological transfer and internalization. For, while one can theorize about what effect the competition of discourses must have had in Cuba, and while there is ample evidence of the ideological debates' being fierce and relevant both within the vanguard and among the many grass-roots activists, the critical question is: to what extent, and how, was this debate (and its radicalizing effects) internalized in the average Cuban, and how did the process of ideological socialization actually occur?

The first part of the answer must lie in the collective milieu of the revolutionary transformation, for not only was this a new experience for most Cubans, but a profoundly liberating and empowering one. Moreover, the internalization of an ideology must necessarily be a dialectical process between the collective context and the individual conversion, for what is necessarily an individual act of cognitive identification, persuasion and then commitment is also one that seeks to lose the individual within a collective definition, since ideology can only be about a shared vision and will therefore always define itself, and seek uniformity, within the collectivization of belief. An individual ideology makes no sense; ideology is always collective. It therefore follows that an effective process of internalization of a shared ideology depends on the extent of the consensus of the collective context and the social and political processes that constitute that context.

The starting-point for any explanation of the process of internalization in the 1960s must, therefore, be the deeply traumatic collective experience of a movement for social reform that revolutionized everyone's world, preconceptions and sense of identity, the experience of a collective sense of shared sacrifice for the greater good, of a shared struggle against overwhelming odds, of being given responsibility for the defence, education and liberation of the wider society and the future nation, and of real, furious and unprecedented debate. The whole experience created a deep and lasting sense of community – a community of suffering, of celebration, of hope and of work – always within an atmosphere of heightened excitement, alert and pressure. In such a context, the reaction of many newly politicized, and often newly literate, Cubans was to respond to their new individual historic responsibility by losing themselves within the collective struggle.

However, this process of self-liberation was taking place within forums (CDRs, militias, cooperatives, literacy brigades and so on) where the leading and most attractive discourse was the 'inwardly-orientated' version that posited self-reliance and self-belief, which indicated that, while the 'problem' lay outside (and not 'inside', as they had been encouraged to believe), the 'solution' lay within – within Cuba and therefore within each Cuban. It was a voluntaristic ethos that, in its immediacy, urgency, determination to break from orthodox norms, and self-belief, prefigured, or reflected, the related simultaneous movements for radicalization that were emerging elsewhere on the Left, to be characterized loosely as the 'New Left', in which the fatalism, conservatism and objectivism of the traditional forms of dissent were challenged by younger, more impatient and more self-confident interpretations of the dissident traditions. In Cuba, the mixture of a novel self-confident discourse, the daily experience of empowerment and the new sense of community all combined to intensify the radicalizing thrust of the discourse.

In this context, therefore, the actual mechanisms of socialization were perhaps more effective than one might otherwise expect. One outstanding example is the series of manifestos issued during the rebellion, which still remained as the

Revolution's guiding documents, especially given the steadfast refusal to institution-alize through a constitution and the preference for the somewhat *ad hoc* Basic Laws (*Leyes Fundamentales*) of 1959, which – despite the fact that (or perhaps because) they were modified nineteen times by December 1962 (Azicri 1988: 97) – largely codified the empirical process of reform and the underlying principles articulated by Castro in 1953. Given that that 1953 speech had, at that critical moment, responded to most Cubans' readiness to dissent from the discredited system, evoking a whole effective programme of *cubanía* by its explicit and implicit expression of the *cubanista* codes, the close relationship between it and the Revolution's first laws confirmed that pattern of popular identification.

A second set of mechanisms was therefore the universal manifestations of visual and written propaganda after 1959, exploiting both the artistic vanguard's talents and new commitment and also the population's newly awakened enthusiasm. Highly attractive and openly committed posters and hoardings sprang up every-where, television and radio repeated the images of change, slogans abounded (even on bus tickets), usually reinforcing the Revolution's *cubanista* pedigree and the collective mood of determination, and the new press was full of revolutionary news, propaganda, advertisements, calls for action and articles about Cuba's past and the new achievements. The commitment of the popular weekly *Bohemia* was fundamental to this process, becoming a vital tool for the popularization of the Revolution's concerns, while the more predictably committed dailies – *Revolución*, *Noticias de Hoy*, and then *Granma* – carried a full diet of items designed to raise political and historical awareness, and to keep the momentum going to revolu-tionary effect.[49] In a population that had always read newspapers extensively, the new literacy meant an even greater propensity for reading, and a ready audience for press propaganda.

A further mechanism was the first decade's experience of cultural revolution, with the initial enthusiastic explosion of frustrated talent paralleled by a new public for the new art, encouraged to have unprecedented access to the hitherto elitist genres and even to participate in the creation of art (see especially Casal, 1971; Matas, 1971). For the Revolution's new art and literature was doubly democratic – in its desire to bring art to the masses and be visibly committed, and also in its encouragement of a more participatory style of artistic creation. Poetry workshops abounded, most small towns had their *Casa de Cultura* (Culture House), theatre companies such as the Grupo Teatral Escambray (as in the early Soviet Agit-Prop experience) toured the countryside to propagandize (Medin 1990: 131–7) and also involve, and literary contests flourished to stimulate quality and commitment. The result was further empowerment, as people hitherto excluded from art and literature

49. For much of this discussion I am indebted to the unpublished M.Phil. thesis of Grail Dorling (University of Wolverhampton).

now belonged to a society where these things were open to them and their involvement was encouraged, and as they were told that they too could create, that their work was as valid as that of any exponent of 'high culture'. In a context where readership had expanded out of all recognition and where there was a new hunger for literary products, the new artistic focus on *cubanidad* and on the popular aspects of the Revolution drew the uninitiated closer to the core *cubanista* values of the process. There were also other empowering and radicalizing aspects of the artistic revolution in the significant implicit shift from people as object (as theme or as consumer) to people as subject (paralleled by the wider shift of the period); the generally exorcizing tone of much of the early literature (reinforcing the overall rejection of a negative past and the celebration of a positive present); and the tendency of much of the new work to focus attention on the ordinary, the everyday and the *hombre común* ('common man').

In this whole experience, cinema was fundamental, especially given the popularity of the medium in pre-1959 Cuba, to the extent that most urban Cubans were already familiar with it as a medium of entertainment and communication. Now, the new cinema – centrally directed by Castro's former student colleague, Alfredo Guevara, the head of the new ICAIC (Instituto Cubano de Artes e Industrias Cinematográficas – Cuban Institute for Cinematic Arts and Industries), whose foundation in March 1959 showed the medium's importance – responded fully, making itself the most popular, radical and committed form of cultural expression and helping to shape the new consciousness with its emphasis on documentaries, and its epic themes of rebellion, Cuban history, struggle, exploitation and popular life (Matas 1971; King 1990; Medin 1990: 87–99). The changes in the films shown then show the new political goals: in 1959, of 484 films on public release, 266 were American and only 3 from the Socialist Bloc; but by 1970, of the 120 released, 49 were from the Socialist countries and only 11 American (Medin 1990: 92).

The third arm of the ideological process was unquestionably education, one of the Revolution's most public priorities, and already extolled within the *cubanista* codes. The education revolution's whole thrust was, throughout, popular and democratic, with the educational use of abandoned bourgeois properties sending a clear and radical message that expropriation meant the nation's cultural and human enrichment. The seminal Literacy Campaign did more than any other early campaign to strengthen, deepen and radicalize the perceived symbiosis between Revolution and people, creating a new base for the social transformation, as articulated by the rebel leadership; even the basic literacy textbook, *Alfabeticemos* ('Let Us Make Literate'), implied a collective effort for progress. Beyond that, every mass organization became daily involved in the education process, always in an implicitly radical manner, through either collective action, or empirical learning, or the overtly political content of the textbooks (see Medin 1990: 67–84). The literacy primer, for example, had twenty-four key topics, all of them self-consciously political, while the militia's *Manual de Capacitación* (Training Manual) reinforced a *cubanista* definition of revolution, through chapters such as *Carácter Patriótico de la Revolución Cubana,* which explicitly placed the Revolution in a Cuban and a Latin American, rather than a world, context, and talked of unity behind the *programa patriótico de la libertad nacional, el progreso y la democracia* ('patriotic programme of national liberty, progress and democracy') (Departamento de Instrucción, MinFAR 1960: 17). The manual was also divided revealingly into seven sections: on the Revolution, the agrarian reform, industrialization, economic geography, Cuban history, *doctrina martiana* (Marti's doctrine) – consisting of a series of quotations – and *moral y disciplina* (morale and discipline) (see Judson 1984: 232–8).

As with the art, this was all carried out within the context of general enthusiasm for, and gratitude to, the Revolution that had brought this liberation, meaning that those thus educated tended inevitably to be more willing to absorb uncritically the messages that the whole process conveyed and that seemed to reflect their own desires, experience and deep-seated ideological convictions, either pre-existing or developing each day.

Even at the level of the activists, political education was vital, a task carried out mostly through the CDRs and the EIR – where the texts and the message were radical and increasingly Marxist, and where the staff were mostly either from the PSP, the more politically aware of the 26 July Movement's cadres or those among the many foreign sympathizers who came to Cuba to lend support whose judgement and expertise could be used and trusted. While the overall message may not have been uniform (since they too were affected by the 'competing discourses' and the early tensions), the underlying impulse for radicalism was.

These three contexts and mechanisms for radicalization – the collective experience, the cultural revolution and the educational changes – were perhaps to be expected in any revolutionary experience, and certainly in the Cuban case at that time, and they constituted a firm basis for the collective transformation of consciousness. There was also a fourth factor that deserves attention. For, in the specific context of a Cuba where the 'alternative project' was offered by an already radical and radicalizing *cubanía* and where the institutional vacuum had, as we have seen, created a context where this discourse could be effective, its role was more fundamental than might otherwise have been expected. This fourth mechanism for internalization was myth, which is the subject of the following chapter.

Part II
Myth and Ideology

–3–

Myth-making and *Cubanía* in pre-Revolutionary Cuba

If we examine the two pre-Revolutionary centuries in Cuba for signs of the origins of the myths that would later become so significant in the process of radicalization and survival, the most obvious fact is that, until the twentieth century, the ground was relatively sterile, with few myths being evident and with, at best, a small number of 'pre-myths', with the potential to possess a 'story-line' but lacking the substance, the conviction and the context to develop them in coherent form. This is not surprising, since, for much of that period, there was little consensus on the need for any such myths and little clear sense of social identification to provide the ground for myth-making or an audience to which the myths could be interpreted and repeated.

Certainly the period between the 1750s and the 1860s, though critical in the Cuban historical development between a clearly hegemonic and largely unchallenged Spanish colonialism and the start of a sense of *cubanía*, could hardly be described as a 'national' society, or even a 'pre-national' one (one with an ability to produce a viable set of hegemonic or counter-hegemonic myths). Without a sense of 'nation', the lack of social cohesion in a 'pre-national' society leads either to an essentially disaggregated social fabric, with no need even for hegemonic myths on behalf of the colonizing power, or, alternatively, to a coherent and unchallengeable myth-system developed by the dominant ideology. In Cuba, given the island's relative pre-1762 economic, military and political marginality within the Spanish Empire until sugar began to become lucrative and a basis for Spanish intransigence, one cannot really talk of such a coherent myth-system, since a 'Cuban society' was largely an amalgam of Spanish settlers, allied to a relatively small number of families that might constitute a *criollo* oligarchy, together with either a transient urban population or a poor farming sector. Given the early absence of a notable indigenous population – on which to base an 'imagined community' (Anderson 1991) or against which to build a defensive white identity – and even the lack of a significant slave population, there was simply little perceived need for either a hegemonic or a counter-hegemonic system of myths.

In this context, then, any myths that are now identifiable for that early stage were necessarily pre-organic, in that they were not focused on collectively acceptable figures or events, but, rather, on ideas and concepts that might be considered 'mythic' in that they already had a range of perceived but not rationally understood implications. In other words, such ideas might be said to cover all that it was necessary to know about a given society, without specific references and certainly without a 'story-line'.

There were other reasons why this period should see no evidence of clear myths. In a situation where a colonizing power conquers an existing society and then proceeds to dominate it colonially, the resulting colonial society needs to be convinced hegemonically of the justice and naturalness (the organicity) of its state of domination through both an overwhelming and overriding ideology and therefore through the necessary myths to reinforce and distil this. One can find ample evidence of such myths, for example, in the Spanish control of both Mexico and Peru, where there was a clear need to control the previously vibrant mass societies to ensure passivity, acceptance and submission. In the Cuban case, however, genocide had rapidly eliminated a coherent pre-Columbian indigenous society and culture, leaving something of a cultural *tabula rasa* in comparison with the societies where far greater numbers of indigenous Americans still survived. With the evolution of a highly variegated colonial society, almost lacking in social cohesion and resembling more a mixture of a settler enclave, a garrison town and a disaggregated layer of small farmers, there was therefore less of a compelling need to construct a cohesive hegemonic ideology on the part of the Spanish authorities and elite and, hence, no need for any myth system to enforce such an ideology.

Equally, it follows that, if there is no counter-hegemonic challenge to colonialism mounted by a self-confident and nationally-conscious counter-elite, then there can be no compelling need for any counter-myths to enhance that challenge, not least since, in such a society, there can be no necessary 'story-line' – based on a past glory (perceived or real, and now suppressed), on some defeat that has created the present situation, on a history of post-conquest suffering, struggle and resistance, or on some perceived and shared sense of a 'destiny'. One basic feature of politico-historical myths is that they tend to be all the more powerful and evident in those societies where a perceived 'story-line' is evident and acknowledged, running counter to an aspiring hegemonic version. A society seeking to discover, define, protect or rescue a lost sense of 'national identity' (by definition, a conquered society) will produce its organic myths to express the ideology underpinning that claim; there must necessarily be a consensus, in a sufficient number of groups or layers of the colonized, defeated, subdued or satellite society, that there is a 'nation' to discover, define, protect or rescue. In pre-1860s Cuba, no such consensus existed; therefore, there can have been no such counter-hegemonic ideology, and no politico-historical myths.

Once sugar began to become the basis of Cuba's economic and colonial value, and after Spain had lost its mainland colonies, a more conscious Spanish attempt was made to create a hegemonic ideology of loyalism and natural colonialism, based on myths that supported Spain's claim to legitimacy in Cuba (such as those largely adhered to by Saco and the early *criollo* Reformists) (Schmidt-Nowara 1995a: 110–12), and on notions such as those suggested by the often repeated epithets for Cuba, *la perla del Imperio* ('the pearl of the Empire'), *la perla de las Antillas* ('the pearl of the Antilles') and *la isla siempre fiel* ('the ever-faithful island'). By definition, therefore, this new situation should have engendered obvious possibilities for the creation of a counter-ideology, most notably through a series of counter-myths, especially given the social and political divisions that now arose in Cuban society. However, this did not really yet occur, because of the weight of both Spanish oppression and Spanish numbers, making the *criollos* in Cuba less able to claim to represent a majority struggling for liberation from an insignificantly small minority occupation force or population. Moreover, Spain actually did expend relatively little energy during this period in seeking to convince Cubans of the justice of their own oppression, partly perhaps because Spain itself was unconvinced of its own case (with Liberal–Conservative tensions in Spain confusing the colonial project and with a self-image of instability) and partly because the rationale for the persistence of colonialism was so clear and pragmatic – to protect slavery and the white population, and to control the increasing sugar revenues. Thus, there was not even an attempt to enlist the Catholic Church in the colonial project, since that institution remained largely Spanish, urban and bourgeois, with few inroads into, and little interest in, the lower social orders and the growing slave and *mulato* populations.

That issue, however, brings into focus the one area of Cuban life where underlying myths were evolving – in the many Afro-Cuban religions that, syncretically, were beginning to provide solace, cultural identity and social cohesion to both the slaves and the growing layer of *mulatos*. That is not to say that these myths were yet able to offer a counter-hegemony sufficient to represent an idea of 'nation'; but rather that they did, collectively, begin to present a conscious alternative to white Spanish society, as an expression of the 'other' that any counter-hegemonic ideology or myth must encompass. Restricted as yet to Afro-Cubans, the myths of *santería* could not yet constitute such a unifying myth or myth-system, but they already provided the basis for future evolution.

Moreover, slavery itself now began to lay the ground for an eventual 'pre-myth', for the early arguments around slavery tended to focus on Cuba's nature, status and destiny. At a time when the concept of 'nation' was only just beginning to emerge amongst separatist-minded *criollos*, the debate's focus on slavery was indicative, since that institution did indeed lie at the heart of Cuba's continuing domination by the remnants of a Spanish Empire.

Thus the dominant loyalist, conservative, or simply pragmatic constituency argued that slavery was the key to survival, and attempted half-heartedly to construct a viable argument for the naturalness both of slavery as an institution and, alongside that, of Cuba's Spanish links. This is when there was some sympathy in Madrid, although never in loyalist circles in Havana (which tended always to a more intransigent settler mentality) for concessions to Cuban demands for greater autonomy or representation, and when many *criollos* responded by arguing for, and even believing in, the justice of a situation where a more autonomous Cuba would be an accepted part of the Spanish system – perhaps another province of the metropolis (as the Spanish Republic's 1873 constitution indeed stipulated).

Against this was set that argument proposed above all by Varela, that slavery was the expression of an inherently unjust colonialism and that, just as slavery was unnatural, so too was colonialism. At one level, this was simply an astute reflection of slavery's long-term economic weakness, but it also reflected a deeper philosophical and ethical position that would soon become an incipient *cubanía*. Increasingly, 'anti-slavery' became 'a central site for the articulation of elite national identities' (Schmidt-Nowara 1995b: 442), even if that was an identification by denial rather than a clear-cut, consensual belief in abolition. In this context, the victims of the Escalera massacre became mythic heroes for black and white alike, 'resurrected as proto-martyrs' (Paquette 1988: 265).

The ambiguity of this debate was then reflected in the 1868–78 war. Although the first act of the war (Céspedes's freeing of his slaves) was largely practical, as was the subsequent Spanish decision to concede conditional freedom, it also responded to an awareness that, as colonialism meant slavery, then independence could not in principle be based on that same institution. That was the rationale that lay behind the rebel leaders' acceptance of peace terms in 1878, recognizing that the ideas of independence and abolition had become so intertwined among the rebels that a continuing relationship with Spain again made practical sense. Thus, although their position too was largely pragmatic, it also reflected a philosophical posture, as did the counter-argument of the more radical rebels. Indeed, Maceo's symbolic resistance at Baraguá (as a *mulato*) reinforced that reality. The war, however, broke the power of the argument for slavery, which was clearly no longer as necessary as before, being economically moribund, especially in view of the fact that, once the idea and process of emancipation had begun, the momentum of abolition meant that it was only a matter of time before complete freedom came about, especially after the victory of the abolitionist Union in the American Civil War.

The debate had, however, contributed to the construction of an ideology of national identity and to myth-creation in Cuba, for from the debate had come a sense of 'anti-slavery', the notion that slavery had been an unnatural obstacle to the emergence of a 'natural' Cuba – a position containing the seeds of an eventual *cubanía*. Alongside that notion the basis of a later myth now evolved, encapsulating Cuba's awareness of its Africanness and of the iniquity of slavery. This was the myth of the *mambí*, seen as the archetypal Cuban rebel who had fought heroically to the end for his, and Cuba's, freedom. The fact that this figure had a 'story-line' – with a trajectory of uprooting, oppression, self-liberation, *lucha*, and heroic self-sacrifice – gave it a mythic quality that would remain in the cosmology of the eventual *cubanía*.

It might equally be argued that a further 'pre-myth' was evident in the whole question of American annexation; this time, however, it was an idea put forward not by the colonial power to cement its hegemony, but rather by those among the colonized who were not yet prepared to contemplate total separation or who could not yet conceive of an argument for independence. Few Cubans were genuinely annexationist by conviction, with most annexationists being either confused, realist, or opportunist. Amongst the most committed opponents of Spanish colonialism, annexation was believed in through a process of reductionism, whereby, since colonialism was by definition illiberal and the republican United States by definition liberal, then annexation allowed them to adhere to a liberal myth as a vehicle for liberation. Even as a 'pre-myth', however, it had little depth or tenure, unable to exercise any motive power beyond a small group of often masonic conspirators. Certainly, by 1868, the idea was dead, and its mythic potential partly died with it, not least because it always lacked even a potential 'story-line', being associated neither with a real nor an imagined past Cuban success (to which to cling) nor even some past defeat.

However, if annexation did not survive beyond this embryonic stage of mythification, then the United States as an idea certainly did, exercising a powerful attraction and inspiration for countless oppositionists in colonial Cuba until 1898, and even more realists or opportunists after 1902. Here the 'story-line' was convincing – of a postcolonial society that had achieved everything that Cuba could never achieve in terms of success, power, cohesion, self-belief, progress and advancement. To this end, many of the American nation-building myths were imported as part of the new ideological baggage of accommodationism, always to reinforce a potential (and then real) new hegemony after 1902. To the American ethos of achievement was contrasted the Cuban self-image of failure and, while America's frontier myths were taken as proof of an inherent strength in American society and of the rightful power of the *Norte*, Cuba's 'frontier' was always seen, in certain quarters, as a weakness, as proof that Cuba was never far from 'barbarism', especially as positivist notions of 'civilization and barbarism' took hold in the late nineteenth century.

Underlying this myth, and others, was a whole evolving mythology around sugar, and the naturalness or unnaturalness of Cuba's affinity with the crop to which it had been committed since the 1760s. Essentially, two distinct competing myths evolved around the issue. On the one hand there was the myth of Cuba's 'natural' identity and future lying in a full commitment to, and domination by, sugar – a myth made powerful because it was held and propagated by the dynamic, and then dominant, entrepreneurial interests in the colony. As we have seen, it was in the *sacarocracia*'s interest to present the idea that, before sugar, Cuba's 'pre-history' was characterized by *tiempos primitivos* ('primitive times') (Moreno Fraginals 1977: 127), from which developed the ultimately convincing argument that 'real' Cuban history began in 1762. The myth was perpetuated by a whole arsenal of arguments – economic, social and political – that were difficult to counter, given the wealth, stability and confidence arising from Cuba's cultivation of and headlong rush into, the new crop. The familiar phrases about Cuba's being *la perla del imperio* or *la isla siempre fiel* reinforced this, for they assumed that the island's prosperity and loyalty were intimately tied together, a juxtaposition in which sugar (and slavery) was the key. From that flowed the many sayings that were summarized in the often-repeated saying *sin azúcar, no hay país* ('without sugar, there is no country').

The alternative myth, however, posited a genuinely Cuban future in a sugar-free economy. Always a theme of patriotic laments and economic assessments at times of sugar crisis, this was manifested most coherently by Fernando Ortiz, in his notion that Cuba's history was characterized by an essential 'counterpoint', between sugar and tobacco. This was an idea that struck deep chords in many Cubans, and contributed to an ambivalence (after 1921 and 1929) towards sugar. According to Ortiz, the old idea of sugar's being equated with Cuban success was an illusion. On the one hand, Cuba had previously possessed a tobacco cultivation based on an indigenous plant, which was produced labour-intensively and therefore led to employment and a personal identification between farmer and crop and was cultivated by free and largely white labour; its quality gave it its comparative advantage. On the other hand, sugar was an imported crop that was based on slave labour and technology, whose comparative advantage was in its quantity, all of which led inexorably towards greater vulnerability to other producers and other sources (such as beet) and to market cycles. In this light, argued Ortiz, the nineteenth-century battle between sugar and tobacco was unequal and decisive; with tobacco's decline and sugar's rise Cuba's chance of independence disappeared.

The idea, and the myth, which Ortiz's supposedly solid historiographical arguments partly represented but also helped to codify, was attractive in its simplicity. The twin facts that (as Stubbs has shown masterfully) the reality of Cuba's tobacco industry was far from idyllic – displaying proletarianization, capitalization and monopolization, all of which peripheralized and de-industrialized Cuba's production (Stubbs 1985: 52–61) – and that tobacco was not really in decline meant little to those Cubans prepared to believe that sugar was the root of all Cuba's ills, its 'curse' rather than its 'blessing'. Interestingly, even recently one writer was still able to present a broadly similar argument, maintaining that, in the eighteenth and nineteenth centuries, *cubanidad* focused on the question of sugar, with resistance to its expansion and opposition to slavery being linked on the one hand, while, on the other, was ranged the 'power theme', to perpetuate sugar's hegemony (Benítez Rojo 1986: 14). This latter variation of the theme sees an essential division between *Cuba Grande* – 'authoritarian, proud and insensitive' – and a *Cuba Pequeña* ('small Cuba'), which 'looks inward, toward the land, and its culture' (Benítez Rojo 1986: 15). Therefore, although it was some time before Ortiz wrote down his theories to codify the myth, as a myth it clearly existed in the thinking of many Cubans.

In the trajectory of Cuban myth-making, however, the turning-point was clearly the 1868–78 war. Before that, there was little consensus on the idea of rebellion, let alone separation, and, as has been seen, little perceived need among the colonizers to convince Cubans of the naturalness of their subjugation. After 1878, however, the umbilical cord had been ruptured and many watersheds passed – in slavery, annexationism, the idea and deed of rebellion, and ideologically. Thereafter, ideology and, with it, myth, would begin to play a role. After 1878, both the Spanish colonizing society and the newly politicized Cuban counter-society began to produce coherent and identifiable myths; but, given the still as yet not fully formed nature of the political culture in which they operated, these could only at best be pre-myths, based on ideas rather than more powerful and consensual figures or events.

On the Spanish side, there was a clear need now (after rebellion had proved to be a real threat) to convince the defeated Cubans of the organicity of continuing Spanish rule. This was above all achieved through appeals to pragmatism, without myths, as the familiar arguments about the threats of abolition and slave rebellion were again brought out, and as a case was made for some autonomy (based largely on the recognition that many *criollos* had proved their continuing colonial mentality in their preference for surrender rather than an increasingly dangerous separatism). According to this perspective, Cubans would be second-class citizens and prepared to accept that.

If there was a myth to reinforce this claim it was the sense of 'family' that now prevailed, as Cubans were treated culturally as a 'prodigal son' who, having strayed from the family hearth and loyalty, would now be punished but brought back into the 'natural' fold. In the myth, the 'story-line' was clear: the Empire boasted both past glories and an inherent 'spirituality' (set against the crass and non-Hispanic materialism of those who threatened the new 'family' and also against the divisive intentions of a supposedly anti-Hispanic liberalism), while Cubans and Spaniards shared a common religious and racial heritage. This was contrasted to the Protestant societies that interfered repeatedly with the family unity (and to the anti-Hispanic religious beliefs of the 'threatening' black population), and prolonged old concepts of *limpieza de sangre* ('blood purity'), implicitly binding white Cubans with Spaniards against the 'threat' from below. With peninsular immigration increasing, the 'family ties' would be fortified further.

On the Cuban side, too, myths now developed, especially what we could call a myth of a 'pre-nation', in which the now powerfully mythic figure of the *mambí* played a vital role. This was a startling new development, set against the preceding ideas of *cubanidad*, which had invariably excluded the slaves from a vision of 'otherness'. What *nación* mostly meant now was rarely a clear-cut concept of a free, independent and different Cuba, but rather a consensual and emotional identification with an entity that had been glimpsed in the struggles and hopes of 1868–78 and seemed to be represented by the *mambí* – seen less as an Afro-Cuban and more as a free spirit, close to nature (in all its senses – romantically positive and barbarically negative) and an essentially communal being. This new concept of *nación* also involved a sense of rescue, not of a lost 'nation', but rather of a lost precolonial innocence (as the destruction of the indigenous population began to be lamented in literature) and of a 'natural' existence represented by the *campo*. One interesting parallel development in the whole process of myth-making, simul-taneously, was the evolution of the popular myth of the legendary figure of Manuel García, the Robin Hood-style rebel-bandit (the *bandolero*), the so-called *rey del campo* ('king of the countryside'), whose exploits were recorded in oral history and popular culture, and whose legitimacy clearly derived from his participation in the Ten Years War, of which those same exploits were seen as a continuation.[1] Indeed, the war itself was the subject of an incipient myth-making process that would take greater shape after the failure of the second war in 1895–8.

This vague concept was, necessarily, the shared 'lowest common denominator' vision of Cuba. At an individual level, there were many Cubans with clearer, and usually more ideologically driven, visions of a genuinely free nation. Indeed, as the war's social dimensions began to play out after 1878, with new classes, new conflicts and a new awareness, the idea of *nación* began to take shape as an evolving inchoate sense of social identity, rather than an imagined cultural community, in which *nación* was seen as 'we the people', as a fusion of the negated elements of Cuba – the Afro-Cuban, the liberal, the eastern and the rural Cuba that the rebellion had essentially represented. In this sense, the *mambí* became a powerful symbol and a myth in its own right – with a 'story-line' that evoked images of freedom, rebellion, and intransigence.

The evolving idea of *nación* was strengthened by the new experience of mass emigration. Hitherto, emigration (or exile) had been a path trodden by bourgeois intellectuals and political dissidents; now, however, with the translation of a large part of the tobacco industry to Florida, there was a new mass working-class emigration, which meant particular features once it evolved into a definable community. Firstly, it meant a greater likelihood of a genuine and identifiable

1. Interestingly, Cuba's first feature film in 1917 was about García, and, much later, both a radio serial and a comic strip magazine were dedicated to him.

Cuban community than any previous Cuban émigré settlement, with its own structures, linguistic boundaries and cultural forums, a community always more likely to be able to preserve a sense of *cubanidad*. Secondly, as we have seen, it meant a more radical political and social vision of *cubanía*, since the openness to outside ideas that emigration brought, and also the special sense of communal identity, began to change the workforce's political thinking. Therefore, *nación* now evolved as never before, as both a conjunction of values, images and desires (as for those inside Cuba), but also an accentuated sense of both nostalgia and hope for the future, a curious mixture of an imagined entity (perhaps inevitable among economic or political émigrés) alongside the sharper awareness of the fundamentals of the Cuban reality that distance offered.

Therefore it was largely among the émigrés that a clearer sense of *nación* – as *Cuba Libre* – began to emerge and, with it, a clearer context for politico-historical myths that would now have a potential for a 'story-line' of oppression and denial, struggle and emigration. In this context, indeed, *Cuba Libre* became a pre-myth, a symbol, by evoking emotionally and simply a whole narrative of Cuba that was instinctively understood by its adherents and taken to refer to a wider range of more complex, and even contradictory, events, issues, beliefs and programmes. The term (first used in the early-century radical conspiracies, inspired more by French revolutionary concepts of *liberté* than any clear notions of independence) now became a shorthand referential symbol of past struggle and future liberation, avoiding precise definition. To the émigré radicals, *Cuba Libre* conjured up images of past struggles and a destiny where *libre* meant social, as well as political, liberation. However, the only cloud on the horizon of this particular pre-mythic symbol was the fact that, as most emigrant workers were white, this vision did not yet always explicitly include the Afro-Cuban element of national identity. That this early notion of *Cuba Libre* owed much to European Romanticism was not surprising, given the attraction of Western European ideas and intellectual fashions for much of the century; indeed, a good part of the more intellectual and cultural concept of *cubanidad* in the *criollo* bourgeoisie echoed European ideas of the *Volksgeist*, which became fashionable in Spain and Spanish universities in the first half of the century.

Thus, by 1898, there was no clear national consensus of either ideology or myth. *Cubanidad* was beginning to evolve into a more political and ideological *cubanía*, and *nación* was beginning to evoke, and to be distilled in, the pre-myth of *Cuba Libre*; but, while the political struggle was unified until the final stages of the war, the vision behind that struggle was not. After 1902, therefore, the reality of a divided and demoralized nation, following the expectations of 1895, meant that two kinds of myth or pre-myth emerged.

On the one hand, the pre-1895 myths evolved further, but now, in new and less optimistic circumstances, changed their nature, while new counter-myths began to evolve more clearly. Of the old pre-myths, the recently created one of *nación* became understandably ambiguous, characterized by both a lack of clarity and an underlying loss of confidence. It was understandable because the divisions of 1898–1902 and the necessary readjustment after 1902, with its choices between accommodationism and 'betrayal' (the latter already becoming one of the 'patterned categories' of Cuban dissident discourse (Valdés 1992: 217)), on the one hand, and a nostalgic, stubborn, but perhaps costly, resistance, on the other, had destroyed the necessary consensus. If there was no unified social context, there could be no unified myth, and *nación* often came to mean whatever the adherent wished it to mean.

Thus, for an unreconstructed radical, it could still mean the long, unfinished struggle to create *Cuba Libre*, while, for a more pro-American Cuban, it could mean the present 'story-line' of a now liberated Cuba, in which the prosperous present was a continuation of the heroic past. Certainly all those 1895–8 veterans who now adjusted their views to accommodate the new reality needed such a myth to justify that adjustment, and, in this context, *nación* began to be appropriated by the aspiring hegemonic elite of the new Cuba – the 'managerial', dependent, pro-American elite that still paid lip-service to the 1895 ideals. Equally *Cuba Libre* itself became ambiguous, functioning as both a hegemonic and an aspiring counter-hegemonic myth. For the radicals, it was a memory of a heroic struggle and a symbol of the Cuba that might have been, and could still be – although few actually believed the latter in the post-Platt demoralization; for the elite, and other realists, it was a safe reminder of the recent but essentially historical struggle, with no future implications at all, referring at best to the present reality.

Finally, the *mambí* myth became weakened and equally ambiguous, referring both to the symbol of the past struggle (either thankfully forgotten or nostalgically and officially remembered) and also to the pre-1860s 'threat' of the supposed savagery below the surface. For those who aspired to 'Americanize' themselves and Cuba, and to become recognized as a part of the urban civilized world, the *mambí* was a useful symbol of a past that had been necessary to establish the supposed *Cuba Libre* of the present, now building its prosperity in the equally necessary American shadow, but was also a permanent reminder of Cuba's essential 'inferiority' and incapacity if it gave in to its 'natural' self. Indeed, after the end of the war, a conscious attempt was made by white intellectuals to present the *mambí* as a racially unthreatening colour-free Cuban (Ferrer 1995: 215–68). The *mambí* was thus two things. On the one hand, it was the hidden ex-slave behind every Afro-Cuban, the ruthless and bloodthirsty rebel behind any hint of radicalism and the quaint and safe (because no longer present) symbol of a distant 'barbarism'. Thus one could evoke the *mambí* with official and rhetorical vigour while, secretly, breathing a sigh of relief that such things were past. On the other hand, as we have seen, the post-1902 political legitimacy of the war veterans, the *caudillos*, was partly reinforced by their adoption of the label of the *mambisado*. Mostly white officers from the 1895–8 struggle, these politicians did nonetheless gain some measure of credibility from their association with the term *mambí*, and membership or leadership of the equally ambiguous Asociación de Veteranos.

These ambiguities – reinforcing the developing and often deliberate view that racial problems had disappeared with the victory of 1898 (Ferrer 1995) and interwoven as they were with each other – were further complicated by the 1912 PIC revolt, which, as we have seen, so frightened white Cuba that it led to an official amnesia about the past role of the slaves and ex-slaves. Thus, *nación* and *Cuba Libre* could both now be taken to refer to a necessarily white Cuba – past or present – as the consensus on 'blackness' ended.

With the whole question of *cubanía* now open to variable interpretations (arising from the need to either rescue, and redefine, the essence of the denied *nación*, or resurrect old definitions), the once potentially solid and unifying myths now began to break down. At one level, the three pre-1898 pre-myths, or symbols, became fused into one complex and contradictory pseudo-myth, where the boundaries became indistinct, the meanings ambiguous and the uses multifarious. At another level, these also broke down into a number of 'sub-myths', with, for example, the emergence of mythic connotations around the notion of *Oriente* (identified as almost a mystical Avalon and as the 'real' heartland of the patriotic nation) and also of the land, now often seen romantically as the basis of a 'natural' Cuba. It was almost as though the weight of neocolonialism, the ills of the new Cuba and the overall collective depression of expectations meant that even an aspiring dissident *cubanía* could not muster the collective strength to sustain coherent and clear myths, with clear 'story-lines'; instead, refuge was sought in half-myths, in images that did not even aspire to the status of pre-mythic symbols, lacking even the cohesion of a proposition. At best they were symbols that recalled the past and banished the future to the world of illusion. Thus, for example, both *Oriente* and *tierra* (the land), or the *campo*, could be contrasted (as 'naturally' Cuban) to the venality of the white, urban, corrupt and accommodationist western half (which had always been more Spanish and loyalist), but could also be seen as closer to the land-based guerrillas of the Liberation Army. It was now that the mythic qualities of the *guajiro* began to be extolled in literature and in popular verse and song; it was no accident that this figure, seen as the embodiment of the Cuban's supposedly natural affinity for the land, was implicitly white, almost the unthreatening, but also unheroic, version of the *mambí*.

One significant new myth did, however, begin to evolve at one level – the myth of Afro-Cuba and, with it, of the *ajiaco*. Just as political Cuba was beginning to write Afro-Cuba out of the history books and the political project, cultural circles, led by Ortiz, focused attention on this forgotten element, constructing an idea of a present-day Cuba that was, culturally (if in no other way), a fusion of the African and Hispanic roots in religion, dance, music and mythology. In what was effectively the mythic distillation of the emerging current of *cubanía cultural*, this led to Ortiz's concept of Cuba as the *ajíaco*, the particularly Cuban stew consisting of ingredients that were essentially American, Iberian and African in origin. As Ortiz put it, '*cubanidad* is not only seen in the outcome but also in the complex process itself of its formation, disintegrative and integrative, [. . .] in the environment in which it operates and in the vicissitudes of its evolution' (author's translation) (N. Suárez 1996: 12). It also led to the development of cultural *negrismo*, the surrealist art of Wilfredo Lam, the poetry of Nicolás Guillén and other *negristas* and the novels of Alejo Carpentier. *Negrismo* was itself characteristically eclectic, responding to Cuban circumstances and ideas and European fashions of 'primitivism'; but, at a deeper level, it responded to this new myth, which both rescued something of the old folkloric search for *cubanidad* and adhered to the *martiano* notions of a 'colour-blind' Cuba, legitmized by comfortingly repeated quotations from Martí, such as his 1891 words from *Nuestra América*, describing a somewhat idealized vision of the Latin American reality – 'no hay odio de razas, porque no hay razas' ('there is no race hatred, for there are no races': Martí 1975: 100) – and his 1893 assertion from *Mi Raza* – 'Cubano es más que blanco, más que mulato, más que negro' ('Cuban means more than white, more than mulatto, more than black': Martí 1991b: 299). It corresponded, moreover, to the evolution of a more coherent set of beliefs, customs and rituals around the main Afro-Cuban religions and to the reality that these evolving manifestations were beginning to attract white adherents. Thus the political and cultural myth of Afro-Cuba matched the newly unifying myths of religion.

However dubious some of the assumptions might have been around this myth, and no matter how artificial and even somewhat racist the deliberate myth-making might have been – not least in the hands of Ortiz, whose underlying intellectual inspiration continued to be positivism and whose theories of atavism betrayed a disparaging view of the essentially 'barbaric' side to the African element – it nonetheless played a role in the formation of the evolving nationalism and in the evolution of a national intelligentsia. One later example, as we have seen, was Ortiz's influential argument on the mythic 'counterpoint' between sugar and tobacco.

What then of new myths in the new post-Platt Cuba? The first was the emergence of a multifaceted myth about the 1868–78 war, for one way in which the discrepancies around the recent struggles were conveniently manifested as consensual myth was the tendency to mythify that war, now increasingly referred to as the *Guerra Grande* (Great War) or simply the Ten Years' War. These references served several purposes – both hegemonic and counter-hegemonic. On the one hand, by extolling the glory of the first war, the new political elite could distract attention from the more controversial and too recent second war – which, through its length alone, could not aspire to the epithet *Grande* as deservingly as the first – and yet could bestow some vicarious legitimacy on the second war by presenting the first as the real, heroic and historical war for liberation of which the second was the natural culmination. That continuity was helped by the similarity in strategy, fighting and Spanish reaction in both wars, as well as the continuity in the presence of the *mambí*, of Maceo and Gómez in the military leadership and of the commitment of Martí. On the other hand, those who dissented from the new post-1902 regime could also see the first war as the *Guerra Grande*, since it had ended not in humiliating and demoralizing betrayal (as had the second) but, rather, in Maceo's glorious decision not to accept the surrender terms negotiated by the (white) leadership and to fight on, with his now mythically famous Protesta de Baraguá.

There is, moreover, a further, more sinister, significance in the term *Guerra Grande*, in that it stood in implicit contrast to the so-called *Guerra Chiquita* of 1879–80, the war that was largely marginalized in the historiographical canon because of its racial, and thus 'threatening', implications, but that was, evidently, a significant struggle, and deservedly considered by some as the real 'second war', rejecting the conventional tendency to attribute that label to the 1895 war. Even the use of the diminutive *Chiquita* rather than *Pequeña* or *Chica* reinforced that implicit marginalization.

In this second current of thinking, however, there was ambiguity, since this earlier second war was so clearly more inherently, more purposefully and (to the elites) more frighteningly revolutionary than the *Guerra Grande* and, therefore, should perhaps have been expected to be seen as a glorious episode too. The frustration and disappointment of the outcome were, however, enough to create an ambivalence about the second struggle and, in the process, to create a greater mythification of the first. The *Guerra Grande* thus entered popular and official mythology as a strangely unifying myth.

This dual-purpose myth therefore provided a bridge between the would-be hegemonic myths of the second war as a successful struggle and those that were now proposed by a dissident *cubanía* to challenge that hegemony. The most obvious of these counter-myths was, from the start, that around the Platt Amendment.

As Cuban political life began to degenerate in the first twenty years after independence, one alternative to the hegemonic explanations of Cuba's dilemma – in other words, those that sought to explain, and justify, Cuba's prostration as a satellite of the new American metropolis, through either variations of pragmatism or theories of Cuban inferiority and lack of preparedness – was the notion that all Cuba's ills were attributable to *la Enmienda* (the Amendment) and all that it represented. According to this perspective, the Amendment (often simply referred to as *Platt*) was not just the instrument for the United States' neocolonial hold over Cuba and a pretext for constant intervention, but also the symbol of the preceding years of occupation, humiliation and Americanization. It therefore became a referential symbol of Cuba's new perceived dilemma of a questionable independence, a systematic conspiracy to deny Cuba's national identity and a new economic, political and cultural servitude, but, precisely because it had an inherent 'story-line' and even the necessary 'interpreters' (not least in the self-appointed *mambisado* and organizations such as the Asociación de Veteranos and the Liga Antiplatista), it acquired the status of a counter-myth, expressing the essential negativism of the disoriented nationalist constituency.

Thus, while *cubanía rebelde* struggled to find its *raison d'être* and a positive set of symbols around which to rebuild its sense of destiny and nationhood, *Platt* offered a comforting explanation of defeat, one that told a 'sacred tale'. This related the whole trajectory of, firstly, heroic collective struggle led by the incorruptible Martí, then betrayal (by both neo-annexationists and a United States that claimed to liberate but then enslaved), then conspiracy (between Washington, Madrid, Spanish loyalists and new opportunists), and finally coercion (to persuade the Constituent Assembly to sign its own death-warrant) in the genesis and imposition of the *Enmienda*. It also went on to relate the story of further betrayal, corruption and invasion.

As a 'story-line' that convinced through its visible manifestations (the monument to the *Maine*, the American-established institutions, the occupation troops), it challenged the view of inferiority that underpinned the self-deprecating self-image of many Cubans after 1902, by placing the blame on Washington and others, although, ironically, it still objectivized Cuba, implying that the nation was essentially the object, rather than subject, of its own history. *Platt* became the equivalent of *antinación* in nationalist discourse, and the term *plattista* became a synonym for 'treacherous', 'unpatriotic' and *vendepatria* (literally 'selling the country'). Thus, when later historiography characterized the first three decades as the *república plattista*, no effort was needed by Cubans to see what this implied – an inherently anti-Cuban political structure. However negative the myth may have been, it thus offered a perspective to which to cling in the depression of 1902–23, after which it had already acquired sufficient mythic substance to become a wider symbol of betrayal that transcended the narrow and negative perspective of the early years.

Platt implicitly challenged the resurgent myth of the *Norte*, which had evolved from annexationism, through the post-1870s pro-Americanism and the neo-annexationism of the 1890s and the occupation, to gain strength through opportunism, resignation and conviction. According to this myth, Cuba's history of failure (to gain independence simultaneously with its neighbours, to win either war against Spain and to resist American domination and control) was contrasted with the American myth of success, now even more evident after the embarassingly easy and rapid defeat of Spain (the first defeat of a European empire by the New World power) and then, after 1918, the victory over the Central Powers. The myth that equated *Norte* with 'success' – both in its own history and in the promise of personal success that it held out for individual Cubans either by association or by emigration – was a powerful and convincing one in the Cuba of the *seudorepública*.

The second new counter-myth, which began to take more definable shape around the 1920s, was the myth of generations (see especially Valdés 1992: 207–13). There are several reasons why dissidence within a political culture such as Cuba's at that time should have gravitated so evidently towards the motivating power of such a myth. In any society where there is a sufficient popular or intellectual consensus about the notion of national renewal or rebirth (a society that has a pre-existing history to which to return, or on which to rebuild, after some disaster, invasion, occupation or defeat) or in any society where there is a similar consensus on the notion of national unification or reunification, the power of the generational myth is clear. In such a context, where the concept of renewal is fundamental (not least to the society's collective self-belief), generations, and the accompanying notions and implications of re-generation, have the ability to justify both the faith in change that is implicit in the self-image of revolutionary legitimacy and the need for continuity. Faith in change, on the one hand, implies the hope for a future that will correct the failings of the present generation; while continuity, on the other hand, links the present dissidence to a past that is perceived to contain the essence of the denied nation. According to this perspective, each succeeding generation can be seen as taking up the preceding generations' struggle, which has been betrayed by the intervening one. Generationalism therefore offers, simultaneously, optimism for the future and pessimism about the present, a revolutionary viewpoint of change alongside a traditionalist memory of the past; for a dissidence that seeks to be organic, linked to a perceived national past, different from the present denial, the myth of generations offers much and has a clear motive power. Furthermore, generationalism links with other critical notions – such as vanguardism and subjectivism (Valdés 1992: 212–13) – to reinforce their motive power.

In the reawakened and more radical Cuba of the 1920s, the recourse to such a myth was natural, offering a 'story-line' of failure and renewal that was the essence of the evolving dissidence, of the permanent dilemma between rupture with the present and continuity with the past, and of the *cubanista* tradition of cyclical struggle. The concept, and image, of renewal was, indeed, essential to collective self-belief and faith in the eventual destiny of the Cuban nation, for despair was only prevented by a belief in the ever-present possibility of a coming attempt to rescue national identity and pride. The myth of generations therefore now exercised a special motivating and mobilizing force.

Of course, the power of the concept of generations was by no means unique then to Cuba, and many have theorized that the idea is endemic in Hispanic cultures. However, the evidence for a Cuban tradition of generationalism is overwhelming, in historiography, cultural theory and popular mythology, with repeated references to the Generations of 1895, 1930 and, most evocatively, the *Centenario*.

A powerful third myth now evolved to overlap and intertwine with *Platt* and the generational myth – that of José Martí. As we have seen, Martí's death in the first weeks of the 1895 war had removed a significant element of leadership, direction and unity from the liberation struggle; but, in death, he now predictably became a powerful symbol of *cubania*, central to the collective self-image of a defeated but still resistant patriotism. However, between the end of the war and the new 1920s dissidence he was all but ignored, commemorated in a formalistic but somewhat unenthusiastic manner (as on the first Cuban coin in 1912) by the *mambisado* that had survived him to inherit the new Republic. For example, in 1899, only 16 of 105 leading Cuban politicians and intellectuals consulted chose Martí to be the first Cuban leader to be represented in a statue (Santí 1996: 55), and only in 1915 was his first statue erected, in the Parque Central, and that was through public subscription.

This was unsurprising, as his image, and the memory that was retained of him, contrasted so starkly with the corrupt and self-serving reality of the *república plattista* that it was hardly in the interests of the *mambisado* to revive his memory too much. Therefore, what was commemorated was his poetry, his lifelong commitment to *Cuba Libre*, and his death – a self-immolation that had eventually won Cuba its long-cherished independence. All three issues were relatively safe in not challenging the new political situation. What was, however, decidedly not commemorated was his extensive political and social writings, his political activity with the radical Florida workers, the importance of political unity enshrined in his vision of the PRC and his evolving anti-imperialism. There was some acknowledgement of his fears of Washington's imperial ambitions, especially because it suited the Partido Nacional's claim to have inherited the *cubanista* mantle that they present themselves as opposed to the *Enmienda*. Thus Martí's final words about the *monstruo* were remembered and repeated officially by the 'nationalist' camp, as a touchstone, to give rebel authority to those officially associated with Martí's position and to ritualize the underlying discomfort that the accommodationist nationalists felt.

Below the level of formal politics, however, Martí's deeper significance was indeed preserved, especially among those with whom he had identified. For the unionized workers who emerged after 1902, and for the radicalized rebels of the old PRC, Martí was more than a heroic figure and a symbol – he was a political prophet, a deep political and social thinker, and the person whose project most expressed the essence of *Cuba Libre*. Thus, while there was formally an artefactual mythology being created around the figure of Martí, at the level of the residual *cubanía rebelde* Martí was remembered in popular culture – Ibarra cites seven *décimas populares* (ten-line popular verses) that lamented the betrayal of his ideals (Ibarra Cuesta 1994: 200), and a new powerful, more organic, political myth was being created that presented a 'story-line' of Martí's life and death as the manifestation

Figure 1 The first statue to be erected in honour of José Marti, in Parque Central, Havana

of the self-image of *cubanía rebelde* – a story of life, struggle, death and betrayal that seemed to encapsulate the hopes, defeats, frustrations and disillusion of those who adhered to a radical version of *Cuba Libre*. According to this evolving myth, Cuba, like Martí, had struggled since at least 1868 – heroically, in a unified way and with a clear vision of the future – only to be killed (Martí by a Spanish bullet, Cuba by the Platt Amendment) and then betrayed by his fellow leaders.

The myth was all the more powerful for being phrased in such moralistic terms; 'life' also meant vitality, purity and vision, 'struggle' meant heroism and commitment to the cause, while 'death' meant sacrifice and martyrdom, and 'betrayal' laid the blame for Cuba's ills not at his door but at the feet of those whose ambitions meant a rejection of all that he – and Cuba – stood for. It is significant that the later term *apóstol* (apostle) was first coined of Martí by the Tampa tobacco workers after his death.[2]

The myth, however, lacked the necessary 'interpreters', with authority, legitimacy and a platform, to ritualize it, and it thus remained at the level of sub-culture, undeveloped and stubbornly resistant. The year 1923 was to bring such 'interpreters' to the fore in the form of the dissident students who took up the *lucha*. Their fight against corruption – identifying themselves with a key issue that separated the new republic from Martí – placed them firmly and publicly within a *martiano* tradition, and their status as students echoed the intellectual commitment that Martí had represented and legitimized. Their youth, equally, made for an easier identification with images of purity and vision, and, finally, their willingness to act in pursuit of their ideals and of the 'essential' Cuba that they felt had been betrayed by the Generation of 1895 all made them the perfect 'high priests' of the myth.

Therefore, when Mella, the principal and most charismatic student leader, specifically sought to rescue the ideas and the political message of Martí's writings and then, by giving his Universidad Popular Martí's name, identified the ever more radical spirit of the new dissidence with his figure and ideas, the myth began to take clear and powerful shape, for the 'story-line' – life, struggle, death and betrayal – now had text to support it and, significantly, a new young generation to act as its 'interpreters' and rescuers, strengthening the myth and also their identification with it. Moreover, his ideas, though now so exalted, were, importantly, still not clear, for Mella's version was a deliberate selection of those aspects that suited his own purposes and vision – radical, popular and anti-imperialist. Many Cubans were therefore still not really familiar with Martí's developing radicalism, his social vision and his many critiques of American society and mores, and of Latin American social and political realities. Furthermore, there was almost no awareness

2. I am indebted to Cintio Vitier for this information.

of his economic ideas, despite the fact that he had made great play of the significance of such issues as diversification, the land, currency reform and protectionism. Mella, and the student *martianistas*, had brought Martí's ideas closer to many Cubans' concerns, but had left much undiscovered.

However, the little that had been revealed was powerful enough to reinforce the myth – with Martí's warnings about the *monstruo* given new force and anti-imperialist meaning and with his vision of *Nuestra América* coinciding with a greater student and worker awareness of contemporary radical struggles outside Cuba. In this way, the myth represented not only *Cuba Libre*, but also a possible *Nuestra América Libre*, which endowed it, and the student rebels, with an even greater legitimacy and historical importance. Hence the imprecision of the awareness of Martí's ideas – now talked of as an *ideario* rather than an ideology or argument – was a help rather than a hindrance to the myth.

Those same 'interpreters', armed with this myth and its *ideario*, then went on to challenge the whole system with their assault on the disappointing *machadato* from 1927. The FEU became the DEU, but the idea of the young intellectual rebels carrying forward the torch of *cubania* and rebellion remained powerful, especially when Mella was murdered in Mexico in 1929 – thus adding further credibility to both the generational and the *martiano* myths, with a new cycle of 'life, struggle, death and betrayal' to add to the 'sacred tale' of Martí. In turn, all of these features of the 'tale' were forcefully enacted in the four brief months of the 1933 Revolution, with its images of student rebels successfully assaulting the citadels of power, the deliberate attempt to create a 'clean' government of intellectuals, the recurrent images of *lucha* throughout late 1933, and, ultimately, the 'betrayal' by Batista's coup, Washington's collusion and, in 1935, the death of the young and popular Guiteras (a further echo of Martí and Mella). Moreover, the whole 1933 platform could justifiably be seen as *martiano* in inspiration, if not in detail. Even the somewhat questionable '50 per cent law', which resulted in unemployment, discrimination and poverty for many Haitian and Jamaican immigrants and which had its racist overtones – was presented by some as in keeping with Martí's ideas of protectionism and the full employment of Cubans.

The whole question of myth came sharply into focus in 1934 when, with the defeat of yet another 'generation' and yet another *lucha*, the Platt Amendment was successfully abrogated by agreement between post-revolutionary Cuba and a cooperative United States. The sudden removal from the Cuban political culture of such a powerfully mobilizing myth meant a partial vacuum within the mythic structures of *cubanía*, especially when this coincided with Batista's successful efforts to present his reforms as the realization of the whole 1933 programme without the attendant chaos and bloodshed. Indeed, at a stroke, one *cubanista* myth disappeared from the arsenal.

As has been seen, however, the new post-1934 arrangement and relationship with the United States was an illusion, with the old openly neocolonial control now replaced by a more subtle indirect control through the new Reciprocity Treaty and the quota, about which there was no clear consensus as there had been with *Platt*. While bad years thereafter could be attributed to the baleful influence of the quota, years of stability and economic security could also be seen in that light. *Platt*, of course, could never be presented in a good light, as its very existence was a slight to nationalist beliefs and as the effects of its existence, in interventions and in the ever-present role of the American ambassador, could rarely be presented as beneficial to Cuba's self-belief.

There was therefore a double need to fill the mythic vacuum: on the one hand, the inheritors of the 1933 revolution needed to create a myth of that episode as both part of the long *cubanista* tradition of *lucha* and as successful, while, on the other hand, the dissident constituency needed something tangible and consensual to replace *Platt*. The former myth-making was made all the easier by the actual events of 1934–44, where 'success' was easily measured by reform, nationalist protection measures, the alliance with the communists and the *Enmienda*'s disappearance. Indeed, so clear was the regime's achievement that conscious and coherent myth-making was actually unnecessary, since there was an unwritten acceptance at many levels of Cuban society that Batista had somehow 'rescued' the 1933 revolution, by first defending the rebellion and then seizing power and restoring a necessary unity and stability, and preventing a destructive American intervention, but also, after 1938, by constructing his 'patriotic' coalition, his version of the Popular Front, and making Cuba a more comfortable and socially progressive place. It should not be overlooked, in the negative images of the second *batistato* after 1952 and in the inevitable post-1959 tendency to excoriate his whole political contribution, that many Cubans in the 1950s looked back to 1938–44 as a 'golden age'. Batista's claim to be an 'interpreter' of the evolving myth of 1933 was thus guaranteed until he destroyed it in 1952. Indeed, the 1940 constitution (on the basis of which he was then elected) retained some mythic power in the Cuban political system until 1958, Castro himself referring to it repeatedly from 1953 and using it as the yardstick by which the rebellion and the new Cuba after the victory would be measured.

Thus, in the ranks of a dissident *cubanía*, what myth-making there was in 1934–48 tended to focus on the events of 1933 – once again 'betrayed' by an unholy alliance of entrepreneurs, Americans, the Right and the post-1944 *Auténticos* – and the constitution, especially as its major radical and social provisions were so flagrantly ignored after 1944. The apparent vacuum was helped by the fact that the Left, after 1935, tended anyway to seek solace and identity outside Cuba, in the huge and impressive commitment to the Republican cause in the Spanish Civil War, when the only voices in favour of the Nationalists came from a discredited Catholic Church and the pages of the conservative daily *Diario de la Marina*.

In the battle of myth-making, therefore, the field was left somewhat clear for the new political elite, whose need for myth was evident since it lacked a real economic basis for its claim to hegemony and for any lastingly successful populist project to function. So long as Batista enjoyed the opportunity afforded by 'Popular Frontism' and then the lucrative war years (which provided, after 1941, both a guaranteed and demanding high-priced American market and the image of a friendly Soviet Union to legitimize further the association with the communists), the success of his populist project was assured. After 1945, however, with the Cold War beginning to escalate and with global sugar production beginning to recover, the effects of the quota and the emptiness of the claim to 'Cubanization' began to become evident.

When the PRC-A came to power in 1944, they therefore needed a rallying myth to legitimize their claim to hegemony. The answer lay in the claim that they had already laid as heirs to Martí, by assuming the title of his PRC and adding *auténtico* as a specific rejection of Batista's claims to be *martiano*. Now, after 1944, they built on that claim by a naked manipulation of the rescued Martí myth; with great fanfare they sought to 'martianize' Cuba, building even more busts of the *Apóstol* throughout Cuba's squares, schools and nurseries, encouraging hagiographic studies of the newly sanctified *Maestro* ('master', or 'teacher'), studies that spoke of Martí as the 'celestial star' and 'chemically pure' (Kirk 1983: 6) and, fundamentally, iconizing the myth of the 1920s, enshrined for the purposes of veneration. Thus there were official references to Martí as the *santo de América* ('saint of America'), the *Cristo americano* ('American Christ') and the *místico del deber* ('mystic of duty') (Santí 1996: 56), and the whole myth became 'statuesque' (Kapcia 1985: 60).

The myth of Martí, which, as myth, had had a 'story-line' whose purpose was to distil the 'message' of *cubania* and to encapsulate the perceived 'story-line' of the betrayed and struggling *nación*, now became a deliberately static icon, lacking a 'story-line' and presented as an object for admiration; Martí ceased to be presented as a 'model for action', as he had been in the 1920s and 1930s struggles (since 'action' would inevitably have destabilizing effects in the fragile balance of the flawed 'new Cuba') and became an anodyne 'model for being', a figure almost to be worshipped in the abstract.

If iconization is to succeed, however, an 'infrastructure' of legitimacy is even more necessary than with myth; in the latter case, the very fact of its organicity allows, and indeed depends on, a measure of flexibility and reinterpretation, wherein the political circumstances and the ideological context of the mythic empowerment are essential determinants of the effectiveness of the myth. Icons, however, need a clearer and almost institutionalized 'priesthood', since the necessary process of alienation (for the purposes of proper and controlled 'veneration') needs a class of acceptable initiated 'mediators', to interpret what is necessarily beyond easy comprehension by the 'mass'. In this context, one of the obvious features of post-1944 Cuba was the lack of any such credible 'mediators'. The veterans of 1933 might perhaps have been able to adopt such a role had their claims to have inherited the mantle of *cubanía* and its specific 1933 manifestation not been increasingly disproved by their behaviour in office. They could in the end lay no credible claim to being revolutionary, honest or nationalist, and were daily becoming a factor that not only lacked such credibility but was damaging to the system's credibility. The other possible *cubanista* 'priests' might have been the students; but they too were writing themselves out of the script through the degeneration of student activism into *bonchismo*.

All of this meant that the whole project of iconization was not only flawed but essentially counter-productive and dangerous, since the more the icon contrasted with the reality of an increasingly disillusioning Cuba, the greater the potential for a new reinterpretation of the underlying myth. In this respect, the emergence of a new pre-mythic symbol, which encapsulated many of the existing dissident myths of the pre-1934 years, was especially significant. This symbol was the idea of *historia*, which now received greater attention than ever in a very particular way, and began to acquire a popular significance and a politically dissident role.

The reasons for this lay in the particular conjunction between the dominant counter-myths – of *Platt*, generations and Martí – and the circumstances of the time, with a heightened awareness of the coincidence of various overlapping anniversaries as the PRC's period in office proceeded. In the 1940s, many Cubans – already in a culture that systematically sought celebration or commemoration in historical anniversaries – were acutely aware of the approaching anniversaries: the eightieth of 1868 (in 1948), the fiftieth of 1895 in 1945 (recalling both the start of the second war and the death of Martí), the fiftieth of 1898 (in 1948) and of 1902 (in 1952) and, towering over them all, in 1953 the centenary of Martí's birth. Such a coincidence would, in the most relaxed of circumstances, have been significant and unprecedented; in the circumstances of disillusion, frustration and disguised politicization, it was explosive and helped to mould the three myths together in a complex and powerful myth-set that explicitly extolled the redemptive power of *historia*.

The three myths, collectively, served the purpose of developing a complex, changing, always variably interpretable, set of belief-systems that helped to clarify, explain, and act as metaphors for the much larger, more cosmic, ideology that *cubanía* represented; as such, they were not mutually exclusive, but overlapped, reinforced each other and, together, presented a coherent set of images that made the abstract more comprehensible. If the codes were the building-blocks of the ideology, then the myths were its cement.

However, all of them – codes and myths, bricks and cement – focused individually and collectively on one thing that united the whole ideological apparatus:

history. For all of them had, as a purpose, individually and collectively, the explanation of Cuba's perceived past and its present, and the justification of both, together with the vital role of positing an 'essential' Cuban future. In other words, *cubania*, like all ideologies, offered a collectively viable, acceptable and variable explanation of Cuba's past context, its present dilemmas and subjugation, and its potential future (the world as it was, is and should be), and, within that vision, offered a programme for action to achieve that future. Within this global purpose and focus of the *cubanista* ideology, the individual myths that distilled it all had history at their core, all had history as their definer and all had history (as past, present and future) as their purpose.

The reason is clear – quite apart from the essential purpose and function of any ideology of national identity. All the myths were focused on, served and were evolved from the essential issues of identity and nation, an 'imagined community' whose self-image was one with a past of national humiliation (a past all too uncomfortably recent), which had resulted in the distortion, betrayal and non-fulfilment of Cuba's historical destiny. In other words, like any personal psychology, those who perpetuated, propagandized and believed in *cubania* needed to come to terms with that past, or, alternatively, create a mythology about a past that was equated essentially with 'non-nation' or 'anti-nation'. History, then, was essential to the whole purpose, success and continuation of *cubania*; indeed, without a sense of history, *cubania* was meaningless, and any danger of meaning's disappearing from the Cuban identity had to be countered by periodic reaffirmations of Cuban history – or at least a view of Cuban history that reinforced the *cubanista* message.

History, however, was even more central than that, for it could be said to be a myth in itself, or at least what we might call a 'myth-system'. Firstly, this was so because the perspectives of *cubania* grew fundamentally out of several intertwining strands of nineteenth-century thought, which all shared a view of history as progress (Darwinism, social Darwinism, positivism, Krausism, Hegelianism, and of course Marxism). From this complex mix of intellectual influences came a view of nationalism (also a nineteenth-century perspective itself, offering a view of history as progress) as essentially social, rooted deeply in Cuban society, urban and rural, white and black, rich and poor, but one that still, despite its affinity with later twentieth-century liberation struggles, was petrified within a nineteenth-century intellectual framework. Such 'petrification' arose both out of a Spanish colonialism that largely survived only by default, and also out of the mimetic tendencies born of dependency, which sought to import perspectives to explain a past that ought not to have happened.

Secondly, history became elevated to mythic stature because, by the 1940s, many Cubans saw themselves as victims of their own history, as objects of historical processes that did not belong to them and over which they had had no control, despite generations of heroic struggle. This tendency towards objectivization and victimization meant, by definition, that no blame was attached to Cuba itself, in a view of Cuba as a suffering entity, and in an essentially negative view of Cuba's past and present, a denial of its 'true' identity.

How then did this myth actually express itself within Cuban political and intellectual life? On the one hand, within the political sphere, *historia* began to play an autonomous role, expressed in three themes. The first, as we have seen, was the essentially historicist myth of cyclical generational renewal, with all its ambiguity and fusion of radical hope and absolution of responsibility for past errors. The second was the as yet only intimated theme of '100 years of struggle', with its implications that 1868–78 was the real awakening of a mass national consciousness and that, within that century some sort of fulfilment of the nation's destiny would be achieved – although, interestingly, this perspective dated the struggle from the first mass rebellion organized by whites, ignoring the many preceding slave rebellions. This theme brought a comforting continuity to the 'present' struggle (at whatever time), placing each generation within a historical tradition and investing it with a future historical significance. The third theme was, inevitably, the repetition of heroism, the sense that Cuba's struggle was based on the action of heroic individuals and groups, rather than classes. All three themes pointed to one simple reality – that all nationalist rebellion had, by definition, a proven historical legitimacy.

Meantime, in the academic and intellectual world, the study of history became a respected, and even 'sacred', discipline, receiving greater scholarly attention from historians who were increasingly being seen as 'keepers' of the national conscience and consciousness; even non-historians dabbled publicly in essays on historical themes. Historians whose work was well respected and whose academic approach was to use new archive material and sources increasingly saw themselves as political activists, serving a valuable patriotic role; Guerra y Sánchez and Roig de Leuchsenring stand out in this respect, their seminal studies from the 1921–35 period (the former's *Historia de Cuba* in two volumes between 1921 and 1925 and *Azúcar y Población* (1927), and the latter's 1935 *La Historia de la Enmienda Platt*) – remaining still the perceptive classics that they seemed to be then, but their purpose and impact going well beyond the 'ivory tower' of academia. The historian was now expected to be committed, obeying certain 'organic' rules and performing a clear organic function. They were, in short, playing a role as 'priests' of the new myth, and their efforts served two purposes – to bring attention to previously neglected themes, periods, characters and events of Cuban history and to raise the popular awareness of history and the status of historiography within Cuban society.

This, then, was the situation of politico-historical myth up to the eve of the *batistazo*. We have already seen how *cubania* had by then become more coherent, with more fully developed and powerful codes, and also how the rebellion then went on to reflect and strengthen that. Now, when we look at the role of myth in general and specific myths in particular, we can see the same process happening.

For a start, as has been observed, the coincidence of so many historically significant anniversaries between 1945 and 1953 made that period especially evocative and redolent, with an unusual potential for myth-making and myth-fortification. Moreover, the specific order of the 1952–3 anniversaries was especially significant, since the reminder of *seudoindependencia* in 1952 coincided uncomfortably with Batista's coup – both now seen as humiliating experiences, ending hope and vision, and contributing to the negative Cuban self-image. On the other hand, 1953 saw a reminder of hope – the birth of Martí – coincide with Castro's bold and mobilizing heroic action, intended and seen as a call to arms, both eventually bringing out the best in Cubans' self-image. The fact that Batista chose to justify the coup through reference to Martí's centenary only fortified the positive image of the youthful rebellion. Thus the order was a powerful reminder of the positive over the negative.

In this sense, the inevitable popular tendency to see that rebellion as the work of the 'next generation' powerfully fortified the already significant myth of generations and endowed the young rebels with even greater mystique. Again, the similarities between Moncada and other historic episodes – notably the 1868 and 1895 rebellions and Guiteras's 1931 attack – and the openly *martiano* tone of Castro's speech reinforced the cyclical nature of this particular generation's actions and its historical legitimacy. Moreover, the use of the term *centenario* almost certainly invoked images of millenarianism, both terms imbuing the struggle with a sense of a glorious past (with 1968 promising to celebrate a century of struggle) and also a destined future.[3] The epithet 'centennial' therefore worked on several levels – celebrating and taking legitimacy from Martí, rescuing the betrayed tradition of struggle, representing the renewed hope of a new generation within the tradition and promising to realize the long-postponed 'millenarian' and 'millennial' destiny of *Cuba Libre*. *Centenarismo* thus reinforced the already powerful appeal of this latest generation, unifying past and future in their particular heroism, a theme that Castro's defence speech took up rhetorically but effectively; when he proclaimed that a future *historia* would 'absolve' his actions, he was consciously and unconsciously invoking a whole tradition of *cubanista* thinking and laying a legitimate claim to be the 'interpreter' of this particular powerful myth. It might reasonably be argued that the three dominant counter-myths, wrapped up in the evocative 'myth-system' of *historia*, reached their culmination in the action of Moncada and, specifically, in Castro's finely tuned 1953 speech.

---

3. Although the phrase 'one hundred years of struggle' was not publicly coined until 1968 by Castro himself, it had been prefigured in the whole anniversary-conscious political culture of 1952–68.

In this way, the pre-existing myths of generations, Martí and history became more legitimate and more 'sacred' and, in the process, even more capable of distilling the ideology of *cubanía*, enabling it to be internalized more generally. It was therefore inevitable that, in the circumstances, many Cubans would respond to this act of defiant, if apparently futile, heroism and self-sacrifice by seeing it not as irrelevant (as the PSP did) but rather as belonging to a hallowed tradition of dissident *cubanía* (*cubanía rebelde*), thereafter seeing the 26 July Movement (with its evocative titular reference to a presumably historic date) and the young ex-student leader as valid representatives of the 'millennial' tradition.

There were, however, two critical features that distinguished this rebellion from those that preceded it in the tradition, which would soon turn this latest generation into a point of departure and a renewal of the old, at one and the same time. The first (as we have seen) was Castro's critical decision not to follow the traditional exile route to Miami, but rather to head for Mexico, thereby placing himself outside the perhaps discrediting environment of traditional ineffectual dissidence. The second was the image of success that thereafter characterized the rebellion, with repeated survival (against all the odds and the most devastating blows) – an image that clearly undermined the traditional *choteo*. Moreover, once the guerrilla campaign started, new myths began to form – in the survival of *los Doce* ('the Twelve'), in the renewal of the struggle of the *mambises*, in the rebellion in Oriente, in the guerrilla itself, and, of course, in the 'sub-myth' of youth that the whole mythology of generationalism implied and that the struggles of 1923, 1933 and now 1953–8 all made clear.[4]

In this way, just as the pre-1959 years saw the evolution of the whole radical and dissident ideology of *cubanía*, with its clear potential to rally, point the way towards action and a possible future, and explain the past tragedies, the present sufferings and the future liberation, so too was this period especially fertile for the creation of the necessary myths, all of them rooted deeply in the past and all of them powerfully usable for the new Cuba that was about to emerge from the ashes of the *batistato* and the insurrection.

---

4. 'The Twelve' was the title of Carlos Franqui's account of the Sierra struggle written soon after the victory. As we have seen, the numbers of rebels from December 1956 was never clear, and it is almost certain that there were only the mythic 'twelve' for one short moment of the early campaign.

-4-

Revolution and the Radicalization
of Myth and *Cubanía*

The preceding chapters have traced the evolution of a definite, consensual and organic ideology of *cubanía*, in which the *rebelde* definition had become counter-hegemonic by the late 1950s and then, after 1959, became hegemonic, guiding the whole revolutionary process and contributing to its radicalization. They have also demonstrated the existence of a tradition of myth that, until 1959, was fundamental to the cohesion, transformation and permanence of that ideology. In 1959, therefore, the now victorious and *cubanista* revolutionary forces possessed a system of myths, old and recent, on which they were able to build the instruments for ensuring the socialization and internalization of an ideological consensus.

Moreover, the Revolution enjoyed a particular context in which this process could initially be especially effective. Firstly, there was a widespread self-belief and enthusiasm, whose force could only partly be explained by the end of the *batistato* and the arrival of the young guerrillas; for, after decades of increasing collective self-doubt and self-denigration, the positive message of *cubanía* now emerged, with a vigour that reflected its essentially visionary and millenarian impulses. Secondly, the new context was one of collective involvement and mobilization, reinforcing, as we have seen, the organic nature of the revolutionary ideology and radicalizing the demands on, and the direction of, the whole process. The third aspect of the new context was, especially after mid-1959, the external hostility, which both furthered the Revolution's radical tendencies and created a powerful sense of community. All of this, therefore, meant a clear, but new, role for myth, as part of the necessary processes of internalization and transference (from an essentially negative context to a positive one). This meant the need to move from 'mobilizing myth' to 'sustaining myth' (Judson 1984: 15), and, thus, a need for two particular kinds of myth.

Firstly, it meant the need to identify, preserve and enhance the traditional organic myths that would link the new *cubanía* with the tradition of *cubanía rebelde*, which now gave the Revolution much of its historical legitimacy, direction and purpose and a historical basis of continuity on which to build and through which to break with the past, without losing touch with the Revolution's roots. This need meant a historical context of certainty and of a perceived heroic national past, seen as the key to the achievement of the 'real' future for *cubanía* and the *nación*. This was especially because, by the 1950s, *cubanía rebelde* had actually become the necessary 'alternative project' to challenge the flawed hegemony of the old society, and would therefore be the basis for the new. In this new context, the vanguard – the accepted interpreters of the myths, recognized the need to keep faith with that historic project to link the Revolution both to past heroisms and *lucha*, and to the destined *Cuba Libre*.

The second mythic need was for essentially new myths for the new society soon to be realized by that project. In a process of revolutionary transformation, by definition, certainties disappear rapidly and change can destabilize even the new society itself; such new myths were therefore necessarily those that would project a positive self-image and would express a society about to change, rather than, as in the past, seeking to preserve some 'betrayed' and lost 'essence'. Therefore, alongside the essential old myths to provide a stable historical basis for the new transformation was a need for new ones to complement and support these.

In such a context, the most obvious recourse would be to the *rebelde* myths of Martí, generations and history, and also the newer, pre-mythic, symbol of the guerrilla – for the insurrection's mythic potential was considerable, focusing on the Sierra itself, the *campo*, the image of youth, the victorious struggle (itself a new phenomenon), the leaders and (once again) *Oriente*.

At one level, the use of the Martí myth was relatively easy, since the close identification between the struggle and the Moncada's *autor intelectual* was so explicit and universally accepted that it hardly needed to be elaborated.[1] In the euphoria of victory, the new Revolution was seen as the culmination of the betrayed and frustrated *martiano* project, the fulfilment of his hopes and the justification of his death. In a sense, the ashes of the old society from which the new one was being created included the ashes from the self-immolation of so many fallen heroes, including the new martyrs of the insurrection – Abel Santamaría and Frank País – together with the charismatic Camilo Cienfuegos, whose death after only a few months of the victory deprived the new Cuba of one of its leading figures.

In this respect, therefore, the post-1959 evolution of the Martí myth was organic, in that it responded to both the vanguard's public identification with the ideas, figure and action of Martí and also the populace's willing acceptance of that identification. In both cases, the recourse to the myth was inevitable and natural, especially in a context of deep, and often painful, redefinition of community, nation

---

1. Interestingly, the label *Apóstol* seems to have been dropped from regular use from early on in the Revolution and replaced by *Héroe Nacional* (national hero). One can speculate that this might have been because of the original term's religious connotations and *auténtico* and right-wing associations (although, as we have seen, it was Tampa radicals who first coined it), and also because of the nationalist connotations of the new term.

and identity, where the attraction of a critical unifying figure (and 'story-line') provided a vital element of stability and a permanent point of reference. This was especially true as the increasing isolation obliged the leadership, the intellectual elite and much of the population to become somewhat inward-looking, focusing on autonomous criteria and a reassessment of Cuba's own traditions, past, and character. Once again, the atmosphere was one of 'Cuban solutions for Cuban problems', and, in this context, the recourse to Martí was significant.

There therefore began a double process of mythification. Formally, in the newly 'official' discourse, the Revolution looked for its unifying legitimate and popular myth explicitly to the one that had guided the rebellion and crucially identified it with the heroic past, and consciously attempted to identify Martí's relevance to the new revolution (Kirk 1983: 12). The study (rather than, as before, the exaltation) of Martí was encouraged on an unprecedented scale, while numerous publications were produced explicitly linking the *Maestro*'s writings and ideas with the new reforms, especially as the authors – the new intellectual vanguard – saw themselves as the natural heirs to the *martiano* tradition of politically committed men of ideas (see especially Fernández Retamar 1967b; Desnoes 1967b). This was reinforced by the repeated image of, and quotations from, Martí on posters, tickets, leaflets, advertising hoardings and any number of unexpected places. Medin contends that the 1966–9 period saw two parallel processes, a weakening of the image of the Soviet Union and an intensification of the image and projection of Martí (Medin 1990: 56).

However, the scale of the process did not yet iconize the myth, since it was welcomed by most Cubans – a fact recognized by those émigrés who, in Miami, developed a parallel mythification of the person whom they too started to call the *héroe nacional,* as a point of historical reference, source of legitimacy and point around which to rally the divergent political interpretations of the evolving community.

The reason is that alongside this was the growth of the popular myth of Martí, a popular and less tangible identification between *la Revolución,* as a collective, lived experience, and the figure with whom most Cubans had become familiar since childhood. Everything that the myth represented for the average Cuban now seemed to be reflected in the new Cuba – equality, independence, dignity, heroism, self-sacrifice, intellectual liberation. What also prevented iconization in the early years was the incontrovertible fact that so many of the policies, reforms and experiences of the Revolution did indeed correspond closely to the ideas, representations or image of Martí. There was none of the alienation so necessary for iconization.

Within a decade or so, however, a problem evolved that few had foreseen, namely the simple fact that the myth's 'story-line' (life, struggle, sacrifice, death and betrayal), which had been so powerful after 1933, no longer worked in a Cuba where, for all the setbacks, invasions had been resisted, reforms enacted changing the lives of most Cubans, living standards raised, and so on. In other words, the Revolution's very success – especially in the 1970s, as standards rose and confidence increased – militated against the viability, organicity and legitimacy of a myth that had before so powerfully represented the self-image of an essentially frustrated, defeated and oppositionist Cuba. Throughout the 1960s siege and struggles, this danger was minimal, as Cubans could still justifiably see themselves as an embattled enclave fighting against a hostile world for 'purity' of revolution, national integrity and sovereignty, and genuine social equality. Furthermore, as Cuba emerged from the worst of the 'siege' and began to move towards more orthodox interpretations of Marxism, showing the growing influence of Soviet paradigms, the emphasis on Martí seemed to be relegated, locating him in history as more of a 'precursor', a representative of the 'progressive bourgeoisie' of 'prehistory' than the ever-present *autor intelectual.*

Even more than with Martí, the myth of generations (so fundamental to the legitimacy of the 1953 rebels and to the atmosphere of renewal in the 1950s) had a limited use after 1959, given that its inherent meaning, and 'story-line' – of cyclical regeneration, rescue and rejuvenation of a perhaps doomed ideal – simply did not fit comfortably within a Cuba now successfully led by the latest generation, seen to be realizing the preceding, lost, generations' dreams. Given the leadership's youth, the implications of cyclical betrayal were either meaningless or, more dangerously, full of the wrong sort of meaning for a vanguard that either had no intention of betraying rescued ideals or no desire to be seen in that light. With the émigrés and many external analyses presenting the Revolution's radicalization, and its turn towards communism and the Soviet Bloc, as betrayal, recourse to a myth that implied cyclical betrayal was of no use. It therefore disappeared from the armoury, at both leadership and popular level, being replaced eventually by the value, which acquired mythic status, of 'youth'.

Historia, on the other hand, presented no such problems, as it so clearly looked both back (to a past that could be rescued by the present, 'real', Cuba) and forward (to a Cuba that the present system could be seen as creating). Several processes therefore began within days of the victory. Firstly, the newspapers – especially *Noticias de Hoy* and *Revolución* – began what became a tradition of a series of short articles on episodes, events, figures and issues from Cuban, Latin American and world revolutionary and (especially with *Noticias*) socialist history. Secondly, historiography itself was ascribed a critical role in the collective task of nation-building, in the rescue, reconstruction and exaltation of a lost national identity, and in the national goal of education. Indeed, of all the academic disciplines, it was perhaps the most encouraged, vaunted and independent, a process helped by the fact that so many respected historians remained in Cuba and, with official encouragement, began to rewrite history in an explosion of books, pamphlets, articles and courses. Thirdly, the general awareness of the 1953–9 years as a dramatic lived historical experience that needed to be recorded for posterity gave rise to a wave of memoirs, narratives, and books about the struggle, not least Guevara's *Pasajes de la Guerra Revolucionaria;*[2] this, in turn, led to the realization that the ordinary Cuban's daily struggles before the victory were a rich source of educational, historiographical and political material that needed to be recorded, ranging from memoirs of the 1895–8 war, and the various later struggles, to the accounts of daily life in Cuba, in exile, at work, at home and so on. Stimulated by the new focus on the *pueblo*, this produced a conscious drive to seek and record *la historia de los sin historia* ('the history of those without history'), to which historians were encouraged to devote themselves, and also the popularity of a whole new genre of *literatura de testimonio* (testimonial literature), the most famous being the 1966 *Biografía de un Cimarrón* ('Biography of a Runaway Slave') (Barnet 1983). Furthermore, this whole campaign was given different levels of encouragement by the creation of the Instituto de Historia, the History Section of the FAR, and innumerable popular history projects across the island (see Ibarra Cuesta 1995b; Moreno Fraginals 1983).[3]

In this sense, it is useful to see Cuban historiography in the context of the literary genre of, and debates around, autobiography. It could be argued that a specifically Cuban historiography, before and after 1959, was nothing if not a collective desire for national autobiography. Leaving aside competing theories of autobiographical writing, it is worth considering here three different purposes of autobiography: catharsis or confessional expurgation, the desire to enhance an understanding (one's own and others') of one's own past, and, lastly, the desire to justify to others (and oneself) a given past, which, in the case of a 'marginal', could be either a past as victim or a past as victor.

It is revealing to see how many of these were equally applicable to the tenor and purpose of pre-1959 Cuban historiography, especially considering that we can understand 'the life around which autobiography forms itself [. . .] as participation in an absolute existence far transcending the shifting, changing unrealities of mundane life' (Olney 1980: 239). When we bear in mind the general, if stylized, Cuban perception that, firstly, the reality of pre-1959 political and cultural life was mundane when compared to the hopes vested in independence by repeated generations and, secondly, that that reality was essentially false (a negation of the 'real' Cuban destiny of an independent existence), then a transcendental purpose to national 'autobiography' becomes both desirable and likely, and certainly helps

---

2. These were published in English as *Reminiscences of the Cuban Revolutionary War* (Guevara 1968).

3. I am once again indebted here to Grail Dorling for the ideas expressed and argued in her unpublished M.Phil. thesis (University of Wolverhampton, 1999).

us to understand the otherwise complex and contradictory attitudes to Cuban history.[4]

Such an autobiographical focus can also aid our understanding of the new, post-1959, historiography, if we consider the purpose of autobiography from the point of view of a marginal entity. If the accepted, hegemonic, biography (history) has consistently and systematically marginalized the author (in this case, culture), then the perceived need of autobiography is to ensure that the denied identity is placed centre-stage, at the centre of consciousness, while still seeking to explain and justify the previous marginalization. In other words, historiography (as national autobiography) has a double purpose: to objectivize identity (and thus explain past victimization) and, with greater confidence if not yet real self-awareness, to subjectivize one's own identity.

Autobiography is different when written from the point of view of a 'marginal' (whether a person or a whole culture). Indeed, it is perhaps only possible for a 'marginal' with a sense of, or aspiration to, an identity to embark on successful autobiography. Thus, if autobiography from the margins is always 'a house divided against itself' (Schons 1926: 158), then so too is the historiography of a denied national identity, in which case, it is apposite to ask – and any 'national' historian is obliged to ask – which 'voice' is used in such an exercise, that of the dominant culture or some sort of 'authentic' one? If the latter, then the next logical question is what 'authentic' actually means and how such a voice can be identified, for the simple reason that one cannot easily know what the 'authentic' identity is when such an identity has, by definition, been systematically denied. Moreover, to pursue this, one might justifiably ask if one can, in these circumstances, know oneself, whether personally or collectively (and nationally). If the answer is affirmative, then the subsequent question is whether honesty is either possible or even desirable. Indeed, as has been observed (of autobiography), 'the self appears organic, the present the sum total of the past, the past an accurate predictor of the future' (Gusdorf 1980: 35). In other words, as national consciousness struggles to know itself, it is perhaps inevitable, and even desirable, that a high degree of self-justification, and *post hoc* rationalization, will become central to the process of 'writing the (national) self'.

In the context of the new historiography in revolutionary Cuba, Olney's words ring true – that 'life [. . .] does not stretch back across time but extends down to the roots of individual being; it is atemporal, committed to a vertical thrust from consciousness down into the unconscious rather than to a horizontal thrust from the present into the past' (Olney 1980: 239). The search for the 'essence' of a denied, distorted, betrayed *cubanidad* was central to defining, and celebrating, the new reality, and to linking that 'now' to a perceived heroic current of 'then'.

4. In this discussion of the relationship between historiography and autobiography, I am indebted to the ideas offered in papers by my colleague, Parvathi Kumaraswami.

All of which leads logically to the conclusion that, in both the pre-Revolutionary and post-Revolutionary periods, the historian in Cuba enjoyed a special place, seen as fulfilling a special role within the national psyche and the national evolution. This applied equally to the pre-1959 historians (such as Julio Le Riverend, Raúl Cepero Bonilla and Herminio Portell Vilá) and the new generation of experts (such as Manuel Moreno Fraginals, Jorge Ibarra and José Tabares del Real). On the one hand, historians were the accepted authors of the collective, national, autobiography, part of the national struggle for self-determination and the rescue of a lost, betrayed, identity, with a vital function, for, in a sense, the future of Cuba was in their hands. Meantime, on the other hand, they were also the accepted 'interpreters' of the renewed and now revolutionized national myth of *historia* itself.

The new environment, however, which reinforced some inherited myths and made others less tenable, needed fundamentally new myths, preferably arising from the recent experience, which could continue to motivate and provide a legitimate collective point of reference. Thus, while there was an inevitable myth-ology (in the common sense of the term) created out of aspects of the struggle, cemented in posters, films, anniversaries, biographies and autobiographies, it was not so much the struggle itself that became a new myth as the figure (and implied 'story-line') of the *guerrillero* (guerrilla).

The mythification of the guerrilla – as figure, symbol, 'story-line', idea and history – was inevitable, as it linked smoothly with at least three existing myths and all the established codes of *cubanía*. The most obvious of the precursor myths echoed was that of the *mambí*, an identification already implicit in the popular reaction to the guerrillas and explicit in the Movement's manifestos and declara-tions. In previous decades, as we have seen, the *mambí* had been represented as a patriotic, popular and largely ill-defined figure (reflecting the deliberately shadowy nature of the nameless fighter whose hit-and-run guerrilla tactics had been charac-teristic of the strategy of both wars of independence), implicitly close to nature, heroic, communal in struggle but individualistic in his valour, resourceful and intelligent (usually meaning cunning rather than intellectual). That figure, and myth, represented much of the desired self-image, even the would-be *alter ego*, of a largely prostrate, defeated and self-doubting population. Now, after the victory, the *guerrillero* (seen increasingly as a timeless and placeless entity, not necessarily identified with the specific 1950s struggle) was seen as a newer, successful version of the *mambí*, given a revolutionary legitimacy that the latter lacked explicitly, and seen as the deliverer of the new freedom that was realizing, finally, the long-cherished *Cuba Libre*. Here the idea of *los Doce* furnished the myth with an aura of the 'sacred'.

The second myth into which the *guerrillero* inserted itself was the problematic one of generations, since the specific guerrillas of 1956–8 were seen as universally young rebels, ridding Cuba of the old system, and, with it, the hopeless ethos and failures of preceding generations. This was especially true as the myth tended increasingly and necessarily to blur the edges of the definition, including the young heroes of Moncada with the Sierra rebels. The fact that this latest generation included several 'martyrs' (notably the charismatic and popular Cienfuegos, whose image – rather than those of the living Fidel or Che – appeared all over Cuba after his death) helped reinforce the generationalist aspects and legitimacy of the new myth. Furthermore, there were implicit echoes of other mythic issues, especially the association with *Oriente* (an entity already mythified as the crucible of the 'real', hidden *nación*, and, within that, linked to a whole global mythology of 'new life' and renewal coming out of the east).

The third pre-1959 myth with which the *guerrillero* was linked was, surprisingly, the distant myth, and myths, of Afro-Cuba. It was surprising because so few of the rebels were black, but the fact was that many of the immediately mythic representations of the guerrillas – in art, literature and popular imagery – were unmistakably Afro-Cuban. At times this was a matter of the general image of the liberators 'coming down' from the mountains (with the *monte* having particular resonance in Afro-Cuban religious myths), and the immediate identification with existing mythology that Castro seemed to attract, not least when a dove reputedly alighted on his shoulder during an early rally. At other times, it was explicit, as in Pablo Armando Fernández's series of poems in *Libro de los Héroes* ('Book of the Heroes'), which pointed towards new directions in the Revolution's early poetry (towards more confident and forward-looking themes and away from the inevitable discourse of the purged past), and which explicitly sought to mythify the new process:

> Duermen en la tierra de los antiguos mitos,
> doce presagios de los ríos, doce
> augurios de la primavera.
> Cuando despierten serán guerreros
> De olvidada tradición. Sus memorias inauguran
> El tiempo señalado por los poetas.
> (*Doce,* Fernández 1963: 29)

(*Author's translation*: 'In the land of the ancient myths sleep twelve premonitions of the rivers, twelve auguries of the spring. When they awake they will be warriors of a forgotten tradition. Their memories initiate the time signalled by the poets.')[5]

As for the codes of *cubanía*, the myth represented almost all those constituting the discourse in 1959. Agrarianism was implicit in the guerrillas' perceived natural

---

5. Fernández had the prestige of being Deputy Editor of *Lunes de Revolución*.

identification with the countryside and the peasant, while collectivism was expressed in the much-vaunted camaraderie of the small rebel band (from Moncada and the Isle of Pines, through the *Granma* and the days of the 'Twelve', to the few survivors who were the 'historic' core of the Sierra), which was repeatedly represented in the early literature, film and newspaper coverage. Moralism was, of course, implicit in the images and examples of commitment, self-sacrifice and purity of the 'reborn' and young neo-*mambises*, having come untainted from Mexico (rather than Miami) and having 'purified' themselves in the struggle in Oriente. Activism was obvious, and reinforced by the militant and warlike imagery of the struggle, which public Cuba now repeated.

Three other pre-1959 codes were also manifested in the myth. The first was culturalism, strengthened by the accounts of the education campaigns in rebel-held territory and of Guevara's role in educating the untutored, or less politicized, guerrillas, and this was developed further when the guerrilla ethos was explicitly invoked for the 1961 Literacy Campaign, with the militant discourse of *lucha* in all the organizations and mobilization. Even the embryonic internationalism of the late 1950s found an echo, with Guevara's commitment (as an Argentine) often compared to that of the Dominican Gómez in the two independence struggles, as well as the evolving rhetoric and realization of anti-imperialism, which, as the decade progressed, became so characteristic. That this ethos was now more clearly Marxist hardly detracted from the code, as, by then, the two levels of ideology had become so clearly intertwined as to make the relationship seem, and feel, symbiotic. Finally, revolutionism was implicit and explicit in the whole guerrilla myth, especially as they had experienced a process of radicalization and were now engaged in a campaign to revolutionize Cuba, refusing to compromise ideals and taking the Revolution 'to the people' in so many senses. Only statism among the pre-1959 codes could find no clear manifestation in the guerrilla myth.

The 'story-line' of the myth was equally clear: a battle against all the odds, snatching survival and even victory from apparent defeats, and leading to a growing community of shared struggle, suffering and victory (seen as the nucleus of the 'new society'), through acts of daily and often unsung heroism, and hence to an organic symbiosis with the *pueblo* and eventual, inevitable, liberation. The latter points were crucial to the myth's power, departing from the 'story-line' of so many pre-1959 myths – that liberation had actually happened and, being inevitable, because right and just, was a culmination of Cuba's history. In this way, the myth also linked naturally and significantly with *historia*, as the guerrilla both looked back to Cuba's heroic past and forward, to the *Cuba Libre* that could now be built at last.

The myth's political effects were far-reaching. The first was what some have misleadingly seen as a 'militarization' (of society, language and image), as the universal images of the young *barbudos* ('bearded ones') were taken to represent the whole Cuban revolutionary struggle and as political programmes were presented as *campañas*, through *brigadas*, *asaltos*, *luchas*, *batallas* and a generally militant vocabulary of weapons, defences, marches and armies. Even the new army remained the Rebel Army (preserving the link) until it became the FAR, but with the original guerrilla rank of *comandante* – major – being retained as the sole officer class, while the militias were the epitome of the image of a *pueblo en armas*. Beyond the inevitably 'military' structures, so much of Cuban society was 'militarized' in image, uniforms and structures, including schools and the young *pioneros* (Organización de Pioneros de José Martí), founded in 1966. Finally, Castro's and other leaders' continuing use of the familiar olive-green rebel uniform meant a permanent identification with the *guerrillero*, while the FAR magazine significantly carried the name *Verde Olivo* ('Olive Green').

Thus, even during the Bay of Pigs, the struggle was represented less as a land battle than as a *pueblo en armas*, through the CDRs and the militias, immediately identifying it with the whole global history of guerrillas, from 1808 Spain, through the anti-Nazi struggles after 1939 to the more recent Vietnamese uprisings. Then, when American policy shifted towards support for covert subversion, the resulting campaign was again represented as a guerrilla battle, redolent of the narratives of the 1956–8 war.

In this context, one should not overlook the role played in the whole myth-making exercise by the Revolution's early literature. The combination of, on the one hand, the literary explosion that the victory released (affecting both pre-1959 writers and those now given their first opportunity) and the literary hunger of the newly literate created a natural tendency for the one to produce works – especially in poetry and the short story (the more immediate genres, better able to be published in magazines) – and the other to demand them, works dealing with the recent struggles and the continuing battles against the counter-revolutionary forces. Thus the figure of the *miliciano* (militiaman), seen as the continuation of the guerrilla, abounded in the early poetry, and the early literature was full of such themes – Felix Pita Rodríguez's *Las Crónicas* (1961), explicitly portraying the *milicianos*, the popular stories of Jesús Díaz's *Los años duros* (1966), Raúl González de Cascorro's *Gente de Playa Girón* (1962), Eduardo Heras León's *La guerra tuvo seis nombres* (1968), Norberto Fuentes's *Condenados de Condado* (1968), and Hugo Chinea's *Escambray 60* (1970).

'Militarization' was, however, an inappropriate term, implying a domination of civil society by a separate military caste or structure, while the Cuban case was closer to that of pre-1967 Israel, where military and civil societies fused more organically in very unique circumstances. Instead, a more accurate term might be a 'guerrilla mentality' (González 1974: 109) that we might call *guerrillerismo*, since now another effect of the myth was to universalize the ethos of the guerrilla into all aspects of life.

The adoption of *guerrillerismo* was both deliberate and inevitable. It was deliberate for the reasons indicated already – to strengthen the new myth and the legitimacy of the guerrilla-led revolutionary process, especially as, from 1959, the internal battles or debates created a need for a mythic legitimization of what we could call the 'inward-oriented' perspective. The strength of the guerrilla myth and, with it, the growing *guerrillerismo* – what has been called the 'Sierra Maestra complex' (González 1974: 109) – helped reinforce the *sierra*'s claim to revolutionary hegemony in the public mind, and also, of course, the leadership of Castro himself, who, despite the avoidance of a personality cult, was by implication being represented personally every time the guerrilla myth, imagery and mentality was extolled.

Moreover, the move towards *guerrillerismo* was inevitable, for, as the ideological differences evolved between the Cuban definition of revolution and socialism and the more conventional models of the PSP and Moscow, the evolving *guerrillerismo* helped create the mood of the radicalizing revolution, with its instinctive preference for voluntarism, for insurrection, for the subjective over the objective, and also for speedy responses to the dilemmas in which the Revolution found itself. The parallel between the Cuban self-image – challenging orthodoxy, creating a revolution out of inauspicious circumstances, taking on the might of the imperialist United States in a global 'war of the flea' (Taber 1974), and also the ideological might of the Soviet Union – and the image of the *guerrillero* was so close as to bestow the qualities presumed to be characteristic of the one upon the other.

It was, of course, precisely this image of the Revolution that, understandably, attracted to Cuba the coincidentally emerging New Left in the developed world, for the Revolution represented for many younger West European and North American radicals the archetypal expression of the 'now generation', unprepared to wait until a promised tomorrow and challenging every orthodoxy, including those offered by the 'two imperialisms' (Washington and Moscow). Cuba's relationship with this New Left was, in fact, never simple, and the irony is that the Revolution's attraction for the New Left was based as much on their perception of image as on the reality of any close ideological or political affinity between an apparently 'New Left' revolution in the 'South' and the often disaggregated and contradictory protest postures of the middle-class young in the 'North'.[6]

The effects of this *guerrillerismo* must also necessarily include the whole strategy adopted by the Cuban leadership towards both Latin America and Africa. Needless to say, that policy did not respond to *guerrillerismo* alone, or even in large part; as we have seen, the Cubans' decision to encourage insurrection and revolution abroad in those years was the result of a range of different motives and calculations. It responded, for example, to the recognition that, with isolation complete and

6. I am indebted here to the work and insights of my doctoral student and colleague, Kepa Artaraz.

with the resulting need to break the encirclement, but also with American guarantees not to invade, Cuba had nothing to lose by fomenting revolution in those countries that were anyway hostile and supportive of the quarantine. There were also internal factors – the strengthening of national unity and a sense of alert and mobilization. Finally, there was an obvious and growing ideological commitment to the whole idea of Cuba's putting its resources – military, human, financial, educational and political – at the service of brother rebels in the rest of the Third World. Indeed, in the latter case, the argument was even stronger, since the various insurrectionary groups to which Havana lent active support were almost all fighting against their colonial masters in a cause with which the Cubans could easily identify, or were, like the Algerians (to whom the Cubans felt especially close), a new and revolution-ary state struggling to throw off the remnants of imperialism and to create a new society based on similar principles.

Nonetheless, *guerrillerismo* considerably helped then to legitimize the whole strategy, as the vanguard sought to portray the island as the *foco* of Latin America and the Third World, a notion helping to strengthen the self-belief of those Cubans who, while not participating in the various struggles, could feel that they shared in such a heroic, historic and global undertaking. The gloss of the guerrilla thus rubbed off on to the most civilian and the least military of office-workers, labourers or state functionaries, who were all encouraged to feel that they were being part of a global 'guerrilla' struggle. Given the simultaneous ethos that militated against institutionalization and bureaucracy, the guerrilla gave the self-image of the Revolu-tion, and those who supported it, a myth to which to adhere.

Similarly, the new *guerrillerismo* helped to give political and mythic strength to the new emphasis on the peasant and the countryside, after 1963, with the agrarian reform and the decisions to shelve the ambitious industrialization plans and opt for the ten-million-tonne strategy. What were rational decisions, responding to specific economic or political circumstances, could be presented as part of a process that was seeking, like the guerrillas, to find its historic roots and reinvigorate itself in the always quintessentially Cuban *campo*.

This myth was also intimately linked to two other myths that began to emerge in the first decade, David and the 'new man'. The latter will be addressed later in this chapter; the former merits attention here, as its emergence was perhaps inevitable given the reality of isolation and the Revolution's success in undermining the traditional collective self-deprecation. Taking its cue, as we have seen, from Martí's universally familiar words, the myth took shape as collective self-belief grew following Playa Girón and the *Crisis del Caribe*. It was a powerful myth, reiterated in literature, the visual arts, posters and slogans, expressing not only the new confidence and determination, but also identifying Cuba with religious imagery and mythology, since, although Catholicism might have been socially weak, most Cubans were familiar with the biblical story. It was thus ideal, being biblical, *martiano* and hopeful (since David – just as Cuba seemed destined to – had won his battle against Goliath), and reflecting the general sense of confidence and moral righteousness.

This myth had other effects, implicit in the growing number of literary and media references to the parallels between Cuba's lonely, brave and principled struggle against imperialism's hostility, and, on the one hand, Britain's solitary resistance in the 'dark days' of 1940–1 against Nazi Germany, and also, often obliquely, Israel's determination survive as an embattled community in a hostile environment – the latter image, indeed, being invoked by Castro himself (Metz 1993: 119). Both parallels had more to do with image and self-image (and also justification of the political choices necessary for survival) than with political identification. For example, Cuba's growing alliance with Arab radicalism (including the PLO) made logical the leadership's formal opposition to a pro-American post-1967 Israel seen to be illegally occupying Arab territory. Revealingly, however, this did not preclude active cooperation between the two countries throughout the 1960s, in trading operations and development projects, and did not lead to a diplomatic break until 1973, once Cuba needed to prove its Third World credentials to the suspicious Non-Aligned Movement summit in Algiers, having heard Castro describe the Soviet Union as the 'natural ally of the Third World'. The parallels with wartime Britain have already been repeatedly drawn in the preceding chapters, and the references to this similarity by writers and leaders alike would indicate a conscious attempt to link the two experiences, not so much politically as at the level of myth. In both cases, of course, the parallel experiences had proved, or (in the case of Israel) were likely to go on proving, to be successful, to be 'Davids' rather than brave failures, and were thus natural parallels to draw as the 'guerrilla mentality' was matched by a growing 'siege mentality'. Here again myth operated, as the image of 'siege' was often expressed by the metaphor of Sparta, with its double connotations of an embattled people defending the last redoubt and of a purifying and hardening austerity (Moore 1988: 135).[7]

This concept of 'siege', while responding to real diplomatic and economic isolation and the need to conserve resources, was to some extent an imagined dilemma, as the 1962 agreement had actually guaranteed security from invasion – although the continuing émigré expeditions from Florida helped justify a genuine vigilance (for the CDRs and the MNR) and also the 'siege mentality'. It also, however, encouraged another, developing, process of self-reliance, stimulating all Cubans to look to their own individual and collective resources for survival. This corresponded to the leadership's awareness that the 1959–63 experiences had confirmed the inadvisability of depending on imported models, and that Cuba's

---

7. Interestingly, one of the two pieces of literature that sparked the 1971 'Padilla affair' was Antón Arrufat's play *Los Siete contra Tebas* ('Seven against Thebes').

development strategy, and ideological definition, had henceforth to be nourished on its own criteria, past and nature. The shift that this encouraged in the arts towards a cultural *cubania* was therefore inevitable; but the signs could already be detected in the early artistic welcome, as writers, poets, film-makers and visual artists sought to rescue their own, and Cuba's, 'real' nature through their expression, asserting (for the first time) or reasserting a lost identity. The 'siege' after 1962 propelled this shift even further, leading, indeed, as we have seen, to a new insularity, as the process of what was effectively described as 'cultural de-colonization' led to a willingness to reject both the once acceptable cultural criteria of the United States and Western Europe, and the eclectic cultural hedonism of the early Revolution.

For the first eight years, therefore, there were two almost contradictory mythic processes under way in Cuba. On the one hand, at least two of the pre-1959 myths – Martí and generations – had become less relevant, although the former still held popular sway. However, as has been observed, even that myth, for all its emotional identification with the Revolution's and many Cubans' assumed *martianismo*, made less sense in a Cuba that now boasted political, social and even military, victories, and where many Cubans felt that they now controlled their own destiny as never before. On the other hand, the new myths exuded and reflected a new confidence and a sense of community that were positive, hopeful and proud.

Both processes were, however, to coincide dramatically on 9 October 1967, in the shock of Guevara's death in Bolivia. Leaving Cuba in 1965, ostensibly to pursue his own and Cuba's goals of spreading the revolutionary example throughout the Third World and to realize the Cuban commitment to revolution, Guevara had disappeared from public view; but the general silence on his activities and where-abouts had, since then, done nothing to diminish public interest in, and affinity with, the charismatic leader, who, for all that he was not Cuban and did not share Castro's ability in public speechmaking and for all that his image was of a demand-ing and self-sacrificing hard taskmaster, had enjoyed considerable popularity amongst Cubans generally and his Sierra *compañeros*. The news of his death therefore certainly shook those comrades, who, for all their political differences with him, clearly felt a deep personal loss, of a friend and a source of moral and intellectual strength.[8] It also, however, had a wider effect, shaking Cuban confi-dence to its foundations, at a time of even greater isolation (with Cuba's quarrels with the pro-Moscow Latin American Communist Parties) and greater fears that Washington's increasing commitment to South Vietnam might presage a renuncia-tion of its 1962 undertakings on Cuba, and also at a time of growing economic hardship and crisis. The brutality and poignancy of his death in the Bolivian jungle only served to heighten that sense of loss, as though his own sufferings, battles and death somehow reflected the loneliness of a Cuba that had been deserted by

---

8. This was confirmed by a number of those interviewed in Cuba in 1995–7.

its allies and was equally surrounded by hostile forces dedicated to its destruction. Moreover, given that many Cubans probably saw the whole continental strategy as a means of ending isolation, the implications of the death and evident failure of that strategy's leading exponent were too awful to contemplate. Indeed, the death was, in many respects, the first real acknowledged setback in a process of apparent success (many of the previous economic failures having been either explained away or turned into positive strategies, making a revolutionary virtue out of economic necessity).

Until 1997 it was perhaps difficult to appreciate the depth of that sense of loss and grief; in that year, however, the obviously genuine outpouring of emotion that greeted the much-publicized return of Guevara's bones from Bolivia (to be buried ceremonially in Santa Clara) gave some hint of it, given that thirty years had passed since his death at a time when many who mourned the returning martyr had not even been born.

Che's death, however, went deeper than practical considerations and political messages, for he had always been seen as Castro's close ally, friend and confidant, his undisputed second in command, as selfless and committed and as something of a guarantee of the essential purity of the Revolution throughout all its twists and turns, compromises and hardships. With Guevara in the vanguard, there was felt to be little chance of corruption, of betrayal, or of a loss of momentum. His departure in 1965 had already led to some unease, and to stories of rifts between the two former comrades-in-arms. Now his death removed a friend, a hope and a direction.

In terms of myth, the result was immediate, both spontaneously and deliberately – a public and popular mythification of *Che*, the fallen hero – with the following year being re-named the 'Year of the Heroic Guerrilla' and with the famous Korda portrait (with its appropriately visionary gaze) reproduced throughout Cuba, on posters, in newspapers and, most impressively, hung on the walls of many Cubans' homes. The new myth was immediate and organic, since it referred most directly to the Cubans' lived and shared experience – *Che* had been Cuba, fighting alone in a hostile world, and his sacrifice had been theirs, and would, presumably, be the ashes from which the new struggle would be born. As one writer expressed it, he became 'an adopted patron saint of the Cuban government after his death' (Domínguez 1993: 118). As yet, however, there was little positive about the myth, with a sombre and somewhat pessimistic mood. Within a year, however, *Che* was being enlisted effectively as a symbol to drive forward the faltering campaign for the 1970 harvest and to revolutionize the economy in the appropriately named 'Revolutionary Offensive'.

The mythification of *Che* now took two related directions: focusing on the figure, life, memory and writings of Guevara himself and feeding into the growth of the new myth of the 'new man' – the latter being predictable, given the close association

Figure 2 The famous representation of Che Guevara's face appeared all over Cuba from the late 1960s

Figure 3 Che's Image preserved as the 'human' rebel, in the Museo de la Revolución

in everyone's mind between the concept itself and *Che*, since he had written explicitly about it previously and could now be seen as its embodiment.

Needless to say, the myth's impact could not be explained just by the simple identification between one man and one piece of writing; the roots of that identification went deeper. Certainly, it was true that Guevara had most clearly articulated the idea, based on the earlier concept of 'New Soviet Man' (born in the young Soviet revolution), that the revolution would necessarily create a new type of being, selfless, cultured, educated, committed to the revolution and to his fellow men. However, he had given it a specifically Cuban focus by seeing such a process of creation as preceding, or paralleling, the economic and political revolution, arguing that, in order to further the revolutionary process and overcome the obstacles of both capitalism and underdevelopment, a new revolutionary consciousness was necessary. Thus the idea of the 'new man' was a manifestation of the underlying voluntarism and subjectivism of Guevara's, and the vanguard's, concept of revolution.

However, the idea was by no means Guevara's alone, for one could find its roots deep in the traditions of *cubanía* and also in the ethos of the whole insurrection and revolution, in *History Will Absolve Me*, in all the manifestos, and in the early 1959 reforms. *Cubanía* had always implied a belief in the creation of not just a 'new Cuba' but also a 'new Cuban', with the permanent and almost millenarian emphasis on renewal, regeneration and heroism and with the existing codes that expressed and reinforced it all – agrarianism (implying 'back to nature' and a return to 'pure' roots), collectivism (implying a new solidarity to posit against the individualizing disintegration of the old society), activism, moralism and culturalism, plus the newer codes of internationalism and revolution. *Cubanía* called openly for a new way of being Cuban, and, however much it rooted this all in an imagined or a lost past, it still implied 'newness' in a way that underpinned every reform, gesture and act of the new Revolution. *History Will Absolve Me*, for example, clearly called for a new ethos, and Castro himself made repeated references to the need to replace old materialist attitudes by a new moral approach.

Thus, when Guevara articulated the idea in his seminal 1965 essay *Socialism and Man in Cuba*, saying 'To build Communism, it is necessary, simultaneously with the new material foundations, to build the new man' (Guevara 1987: 250), locating the model clearly in the Sierra guerrillas, where 'could be glimpsed the man of the future' (1987: 247), a chord was struck immediately in a population already ideologically geared towards such a notion. Moreover, as the 1960s progressed and the Revolution's new political and economic preferences became clearer (the defiant and costly commitment to Third World revolution, the 'moral economy', the 'anti-institutionalism'), the context for an organic inculcation of the idea began to evolve.

Now, with the death of the person who, in most Cubans' eyes, had most represented the ideals that the notion proposed, what had previously been a set of intellectual propositions and emotional postures became embodied in *Che*, the fallen hero and archetypal guerrilla, who had abandoned the relative comfort and security of a government post to risk death and to suffer in the jungles of Africa and Bolivia, fighting to liberate his fellow Latin Americans. With a 'story-line' that reflected Che's – selfless dedication and self-sacrifice, commitment to self-improvement and to the collective good – a double process began, whereby the new *Che* myth became intellectualized through the New Man, and the New Man myth became embodied in *Che*. Both myths therefore became one, powerfully and effectively. At a time of hardship, difficulty and demoralization, the myth conveyed a necessary message of hope, as, although Che's death had dealt a painful blow to morale and hope, his life remained as a model to which to aspire, which, if universalized throughout Cuban society, could offer a real hope of overcoming obstacles. Thus schoolchildren were (and still are) daily exhorted to repeat their desire to 'be like Che', and the myth became a real 'model for action' in a Cuba that needed such a guide.

Briefly, several myths now merged organically – *Che*, the New Man and Martí. By 1967, the problems inherent in this last myth had become clearer, with a less natural, comfortable or organic affinity between its basically self-victimizing 'story-line' and the reality of success and survival (although, with 'siege', hardship and continuing David-like struggle, the contradictions were still not apparent). There was, however, a real risk of iconization, of ritualization of the *Apóstol* in the emblematic references to him as a historic figure whose work was now being realized, especially as there had been, as has been observed already, a slight marginalization of Martí in the face of growing socialism. Guevara's death, and the new mood of demoralization and defeat, therefore enabled *Che*, as 'new man', to be seen as a reinvigoration of Martí, as Martí reborn in a new, revolutionary, context. Obvious parallels were drawn in the press, in posters and in speeches between the two histories of service to Latin America and, within that, of revolutionary peregrination and exile from their native lands, and between the two deaths – heroic, tragic and lonely, in battle and at the head of their forces, but also between the two lives, seen as essentially moral, pure, self-abnegating, committed and almost poetic in their beauty.

Now, however, the context for this new double-myth began to change again dramatically. The 1970 *zafra*, on which so many hopes had been pinned and for which so many sacrifices had been tolerated, turned out to be a failure, delivering a harvest of a record eight and a half million tonnes, but one well below the 'sacred' total, and, with the effort to harvest the crop, involving an expensive mobilization that actually cost the economy three times what the sugar was then worth. The immediate result was yet another period of debate, prefaced by some frank soul-searching and public admissions by Castro himself. Meantime, behind the scenes, other pressures were making themselves felt and other decisions were effectively being made. One such was the successful decision to seek membership of Comecon (in 1972), with immediate implications for economic strategy, since Comecon's previous reluctance had arisen from Cuba's supposed economic heresies. Another was the general toning down of public criticisms of the Soviet Union's attitude towards the Third World and of the insurrectionary strategy in Latin America, a partly pragmatic decision indicated by political changes in the region to more favourable governments.

Thus, by the time the eventual new phase was formalized, in the various moves of 1975–6 – the party congress and new economic strategy in 1975, and, in 1976, the new constitution and OPP electoral system (Órganos de Poder Popular – 'Organs of Popular Power') – it had already become clear that a new set of priorities and a new ethos would have to be developed in a different world context, in which voluntarism and the 'moral economy' (now, anyway, called into question by the failure) would have, at least, to be reconsidered. Most importantly, the imperative then was – at vanguard and popular level alike – a need to slow down, and consolidate, the often bewildering pace of change, to institutionalize, decelerate, decentralize, stabilize and legitimize.

Thus the party was given its first national congress; its membership increased, its purpose was clarified and its leadership saw the entry of two groups – the former PSP activists, largely restored in power and prestige, and younger 'technocrats', trained in the Socialist Bloc. New economic strategies were now increasingly adopted from 1973, with the formal 1975 SDPE (Sistema de Dirección y Planificación de la Economía – Economic Management and Planning System) emphasizing efficiency over need, limited market mechanisms, material over moral incentives and a full integration into Comecon. By 1980, 94.8 per cent of enterprises were inside the SDPE system (Fitzgerald 1994: 77), with impressive effects in terms of growth (annual rates being consistently above 6 per cent from 1972 to 1981) (Brundenius 1984: 40).

Legitimization took many forms – the constitution, the revival of the CTC (whose purpose and credibility had declined somewhat in the years of mobilization), and, above all, the electoral system, which seemed to emulate the Soviet pyramid structure of local direct elections, leading to indirect elections to a short-lived national assembly. The local OPP organs rapidly proved to be more efficient than the CDRs, whose political and politicizing role – so characteristic of the 1960s – now declined further. There were other signs too – the introduction of Soviet-style military ranks into the FAR, the disappearance of the militia, improved relations with Washington and the introduction of an unprecedented level of 'consumerization' as a result of Comecon.

This was an apparent political, economic and ideological *volte face*, a victory for the 'orthodox' arguments defeated in 1962–6, with the Soviet Union apparently exercising a new hegemony, the downgrading of the ideas, and even some of the personnel, of the late 1960s, and a different image being presented to the world and to Cubans alike – of a more stable, less frenetic, more orthodox and more 'Sovietized' Revolution. It was, of course, not that simple, as, although many of these reforms were demanded by Moscow (as the price for bailing out the economy), they were also welcomed by many Cubans and perhaps anyway likely to emerge. Moreover, the new institutions and personnel were often introduced not instead of, but as well as, the old – the CDRs coexisting with the OPP, the political structures simply expanding to include the 'orthodox' elements as well as the Sierra rebels, with the legitimization actually giving Castro (now President) more, rather than less, authority, and, through the constitution, legitimizing all the previous radical changes.

Nonetheless, a new period and context were clearly in operation, with an inevitable effect on the evolution and perception of ideology, and, within that, on the way in which myths functioned, leading to a need perhaps to revise the previous myths or to look for new ones. A myth such as the New Man or the *guerrillero* no longer comfortably reflected the new priorities, and could indeed create tensions. By the late 1970s this was even clearer, as consumerization and the greater emphasis on material, rather than moral, satisfaction (within the new trading system) meant a very different collective self-image.

The most obvious tendency now was a natural 'symbolization' of those myths that no longer fitted easily but survived at some level and were seen as especially useful. Of the resilient pre-1959 myths, *historia* was, perhaps, the most usable and useful; here, however, two different tendencies were detectable. On the one hand, a new scholarly emphasis on rediscovery of the 'lost' history of the Cuban people ensured that the pioneering 1960s efforts were continued by a new genera-tion of rigorous scholarship. Simultaneously, however, there was a degree of symbolization, as institutional historiography gave the 'official' discourse (of the past's being realized in the present) a new focus, shifting attention away from the more nationalist roots of *Cuba Libre* towards histories of the working class, the Communist Party and other 'safer' topics – but steering clear of the ambiguous 1934–44 period. This was symbolization, because the new perspective of history was far removed from the underlying ethos of the 1960s Revolution and, following a new vanguard discourse, ignored the popular canon of *cubania*. Moreover, the new historiography now revised the once contested past in the light of a present that was positive and also, in the process, presented Cuba as, for the first time, the subject of its own history, moving beyond the mythic victimization and objectivi-zation that had ensured the hegemony of the former myth of *historia*.

A similar process also began to happen with Martí. Firstly, the Cuban patriot – of such eclectic, clearly nineteenth-century, views (including liberalism, Krausism and even freemasonry) – fitted uncomfortably within a process that now saw itself as part of a socialist, and largely European, world, wherein a 'progressive bour-geoisie' was integral to a necessary past but had little relevance to a socialist present, defined now by the model offered by the Soviet Union and the eastern European states. Martí therefore, although still lionized and given official admiration, became formally part of the Revolution's 'pre-history', and thus his role became quite different from the message conveyed by the previous decade – that he was present in a revolutionary process that was realizing his dreams. In essence, the myth of Martí – so long such an integral and organic part of the evolving and radicalizing *cubania* – was becoming 'frozen', retreating to the status of symbol, with all the implicit dangers of a subsequent iconization. The fact that a full iconization did not set in, as had occurred in 1934–58, was attributable to the myth's organic and popular roots and the overt resistance that began to be exerted.

Simultaneously, 'underground' work was beginning in the academic and intel-lectual elite to rescue the 'essential' Martí, by studying and publishing his writings (as well as his actions and image), in a parallel process that, not unlike what happened after 1934, countered the more official symbolization. This became more evident as Armando Hart (a Movement veteran, and always part of the 'inner circle') was appointed the first Minister of Culture in 1976, immediately encouraging a revival of *martianismo*, especially in the establishment of the prestigious Centro de Estudios Martianos. A 're-martianization' of the Revolution was therefore integral to the process of either 're-Cubanization' or 're-Fidelization' that was actually under way from the mid-1970s, alongside the apparent institutionalization and 'Sovietization' processes.

What was actually happening was once again less a battle of 'factions', or a 'radicalism-versus-orthodoxy' dichotomy, and more the familiar picture of 'competing discourses' at all levels. It was, therefore, inevitable in the circumstances that this 'competition' should have obtained also in relation to such a potentially powerful and unifying myth as Martí, for the 'officialization' of the myth in the more 'outwardly oriented' 1970s (focused more on eastern European, and thus 'exogenous', models) meant in effect a process of symbolization in official discourse, in that the figure, rather than the 'story-line', of the myth was emphasized, thus necessarily alienating it from the organic base of the myth. Meanwhile, at a less official level, what we might call an 'alternative vanguard discourse' was being developed by those adhering to the 'inwardly oriented' perspective (and therefore focusing on 'endogenous' models and criteria), seeking, with this myth, to develop an awareness of Martí, his life, his actions and his writings, through the creation of study groups and the new Centro. This latter discourse was inevitably closer to the myth's existing organic attraction, given all Cubans' familiarity and identification with certain essential features of the 'story-line', and, in the circumstances, represented something of a cultural resistance to the exogenous ideological pressures. Martí thus became, effectively, something of an ideological and mythic battleground for these competing discourses.

If this happened with Martí, then a parallel process of symbolization happened even more clearly with the more controversial, but newer, myth of *Che*, for which the conditions for potential symbolization–iconization were even greater, given that the whole thrust of policy from 1975 was increasingly contrary to Guevara's ideas, prescriptions and image. Economic policies were now geared to the 'socialist division of labour' (with Cuba principally supplying primary materials within Comecon), to material incentives, decentralization and the efficiency criterion of *cálculo económico* (economic calculation), and political direction was now determined by a closer (and, some felt, more subservient) relationship with the Soviet Union, while domestic structures were apparently akin to those in the Socialist Bloc and were now led more by the old PSP (who had been prominent in arguing against Guevara). Not only were his ideas now relegated or even marginalized (with a decreasing level of publication of those ideas), but all those associated with 'Guevarism' were also marginalized in the new system.[9] In these circumstances, therefore, it was inevitable that any organic mythification of *Che* should be marginalized too, and that, in its place, a formal symbolization should be constructed.

There were thus again, within the competing discourses, two competing approaches to the myth. At the formal level, *Che* was clearly symbolized, by stressing his figure and his presumably historic meaning without pointing to his ideas and writings. In this way, the adherents of the exogenous models hoped to appropriate some degree of the legitimacy bestowed by this palpably revolutionary figure at a time when more and more of the directions pursued seemed less revolutionary than hitherto; however, by deliberately alienating the myth – through symbolization and an emphasis on *Che* as a more static and venerated 'model for being' rather than the more challenging 'model for action' – it became increasingly bereft of any organic meaning and thus of any relevance to the present situation. That situation was increasingly unlike the 1967–70 context, when the combination of demoralization, political pressure and economic difficulty had made more organic an identification with the *Che* myth and its 'story-line'; now, increasingly, the emphasis on material benefits, markets and coexistence meant almost a 'de-politicization' of the political culture and, certainly the emergence of levels and islands of privilege and a gradual undermining of the 1960s commitment to egalitarianism. In this context, the earlier myth of *Che* would have been not only irrelevant but even dangerous and destabilizing, with its essential messages of revolutionary commitment and fierce egalitarianism. Instead, it was important to present *Che*, who could be useful to legitimize aspects of the new order, as a symbol of self-sacrifice and martyrdom that might have been relevant to the past but was now somewhat unnecessary and meaningless. Guevara's image thus appeared in almost statutory fashion, as a hero of the past – of the present order's 'pre-history', alongside Martí and other historical figures; but his writings were increasingly difficult to find and his overt 'disciples' marginalized in the political and academic structures. *Che* as a man of ideas disappeared under the weight of *Che* as a man of action of the past.

Simultaneously, however, the more 'inwardly-oriented' alternative vanguard discourse was challenging this representation. For a start, as we have seen, it is a simplification to present the 1970s as 'Sovietized' and 'orthodox' in all respects (Fitzgerald 1978). In foreign policy, pragmatism (which, as we have seen, had anyway played a part in the apparently 'utopian' confrontational foreign policy) may have determined an abandonment of revolution in Latin America; but new

---

9. One example was the closure of the magazine *Pensamiento Crítico*, which had, from 1968, flown the flag of radicalism, 'Guevarism' and a somewhat unorthodox interpretation of socialism, Marxism and revolution.

opportunities in Africa allowed the ethos of revolution to emerge, as Cuba, as a 'revolutionary state', aided liberation struggles and empathetic governments. Even in the economy a degree of the old voluntarism still remained, and was even institutionalized in the *microbrigadas*.[10] In the political structure, as we have seen, there were contradictions, or tensions, between the apparent 'Sovietization' of the system and the residual power and function of the CDRs, and between the return of the PSP and the survival, and even resistance, of the *sierra*. Finally, in social policy, the 'inefficient' devotion of resources to the massive expansion of health provision and educational opportunity, not to mention the new Third World 'internationalism', all bore a closer resemblance to the 1960s ethos than to the new dispensation.

Beyond the official levels, therefore, especially among those Cubans where the alternative discourse still held some sway, the organic myth was retained, often as a memory of the fallen comrade held by his former co-revolutionaries, who were now more marginal but also themselves beneficiaries of the symbolization process itself. The more that *Che* was held up for veneration, the more they as a group were legitimized vicariously; the more that photographs of Guevara alongside Castro or any others of the Sierra were paraded publicly, the more the former guerrillas were associated in the public mind with *Che*. Moreover, the greatest image in the symbolization–iconization process (the Korda portrait – replicated in enormous public detail in the Plaza de la Revolución) came, as many Cubans were aware, from a particular period – and even a particular moment – in the 1960s; and, with his beret and longer hair, and visionary gaze, the *Che* that was represented was one that recalled those days, rather than the present less heroic and less revolutionary period. Furthermore, every time that a national rally or parade was held in the Plaza, the link between Fidel and the image of Che was all too visible to ignore.

A strange counter-process thus became evident, whereby the 'outs' of the alternative vanguard discourse did not actually need to articulate their views coherently to maintain themselves in public consciousness, for the symbolization of *Che* was a constant reminder of their claim to hegemony. Moreover, as enough aspects remained of that discourse – the commitment to African liberation, the new 'internationalism', the continuing voluntarism – that were redolent of the previous decade, the *Che* connection also helped to identify one level of popular awareness with the organic aspects of the continuing myth. In this respect, too, the Revolution's practice of simply marginalizing the 'outs' after a 'debate' guaranteed 'spaces' for the alternative discourse to be maintained openly and organically.

---

10. These were an attempt to solve the growing housing shortage by encouraging enterprises to release or second volunteer workers to form 'brigades', which would, with expert advice and direction, construct new residential blocks (especially in the eastern suburbs of La Habana del Este).

It also, however, survived popularly in a way characteristic of the necessary contradictions of the evolving system. Throughout the 'good years' of 1972–85, when material living standards were visibly improving and when the frenetic political pressures abated considerably, many Cubans seemed to respond positively to the memory offered by *Che*, as though it enabled them to identify with a period that, though it had implied constant mobilization, pressure, economic shortages and eventually demoralization, had also meant a sense of community, shared suffering, collective heroism and pride, and even a moral dimension to the whole effort. For these (especially older) Cubans, maintaining the memory of *Che* was thus a valuable link with a period that had perhaps felt closer to the 'essence' of the Revolution than the present period; the contradiction lay in the fact that this same nostalgia could be felt by those who enthusiastically pursued material benefits, professional opportunity and even party position in a structure where membership could now (as it could not during the 1960s) be seen to bestow more benefits than demands. For these Cubans, nostalgia meant an identification with a part of themselves that had gone but about which they still felt good – albeit those same Cubans might also be relieved that it had indeed gone – not unlike the 1960s British nostalgia for the community spirit of 1940–45.

Simultaneously, the new dispensation also meant a need for new myths, some of which emerged organically and others of which were more artefactual, to meet the new demand. Two in particular stand out as representative of both categories. The first was a revival of the myth of Afro-Cuba, which was given a boost by the pride around the military commitment to, and involvement in, Angola. Whatever motivations lay behind the Cuban decision in November 1975 to commit troops to defend the new MPLA government in Angola against the South African invasion, it rapidly became a popular and prestigious action, both inside Cuba and more broadly within the Third World (see Connell-Smith 1979; Domínguez 1978b; Gonzalez 1977; Gunn 1980; Kapcia 1979; LeoGrande 1980; Moore 1988; Thomas 1977–8; Treverton 1977; Valenta 1978). Within days, the involvement was being extolled as the 'return of the slaves', the press and speeches were full of references to the Angolan origins of many of Cuba's slaves in the last century, and the whole episode was being presented as Cuba partly helping to pay off the world's debts to Africa for the ignominy and iniquity of slavery. As success followed success in saving the new government from an enemy seen universally as both evil and racist – and thus anti-African – national pride grew dramatically and the initially volunteer commitment to the military struggle needed little encouragement (although, more prosaically, those that volunteered did receive tangible material benefits that might otherwise have been less available). By 1976, there were between 15,000 and 36,000 troops (Pérez 1988: 378), by 1977, 30,000 (Mazarr 1988: 385); by 1979, with over 15,000 Cuban troops having also fought in Ethiopia (Pérez 1988: 378) – although in a less clear-cut struggle of 'good against evil', and with the initial threat to the MPLA's having been deterred, the image of a syncretic Cuba going back to its roots and restoring pride in Cuba, Afro-Cuba and Africa, was powerful and popular.

Moreover, this coincided with, and partly stimulated, a new cultural emphasis on Afro-Cuba that aspired to go beyond superficial identification with folklore and that in historiography, for example, attempted to rescue a forgotten African and slave past. The old myth of Afro-Cuba was therefore revived, progressing yet again along its trajectory – from the earliest folkloric representation of the pictures-que, through the greater political and anthropological emphasis on the mixed nature of Cuban society, to its most recent manifestation of pride and, more importantly, human and military commitment to secure that identification.

This, however, does introduce the sensitive issue of race and Revolution, never a clear-cut issue and often a subject of passionate controversy. Alongside the evident material and legal improvements for Cuba's black population after 1959 – which saw them benefit proportionately more from reform and integration than the white population (if only because blacks represented a greater proportion of the hitherto poor and marginalized), and which evidently saw blacks emerge as the Revolution's most enthusiastic supporters (80 per cent compared to 67 per cent of whites: Zeitlin 1970a: 77), especially after Castro's much-publicized visit to New York's Harlem in 1958 and Sekou Touré's visit to Cuba in 1960 (Moore 1988: 97), there was an alternative case being made by critics of a still discernible institutionalized racism. The most vociferous, but also partisan, of these critics, Carlos Moore, even condem-ned the 'manipulation' of Afro-Cuban culture – seen in the emphasis on its 'exotic' aspects enshrined in the Instituto Nacional de Etnología y Folklore (1961) – and of Afro-Cubans generally to legitimize foreign policy and to cover what he saw as the 'denigration' and 'divide-and-rule' repression of Afro-Cuban religion (Moore 1988: 100–3, 304). What is clear, beyond polemic, is that the Revolution's official 'colour-blind' policies - designed to emphasize unity and universal improvement, rather than affirmative action (Pérez Sarduy and Stubbs 1993: 11) – have tended to under-emphasize the undesirably high proportion of crime and lingering poverty among the black population, and their under-representation in the political system.[11] This latter fact was even publicly acknowledged by Castro in 1986 (Kapcia 1986: 198). Whether this constitutes institutional racism is questionable, but it certainly reflects an ambivalence – official and popular – towards issues of race, which makes the question somewhat sensitive and makes conclusions difficult to draw.[12]

11. In 1978, for example, Cuba counted only five black Ministers (out of thirty-four), four black members of the Buró Político (out of fourteen), sixteen black members of the party's Central Committee (out of 146), and no black generals in Angola (though most of the troops were black) (Moore 1988: 333).

12. One of the most obvious problems here is the statistical information, largely based on self-classification, which, in 1983, indicated only 12 per cent as black and 22 per cent as *mulato*, while other estimates put the black and *mulato* figures as high as 50 or 60 per cent (Moore 1988: 333).

Certainly, however, there is no consensus in contemporary Cuba about the prominence of black 'heroes' in the *cubanista* pantheon; apart from Maceo, who towers
over the rest in terms of mythification (and is, indeed, perhaps the only black
figure to acquire real politico-historical mythic status), other leading black fighters,
intellectuals, and activists (such as Juan Gualberto Gómez, Quintín Bandera, Carlos
Baliño, Lázaro Peña and Jesús Menéndez) tend to be acknowledged for their role
in the long struggle, but are rarely noted for their 'blackness', while the majority
of the mythic 'heroes' do still tend to be white.

Whatever the reality of the question of race, however, the Angolan intervention
also revived another 1960s myth – the guerrilla. Firstly, the image of Angola that
was presented externally and domestically was of a commitment without counting
the economic cost. As the first troops were ferried in battered Britannia aircraft,
with rudimentary weaponry, the images recounted in the press and in the early
reports were redolent of the 1960s and even the 1950s struggles, of self-sacrifice,
of David against Goliath, of a fundamentally human and humanistic commitment
against the armed might of the greatest racist power in the world – often, implicitly,
identified with American imperialism, since, although Washington did not generally
support South Africa,[13] it did aid UNITA and the FNLA, the MPLA's two rival
forces. Furthermore, the intervention was largely seen as a military commitment
(thus also continuing the theme of *lucha*) led, directed and planned by Castro and
the other Sierra veterans; thus, as in the Escambray campaign of the 1960s, a
land-army's fight against counter-revolutionary guerrillas could be presented as a
continuation of the guerrilla. The sheer numbers of Cubans involved in this latest
manifestation of *conciencia revolucionaria* – 300,000 having served in Angola
and Ethiopia by 1988 (Domínguez 1990: 45) – increased the myth's power, as
many more Cubans than the original Rebel Army had now become heroic *guerrilleros*.

Alongside this was the reinforcement of the myth, and so many *cubanista* codes,
by the new 'internationalism' that had become so prominent in the 1970s and
would, in the 1980s, become a source of pride (and opportunity) to so many Cubans
(see Erisman 1991; Richmond 1991; Levine 1983). For, with between 11,000 and
20,000 Cubans serving on 'internationalist duty' in up to thirty-seven countries
by the 1980s (Erisman 1991: 140), this was an experience that impressed itself on
thousands of mostly young Cubans who, besides having their eyes opened by
contact with countries that were mostly poorer than Cuba, could feel a sense of
pride, participation and belonging that enabled them to identify with *guerrillerismo*,
and the codes of collectivism, activism, culturalism and, above all, internationalism
now made concrete.

The third myth that was now given a new boost and direction was the somewhat
forgotten myth of generations, now given new clothes as the emerging myth of

13. Indeed, in January 1977, Andrew Young, the American UN Ambassador, acknowledged the
Cuban presence as contributing to 'stability and order' in southern Africa (Mazarr 1988: 389).

youth. The image of the Revolution as an essentially youth-led and youth-oriented process was integral from the outset – from the inherent generationalism of the 1950s, and from the evident youthfulness of the guerrillas, together with the underlying and explicit references to renewal and a 'new Cuba'. The stress on the education of the young throughout the 1960s – with the Literacy Campaign being largely staffed by the young – reinforced this identification, as did the fact that the construction of the early Revolution so obviously lay in the hands of younger Cubans – not least because so many emigrants, whose places the new generation urgently needed to take, were older, or seen to be older. The importance given to the *pioneros* reinforced this emphasis.

As the process aged a little, however, and as the *sierra* generation remained in power beyond their visible youthfulness, the concept needed to be addressed somewhat differently, which the new myth proceeded to do. From the early 1970s, the implicit stress on youth was now made explicit – the young were seen as the essence of the process (in the past and in the future direction and purpose), youthfulness was presented as the characteristic of a fundamentally renovatory transformation, and youth was seen as the emblem and symbol of the whole Revolution. The Isle of Pines was therefore renamed the Isla de la Juventud (Isle of Youth) in 1976, and dedicated almost entirely to the 'internationalist' education of Third World youth and to work-camps designed to reinvigorate the new genera-tion as the older ones had been through the 1960s struggles and mobilizations. Equally, the UJC was strengthened and its profile raised, and the posters of the island extolled the Revolution's commitment to its young.

Related to this new emphasis was a new pride in Cuban sporting achievements – themselves, as with the Angolan episode, a new experience for a culture raised on an essentially self-denigrating self-image (Griffiths 1979: 247–60; Bunck 1990). The themes were related simply because of the universal identification between sport and youth; yet sport soon took on a political importance of its own, being a source of pride and nationalism, and a focal point for political activity – as, for example, in decisions to stage the Pan-American Games in Havana in the depths of the 1990s crisis or in the celebration of Olympic baseball victories against the United States, and the May 1999 victory against the Baltimore Orioles.

Mostly, however, these new myths could not justifiably be called myths in the use of the term in this study; they were at best pre-myths, or myths in formation, not least because they did not yet demonstrate any deep organic identity. They were, in short, mostly symbols, since, apart from the 'return of the slaves' message explicit in the Afro-Cuba myth, they lacked the necessary 'story-line' and, instead, each represented a value that operated almost totemically in the political culture – if a totem is defined as a symbol that is believed, or said, to identify the group. In part this ascendancy of values (over myths) can be attributed to the fact that the Cuba of the 1970s was a more confident and less mobilization-oriented society and thus less amenable to organic myths; in part it was because the period was actually something of a hiatus between mobilizations, a period of ideological uncertainty where one of the competing discourses – the 'outwardly-oriented' one, which sought guidance in exogenous models – was politically and economically dominant but unable to convince organically, while the alternative discourse was to some extent in temporary retreat and unable to challenge the pragmatic dominance of the rival version. In such a context, the leading (but not yet hegemonic) discourse was unable to create the convincing 'story-line' necessary to form a myth, while the discourse in retreat was unable to challenge for political reasons. Moreover, the social context for the whole 'competition' was of a need to consolidate ideologically and rely on a moment of unprecedented material satisfaction. In such a context, myths can all too easily 'retreat' to the status of symbols.

All this held true until the mid-1980s, when the multifaceted crisis and the subsequent process of 'Rectification' began, again throwing the Revolution into the ideological melting-pot and again bringing the dormant issues to the surface. This was particularly so as the origins of the crisis were fundamental to the underlying 'competition'. Long before the 1989–91 collapse of Comecon, the Socialist Bloc and the Soviet Union had created the deep crisis that so threatened the Revolution: the system was already undergoing, and addressing, a more structural series of deep challenges, which came effectively in three separate stages.

The first was an unseen, but underlying, weakness and inefficiency in the preceding decade, with a crucial combination of economic circumstances throwing into question the economic successes upon which the new ordinance had based its political legitimacy (Roca 1986). Those circumstances began with a sudden fall in the price of both oil (which Cuba was by then re-exporting profitably) and sugar, to which a more market-oriented Cuba was now more vulnerable. That was followed by rising interest rates, to which Cuba was also newly vulnerable, having, at the Soviet Union's behest, opened up to Western credit and also trade with the West (41 per cent of total trade by 1974) (Eckstein 1994: 47). Then came a fall in the dollar (further reducing oil earnings) and, finally, the rise to power in Moscow of Gorbachev.

This last event was of considerable economic significance, since the new Soviet leader made it clear that when Cuba's already rescheduled Soviet debts fell due (many in 1989), there would be no rescheduling as before, but instead a more commercial relationship based on real prices and hard currency (Shearman 1990). Since 1972, Cuba's debts had been largely repaid in kind, which occasionally reduced the export-earning potential of Cuban sugar but generally cost less than commercial transactions; now that relationship was to be ended. All of this meant that, after the impressive 7.4 per cent growth rate in 1984, the economic planners had to contemplate an imminent external context in which the reliance on Comecon could not continue and in which Cuba would find itself earning less and owing more. The implications for the largely exogenously generated economic model were far-reaching, especially as, by then, Cuba's sugar production suffered from many inefficiencies, under-using mill capacity, land and some labour and over-using other lands and other labour (Brunner 1977: 6–8).

The second crisis was political, arising partly in response to these new challenges, but also from the sins of the past decade. The new external context was obviously problematic now in several respects. Firstly, Cuba now faced a different United States, under Reagan, set on reversing recent international setbacks and, specifically, containing Cuba's recent successful diplomatic offensive in the Third World and the Caribbean Basin region. Gone was the brief space provided by both post-Watergate trauma and isolationism and the rise of a more radical or nationalistic region. Instead, Reagan made it clear in his 'Caribbean Basin' strategy that the source of the 'contagion' was Cuba, to be dealt with afresh; while no one believed that invasion might result (since Pentagon studies had repeatedly indicated that military action would be impractical and costly), the signs pointed to a new 'siege', renewed pressure, and 'the revival of vendetta politics' (Morley 1987: 317). The militias were revived, as the Milicias de Tropas Territoriales (MTT – Territorial Militias), which meant increased budget strains and the risk of increasing demands on a population that, although mobilization had decreased, had still already seen a high number of casualties in Angola – estimates varying between 1,000 and 10,000 (Habel 1991: 133), but probably closer to Eckstein's 2,016 (Eckstein 1994: 202).

Secondly, the Kremlin changes were indirectly worrying, since talk of, and pressure for, *glasnost* and *perestroika* had dangerous implications for the Cuban leadership, which viewed with alarm the mood of uncontrolled debate, the opportunities given to non-communists and, above all, the warmer relationship with Washington and an apparent economic liberalization (no longer as acceptable in Cuba as before 1985). Castro's arguments against the new Soviet politics were clear enough – whatever justification they might have in the Soviet Union (which had, he felt, always been more inherently bureaucratic and exclusive than a more participatory Cuba), they were dangerous for Cuba, which was now again the front line of communism and the Third World against American imperialism. Cuba could thus simply not afford to open up its defences against Washington. Therefore, when some within the Cuban party – seeing a reformist Moscow as their alibi and a possible ally in a bid for reform – made clear their preference for similar principles in Cuba, and when disaffected younger Cubans began, unprecedentedly, to buy up copies of Soviet newspapers, Castro and the other leaders had to respond.

The context for that response was created, however, by the third crisis, which underlay the other two, within Cuba itself – the growing crisis of party legitimacy created by the recent internal changes. The combination of, on the one hand, growing materialism and consumerism, and, on the other, consolidation, institutionalization and bureaucratization as the party was restored and grew, had meant a steady rise of a new party elite and 'bureaucratic class', both nationally and locally, as well as a growing bureaucratic inertia (Habel 1991: 57–65; Bengelsdorf 1994: 91–4). Some who recognized the potential of these changes realized that, as in Eastern Europe, the party was as a result an obvious new source of privilege, power and advancement, and therefore used their position to achieve that. In a Revolution whose first decade had been characterized by a fierce egalitarianism and a shared suffering, such a development was a cause of public resentment and official concern, both often expressed through the mass organizations that still thrived, as well as through both the (new) OPP feed-back meetings (the *rendición de cuentas* – 'rendering of accounts') and the (old) CDRs.[14]

Two small crises then erupted in the process of gradual liberalization. The first was the furore over the effects of the partial liberalization indicated in the creation in 1980 of the *mercado libre campesino* (free peasant market), which then gave rise to a small and resented layer of richer retailers, leading to the closure of the markets in 1986. The second arose from similar arguments over limited and controlled house sales, abruptly halted in 1988, after only four years of operation. In the face of these affairs, which highlighted underlying social tensions (see Stubbs 1989), the political tide began to turn, and, thereafter, pressure was exerted gradually within the party to correct the new direction of the system. The external changes now gave the 'old guard' their cue, the first moves becoming evident in 1985 with the partial demotion of a long-standing member of the 'inner circle', Ramiro Valdés Daussá, who (despite being a veteran of Moncada, the *Granma* and the Sierra) had, as Minister of the Interior, become close to Moscow and inadequate in his response to the increasingly evident corruption.

The stage was thus set for the full-blown drive for 'Rectification' (in full, 'Rectification of Past Errors and Negative Tendencies'). This was launched officially at the Third Party Congress of 1986, which indicated the scale of the internal tensions by having to be spread across two sessions, one in February and the other in December, officially to allow for full public discussion of the proposals outlined in February, but also to ensure that any February opposition was suitably outflanked by the end of the year (Kapcia 1986, 1987).

'Rectification' was, therefore, a renewal of old tensions in a new context of economic and political crisis, internal and external. Although some saw it as a 'return of ideology', and thus partly a return of 1960s modalities (Mesa-Lago 1988: 59–100), the picture was actually more complicated. Those often seen as the 'old guard' (largely, but by no means exclusively, the former *sierra*) – geared more towards the 'inwardly-oriented' vision and endogenous models – took their

14. These are six-monthly public meetings at which OPP delegates are obliged to defend their performance in the various assemblies and that can result in the instant recall of 'unsatisfactory' representatives. They were a mechanism originally developed in the 1960s Poder Local system.

cue from the crisis to retrieve a lost vanguard hegemony, to prepare Cuba for the hard economic choices ahead, to distance Cuba from the 'contagion' from Moscow, to purge the party of its 'rotten apples' (40 per cent of the Central Committee being renewed), to streamline decision-making and stress efficiency, and to attempt to restore something of the ethos of the 1960s. It therefore had a firm economic, as well as political, function and motivation (Fitzgerald 1994: 153–70; Pérez-Stable 1993: 153–73; Mesa-Lago 1990; Eckstein 1994).

This then was yet another of the cyclical 'debates' characterizing the Revolution's long trajectory, between competing discourses and competing perspectives on the nature of socialism in an underdeveloped society. It was now, however, taking place within a new context of more serious crisis, for the threat to the party's legitimacy was a new phenomenon, and the Soviet changes far-reaching in their implications for Cuba. Even so, the expected shift to a 'hard line' (supposedly reflecting the stern tone of 'Rectification'), turned out not to be so, as the need for debate once again opened up forums and broadened parameters for discussions at several levels. Thus, while the vanguard was debating within, and between, the two sessions of the 1986 congress, an extensive grass-roots debate was indeed encouraged (in workplaces, CDRs, party cells and in the OPP forums), as was a debate within Havana intellectual circles, now encouraged to rethink orthodox interpretations and positions. The result was the gradual reincorporation from the margins of those most closely identified with the 1960s 'inwardly-oriented' ethos and policies and with Guevara, and, simultaneously, a revival of academic and political interest in, and awareness and publication of, Guevara's writings.

One significant outcome of this whole shift came, in July 1989, with the arrest and trial of one of the Revolution's leading Angolan generals and one of the few *Héroes de la Revolución*, the Sierra veteran Arnaldo Ochoa, who had been allowed a somewhat free rein to direct the vital sanctions-busting operation. What he was tried for was corruption, abuse of power and involvement in the Colombian-based drug traffic – all sufficient to earn him a death-sentence; but what may also have been behind the decision, besides the truth of the accusation (which Ochoa admitted), was – besides the possibility that he had mounted a challenge to Castro, as some believe (Rabkin 1991: 185) – the need to send warning signals to two groups of people. Firstly, it warned those adherents of the 'outwardly-oriented' discourse who were still in influential positions, perhaps able to mount a counter-offensive, that the new ordinance was in control and that orientation towards either a reformist Moscow or an intransigent Washington was out of the question. Secondly, it warned the FAR that, despite Angola, they were not a separate power group – a message perhaps reflecting fears that the returning officers, used to a degree of autonomy and prestige and many of them Soviet-trained, might become frustrated at finding not a 'land fit for heroes' but a crisis-ridden and again besieged Revolution (see Habel 1991: 177–99). The fact that the FAR and MININT (the Interior Ministry)

– both with independent power-bases and both close to Moscow in training, equipment and thinking – were the forces most affected by the fall-out from the affair (in terms of high-level executions and dismissals) would strengthen that perspective.

Even before the post-1989 crisis in Eastern Europe evolved, therefore, the Revolution was in the throes of both its own triple crisis and a process of self-questioning and debate, which, indeed, may be one reason for the system's eventual survival beyond that new and frightening challenge (which, on the face of it, ought to have propelled Cuba into terminal collapse, in the wake of the rest of the Socialist Bloc). While the post-1989 crisis was enormous, it was actually wider and older than it seemed, with its roots in internal tensions, problems, debates and crises that were somewhat familiar to many Cubans and were already being addressed along familiar lines. In that sense, the real crisis point for Cuba was not 1989 or 1991, as it seemed, but 1984–5; once the cycle of debate and contest was under way from that date, the adjustment to the supplementary crises, although more urgent and more extreme than any had imagined, was actually just that – adjustment of the existing strategy, and not so much a fundamental revision.

The 1989–94 crisis was, however, deep. Imports from Comecon (84 per cent of the 1989 total) fell by 90 per cent by 1992, with oil supplies falling from 13.2 million tonnes (mt) annually to some six million tonnes, and much-needed supplies of fertilizer and animal feed falling from 1.3mt and 1.6mt respectively to 0.25mt and 0.45mt, and with the prices of imported oil and food rising by 40 per cent and of exported nickel and sugar falling by 28 and 20 per cent (Kapcia 1995: 6–7). As a result, the sugar harvests went into decline, from the 8.4mt figure for 1991 to 6.2mt in 1992, 4.3mt in 1993 and 3.8mt in 1994.

Although the leadership's response was visibly dramatic – declaring a 'Special Period' ('in Times of Peace') in September 1990 and talking defiantly of *Socialismo o Muerte* ('Socialism or Death') instead of the familiar *cubanista* slogan of *Patria o Muerte*, in essence the initial responses were simply continuations of 'Rectification', which, as has been seen, had always had an economic motive (to streamline, batten down the hatches for the coming storm, and return to some of the previous values of austerity and voluntarism), a political purpose, and an underlying ideological inspiration and direction. Thus, for example, the revival of the writings and study of Guevara was accelerated (not least to seek ideas of relevance for the new crisis), and greater attention was paid to youth, to the Revolution's nationalist pedigree and past, and to the decade of the 1960s – all of which had been either initiated or prefigured in the debates of the 1980s, but all of which now acquired a new urgency and relevance.

For, essentially, the leadership recognized an important fact – that the causes of all of the post-1985 crises lay deep in the preceding decisions, patterns and system, and needed to be addressed in particular ways. Most fundamentally, there is an inevitability and a structurality about crisis that cannot be ignored in any analysis, for all revolutions must by definition be in a process of permanent crisis, given the inevitability of internal and external threats (which the history of most revolutions proves) and the constant need of the revolutionary process to redefine itself in the light of the equally inevitable changes that the process itself generates. The more successful a revolution in transforming the social environment, the political structure and the economic orientation of a society, the more the process must examine its direction, nature, purposes and ideological impulses in the light of those changes. A revolution does not, by definition, stand still; neither, therefore, does the need for self-definition. That fact creates an inherent propensity for crisis, in the danger of a disjuncture's arising between shifting popular aspirations and the declared ideology, policies and strategies of the revolutionary leadership. Moreover, success or failure can easily result in either, on the one hand, increased, and unrealizable, expectations or, on the other, growing discontent and frustration. In Cuba, all this was demonstrably true from 1959, the constant process of ideological redefinition bearing witness to the flexibility and organicity of the underlying *cubania*.

Equally, success and failure have both had their costs. One outstanding example of the 'costs' of success was the general rise in popular and youth expectations in the 1970s. In the previous decade, a degree of alienation had, as we have seen, resulted in some difficulties between the often seemingly puritanical authorities and younger non-conformists. Now, however, the potential problem had been addressed by a more market-oriented leadership through the increase in consumerism and the stress on the opportunities for professional advancement – a policy that did indeed reap dividends, as more and more young people made their way up through the social system and came to expect benefits as a matter of course. Even the politically motivated 'internationalism' of the period was also a means to give these otherwise disenchanted and frustrated young people the opportunity to travel, broaden their horizons and see the outside world. The most eloquent illustration of this was the expansion of higher education – from five centres in 1974 to forty-six in 1984, and from 35,137 enrolled students in 1970 to 240,000 in 1984 (Fitzgerald 1994: 88), leading to a 'new professional' class (Fitzgerald 1990) now employed in the burgeoning bureaucracy.[15] As is logical, however, the danger in this approach of material satisfaction was that the young particularly,

---

15. Habel talks of an increase in administrative employment for 1977–87 from 90,000 to 248,000, with 'managerial' employment rising by some 41 per cent (Habel 1991: 37). Moreover, there had been a shift in higher education from the humanities (32 per cent in 1956–7) to the sciences, technology and agriculture even by 1968–9 (11.3 per cent, 28.4 per cent and 11.9 per cent respectively) (Valdés 1972: 437).

knowing no other context, came to develop ever higher and ultimately unattainable social and economic expectations.

As well as creating a serious labour shortage in agriculture, these rising expectations led to a 'consumerization' of ambitions among young Cubans, who were encouraged to think in terms of 'Second World' aspirations (as a result of the beneficial Comecon links), while the Cuban economy continued to show evidence of its essentially Third World weakness. That conflict between unrealizable expectations and reality came to a head in the mid-1980s, when Cuba's apparently solid growth was confronted by the effects of increased borrowing, increased trade with the West and the limitations of the structural trade dependence on the Socialist Bloc. When the system then failed to deliver sufficiently to meet those expectations, the potential for conflict was considerable, with a real threat of widespread youth alienation at a critical time (Rabkin 1988; Domínguez García 1998).

That threat was, however, more deeply-rooted than the sudden economic downturn of the 1990s, having much to do also with the tendency towards bureaucratization, privilege and even corruption within more opportunistic layers and sectors of the political structure. Thus, an increasingly young Cuba found itself frustrated by a system that seemed to have stagnated and become less inclusive, a system still led, moreover, by those who, having come to power in 1959 had then seemed to age in office, while still using the same language, a vanguard that they tended often to consider as irrelevant to their needs, out of touch with the outside world, hanging on to power too long and speaking a political language that no longer meant much to them. To these young Cubans, talk of the heroic days of the insurrection, of the hardships of the 1960s, and of revolutionary commitment had little appeal.

After Gorbachev's rise, the contrast between their perception of Cuba and his image of exciting change became briefly a cause of resentment and discontent. Once Gorbachev's project collapsed in 1991, these same young admirers either bottled up their resentment or directed it towards the apparent failings of a system that was now showing all the signs of a similar collapse and beginning to rationalize its problems as attributable to the previously trusted Soviet link and model. For them, the parallel between the stagnant and gerontocratic pre-Gorbachev Soviet Union and the Cuban case was attractive, and compounded by the Cuban system's long exaltation of the myth of youth while, to them, denying youth its true place in the leadership.

The crisis of 1989–1991 therefore compounded the underlying problem; if this generation expected too much and were being partly, but visibly, alienated from, or disenchanted with, the Cuban process, which was, again, led by the ex-guerrillas, then the prospect of a new austerity and new appeals to mobilization, sacrifice and the ideals of the older generation's years held dangers of an even greater distancing. This alienation remained mostly under the surface early on, but evidently played a part in the dramatic and worrying events of August 1994, when the growing flood of 'informal' refugees (taking to the sea in largely home-made craft – *balsas*), which had reached 3,335 for 1994 by June (compared to 2,857 for the whole of 1992 and 3,541 for 1993), now began to explode, reaching 8,116 by 20 August (and 1,189 on that day alone) (Kapcia 1995: 28). In all, in 1991–4, 45, 575 *balseros* (rafters) were picked up by the American coastguards (Ackerman 1996: 169), and the episode was accompanied by an increase in street violence, embassy occupations and armed hijackings of vessels. Although the exodus had other causes too (not least the measures designed to weaken the developing black market), it partly reflected the sense of frustration and alienation felt by sectors of relatively marginalized Havana youth; indeed, 43 per cent were aged between twenty and twenty-nine, 31 per cent were from Havana, and 56 per cent were professional or skilled (Ackerman 1996: 169–86). To these, the alienation was so great that, even when the Cuban government visibly told the truth about the economic crisis, or the differences with the United States, or the difficulties that the post-communist countries were experiencing, they would refuse to believe it, assuming that Castro was the problem and that the system could not be changed. Such views were, by definition, extreme, and by no means shared by all their generation; but they did reflect the tip of a more worrying iceberg of discontent, distance and mutual incomprehension – and may well have been reinforced in their extreme reaction by the inevitable recourse to the old 'outwardly-oriented' perspectives that always assumed that the problem lay within and the solution without.

The warning was then well taken, since the Cuban leadership, aware of the dangers of ignoring the young, began a process of introducing younger activists into positions of authority (covered in Chapter 6), of rejuvenating many of the middle layers of the bureaucracy and management, and of paying much more public attention to the leading actors in the UJC and the FEU.

There were thus, in all these shifts, clear implications for myth, as for ideology. Firstly, the new emphasis on Guevara coincided with a perceived need, at several levels and for many different and often contradictory motives, both to reinvigorate the Revolution's ideological thrust and to revive the legitimacy of the neglected 1960s, now seen as encapsulating the 'essence' of the 'real' Revolution and the period where the answers to the whole recent, and deeper, crisis might be found. Thus a shift that was sometimes presented as a cynical move by an ageing leadership to clothe itself in the legitimacy of the fallen and forgotten hero actually turned out be more organic in its appeal and response than many might have expected. The reception given to the revival of Guevara's image and ideas seemed to indicate a deeper desire among many Cubans, including the young, for a degree of 'spiritual' authority and solidity. Thus the *Che* who was now paraded almost sacrilegiously on T-shirts, key-rings and commercial objects, for the benefit of the new wave of tourists, actually did evoke a response among Cubans, in two different ways – and, indeed, seems to go on evoking those responses.[16]

On the one hand, the older generations who today either remember Guevara or grew up learning about him (and ritually promising daily to strive to be like him) have responded eagerly to the new interest by buying books, reading articles, and using the commercial objects as a means of signalling their continuing adherence to his memory – while, all the time, either condemning the disrespectful commercialization of the hero or justifying it to themselves as a means of spreading awareness of him. Their motives have been fairly clear: for their part, at a time of uncertainty, bewildering change and unprecedented and destabilizing reforms, not to mention demoralization and fear for the future, they seem to feel a clear collective need to cling to a consensual symbol of the decade that, for all its difficulties and faults, did at least offer a shared vision, a collective identity and, above all, a revolutionary certainty. *Che*, for them, means the Revolution with which they grew up or to which they adhered after 1959, and that many of them wish to preserve in some form or other. For them therefore, the old myth – partially symbolized in the 1970s but always maintained more organically at a deeper level in the 'alternative' vanguard discourse – has now acquired a new meaning, a new importance and, therefore, a new organicity.

That process – of what is effectively the 'rescue' of the symbolized, 'frozen', myth – has, indeed, gathered pace as the years since 1995 have seen the steady retirement of many of the guerrilla generation and their replacement (in the party, the civil service, academia, and elsewhere) by a much younger generation of activists, leaders, technocrats and bureaucrats, but has also proved to strike a deeper chord. Surprisingly, it has been the myth of *Che* that has been seized upon since 1995 by the younger, otherwise more discontented, Cubans to be their emblem.

16. What follows are largely the findings of a research project conducted jointly with my colleague, Professor Jean Gilkison, of the University of Wolverhampton, in two fieldwork visits to Cuba in September 1997 and May 1998, involving semi-structured interviews with nine different groups of people, covering different ages, social groups, levels of education and manners of political involvement. The interviews consisted of a series of questions posed about images of, and reactions to, José Martí and Che Guevara. The results – running to some twelve hours of tape – were then analysed from the point of view of both linguistic form and conceptual content, to determine the extent to which the responses contained evidence of what we called 'customization' of the myths, to enable the respondents to adapt to potentially destabilizing changes and legitimize their own political responses to the leadership's policies. The result have been progressively expounded in papers given at conferences at the University of Braga, Portugal (annual conference of the Association of Hispanists of Great Britain and Ireland), in September 1998; the University of Wolverhampton (School of Languages and European Studies Seminar Series) in February 1999; the University of Cambridge (annual conference of the Society for Latin American Studies) in April 1999; and the University of Havana (second joint conference of the Forum for the Study of Cuba) in April 1999. The final exposition of the full results and conclusions is expected to be published in 2000.

The evidence is that not only have younger Cubans chosen an extensive identification with the familiar images of Guevara, but also, in adhering to the myth of *Che*, have been doing several, often contradictory, things. In the first place, many have been attracted by a figure who represents a permanently young face of the system, someone from a 'heroic' age who tragically (like many a young idol) died young in pursuit of his ideals; this figure may be from the same generation as Castro and the other ex-guerrillas, but he seems untainted by the marks of failure, ageing and disillusion that his surviving ex-comrades inevitably bear. By clinging to *Che*, the young can therefore be 'revolutionary' and still distance themselves from the present leadership.[17]

To some of these young Cubans, therefore, identification with *Che* has been a means of protesting against aspects of the system, rather than simply supporting it. On the other hand, other young Cubans seem to have approached it more positively, identifying with the myth in ways that stress their underlying commitment to a concept of 'revolution' but that also distinguish it from the more staid and less revolutionary system to which they have become used. To them, *Che* is the Revolution to which they would have adhered had they been alive in the 1960s, and identifying with him is thus a way of being both committed and dissenting. In this, they are also following an interesting trajectory.

17. This raises the inevitable question of a possible myth of Fidel Castro himself. It is inevitable because the casual observer of modern and contemporary Cuba is so mesmerized by the personality and apparent dominance of the Cuban leader as to expect, and therefore see, a process of mythification of the *Jefe Máximo* in most Cubans today and throughout the revolutionary process. Indeed, the very use by all Cubans of the term *Fidel* rather than *Castro* seems to imply such a mythification. However, the omission of Castro from this study of contemporary myths of the Revolution is, in fact, quite logical, and in keeping with the definition established earlier. The reason is simple: Castro is still a living, active leader, and thus incapable of being truly adopted as a politico-historical myth, since such myths necessarily depend on the distance of time and death (which allows no future behaviour to spoil the 'story-line' and separates the subject of the myth from the living adherents). That is not to say, of course, that there are not already a number of artefact myths about Castro, in Cuba and in Miami; there are, and they multiply each day, and already play a role in either cementing support for the Revolution (often anthropomorphized through *Fidel*), guaranteeing continued hope (the belief that 'Fidel will find a way'), or in any allocation of blame. Furthermore, one encounters among thinking supporters of the Revolution in Cuba a myth-making tendency to abdicate any requirement for analysis of new and challenging developments by simply seeking the judgemental *imprimatur* of one of Castro's statements. Moreover, there is already a tendency to mythify Castro's past, to separate the Castro of 'here-and-now', dealing with the daily challenges of the process, from the Fidel of the insurrection and the early 'heroic' years. Equally, there is no doubt that once Castro has either left power or died, so long as 'the Revolution' survives, a whole mythic universe will arise organically around him. Thus Castro will clearly be a myth of the future, for which the groundwork is already being laid, both deliberately and naturally, but cannot, by definition, be one of the present or past.

By adopting this position, what these young people are actually doing is to express a radical political commitment that is also 'safe', for they are subconsciously reflecting the 'alternative' vanguard discourse that has been competing for hegemony all along but that has emerged more openly since the early 1990s, challenging the discredited, 'outward-oriented' version and stressing the alternative's 'autochthonous' nature and identification. In other words, the familiar competition of discourses has given the young a space in which to express their criticisms of the existing system and to identify with a period of recent history that seems to them to offer more hope, more direction and more autonomy. This oblique criticism is evident in a tendency to imagine a Che who, having returned from the dead to present-day Cuba, would criticize the same things of which they themselves are critical (the new inequalities, the previous orientation towards 'alien' models, the commercialization of national symbols, and so on); *Che*, therefore, has given these critics a voice with which to take up a discordant position within, and not outside, the basic ideological framework.

It is a remarkable recourse to a rescued, and renewed, myth that has been, and is being, consciously used by different groups and generations to provide succour, identity, a platform and a means of belonging. As such, whatever intentions the vanguard may have had in reviving Guevara's memory and ideas, it cannot have imagined such a successful adoption of the newly organic myth.

Furthermore, the vanguard's new public reorientation towards, and recognition of, a more nationalist, *cubanista* and *martiano* projection of the revolutionary process (past, present and future) has also found similar popular echoes. The various formalizations of this shift – in the 1986 (Third) and 1991 (Fourth) Party Congresses, and in the 1993 changes to the constitution (a revision echoed also in the renewed attention given to pre-1959 and 1960s history in the press and academia) – have been paralleled in the revision, rescue and revival of the somewhat symbolized myth of Martí, a revival akin to that identified with *Che* and for much the same reasons. It has been possible to identify – especially among more middle-aged Cubans – a similar process of recourse to, and expression through, the image and critical ideas of Martí, as a means of finding ideological solace and identity (in a changing environment), of identifying themselves and the Revolution with an acknowledged and consensual *cubanista* figure, and of offering hope and direction in a moment of uncertainty. Indeed, it is also possible to identify a willingness in the young to see the new desired direction of the whole revolutionary process – towards a more definably *cubanista* orientation – as reflected by their affinity with, admiration for and image of Martí. With Martí, as with *Che*, the myth has been visibly, and organically, revived and reconfigured as a means of confronting, understanding and surviving the new crisis.

There can be little doubt in the Cuba of 2000 that, for all the expressed confidence, loyal and tolerant sectors of the Cuban population, as well as the more politically aware and active, are beset by something of an ideological dilemma. It is not, as is often maintained, the supposed loss of faith and ideological direction arising from the collapse of Eastern Europe and the Soviet Union; indeed, if anything, the ideological effects of that collapse were its least problematic aspect, especially because of the continuing tension between the inherently Cuban, 'inwardly-oriented' vision of socialism, revolution and the world, on the one hand, and, on the other, the very different Soviet or East European versions. Many Cubans responded to the crisis by welcoming – perhaps whistling in the dark – an ideological liberation that left them free to criticize those aspects of their former allies that they had never liked or accepted, and that they had often felt obliged to adopt. The extent to which the economic problems of the 1980s were seen to have been caused by those allies' subordination of Cuban plans, interests and identity to the demands of the 'socialist division of labour' helped reinforce that view.

Instead, the ideological crisis has been a crisis of hope, a critically new phenomenon in the whole revolutionary trajectory. Throughout the austerities of the 1960s, hope sustained the majority of the hard-pressed population – a hope that the reforms would continue to improve living standards, that the siege would end, that Soviet aid would help and that collective action would overcome the daunting obstacles. Only in 1967 was that hope dented; but it was then strengthened in the following decade and a half, as improvements materialized and as national pride grew in the light of sporting, political, military, economic and social achievements. In the mid-1990s, however, Cuba for the first time faced the new and deepest crisis completely alone in the world, abandoned by its erstwhile allies, neglected by some of its new European friends and now besieged again by a triumphalist, unfettered and hostile United States, which in 1992 (with the Torricelli Act) and 1996 (with the Helms–Burton Act) turned the screw of the previously tolerable but expensive embargo. In that sense, the collapse of one pole of the global ideological conflict was indeed a crisis, since it meant a need for several concurrent and overlapping processes of redefinition, with the only real affinity being found with those parts of the Third World that were not clamouring for inclusion in the North's economic agenda.

It has been in this context that the current internal debates about ideological definition and direction have been realized, the familiar scenario of competing discourses being complicated by the dismal failure of the last set of exogenous models and the pressure from the new globalized economy to force Cuba into accepting another set, this time capitalist. In this context, the attraction of the endogenous has become understandably great, meaning a new lease of life, and direction, for the myths which belong to it organically and have consistently been used in the pursuit of that 'inwardly-oriented' perspective and interpretation.

However, there is still a crisis, for, in a sense, the Cuba of the late 1990s finds itself in a state of collective postmodernism. After over a century of a 'modernist' canon, in which 'history' has had a linear trajectory and a purpose, with orthodoxy maintaining that the present is the culmination of the past or one 'line' of a past path, the other being the discredited alternative (as with pre-1959 dissidence), such certainties have indeed been weakened, leading to a crisis and a continual questioning, even of the certainty, the canon and the orthodoxy about history. Therefore, if postmodernism can be defined as reflective of, and reacting to, crisis, then it is logical to suggest that crisis can in turn produce a collective postmodernism, leading to a rejection of history as linear and purposeful. If so, it is profoundly disconcerting for a Cuban ideological framework that relies on such a 'progressive' view, which, in a sense, is the nub of the present ideological crisis in Cuba.

Conclusion: *Cubanía* Today: Crisis and the Pursuit of the 'Dreams'

The casual observer of the Cuban Revolution at the height of the August 1994 crisis – probably the lowest point of morale and disintegration since the 1960s – might have been forgiven for assuming that the process was then in its death throes. With three years of deep recession and a cumulative five-year economic decline of 38 per cent,[1] with debilitating power cuts, falling sugar production, increasing unemployment and lay-offs, with many production enterprises operating at 15 per cent of capacity, with food shortages (and the reintroduction of long-forgotten rationing), falling medical provision and a precipitous fall in the peso's value, the economic base of the whole socio-political experiment seemed in terminal collapse. It was easy to assume that the 35,000 *balseros* were simply the tip of the iceberg and that, among the visibly thinner and despondent population, there were many thousands more awaiting their chance or the system's end. Indeed, the 30 per cent rate for abstention or spoiled papers at the December 1992 municipal elections (an unprecedented half of the candidates having to submit to a second round of voting) had seemed to indicate that many Cubans were unwilling even to go through the motions of expressing formal support for that system.

However, by 1999, the worst had not only passed, but some of the old hope seemed to have returned. Economic growth had become permanent since 1994, production had risen steadily, the peso's value had spiralled (from the 1994 low of 120 to the dollar to an average of 20 for two consecutive years) and few depended solely on the rationing system. If August 1994 was a snapshot of the depths of despair of an apparently moribund Revolution, then, in 1998–9, one could find an alternative snapshot in either the public response to the Pope's January 1998 visit or the turn-out of over one million Havanans for the 1999 May Day parade.

Although the recovery is by no means permanent, with persistent signs of an underlying economic weakness (especially in sugar), one can say with some confidence that the Revolution has survived in some form or other. That alone – whatever changes may come in the next few years, under the pressures of globalization,

1. The figures are according to the Cuban system of economic measurement, which, although referring mostly to GNP, also include the pre-1989 measuring system (GSP – Gross Social Product). The figures were zero growth in 1985–9, minus 4 four per cent in 1990, minus 25 per cent in 1991, minus 15 per cent in 1992 and minus 10 per cent in 1993.

'dollarization' and tourism – are enough to make the recovery astonishing, and possibly unique.

Fundamentally, there are two levels of explanation of this survival. Firstly, one must look to the immediate economic and political reforms, the former a series of carefully calibrated measures since 1993, and the latter less obvious and less dramatic, but none the less significant. As was indicated in Chapter 4, the economic reforms have not been designed in a vacuum, or simply as panic measures, having built on the post-1985 restructuring (and on some even earlier reforms) and on the preparations implicit in the 1990 declaration of the 'Special Period'.

The first reform has been the relative opening of the external sector to global market mechanisms and capital. This is the first reform chronologically, not least because its roots lay in the 1982 decision to establish joint venture operations between state enterprises and foreign capital, with further boosts in 1991, so that by 1994 there were 180 such enterprises. Besides these, however, the decision was taken early on to give considerable autonomy to state enterprises in the external sector, hoping to attract capital, function efficiently and expand. By 1995, there were 225 enterprises engaged in foreign trade compared to 80 in 1988 (Kapcia 1996b: 7), and in 1993 the constitution was altered to permit unprecedented foreign access to Cuban property and labour.

The next step, dramatic in concept and effect, was the July 1993 decision to decriminalize the holding of dollars and to allow 'dollarization' to find its natural level. The effects were immediate – the collapse of the currency black market, the rise of the peso and the increase in supplies of food and other consumables. This was followed in September 1993 by the permission to Cubans to engage in limited self-employment activities (reversing the effects of the 1968 'Revolutionary Offensive') – the so-called *cuenta propia* ('own account') sector. This sector now boomed, soaking up surplus labour, directing energies, providing hitherto defunct services, formalizing another part of the informal sector, and soaking up excess liquidity. By 1995, there were 170,000 registered *cuentapropistas* and possibly about one million Cubans either working in, or dependent on, this sector, through their own activities, family networks or illegal employment.

Then, in June 1994, another taboo was broken when the state agricultural sector was dismembered, dismantling the state farms and forming cooperatives – UBPC (Unidades Básicas de Producción y Cooperación – 'Basic Units of Production and Cooperation': see Pérez Rojas and Torres Vila 1998: 83–110). This was followed by the return to the peasant market, allowing farmers again to sell their surplus to the public at market prices in the new *agromercados* (Torres Vila and Pérez Rojas 1998: 148–86),[2] and by the freedom given to *cuentapropistas* to open family-run restaurants, trading in both pesos and dollars (the now-familiar *paladares*).

2. Within two years, private farmers were selling 41.43 per cent of the goods for sale on these markets, the state 25 per cent, the UBPCs 14 per cent and the other cooperatives the remainder (Colectivo de Autores 1996: 188).

Financial and fiscal reforms have also abounded, especially the introduction of more foreign banking operations and the restructuring of the Cuban banking sector, and the introduction of a graduated income tax for the first time since the 1960s. Taken together with a steady programme of cuts in state subsidies, provision and employment, the effects on liquidity and inflation were remarkable, reducing the budget deficit by almost half in one year (1993–4). Finally, of course, there is also the whole question of diversification, though this is less a reform process than the result of the search for new markets and new sources of wealth, the most successful aspect being the development of tourism, growing in leaps and bounds from a negligible level in the mid-1980s to over one and a half million visitors in 1998; but other sectors expanding have included nickel, oil and tobacco.

What then of the question of political reform, often seen from the outside as non-existent and, thus, a source of potential destabilization, given a possible mismatch with such rapid economic change? Overall, since 1992, we can detect a process of such reform at two levels – in institutional structures and in a calibrated 'broadening' of the more informal political system. The first type of reform has meant changes to the electoral system, to the party, to patterns of representation and, finally, to the formal constitution.

The electoral system was, as we have seen, characterized from 1976 by the Soviet-style OPP structures, which, although they may have included a high level of active accountability at the municipal level, had tended by the 1990s to become somewhat discredited by their lack of effectiveness in resolving issues, their mono-polization by an increasingly bureaucratic party and by the fact that the National Assembly was both indirectly elected (and therefore lacking some accountability) and only briefly in session. The reform of the system in late 1992 was therefore long overdue and immediately effective, involving the decisions to make half the Assembly directly elected from February 1993 (although with the other half still appointed through recommendations from the mass organizations), to create standing commissions to operate between the twice-yearly parliamentary sessions and thus ensure continuity and credibility, and to disentangle the party and the electoral system. The reform's effectiveness was proved in February 1993, when abstentions fell from the worrying level of December 1992 to only 100,000 nationally, and when 30 per cent of the final delegates were non-party members (Kapcia 1996b: 16).[3] The subsequent years have seen a consequent process of re-legitimization of the Assembly, with high turnouts and a return to high attendance at the *rendiciones*.

Given the crises of 1985 and 1989, party reform was a clear and urgent priority for leadership and population alike. Building on the post-1986 'Rectification', the

3. At those national elections, 589 candidates were elected at the first ballot in a 98.8% turnout; 83 per cent of these were new to the Assembly. Of the valid votes cast, 88.4% were for the full official 'slate', with some 7 per cent casting blank votes.

1991 Fourth Congress continued the process of revision and self-criticism, preceded by extensive grass-roots consultation and resulting in the replacement of over half the local delegates, the Central Committee, the Buró Político and the Consejo del Estado (Council of State) – the effective executive committee of the Assembly (Eckstein 1994: 115–17). Most significantly of all, whereas the 1986 changes might be said to have begun the removal of the old pro-Soviet elements, these latest changes began a process of 'rejuvenation', also 'retiring' some of the ex-guerrillas – a process already signalled by Valdés's 1985 demotion, but now indicated more clearly by Vilma Espín's disappearance from the Central Committee. The same ethos, indeed, was also simultaneously being pursued at the grass-roots and intermediate levels of the party, where a new generation was being introduced in a clear move to reach out to the young.

Other mechanisms of effective representation were also created, especially the *parlamentos obreros* – the 100,000-strong workplace consultative assemblies introduced to ensure legitimacy for the harsh economic decisions, a restoration of credibility to the trade unions and also feedback from the grass roots – and the new Consejos Populares (Popular Councils). These last mechanisms were based on *ad hoc* experiments in 1983, designed to break bottlenecks in local distribution systems, but were given official blessing in 1988, set up formally in ninety-three pilot schemes in four Havana *barrios* (districts) in 1990, and from 1993 were extended throughout the country (to 900 by the end of that year) (Bengelsdorf 1994: 163–5). A mixture of local elected officials, local representatives of mass organizations and local enterprise managers, they have, through their practical successes, restored some vital legitimacy to the ethos of participation, and are very likely to become a core of the evolving political system.

Finally, the new reform process was given the official stamp with the changes to the constitution (agreed in 1992), sanctioning the economic reforms but also, as mentioned before, indicating a political shift by broadening the potential for party membership and emphasizing a more nationalist ethos and a less stridently socialist one, with the insertion of references to Martí and the replacement of the word 'proletarian' by 'people's'.

All these reforms were both more relevant than they seemed (in a system where changes had come less frequently than in the vertiginous 1960s) and less meaningful than many of the leaders perhaps claimed (given the continuing domination of the party, the CDRs' role in getting the voters out in 1993 and the continuing signs of disenchantment). They were, however, significant simply in that they were proposed (recognizing the need for adjustment) and enacted, leading to a process of expectation and evolution that was bound to have longer-term effects. In this respect, they are also significant as the formal mechanisms that accompany the more informal broadening process that will be addressed later in this chapter.

Such reforms alone, however, would clearly not only not redress the ills of the preceding decade and a half and the growing complaints of the average Cuban, but could not alone explain the survival of political support beyond 1994. For that, we must inevitably look deeper, at more underlying factors that can offer some structural explanations of the willingness of so many Cubans to go on identifying themselves with a system so obviously in crisis.

The first underlying factor is the question of continuity – paradoxically, because at one level, that might be assumed to be a factor acting against popularity, given external media images of an unchanging orthodoxy and an ageing vanguard. Times of crisis can, however, be expected to lead a worried population to cling to, or gravitate towards, the known and the reliable, especially in leadership, ideas, patterns and, as we have seen, ideology and myth. Indeed, precisely because the essence of the Revolution's character (positive and negative) is found in critical elements of continuity, it is worth while here identifying these elements – for they both set the context within which these reforms have taken place and in which they have a greater relevance than might be obvious at first sight, and also help us understand what the 'essence' of the Revolution might be, as so many Cubans at all levels react to the current crises, the reform process and the economic changes by striving to identify what it all means and what is worth preserving.

To talk of continuity, in the context of an apparently ever-changing Revolution, is inevitably to invite surprise among lay observers, used to seeing the process portrayed as a zigzag trajectory, a series of phases implying a tendency to policy switches and changes of direction. For most histories of the Revolution, written, spoken or filmed, fall easily into the temptation to trace its evolution through at least six definable phases. It is tempting firstly because it is not entirely inaccurate, since the revolutionary process has repeatedly come face to face with one basic reality of transformations in the Third World – that Cuba, like any dependent economy and also like any Latin American or Caribbean country within the American 'sphere of influence', has always had to develop reactively within a global economic and political context that has, deliberately or accidentally, consistently shaped its character socially, economically and, therefore, politically. For all that the Revolution may have implied a greater autonomy for the Cuban government in a range of aspects of governance and policy, the fact remains that the country's economic health and character have depended throughout on issues such as the price of sugar, the American embargo and the demands of Moscow or Comecon, and its political path has been obliged to react to the vicissitudes of global superpower relations. The 'history by phases' approach has also been tempting because it becomes easier to explain the contradictions that have characterized the whole process by categorizing periods, hegemonies and directions.

It is therefore useful, at this stage, to codify the processes examined so far by following such a pattern of historiography, largely obeying conventional wisdoms but also refining these to present a particular interpretation of the trajectory (always bearing in mind that such a chronology must necessarily create a clumsy periodization and overlook the inevitable overlapping of characteristics).[4] Moreover, the term 'period' is preferred here, since 'phase' implies a clarity of direction or characterization for each period that is not always useful.

Thus, with appropriate caveats, and on the basis of the information and events already outlined, we can begin with the 1959–60 period, characterized by political pluralism (although some see liberalism or even 'romantic anarchy' (Dumont 1970: 27)), by Keynesian or developmentalist economics and by a fragile, uncertain and eventually disintegrating relationship with Washington, a period with total hegemony exercised by no one group but with the strengthening of the *sierra*. Then came 1961–2, a period of political radicalization, with the PSP rising and then falling within the vanguard, and with mobilization ensuring a deeper process of simultaneous political and social change, with greater economic centralization, radical land reform, the emigration of the middle class, the traumatic break with the United States and the beginnings of a long, uneasy, relationship with the Soviet Union. The evidence is convincing of a third period (broadly 1962–5) of vanguard debate, especially over economic policy and the transformational strategy, in a context of uncertainty about external alliances and internal political configurations.

Commentators disagree about the characterization of the following few years, but is seems logical to posit the next stage as 1966–70, a period of heterodox internal and external radicalization – with the new party largely relegated by the hegemonic *sierra*, with participation through continual mobilization, with an increasingly 'moral' economy aimed at the 1970 *zafra*, and with the leadership challenging both Washington and Moscow in Latin America. The failure of that harvest ushered in a new five-year period of debate, as the vanguard was obliged to change character, restore many of the PSP, recognize the previous stresses and begin *détente* with both superpowers. Then followed ten years (1975–1985) of coherent institutionalization, stabilization and consolidation in all areas except African policy (where 'Sovietization' was belied by independent activism): in political structure, economic policy and external relations (especially with Moscow).

Finally (before the crisis struck in 1990) came the 1986–9 period of renewed debate, belying the impression of ideological certainty created by 'Rectification' – debate about the party (and the inherited 'ills' of bureaucratization and privilege), economic policy (regarding a possibly less secure future and reviving Guevara's

---

4. The most authoritative classification of 'phases' is Mesa-Lago's in 1978: 1959–60 (liquidation of pre-Revolutionary institutions), 1961-3 (attempted introduction of a socialist system), 1963–6 (debate and experimentation), 1966–70 (Sino-Guevarism), 1970–77 (pragmatism) (Mesa-Lago 1978: 2–4).

ideas) and about Cuba's past, seen increasingly as the possible guide to its future, more autonomous, path. This pattern leads us inexorably towards the latest period, from 1990 (and the declaration of the 'Special Period'), with its deep and traumatic crisis, precipitated by the sequence of disasters from 1989 and intensified by the tightened embargo. Alongside, and reacting to, that crisis have come the unprecedented and destabilizing economic reforms, undermining the previous three-decade certainties to the extent that many, outside and inside Cuba, have understandably predicted the decline, or collapse, of the Revolution.

If we accept this pattern, one revealing element of continuity becomes clear in the periods of 'debate' interspersing the periods of certainty in direction, alliances and policy, a factor that portrays a more thoughtful and deliberate pattern of policy decisions than the apparent zigzag trajectory might lead one to suppose. For the Revolution's trajectory has been cyclical – crisis leading to debate, debate leading to certainty, until the next crisis, and so on. Indeed, we have seen that such periods of debate have invariably tended towards ideological introspection, when the uncertainties of economy, external relationships and political direction have meant a greater recourse to the perceived certainties of Cuba's indigenous ideological traditions.

Of the other critical elements of continuity, the most obvious is the question of leadership, since it highlights the continuity of Fidel Castro himself, still in power in 2000 after over four decades, repeated crises and attempted assassinations. His role, nature and importance are the subject of many separate books, and, predictably, complicated by mythology, polemic and falsification; however, whatever doubts might exist about the historiography of 'great men', Castro's domination, ability, survivability and popularity lead many a writer to such a perspective. At one level, his role has been crucial in decision-making throughout whole periods (the 1960s and post-1986), at critical moments (1953, 1955, 1956, 1959, 1961) or in critical developments (the break with Washington, the rise of the PSP, the shift to communism and the Soviet Union, the 1970 *zafra*), although it is not always easy to find evidence of such decisions being Castro's alone rather than his articulation of the feelings of the vanguard. Indeed, there is some evidence that, especially in the 'debate' periods, Castro has either only directed vanguard discussions once consensus has emerged or has been persuaded in these (see especially Szulc 1986; Anderson 1997).[5] However, the fact remains that no decision of long-term significance for the Revolution, no major ideological clarification and no major external move seems likely to have been taken without at least Castro's personal approval, his ideological *imprimatur*.

---

5. This has been confirmed by many veterans of the early Revolution interviewed in the research for this book.

Nor is this surprising, given the vanguard's extraordinary cohesion since the Sierra and the tendency in such circumstances for strong characters to dominate, especially where their judgement, popularity and ability have been repeatedly proved. Thus, Castro was always bound to be crucial within the post-1953 movement, and his repeated survivals certainly enhanced collective confidence in his judgement. Moreover, there is much evidence of his personal charisma, publicly and within the group, his ability to persuade through argument or force of character, his remarkable ability to gauge the public mood faster than others, his willingness to act more flexibly than his intransigent image would suggest and to anticipate popular grievances more readily through policy changes.

Furthermore, abroad, his personal relationships with successive Soviet leaders, Spain's Felipe González, and Third World leaders (Angola's Agostinho Neto, India's Indira Gandhi, Nicaragua's Daniel Ortega, Panama's Omar Torrijos, Grenada's Maurice Bishop, Guyana's Forbes Burnham and Jamaica's Michael Manley) have clearly helped determine alliances and actions. Equally, the symbolic significance of Castro's presence and survival has been an obstacle to many American thoughts of some sort of *détente*.

That, necessarily, leads on to the broader significance of Castro's role, in the question of legitimacy, for, throughout four decades of vicissitudes, his survival, with his oratorical ability, 'common man' appeal, personal charm and resulting rapport with ordinary Cubans, and his perceived history of consistency, have all guaranteed that each passing year endows him with even greater symbolic meaning, as the human manifestation of the 'essence' of an ever more complex and contradictory process, whose ideological *imprimatur* can make or break reforms and who is seen ultimately by the average Cuban as the Revolution's *guru*. That is as true of those who see him as the culprit for all the Revolution's wrongs and the sole obstacle to change as it is of those (especially those over thirty-five) who see in him the symbol of solidity and guarantee of security in a bewildering period of crisis and change. Overall, indeed, whereas early on Castro was significant for what he did and said, as much as for what he symbolized, in the 1990s his role has become more one of figurehead, ideological censor and external relations decisionmaker. Yet his survival is the one critical element of leadership continuity.

However visible he has been and remains, it would nonetheless be a mistake to talk of Cuba as ruled by one man, for the surrounding group, the vanguard whose members have rarely sought the limelight (and have often thus seemed mere disciples), has often exercised considerable authority, sharing decision-making, debating issues and ensuring a degree of collective cohesion. Indeed, given the history of vanguard changes, of 'ins' and 'outs', such a pattern is likely, since these debates have largely determined who is 'in' and who is 'out'. However, as we have seen, one should remain cautious of a misleading discourse of 'factions' and 'purges' – misleading given the complexity of a vanguard with a constant flow of personnel, and with constant contradictions, between 'sides' in debates – those associated with one 'current' occasionally adopting ideas associated with the other. Moreover, it is easy to forget that we are always talking of a small group within a small political and intellectual elite within a small population, where 'factions' have little meaning for long, where personal relationships and antagonisms may develop greater significance and where there are insufficient numbers to support long-term divisions into clear-cut, stable factions.

This is reinforced when one examines the actual composition of the vanguard, characterized by a remarkable continuity that enables us to talk of a 'core'. Thus, in 1958, the nucleus of the 26 July Movement was surprisingly small: the Castro brothers, Guevara, Cienfuegos, Valdés, Celia Sánchez and Hart. That nucleus was expanded in early 1959 to include selected PSP leaders (Rodríguez and Roca) and the DR's Chomón, and also trusted confidants, such as Raúl Roa (the Foreign Minister) and Dorticós. By the 1970s that group had been depleted by death (Cienfuegos and Guevara) but not by defection or purge, regardless of political shifts or changing external relationships; for the PSP's post-1962 'marginalization' or the *sierra's* (after 1975) often meant changes below vanguard level – ministerially, in the economic management team, and in the Central Committee. In 1977, twenty-four of the thirty-five members of the 'Cuban leadership' were identified as ex-guerrillas (González 1977: 7). Only by 1988 was there a discernible shift, with Valdés out of the 'inner circle' (but not the Central Committee), with the deaths of Celia Sánchez, Haydée Santamaría and Blas Roca, and with age steadily marginalizing others. However, even then, those of the 'outer circle' who replaced them often had a guerrilla pedigree (such as Osmani Cienfuegos, Juan Almeida or Guillermo García) rather than a bureaucratic or 'technocratic' past.

Ultimately, it was only age and crisis that produced greater personnel changes at the top, as the vanguard skipped a generation in its drive for visible rejuvenation, introducing younger politicians such as Ricardo Alarcón (previously Cuba's UN ambassador), Carlos Lage and the ex-head of the UJC, Roberto Robaina, and gradually retiring some of the guerrilla generation from active political roles. Even so, what remained was still a remarkable continuity, with the Castro brothers continuing to exercise power in their respective areas – Fidel in overall policy-making, foreign relations and economic reforms and Raúl in the Armed Forces – and the retired veterans were still given politically or symbolically significant roles.

In a catalogue of elements of continuity, sugar is the one obvious factor linking the Cuba of 2000 with the Cuba not just of 1959, but even of 1800. The Cuban relationship with its principal crop is predictably a complex, vast subject, with all manner of implications and dimensions. Certainly, one characteristic of the Revolution seems to have been the Cubans' inability to resolve their psychological problems in relation to sugar, oscillating between policies that (seeing sugar as Cuba's perpetual 'curse' and the prime cause of underdevelopment, colonialism and neocolonialism) seek to break dependency – as in 1960–63 – and strategies that seek to build a whole future on it – most visibly (and damagingly) in the 1966-70 period and then again, more structurally but more vulnerably, after integration into Comecon in 1972.

This permanent love–hate relationship has been intensified by the statistical reality of dependence and its wider effects. By the 1880s, some four-fifths of Cuba's sugar exports went to the United States, with sugar determining continuing colonialism, late abolition of slavery and a gross social, geographical, racial and economic inequality. By the 1950s, sugar still constituted 83 per cent of exports (still mostly going northwards) (Pérez-Stable 1993: 89), but now determined a close, dependent relationship with the United States, a highly fragile economy and employment structure, and a still grossly unequal, antiquated and destabilizing social structure. By 1988, the statistical picture was, superficially, little different, with 76.6 per cent of exports coming from sugar (1993: 89), some 70 per cent of those going to one, admittedly agglomerated, market.[6]

The difference, however, was that by the 1980s the whole economy's dependence on sugar was considerably reduced, as it constituted less than 5 per cent of the GDP by 1981 (Brundenius 1984: 77), indicating a greater diversification and development that rendered meaningless talk of a return to 'sugar monoculture' (Gouré and Weinkle 1972: 72). Nonetheless, when the Comecon market collapsed and the single Soviet market fragmented into fifteen, the economic effects were in some respects as disastrous as they would have been in 1958. Most visibly, the inability to exchange sugar for oil led to the catastrophic decline of oil imports, with predictable concomitant effects on all productive, energy and transport systems. Nothing, it seemed, had changed in terms of the old 'curse'; yet Cuba's only long-term economic salvation seemed to depend, again, on increasing the efficiency of the sugar harvest and the size of the sugar crop.

A further factor of continuity must be the level and nature of popular support for the system, which, although never ceasing to puzzle outside political analysts and leaders, can be relatively easily explained, being attributable to at least four factors.

The first is the obvious, popular and deep response to, recognition of, and gratitude for, the many social benefits that have accrued to most Cubans over the four decades, at least until crisis undermined the Revolution's ability to continue guaranteeing these – although, significantly, the one sector of public expenditure that has been more or less maintained throughout the shortages has been health. These benefits have been many, substantial and well-documented over the years, most characteristically health provision, education, housing, job security, racial and social equality and the raised profile of the *campo* (Dalton 1993).

6. Other comparable figures are given by Brundenius (77 per cent of exports in 1959 and 80 per cent in 1980) (Brundenius 1984: 76)) and Habel (87 per cent in 1976) (Habel 1991: 7).

Of these, health-care provision has been the most consistently acclaimed over the years. Certainly, while there has often been exaggeration and uncritical incantation of successes, there is fully documented evidence of the impressive achievements of the various reforms since 1959. Whether this is in the form of increased expenditure – by 1968, the budget was ten times the 1958 level (Valdés 1971: 329); personnel (with an astonishing 400 doctors per thousand inhabitants in the 1990s); facilities – thirty-eight of sixty-six new hospitals in 1959–64 being built in the *campo* (Valdés 1971: 324); or general preventive care education and provision, most Cubans have become well aware of the value of a free, universal and often sophisticated system. Certainly, knowledge of post-1989 events in Eastern Europe, and of other Third World countries, has strengthened that awareness. Moreover, health plays a valuable mythic role in the Revolution, being a metaphor for the health of the whole process (Feinsilver 1993: 22), a significant part of the 'symbolic capital' (Feinsilver 1993: 15–25) and with the post-1980 universal Family Doctor Programme playing a symbolic and even pastoral role.

Education is perhaps more controversially successful, if only because of the understandable emphasis on quantity rather than quality. Statistically, Cuba's success is outstanding, in literacy, access, gender balance and educational achievement, certainly within the Third World but also even in comparison with a richer North (Valdés 1972: 422–55); sixth-grade graduates doubled in 1975–80, and increased sevenfold at basic secondary level (Medin 1990: 80). While there may well be doubts about the qualitative and pedagogic achievements of literacy successes, about the somewhat regimented approach to pre-university learning, and about a highly competitive and selective tertiary sector, there is little doubt that most Cubans are well educated, well read and generally more culturally appreciative than many of their regional or European counterparts, and, moreover, are well aware of the political importance of this achievement. During the 'Special Period', this sector too has significantly been relatively well protected against cutbacks.

To some, it may seem surprising that housing should be listed as one of the Revolution's social achievements, since a glance at the overcrowded, crumbling tenements of La Habana Vieja, and an awareness of the question's sensitivity at critical moments presents a picture of desperate shortage rather than adequate provision. Here, however, we have one of the Revolution's classic conundrums: that success has often bred expectation. While this has not generally happened in the highly politicized areas of health and education, housing has clearly been the object of much public criticism, because it is the one daily shortcoming, or frustration, with which – until the 1990s crisis generated a similar set of shortages and complaints over food provision – most Cubans have had to deal. Moreover, the early decision to grant title meant the evolution of both a greater proprietorialism among Cubans than one might have expected from an otherwise collectivist

Figure 4 The reality of the state of much Havana housing in the 1990s

Figure 5 The Malecón (sea-front boulevard) includes some of the worst housing in contemporary Havana

revolution and also greater expectations among those without title. These expectations have certainly been fuelled since the start of the 1990s recovery, and there is evidence that housing has now become a leading complaint for many urban Cubans.

The reality is that the 1960s moves to correct the housing shortage were impressive and much appreciated (Butterworth 1980). The abolition of renting, the granting of titles, the recycling of abandoned middle-class properties as multi-occupation dwellings, the construction of workers' apartment blocks all contributed to an immediate and effective attack on this shortage, and the disappearance from the major cities of the shanty settlements that had begun to spring up – a success reinforced since by the continuing non-appearance of such developments.[7] Thus, whatever the subjective frustration continually expressed – about overcrowding, the lack of privacy (especially for newly-weds), the appalling state of disrepair in the older Havana *barrios* – the fact is that the objective material conditions of housing in most of Cuba have, until the late 1980s, constituted a social benefit rather than a social problem (see Hamburg 1990; Luzón 1988). Indeed, one might observe that housing has become more of a political problem than a genuine social one, although deteriorating physical conditions in Havana have recently again made it a real enough social issue. Moreover, the continuing recourse to volunteer labour – over 400,000 participants in 1989 (Eckstein 1994: 64) – the use of *microbrigadas* and then (after 1987) *contingentes* to tackle the problems (the latter consisting of between 23,000 and 30,000 workers by 1989: Eckstein 1994: 64; Fitzgerald 1994: 160) – has a double-edged effect – effective mobilization to tackle an urgent problem, on the one hand, but also a permanent reminder that the problem is urgent enough to require such measures.

A somewhat similar picture can be painted of employment, for some three decades seen as a political and social priority rather than an economically determined need, meaning that most Cubans, and especially the young, were educated into expectations of job security. Indeed, the 1971 criminalization of unemployment reflected the belief that, if the system provided universal opportunities for employment, then the unemployed were, by definition, failing in their social responsibilities. The reality for most Cubans was, however, that they were genuinely guaranteed employment of some sort once they sought work, until the 1990s crisis undermined that guarantee and created an unprecedented, admitted and almost requisite pool of 'reserve' labour.

The other social benefits referred to – grouped together as greater equality between races and classes, and between town and countryside – repeat this picture, with early moves, deliberate and accidental, meaning rapid, visible and tangible progress for the black population, the poor and the *campesino*. The immediate

---

7. It should be said that individual shanties do exist, even in central Havana; but whole settlements composed of shanties have disappeared.

Figure 6 Examples of the bourgeois housing put to common use after 1959

Figure 7 Further examples of the public appropriation of richer housing after 1959, from the *chic* Prado area

abolition of formal racial discrimination, the departure of a largely white middle class by 1965 and the benefits of free health care and education, together with the redistributive and egalitarian effects of rationing and employment, the post-1963 emphasis on the countryside for construction, social provision, and economic investment, all meant that, between the late 1960s and the early 1980s, the Revolution could justifiably claim to have eliminated the worst excesses of racial and social inequality and could boast a greater homogeneity than almost any other Latin American or Caribbean society, and than many Northern societies. Since then a number of developments have conspired to undermine these successes, not least the gradual emergence of a 'new' middle class – both as an educated techno-cratic generation, with expectations of skilled or professional employment (Espina Prieto and Núñez Moreno 1990), and then in the rise of a privileged layer within the reformulated post-1975 party. It has also been undermined by the post-1989 social decline and reforms, with new access to dollars creating clear social divisions between those with access and those without. The reality still is, however, that enough Cubans, especially those over thirty-five, have sufficient reason to be grateful for, or aware of, past successes to want to protect such advances.

Of the other reasons to explain the continuing support, the most obvious is the remarkably high level of popular participation characterizing the whole revolutionary process. While, after 1970, mass mobilization may not have reached the 1960s levels, most Cubans have been unable to escape the effects of the many organizations and campaigns that still characterize the Cuban polity, and all Cubans' experience is bound together by organization. They, for example, will still probably belong to the local CDR (these by 1980 had nearly five and a half million members: Medin 1990: 157), and may still become involved in many of its activities, whether the nocturnal *guardia*, or some local inoculation, street-cleaning or education campaign. They will undoubtedly vote in local and national elections and will even probably attend the *rendición de cuentas* meeting of the local *municipio*, which, between 1976 and 1984, recalled up to 10 per cent of the elected delegates and achieved a turnover of about 50 per cent (Pérez-Stable 1993: 124; see also Harnecker 1979: 128–46). They will probably belong to either the FMC,[8] the appropriate trade union (and therefore the CTC), or the FEU. They may possibly also be members of the party or the equally numerous youth wing, the UJC,[9] or will have been *pioneros* (by 1975 accounting for 98.7 per cent of schoolchildren: Domínguez 1978a: 279), will have been in the education system and may still be

8. By 1970, membership had risen to 1.3 million (Pérez-Stable 1993: 116), rising again to 2.13 million in 1975 (Medin 1990: 157) – the equivalent of 80 per cent of the female population over fourteen – and to 2.2 million by 1977 (Domínguez 1978a: 268).

9. Again, membership rose steadily from its 1960s low of about 50,000, to 100,000 by 1969 (still only 1 per cent of the population), 434,943 in 1980, and over half a million in 1985 (Pérez-Stable 1993: 145), now standing at about 600,000.

attending some work-based or local night classes. They will have served either in the FAR or the militias, and may still be registered in the reserve. Moreover, even the private farmer is not exempt, since membership of ANAP (counting 192,646 in 1980: Medin 1990: 157) is expected and practical. All of this is quite apart from the many national campaigns that are regularly launched, for political involvement, cane-cutting, education, or, most recently, from November 1999, over the perceived abduction of the five-year-old Elián González.

This extensive and systematic involvement means that, while *ennui* or cynicism can all too easily result, not least at the ineffective consultation through all these multifaceted channels of political communication, most Cubans remain relatively well informed of developments and are likely to be daily socialized in ways not evident in most of pre-1989 Eastern Europe. As a result, there is what one writer calls 'a subculture of local democracy' (Bengelsdorf 1994: 83–4), and one can claim that, unlike the 1980s Latin American processes of 'democratization' (characterized by democratization without citizenship), Cuba's system may have questionably democratic structures but certainly encourages citizenship.

Finally, in these explanations of popular support, there is nationalism. Indeed, one of the Revolution's very obvious successes has been to transform what, before 1959, was an occasionally flawed and confused sense of national identity into a new national pride. As we have seen, pre-1959 Cuba was characterized by the tension between an underlying faith in the nation's potential destiny and a resentment against its past and present humiliation, neglect and oppression, and, on the other hand, a corrosive lack of pride in Cuba's ability to be genuinely independent, a caustic self-deprecation, and a love–hate relationship with the *Norte* that often meant a self-effacing mimeticism and admiration. Now nationalism can, and does, transcend political allegiances, with an often contradictory set of reactions to any Washington anti-Castro moves or any perceived heavy-handedness by Spain or the European Union, or, most typically, a high level of unanimous and unprecedented pride in post-1959 sporting achievements, in Cuban culture or music and, most tellingly, in Cuba's African military successes after 1975.

Returning to the question of continuity, we discover one further element that is ultimately revealing, namely Cuba's significance in the outside world and, conversely, the significance of that outside world, and especially of the United States, for Cuba. This equation has evidently been significantly reversed in the last forty years, for, while the outside world (and especially the United States) probably determined much of pre-1959 Cuba's economic development and patterns, and therefore, many of its social and political patterns, one effect of the Revolution has been to put Cuba on the world map. At one level, this simply meant making Cuba a critical part of the Cold War (most frighteningly in October 1962); but, more positively, it meant that, rather than simply being the locus of such conflict (echoing 1898), Cuba became an actor in its own right. Certainly this was true of

Cuba's 1960s policies in Latin America – reinforced after 1975, as Cuba's Third World profile increased dramatically. Indeed, Cuba still remains a highly significant issue for many Latin Americans, not simply for the Left but for all political leaders, economic theorists and students of development issues. The more one looks at this feature as an element of continuity, the more remarkably it separates post-1959 Cuba from the pre-1959 period, providing a telling unity between the early Revolution and the present crisis-ridden years.

Here, inevitably, one must also consider the continuity of Cuba's relationship with the United States. There are two levels on which to examine this – the superficial, or rhetorical, level and the underlying relationship, each as important to the protagonists as the other. Rhetoric has, predictably, dictated the terms of the public relationship since the 1960s – it being easy, although misleading, to see a conflict between two mirror-image posturings, one side being seen to be waging an apparently nonsensical, obsessive and counter-productive war against the other in Cold War terms, the other defiantly maintaining its David-like challenge to the Goliath of 'imperialism', unwilling to compromise, determined to resist incursion, influence and friendship, and apparently clinging to a futile image of revolutionary resistance as the *monstruo* continues its outdated anticommunist rhetoric. While these public positions are not without foundation – the Cuba policy of American policy-makers did persist in Cold War terms throughout the 1970s and 1980s, allowing a Reaganite establishment to resurrect the 1950s rhetoric without difficulty, and the Cuban revolutionary leadership has almost certainly continued to believe firmly in its revolutionary mission to lead the oppressed of the under-developed world against a rampant, and now dominant, imperialism, they do play a valuable role both in preserving a mutually useful hostility and in meeting domestic political demands.

What is useful is the image of an identifiable 'enemy without', which can all too easily become an 'enemy within' in both cases. In the United States, Cuba's survival as a formally communist state allows an anachronistic continuation of an otherwise outdated anti-communism to prevail, permitting an official paranoia to justify 'national security' preparations, albeit not at Cold War levels and not essentially nuclear in their weaponry. As a global view maintained within policy-making circles and within lobbying circles, it also justifies the continuing import-ance of the émigré lobby, not only in the traditionally sympathetic Republican Party (Baloyra 1991: 130), but also as a constraint on otherwise more pro-*détente* Democratic advisers and politicians. In Havana, such a formal hostility both justifies the maintenance of a formal military preparedness (strengthening the FAR's political position and the unifying effects of the militia ethos) and helps maintain the long-standing, nationalist-oriented, 'siege mentality'.

Thus, in American eyes, as long as Castro remains in power, and, in Cuban eyes, as long as Washington maintains its embargo and obstruction, traditional positions are at least partly justified, perpetuating politically useful attitudes, strengthening otherwise weakened arguments, and preventing natural changes from dictating new positions and new adaptations. The end of the embargo could, for example, imply for anti-Castro interest groups within the United States both a victory for Castro and a defeat for, and weakening of, an émigré group that has maintained an inordinate influence and an astonishing cohesion, while, for Cuba, it could reduce the mobilizing effect of nationalism and threaten to destabilize the country economically through raised expectations and increased imports.

Beyond this rhetoric, however, lies another reality. Since 1963, Havana and Washington have actually maintained remarkably 'normal' relations through in-direct diplomatic channels and cooperation between security networks, trading contacts, émigré contacts and so on. That Washington is represented in Havana by an official in charge of the huge US Interests Section of the Swiss Embassy (the largest 'embassy' in Havana) does not mean that that person is not effectively the US Ambassador, for all intents and purposes treated as such by Cuban Foreign Ministry officials and other diplomats alike. Equally, the ease with which semi-official contacts have been made, repeatedly, to settle hijacking agreements, migration accords and drugs cooperation indicates the existence of useful and used channels of communication that belie the formal hostility and actually imply a mutual recognition of the other's existence and the need to deal with the other on a daily basis. In this respect, the classic anomaly is the daily flight from Miami to Havana, which does not officially exist on schedules but which is known to all, is announced officially at Havana airport and is a vital human and financial link between Cubans in the two cities. All of this was made clear in 1994, when Washington finally recognized that Cuban instability was worse than the continuity of Castro's power, and signed a migration accord to stabilize the situation.

Finally, when examining continuity, there is ideology. Just as, in Chapter 2, the analysis of factors leading to the process of radicalization after 1959 ended with what was deemed to be the underlying factor of *cubanía*, so too in 2000 can it again be seen to be ideology that constitutes perhaps the most significant factor in guaranteeing both continuity and survival. By now it is clear that, as at any moment in the Revolution's trajectory, ideology is a question of the whole fabric of revolu-tionary *cubanía* that has evolved throughout the century and taken its particular shape since the 1960s, a shape determined by its basic thematic components in the form of the identified *cubanista* codes. Indeed, it is revealing to see how far those same codes that were identified for 1959, and for various points thereafter, have remained unchanged and how far they may have evolved, or are still in a process of evolution.

To assess, therefore, how far the structure and nature of *cubanía* is intact in 2000, we must ask to what extent these codes are still identifiable in today's political culture. Starting with agrarianism, the answer is that this is possibly the best surviving code, not least because of the public response to crisis in the form of an ethos of 'back to basics', which, in practical terms, meant a return to the 1960s, with people and land recognized as Cuba's basic dependable resources. This meant, in the early 1990s, a forced retreat from mechanization to a revived dependence on human and animal labour for basic agricultural tasks, including cane-cutting and transport. While this was simple economic necessity, it also reflected a political imperative – to reinvigorate a sense of solidarity and defensiveness – and an astute political recognition of the fact that the political 'heart' of the Revolution, and its historic base, and deepest support, had always been in the countryside.

As the combination of crisis and reform began to take effect, a complementary sense began to develop from about 1993 that the *campo* again reflected the 'soul' of the Revolution and the route to an autonomous future, especially as food supply had become a critical economic and political issue and as some of the changes ('dollarization', *cuenta propia* activities and the growth of tourism) had again made Havana into a visibly less 'revolutionary', less moral, and therefore implicitly less *cubanista*, city, with petty crime, vagrancy, prostitution, the black market and an increased individualism all being more evident there than anywhere else. Thus, a Revolution that was increasingly searching for its 'essence', in response to the ideological challenges, was obviously being recommended to search within itself, in the *campo*.

That shift in emphasis (echoing 1962–6) was driven by economic necessity, as the desperate need to increase domestic food supplies and sugar exports meant a series of measures that made the farmer a critical factor in the political equation, not least in the creation of the UBPC, into which much hope has been invested.[10] Nonetheless, agriculture's ideological importance has been signalled by the reluctance to contemplate the entry of foreign capital into this sector; if it is indeed the 'heart' of the Revolution, then it makes ideological, if not economic, sense to keep agriculture Cuban, even if other areas of the economy have become 'contaminated' by either capitalism or non-Cuban capital. In this respect, the continuity of sugar reinforces the code.

The code of collectivism is equally evident today, and is being fiercely defended against what is often presented as the ideological threat – of capitalism, individualism and self-interest – unleashed by the combination of the daily battle for personal survival and the economic reforms encouraging enterprise. This resistance is manifested in a variety of ways – the continuing campaigns (whether against the neuritis epidemic of 1993–4 or to mobilize the vote in 1993), the recourse to popular mobilizations against real or imagined threats (in August 1994, in February 1996 during the *avionetas* crisis, but also in January 1998 for the Pope, a celebration

10. Some 2,600 of these units were set up then, accounting for 36 per cent of non-cane cultivation.

of the nation and the 'Cuban family').[11] It is also manifested in the drive towards cooperativization, not least in agriculture, and in the pressure to give the somewhat declining organs of mass mobilization a higher profile and a more meaningful role.

Finally, the new collectivism (now probably evolved again into a *solidarismo*) is evident in the 1990s strategy to broaden the Revolution's base, appeal, scope and even definition. This 'broad front' has meant four things: the broadening of the party (already described earlier) – to something with clearer patriotic credentials and adhering more to patriotic traditions, described by one observer as a *partido criollo* (Bengelsdorf 1994: 170); the subtle separation of selected para-statal bodies from the system to give them more autonomy and credibility; growing cooperation with non-systemic entities within the country and even outside; and the construction of careful channels of communication with outside agencies.

Already, by 1994, it was possible to detect signs of the second strategy – the partial separation of the main para-statal bodies to allow them greater space within the hitherto closely marshalled system to develop alternative strategies, postures, discourses, and thus act as safety-valves or sounding-boards (Kapcia 1995: 23–4). The three bodies most obviously falling into this category were, and still are, the CDRs, the CTC and the FAR. Needless to say, any idea of full autonomy's being granted to, or desired by, these organizations, or of any tolerance of a challenge to the party's hegemony would be to misunderstand the nature of the Cuban political system and culture. What has, however, evolved is a greater willingness on the part of the leadership, desperate perhaps for workable solutions but also more confident in its renewed *cubania*, and aware of the political need for consultation and inclusion, to allow alternative poles of opinion (discourses) within the definition of the Revolution. Here, the underlying and emerging ethos is one of 'family' or 'community', since the official discourse has, since 1994, shifted noticeably towards a more inclusive definition of *nación* and towards a version of the old collectivism that is more akin to 'communitarianism' or, as we have seen, *solidarismo*.

How far, then, have these three bodies actually been 'cut loose'? The CDRs have recently been partly revived in their anti-crime function, but their scope for mobilization and socialization seems to have been recognized in a greater emphasis on their potential, and the strengthening of the national coordinating leadership. The partial 'autonomizing' of the CTC is a more challenging and more controversial

11. The *avionetas* crisis came in February 1996, when two aircraft piloted by the émigré organization, Hermanos al Rescate ('Brothers to the Rescue') – whose aim was ostensibly to rescue *balseros* – deliberately strayed into Cuban airspace, despite Cuban and American official warnings, and were shot down. The incident, which provided the pretext for enacting the Helms–Burton legislation, was almost certainly designed to provoke Cuban reaction, harden a potentially pro-dialogue Clinton administration, and restore credibility to the 'hard line' within Miami.

issue, especially given the well-known difficulties of socialist systems in coming to terms with workers' representational bodies, and also given past Cuban experience. For we have seen that the 1960s saw the conversion of the unions into either 'transmission belt' organizations or mechanisms for mobilization and production, and also the 'withering away' by 1969 of the experimental Consejos de Trabajo (works councils) (Zeitlin 1970a: xxv). Since 1989, however, the *parlamentos obreros* have undertaken a significant consultative role, often succeeding in changing central government proposals, and the CTC newspaper *Trabajadores* has been at the forefront of criticisms of the reforms, the social effects of the 'Special Period' and the demands for greater purchasing power for Cuban workers. The CTC seems, therefore, to have taken on its new semi-autonomous role with effectiveness and some success.

The FAR question is even more complex still, for the peculiar nature of Cuba's system has meant a real difficulty in disentangling it from the party (Pérez 1995: 82–103). What is true is firstly that the FAR has been severely reduced in size – by about a half, to 105,000, between 1989 (the high point of numbers and morale, with the prestigious victory of South African forces at Cuito Carnavale) and 1995 (Greene Walker 1996: 65); in power – from the high point after 1975, where they were identified as key actors in decision-making (González 1977: 9); and in prestige, after the Ochoa affair.[12] What is also true is that they have since then revived, based on the 'professional core' (Greene Walker 1996: 63), on their critical role in public consciousness of alert, defensiveness and preparation, on their leadership of the 1.3 million members of the MTT militias (up from half a million in 1980) (Greene Walker 1996: 67), and especially on their economic successes. For the FAR enterprises, already streamlined in an ambitious 1980s management reform, now achieve productivity levels above the average and play a significant part in labour mobilization through the EJT (Ejército Juvenil de Trabajo, 'Youth Labour Army'), which, set up in 1973 with about 100,000 members (designed to solve the 'loafing' problem), now organizes successful and popular farm-produce markets (*ferias*) throughout the country once a month, offering goods at as little as 10 per cent of the free market price.

Beyond these three bodies, there is the whole strategy of broadening the system to a more inclusive definition of 'community'. This now evidently includes groups such as the churches (considered later), and even elements of the previously excluded external opposition, a significant and far-reaching shift in ethos, and one heralded by the successive *Nación y Emigración* conferences in Havana since

12. The FAR had some 300,000 soldiers in the early 1960s, falling to 250,000 by 1970 and 100,000 by 1974, and then rising slightly to 117,000 in 1975, with 90,000 active reservists. At that stage there were also 100,000 in the EJT, 500,000 support reservists and 10,000 MININT troops (Domínguez 1979: 55–6). By mid-1990 the numbers were still 180,000 (half of them conscripts) (Eckstein 1994: 29).

1994 (always with a high media profile and official support), as well as by the increasing number of references to the 'Cuban family' and to *la emigración* rather than the decades-old term *gusanos*. Indeed, as egalitarianism has been somewhat undermined by the crisis and the reforms, and therefore become less tenable and more dangerous, there has been something of a shift from internal to 'national' community, with the latter being defined more by *nación* than by *pueblo*. This is a move that has struck a chord in Miami, with concerns about the effects on families of the new privations and with racial, social and generational differences beginning to weaken the hitherto united political front (often now seen as 'frozen' in its 1959 anti-communism and more representative of old, white, middle-class émigrés); now, the Cuban community is blacker than before – especially after the Mariel exodus (of some 123,000 Cubans), when some 40 per cent of emigrants were black (Olson and Olson 1995: 84), more working-class, and younger, with few memories of the exodus. With some 1,146,900 Cuban emigrants in the United States in 1994 (Olson and Olson 1995: 93), there can simply no longer be homogeneity, and personal leadership ambitions after the death of the intransigent Jorge Mas Canosa in 1997 have led to significant approaches to the Cuban government for dialogue (Hernández Martínez 1998: 56–71). In this respect the 1999–2000 Elián González case (the struggle for custody over the five-year old shipwrecked *balsero*, which became a major diplomatic incident) fitted well, presenting him as *nuestro hijo* and equating *Patria* and *su familia* (his family).

This reality leads naturally on to the third identified code, moralism, for one evident way in which this has been redirected recently has been in the shift to 'family' (with all its moral implications of authority, responsibility and loyalty) and in the politically skilful decision to take the improved Church–State relations to their logical conclusion and invite Pope John Paul II in January 1998. Capitalizing on a perceived convergence between the increasingly anti-capitalist moralism of the once rigorously anticommunist and ageing Pontiff, the Revolution's longheld moralistic and often anti-materialist beliefs in dignity, equality and selfsacrifice, and the new image of the 'family', beset by a godless and amoral capitalist materialism and threatened by social disintegration, Castro gambled that not only would such an invitation be accepted, but that the risk of critical statements by an always unpredictable Pope – probably against the holding of political prisoners or the harassment of the Church – would be more than outweighed by the benefits. These were likely to be manifold: further Papal denunciations of the American embargo, approval of the Revolution's social achievements and emphasis on education, youth and morality, enormously advantageous publicity and the possibility of wrong-footing, and even marginalizing, the hard-line émigré leadership.

In the event, all those benefits accrued to the Cuban leadership. Notwithstanding the expected criticisms (which were, generally, less than might have been feared by some, and hoped for by the opposition), the visit proved to be an outstanding public-relations success for the Revolution, as millions turned out enthusiastically in a display of nationalist, rather than simply religious, fervour and as a perhaps irreversible wedge was driven into the heart of the Miami-based political opposition.

This visit was, at one level, simply the culmination of a long history of chequered, but generally improving, relations between the supposedly atheistic Revolution and a once politically conservative Catholic Church, a relationship whose recent low-points (especially after the hierarchy misjudged the situation in 1993 by trying to distance itself from a supposedly moribund system with a critical pastoral letter) disguised a mutual desire for convergence, cooperation and a unified approach to the growing social ills of the beleaguered system (see Kirk 1989a; Crahan 1989). While the Cuban church has never shared the 'liberationist' preferences of some of its Latin American brethren (although Nicaraguan bishops after 1979 did try to shake it out of its Cold War 'time-warp'), pragmatism has meant a coexistence around certain common themes of social welfare, community and unity (see Domínguez 1989b). Thus the decision to allow believers into membership of the party (in 1992) made practical sense in many respects (not least in tapping hitherto untapped sectors of activism) and reflected the rebirth, or redirection, of the old moral impulse (see Kirk 1989b).

Nor is it only in religion where this impulse is felt, for the post-1989 crisis unleashed a spate of critical reassessments of the moral, as well as the ideological, basis of the whole process. Part of that rethink, as has been seen, has meant the restoration of the figure, thought and writings of Guevara, and a reaffirmation of Martí; in both cases, whatever attention is being now paid to their precise ideas, both clearly represent role models of moral integrity and personal commitment that reflect the Revolution's new direction. As the general 'back to basics' ethos took hold after 1990, something of the old 1960s moralism was reborn, with increasing references in vanguard and popular discourse to commitment, suffering, sacrifice, selflessness, responsibility, voluntarism, duty and honour.

The fourth code – activism – thus fits well into this picture too, as the decline in the code's viability and credibility in the more materialistic 1972–86 period has been visibly reversed by the various overlapping campaigns since then. Mobilizations – of labour, youth, Havana residents, militias, women – have increased again, not only in response to specific crises but also as part of the revived ethos of community, and all the slogans of *lucha*, vanguard, unity and commitment have been given new force by the threats against the Revolution – crime, inequality, Helms–Burton, hurricanes, the *zafra*, and any number of other perceived dangers. This also, of course, corresponds to the revival of the myth of *Che*, seen often as more *guerrillero* than the perhaps more 'loving' Martí, and more an example of personal willingness to fight. It also matches the renewed *solidarismo*, in that one critical instrument for the new mobilizations and the new activism has necessarily been the FAR.

In this period of heightened *lucha*, siege, commitment and effort, it might be supposed that the fifth code – culturalism – would have less space in which to exist. However, as in the 1960s, it too has seen a revival (although, perhaps of all the codes, it never really declined, but, rather, developed differently). Firstly, the Revolution's leadership has repeatedly stressed to all that education is, with health, an achievement to be defended at all costs; thus, although crisis and reforms have weakened the efficiency and provision of education, expenditure has generally been maintained and, as a sector and an aspiration, it continues to be seen as a priority. Moreover, paradoxically, its very ideological significance is one critical factor that guarantees that the 'dollarization' process will not be allowed into education (or health); which, of course, also means, ironically and dangerously, that a fundamentally important platform in the system's political strategy is being kept afloat by a workforce characterized by its lack of access to the ever more available and divisive dollar.

This code is also witnessed in other aspects, especially the continuing, and often perplexing, freedom and importance given to intellectuals, academics and artists. Again, those familiar with Stalinist regimes, and even with Cuba in the late 1960s, would perhaps expect something of a neglect of, or crackdown on, the intellectual elite at a time of crisis. In fact, however, academic think-tanks (centres, institutes and foundations) have again been given encouragement to develop new thinking, to 'trade' intellectually with the outside, to seek solutions wherever they might be, to re-examine Cuban history and even the history of the Revolution itself (with previously 'taboo' areas being opened up, such as the PSP's collaboration with Batista and the tensions of the early Revolution) – all of which seems to be proved by the otherwise puzzling political prominence and power of the young, long-haired poet, now the Minister of Culture, Abel Prieto.[13] A further example, has been the national campaign, funded by popular subscription, to create the *Cuadernos Martianos*, a stock of textbooks on Martí for Cuba's schools – a campaign that, given the already extensive supply of materials on, images of, and references to, Martí, must be partly explained as yet another mobilization in the service of culture.

Finally, there is internationalism, a code that reached its apogee in 1975–89 in the Third World, but that financial hardship and greater isolation have obliged the leadership to reduce. However, this code has simply been reshaped, not least as a strategy to break the isolation through new alliances – especially in the United Nations (where the voting against the US embargo has steadily increased to the extent that, in 1998 and 1999, only two countries ritually defended it), and in the

13. It should be remembered that the post of Minister of Culture is more politically significant than in most other systems, having been previously held by the influential Hart; Prieto's appointment is thus important.

Figure 8 Internationalist posters from the 1980s.

generally supportive annual Ibero-American Summits and the various Caribbean organizations, with a campaign to identify with the poorer nations (against globalization and debt), with the continuing commitment to overseas education on the Isle of Youth, with medical aid, and with a new opening to outside ideas. It is evident, however, that internationalism lacks the concrete relevance to daily life that it had hitherto, and now serves more of a symbolic or pragmatic function.

The two remaining 1959 codes, the most recent ones in 1959 and perhaps the most vulnerable in the new Cuba of the 1990s, are statism and revolutionism. The former is vulnerable because of the pressure of foreign capital, globalization and survival strategies to reduce the existing state sector and gravitate more towards the current free-market orthodoxy. With the break-up of state lands from 1994, the shift towards autonomous external enterprises, and the general fiscal and financial debility of the Cuban state, this code seems likely to be the most difficult to sustain. Predictably, however, it is precisely because of that pressure that the code remains not just in force but at the forefront of official and unofficial discourse. It remains because one of the shared values in the current process of destabilizing change is the responsibility of a caring state to protect (weak sectors of the economy and society), to guarantee (a minimum of control and provision) and to unify. Thus the idea of the irreducible 'core' state has been consistently proposed in speeches and economic journals, and, so far, has been realized, with 'strategic' sectors such as sugar, land and energy preserved for the state and still free of foreign or private capital, and with an evident consensus about the need to keep services such as education and health in state hands, not least in order to maintain the provision and to avoid Eastern Europe's post-1989 experience. The whole thrust of statism since Martí had long been the concept of an *estado benefactor* ('welfare state') in precisely the present terms – to protect, guarantee and unify. Thus, by stressing a continuing 'basic' role for the Cuban state, the Revolution's leadership is seen to be following the principles of *cubanía*, and of socialism, the demands of the population and the needs of the economy.

Needless to say, when the *estado* is talked about now in Cuba, there is less of a concept of the all-encompassing state of the 1960s – an idea that may have made sense then, in a semi-autarkic isolation and a drive for rapid development, and given the then contemporary developmentalist and socialist orthodoxies, but has long been superseded by new criteria in world economics, by newer socialist (and Cuban) thinking about a limited role for small and medium enterprises and a limited market, and by political realism. Hence, the concept has shifted from the 1960s model towards an entity that mixes *solidarismo* with *soberanía* to create the newer consensus idea of a protective, guaranteeing and unifying state, defending those areas, people and resources that are critical to the progress and unity of the *nación*. The shift towards *solidarismo* is revealing here, for it seems that it is to some extent replacing the long-standing ethos of egalitarianism, given the impossibility of maintaining the latter in the face of the crisis and the reforms, but also because a new generation has grown up without really seeing the high levels of equality that characterized the earlier Revolution. Thus an emphasis on solidarity is a way of rationalizing the need to ensure that imbalances are not excessive, rather than non-existent.

Equally, one would expect a code of revolution to be under great threat now, especially when the daily grass-roots grind for survival probably means a less respectful concern for the concept than in less constrained and more hopeful times. Certainly, there is considerable evidence of a general decline in feelings of social solidarity, communal well-being and shared sacrifice, sufficient to undermine the familiar values associated in Cuba with *Revolución*. However, vanguard discourse at least has taken up the challenge and chosen to stress the fusion between *Revolución*, *cubanía* and *nación* in people's minds and public slogans, speeches and language. Now, exhortations to defend the Revolution (always capitalized) are synonymous with defending the *patria*, a position that is not pure rhetoric, but rather recognizes the reality that most Cubans do tend to mean much more than 'revolution' when they refer to the *Revolución*.

This is because the term has evidently become a symbolic shorthand reference for a whole process, world-view and commitment, a symbol that works in two ways. It means, on the one hand, individual identification with, for example, the social achievements, the nationalist goals or the internationalist enterprise of the Cuban system over the years and, with that, an expression of a sense of belonging to a social grouping with which the individual shares an ideology (of *cubanía*). On the other hand, it means at formal level the whole system of social provision, national identity, and political participation. To speak of *la Revolución* means not to have to define, redefine and examine at every step of the way what exactly is meant by socialism, or which policy is correct or which ideological trend within the communist canon is recommendable. In short, *Revolución* has come, over the years, to mean 'Cuba', in a deeply organic fusion of *cubanía* and *rebelde*, a fusion with considerable long-term significance for popular support.

All of this is important, because what can easily be seen as ritual or formalistic incantations of *Revolución* in public discourse, with apparently little relevance to ordinary Cubans (whose forays into the black market and whose often-expressed grumblings would seem to indicate a lack of faith in anything 'revolutionary') are actually operating at a more subtle level than that. Indeed, the evidence seems to indicate that the public references to *la Revolución* are far from 'whistling in the dark' and are, rather, both a reflection of a shared desire to cling to the 'essence' of the social, national and political gains of the last forty years, albeit redefining *cubanía* to fit the new situation, and also a powerful rallying cry from the leadership to maintain a level of unity.

However, that is not to say that *la Revolución* as a concept has lost all meaning and has simply become a synonym for *cubanía* (although there is some truth in that); for the term is publicly used still, in official discourse (speeches, the media and slogans) and also by private individuals, to mean fundamentally what it may always have meant in Cuba throughout the changes. For example, it evidently means, in some, a personal way of life, a willingness to re-examine their individual political and social conscience and to remain committed; in this respect, someone who is a *buen revolucionario* ('good revolutionary') is an individual who volunteers for campaigns, takes a lead in local activities, is perhaps a party member, is always seeking to take his or her education further, and so on. Alternatively, *la Revolución* is used to simply mean an emphasis on the poor, the people, the ordinary Cubans, stressing social provision and 'community'. Finally, the concept is evidently used, especially in the evolving language of political activists, to mean a willingness to develop, change, adapt ideas and methods in order to 'save the Revolution', while still remaining faithful to the 'essence'. Therefore a *revolucionario* is also someone who, paradoxically, is prepared to think the unthinkable in order to contribute to the collective good, to travel abroad, study and return with new ideas that might be useful.

It is clear, therefore, that *la Revolución* is actually central to the whole process of the preservation, maintenance and strengthening of the *cubanista* codes, being in practice synonymous not so much with 'Cuba' as with 'essence'. As leaders, intellectuals and ordinary loyal Cubans seek to discover, define and then preserve, the 'essence' of their beliefs, the gains and the system, the recurrent theme of all contemporary discourse at all levels is really the need to define that 'essence'. However, the term 'essence' logically almost never appears, for to talk of 'essence' is tantamount to admitting that the rest (once that 'essence' is discovered and defined) may be less relevant, less important and perhaps more discardable. Hence, 'essence' is actually left unsaid and unwritten in much of the discourse that in fact deals with just that idea. Here, *la Revolución* is actually extremely powerful as a tool, since it has also become a catch-all term to express that indefinable but tangible 'essence'. Therefore *la Revolución* is now less a clear idea of change (as it might have been in the 1960s) and more a belief in the 'essence'.

This, inevitably, brings us once again to the question of identity. For the centrality of the idea of *la Revolución* to current debates, to the present process of search, survival and adaptation, recalls the one critical element of ideological continuity both within the Revolution and between the post-1959 period and the preceding periods, namely the constant search for identity. As this study has demonstrated, that theme has been a constant in most of the political discourse, actions and beliefs since the early nineteenth century. All the pre-1895 Cuban aspirations to equality, autonomy, annexation, separatism or independence were also seeking to define a 'Cuban' identity. All the debates about *cubanidad* were fundamentally searching for a definition of 'Cuba', in an environment that sought to deny such an idea and in which many Cubans themselves had a poorly developed concept of it. As has been seen, this meant a search for a sense of distinctiveness, for a set of characteristics and attitudes that would set *criollos* apart from *peninsulares*, would justify claims for equal treatment and rights, and would engender a collective pride. That produced ultimately the concept of *cubanía* and, gradually, the emergence of a sense of *nación* (going beyond the former, narrowly defined, *patria chica*).

After 1902, that debate and search took a different form, as independence meant economic dependence, political humiliation and a cultural denial of *cubanidad*. The events of 1959, however, brought a new dilemma, for one of the critical aspects of the new mobilizing power of *cubanía* by the 1950s was the clearly organic convergence between the popular political culture, the popular demand for, understanding of, and empathy with, *cubanía* – or at least the separate codes that constituted it by then – and the explicit or implicit *cubanista* platform and challenge that was represented by the 26 July Movement. Moreover, by 1958 it was clear that the evolving concept of 'revolution' had become a code in itself, sufficiently for most Cubans to identity 'revolution' with patriotism, honesty and the path to *nación*.

Therefore, in 1959, *la Revolución* – although not clearly defined then – had become the popular expression of *cubanía*, the channel for the search for identity. In that sense, the pre-1959 search for a *national* identity had been realized, meaning that, after 1959, it was transmogrified into a search for a *revolutionary* identity, as the succeeding decades became a trajectory of internal and external pressures to shape the process of change, of attempts to import models, or devise autonomous criteria, or discover a unique path to revolution. *Revolución* therefore tended to replace *nación* as the focus of the collective political and intellectual search for identity. After 1989, that concern became especially critical, as the collapse of hitherto credible paradigms, and pressures, and the resurgence of old pressures, together with the arrival of new ones, threw Cuba back on its own resources in almost every way, but also gave the 'believers' the opportunity to renew that search in a new context.

It is thus apposite that one discovers that, in the 1990s, the 'national' concerns that seemed to be neglected in the past returned to the foreground, to formal discourse and to political debates. For one outcome of the post-1989 search for urgent, viable, but 'Cuban', solutions to the crisis has been a parallel search for a political and ideological definition to match the new situation, the new problems and the new opportunities – above all one that does not lose sight of, and keeps its roots deep in, the 'essential' values of *la Revolución* (which we may take as the codes of *cubanía*). That has meant, above all, an inevitable organic fusion of the two historical searches – for national identity (seen to be discovered in the Revolution of 1959) and for revolutionary identity (now seen to be rediscovered in the *nación*).

The implication of all this is that 'search' means also definition, for one element of continuity throughout the four decades has been the need to define 'self' at a national level. What else, indeed, is a search for identity but a changing awareness and definition of the national 'self'? With that, given the traditional Cuban concern (or even obsession) with history, has come a parallel process of redefinition of the national 'destiny'. Once assumed to be independence, then, variously, either a loyal part of the American system, a member of the socialist community, or a leader of the Third World, it has become clear that the consensual 'destiny' within all Cuban discourse now is survival of the *nación*, no longer narrowly defined but now associated with the broadest, most inclusive, definition historically, geographically, culturally and even ideologically.

Overall, these searches have coalesced in the current understandable search for 'essence' – of Cuba, *nación* and *Revolución*. Of course, if ideology can be defined as the shared perception of the 'essence' of the values, experience and characteristics that bind together a social group, then the current concern goes right to the heart of *cubanía* and revives it in a way not seen since the 1960s. This is, of course, in direct contradiction of both expectations and current images of Cuba, where ideology would, at first sight, seem to be the most vulnerable, and possibly expendable, aspect of the Revolution's continuity. How can an ageing revolutionary vanguard hope to maintain its equally ageing ideology in the face of the tidal wave of change? The answer, again, is in the even greater use of, belief in, and access to myth.

It was this danger to which the leadership responded in 1986, reinforcing this in the mid-1990s, by its decision to rejuvenate visibly the party and the vanguard. Firstly, it paid greater attention, and gave greater freedom and authority, to both the FEU and the UJC (once rejected by many young Cubans as too dogmatic and irrelevant), allowing them to fuse political commitment and social entertainment, and to voice and reflect greater criticisms. Secondly, as we have seen, the response came in the promotion within the party of younger elements, leaping the intervening (and perhaps 'contaminated') generation. With Lage now effectively Prime Minister (presiding over the Council of Ministers), and with Robaina, until summer 1999, as Foreign Minister, the message was clear of a new generation's opportunity.

We have already seen that, although youth alienation may have contributed to the August 1994 crisis, it was by no means the sole cause, since the problem also reflected a deeper discontent, which has always been a feature of the Revolution, attributable to a range of motives. There have been those opposed on political or ideological grounds, through anticommunist ideological positions, liberalism or often religion, or even occasionally through rejection of the social and racial changes. There have been those whose opposition has been based on more personal grounds – disappointment at work, marginalization, frustration in education, or separation from, or subversive contacts with, family abroad. There have been those, finally, whose rejection of the system has been based on material frustration, either the early loss of middle-class status, possessions, housing or living standards or aspirations towards the commodities and opportunities of the capitalist world, and especially the United States, always tantalizingly across the water and always advertising its offerings through propaganda, émigré visits or the rare experience of travel there. These 'anti-system' Cubans have tended to be concentrated above all in Havana, in the younger population and among those who have been more marginal to mobilization. Interestingly, the size of this sector has probably remained largely unchanged since the mid-1960s, since the end of the mass emigrations, which, if true, is both reassuring and worrying for the Revolution. It is reassuring in that it has rarely been greater than a proportion between a fifth and a third of the population, but it is worrying in that successive emigrations have not 'bled away' the problem sufficiently to remove it all together, but have instead seen that dissident sector recreate itself again.

This introduces the sensitive and complicated question of dissidence. It is complicated firstly by the problem of definition and general use of the term in the Western political science lexicon, since the same word can be variously used to refer to those who voice an organic coherent rejection of a given system's hegemony (in a basic and total opposition), to those who are critics of the extremes, or of aspects, of a system, and to those who individualistically refuse to toe an official line. Secondly, it is complicated in Cuba by the differences between English and Spanish, since in English, 'dissidence' and 'dissent' often mean different things, the former perhaps referring to a coherent, but individual, non-conformity with authoritarian regimes, the latter often referring to a more structural but perhaps less visible opposition to the bases of any system, usually with an 'alternative project' in mind. In Spanish, however, the word *disidencia* covers both categories, leading to a greater Cuban sensitivity towards such categorization, even amongst those who are 'dissenting'.

The question is also further complicated by preconceptions about communist societies and by the fact that, while the whole revolutionary process in Cuba self-consciously grew out of a tradition and ideology of dissent – where dissent was the accepted, and even patriotic, expression of *cubania*, that tradition transformed itself after 1959 into an ideology that, although often continuing to perceive itself as an essentially dissenting process (challenging the orthodoxies of both imperialism and Marxism), aspired to revolutionary hegemony, against which there would inevitably be dissent. Indeed, in the first years of the revolutionary process, there were dissenting alternatives to the new project. However, the 'Great Debate' of 1962–5 perhaps shows more clearly the subtleties of the problem, since the phenomenon was actually an officially encouraged and open debate between different schools of political thought within the current socialist ideological tradition, a debate ultimately settled by *fiat* (Castro's decision to opt for a particular path) and by economic momentum and necessity, but with the 'losers' not being fully marginalized but, rather, waiting in the wings until their turn came again. This then was the first clear expression of what we can call intra-systemic dissent, referring to the tolerance of competing poles of opinion and interpretation (competing discourses) within the broadly defined revolutionary project. As this study has made clear, this tradition has been variously evident throughout the forty-one year process of change and redefinition, especially in the recurring periods of 'debate'. From this perspective, it is perfectly possible to present a picture of the Revolution as a process that has explicitly opened up internal debate when necessary to seek urgently needed practical solutions to significant problems.

This inherent tendency has, however, been countered by a further trend within the Revolution – the creation of a vanguard mentality at the top. Based, naturally, in the Sierra experience (and therefore the *sierra* group), it began as a collective sense of certainty – set against the prevailing uncertainty and confusion of the time and then the threat of counter-revolutionary arguments and alternatives, but was then reinforced by the wider 'siege mentality' that emerged after 1962, rapidly leading to an ethos that saw Cubans in simple terms of 'ins' and 'outs', counterbalancing an 'exclusion' of those who left (or sided with imperialism) against the 'inclusion' of all those who remained and shared the struggle of the 'siege'. This exclusion also, as we have seen, eventually extended to those who 'deviated' from the accepted norms of ideology, behaviour and expression, which, in the increasingly moralistic atmosphere of the late 1960s, could mean the marginalization of pro-Moscow 'old' communists and of those who 'deviated' in dress, lifestyle, artistic attitudes or sexuality. It could also, naturally, lead to periods of harassment and incarceration, although the question of 'political prisoners' is again confused by differing definitions and highly unreliable and partisan evidence – with figures ranging between Castro's own assessment of about 2,000 in the mid-1960s, to one diplomat's somewhat discredited figure of 55,000 for 1969 (Suchlicki 1988: 227).

In this sense, it is important to see the question of 'dissent' as one of 'ins' and 'outs', with periods of isolation and crisis often producing a narrower definition of the 'ins' (resulting in exclusion, and even marginalization and antagonism), but with subsequent periods of 'inclusion' and even rehabilitation. If, then, this is 'dissent' (within the parameters of the system), and if the émigrés' outright rejection of the whole process and system is total opposition, what of 'dissidence'?

The most obvious fact about Cuban dissidence to those who come to Cuba with preconceptions from a familiarity with the Soviet Union or pre-1989 Eastern Europe is that they are often simply unable to find 'dissidents', for they either do not exist in significant numbers or exist only fleetingly and lack popular support. Indeed, until the late 1980s, such dissidents as there were either enjoyed little support outside their immediate groups or found their effectiveness continually undermined by incarceration, harassment or the effects of the familiar 'bloodletting' policy of emigration. This immediately brings sharply into focus one basic, but often overlooked, fact of Cuban political life – that, at any one time, the really organized, popular and financially strong opposition to the system is to be found in Miami, which continues to act as a magnet for successive waves of dissident émigrés, each wave further weakening the already weak base for organized dissent within the island.

After 1991, with the collapse of the old superpower balance and the resulting American triumphalism in the region (already expressed in Panama in 1989 and in Nicaragua in 1990 and now resulting in the Cuba Democracy Act of 1992), internal dissidents were inevitably both emboldened and more actively encouraged from the outside, as human rights moved up the American agenda in international diplomacy against Cuba (most notably in the United Nations). Indeed, the stand-off between the United States government and the European Union over their differing views of the 1996 Helms–Burton Law meant that, when compromise was reached in 1997–8, human rights also appeared in European attitudes towards Cuba, anticipated already by a more exigent policy from the new Aznar government in Madrid. As a result, small dissident groups in Cuba resurfaced or reformed, often defined now as human rights organizations, closely monitored and even encouraged by European governments and often close to, and protected by, the Catholic Church.

The ideological crisis of the 1990s was therefore structural in several senses – in the inherent potential of rising expectations and generational alienation to break down unity, in the tendency for discontent to be more openly, and corrosively, expressed, and in the greater likelihood of this increasing at a time of economic shortage and reduced hope.

It has also meant a crisis in the relationship between myth and ideology. For there are clear tensions, and even contradictions, between the combined effects of economic collapse and the message of reform, on the one hand, and, on the other, the underlying, long-cherished values of the 'Cuban community'. A revolution that from the outset has extolled *eticidad*, community and heroism, and preached egalitarianism, cannot easily retain popular faith in the face of the growing and visible inequalities created by access to the dollar, the growing role of foreign capital, the increasing problems of prostitution and petty crime and the increasing tendency towards individualism inherent in the daily battle for personal economic survival. Moreover, for the first time in the Revolution's history, economic strategies have become separated from political criteria, and thus from the process of revolutionary transformation. In the 1960s, and even the 1970s, the Revolution's myths remained powerful and organic because of the close and coherent integration of economic, political and social structures, and those myths in those circumstances had an overall meaning, which made them identifiable.

Thus, now, in the year 2000, the Revolution's search for a new ideological definition (based on the old, and perhaps rescuing the forgotten 'essence' of the 1960s) implies a basic and challenging task in the area of myth. If, then, we examine this 'urgent and basic task', it should be seen in the context of the permanent tension and 'debate' between the competing discourses of *cubanía*, from both the pre-1959 and post-1959 periods, that have characterized the continuing search for a definition of a Cuban identity, a revolutionary *Cuba Libre* – a *cubanía revolucionaria*, rather than just an oppositional *cubanía rebelde*. In such a definition, myths have become the weapons in the battle for hegemony, and also the 'defence' for each discourse and equally for the baffled population, seeking to adapt.

It must also, however, all be seen within the context of the whole relationship between *la Revolución* (as vanguard, party, system and ethos) and the *pueblo*, an always contradictory, flexible but deep relationship, which, over the years, has consistently gone to the heart of the evolving political culture, changing political definitions, the contradictory political structure and every Cuban's political judgements. The basic fact about the system is that, contrary to stereotypes, it is in fact evidently not monolithic – with competing discourses, levels of debate, contradictions, 'spaces' and 'overlaps'. Moreover, the second basic fact to bear in mind is something that was made clear from the first days of 1959, that the Revolution was thought of then by the vanguard, and has remained ever since, a *proceso* (Pérez 1988: 316), rather than a 'system'. Thus to define and describe the trajectory of the forty years of Revolution in terms of 'phases' actually serves to complicate rather than explain, since the categorization of each phase is countered by apparently contradictory evidence at each turn.

Given the stresses and strains of that process, its economic vicissitudes, hardships and political pressures, popular support cannot be expected to have been either constant or consistent over four decades, and has often been less than openly active, even among the Revolution's most fervent supporters. This is not least because, apart from the 1975–85 period – when economic policy was perhaps at its most stable and the resulting economic benefits were most coherently and reliably provided – the four decades have seemed to many Cubans to be as confusing, as destabilizing and even as disheartening as the whole process has at times seemed to outsiders. Quite apart from the small uncertainties and apparent changes in attitude or policy, one only has to consider the major changes that the average Cuban has, over the years, been asked to comprehend, or to accept without too much questioning, to see why this confusion should arise.

For example, the changing attitude to the Soviet Union can never have been easy to understand, moving from conventional opposition in January 1959 to alliance in 1960, and then ideological identification in 1961, followed by the 'betrayal' of 1962, and an often vehemently critical attitude throughout the years of isolation until 1970. This in turn was followed by a period of *détente*, then renewed alliance (with public expressions of praise and affinity), and then a period when Soviet models, textbooks, study programmes and views of the world were accepted enthusiastically and proclaimed to Cubans. This in turn was followed by Cuban criticisms of the Gorbachev reforms and, finally, after the 1991 collapse, came a period of regret for the passing of an old ally but also the start of growing criticisms of the effects of the whole process of alliance and reliance. With just this one example, it is easy to see how much of an understatement it is to say that the average Cuban has been confused over the years, a confusion that cannot but undermine the consistency of popular support for a process that the average Cuban might understand on a mundane level but whose ideological and political interpretation is often deemed to be unattainable. Moreover, the post-1986 'Rectification' is a case in point, since it cannot have escaped any but the most unquestioning supporters of the Revolution that the very leaders who proclaimed the need for a thorough critique of policies and structures were those who had, hitherto, created those policies and structures and, moreover, had called for similar campaigns of reappraisal on other occasions and at other moments of crisis. Such repetition runs an obvious risk of becoming corrosive, as the credibility of those leaders must necessarily be damaged by the process.

Therefore, a picture emerges of a 'system' that is often far from systematic. If conventional studies of the Revolution have blurred the picture, what explanations can be offered here, given the 'prism' of ideology? To put it another way, if it is axiomatic that the Cuban political system has always been, and still is, more complex than the conventional 'monolithic' interpretations would allow, how might we arrive at a theoretical model for understanding that complexity and for understanding how the system actually functions and, more importantly, how ordinary Cubans actually relate daily to it, to the leadership and to the underlying political culture? On the basis of what has been argued, some characterizations of today's Revolution (and of its evolution to this point) can be offered – its 'horizontalism', its 'argumentalism', its network of spaces, and its revolutionary nature.

The first characteristic – that the system is 'horizontalist' – is that it consists of relatively few, but separate, layers of power, control and operation, between which the channels of communication, expression and empowerment are essentially horizontal rather than vertical. Verticality exists in a number of aspects – in the inherent centralism of the economic decision-making structures, in the perceived authority and legitimacy of the party and, within that, of the revolutionary leadership, and, until 1993, in the pyramidal OPP structure. However, the system is horizontal in other clear respects.

Firstly, at least until the post-1993 strains, the Cuban system's perceived and real egalitarianism has operated in swathes across the structure, with huge peer-groups enjoying a genuine if relative equality of wealth, access to decision-making and economic and educational opportunity. In other words, most Cubans have been daily able to perceive a tangible equality between them and their neighbours, family, work-mates and fellow members of the various mass organizations; at times this may have been an equality of poverty or of mediocrity, but Cuba has largely been denied the characteristic Third World tensions arising from the close co-existence of rich and poor. That equality has worked at all levels, with, for example, most rural workers in a given area, residents of a Havana *barrio*, or, further up, technocrats (although living better than many of their compatriots) all sharing a broadly similar level of existence within each group. Thus one can perhaps talk of 'bands' of egalitarianism, layered close to, but separate from, each other.

Secondly, this horizontalism derives from the fact that the many and diverse channels of communication are mostly indirect rather than direct, with messages, complaints, orders and interpretations filtered up or down between the 'layers', a process that occasionally hides the real communication and may even distort or delay the 'message' (especially, as after 1975, where one of the 'layers' becomes entrenched). That does not, of course, obviate the need for direct communication (radio, television, mass rally or the press), which frequently cuts through these intermediary layers; but such directness is usually reserved for 'global' messages and mobilizing uses of the discourse, rather than specific instructions on precise interpretations of policy.

One essential factor of this 'horizontalism', however, is that these layers are not entirely separate, overlapping with each other to allow better communication, social mobility and space. In this sense, they closely resemble the 1970s 'dual circuits' theoretical model devised for urban Latin America to explain the inter-relation between the 'formal' sector (the recognizable and measurable upper circuit, externally linked) and the 'informal' (the overlapping lower circuit, where the majority live, work and operate daily) (Santos 1979). According to this model, the critical overlap between the circuits is where the 'upper' circuit uses the labour resources of the other, while the 'lower' uses the formal and financial resources and opportunities of the 'upper'.

While it would be simplistic to define Cuba in these terms, since there are evidently more than two political 'layers' or 'circuits' at any one time, the concepts of necessary and mutually useful 'overlap', and of politically 'formal' and 'informal' levels, do help one to understand the Cuban system. Thus, for example, while most Cubans are not party members, will often complain furiously about the party and may even feel alienated from it, they all have indirect access to its effects, its decision-making structures, its channels of communications and also its processes of legitimization. They may daily act 'informally' in their relationship with the 'formal' political structure, but they clearly participate at critical times, and periodically, in the 'formal' mechanisms, usually perceiving the need to do so not simply through coercion or peer-pressure.

The second characteristic for a possible theoretical model – its 'argumentalism' – is related to this: this is the idea of different 'arguments' visibly and continually maintained, tolerated and even encouraged within the overall 'project'. This is the now familiar issue of the need to avoid a discourse of 'factions' or splits to describe a system that is remarkably free of Soviet-style or Chinese-style schisms at vanguard level. Instead, as we have seen, differences within the upper 'layers' of the system have invariably been seen by all concerned as 'arguments', competing discourses or distinct *criterios* (opinions or judgements),[14] within the underlying, unchallenged and consensual 'project' of the Revolution.

This, as we have seen, is especially indicated by two factors: the tendency for periods of certainty to be preceded and followed by periods of acceptable 'debate' (often encouraged and usually extending beyond the leadership 'layer'), and the equal tendency for the 'losers' to become only relatively marginalized within the system (given acceptable posts, maintaining their often high positions and even being allowed to return for the next 'debate', in which they may become the 'winners').

14. The use of the term *criterio* (literally 'criterion') is interesting within the Cuban political culture. At one level it is used to mean (ideologically neutral but personal) 'opinion', but it can also mean (ideological) 'interpretation', and a debate can find contributions prefaced by *comparto los criterios de . . .* (I share the *criterios* of . . .) which then proceed to demolish the arguments represented by those other *criterios*. In other words, 'I share the *criterios* of "so and so"' is actually a way of identifying with the interlocutor within the overall 'project' while differing from their interpretation.

This essentially 'argumental' system operates in different ways at different levels. At the top it is normally kept within the group, with a very low degree of subsequent marginalization; in the intermediate 'layers', it can be expressed in the periodic and often relatively surprising level of open debate allowed to and encouraged in academic 'think tanks', and in the mass consultation exercises within the party, the OPP networks or workplaces preceding key decisions; at the bottom, it can be participation in these exercises or simply the constant safety-valve of complaint, grumbling and what has been described as 'foot-dragging' (Eckstein 1994).

The third major characteristic of the Cuban system is its network of interlocking mobilization mechanisms by which communications are transferred and the population is regularly involved. This network has expanded over the years, to leave no single structure or organization to which all belong or in which all participate; instead, from the relatively simple participatory systems of the 1960s, the Cuban system has developed into a number of structures and organizations that have been additional to, not substitutes for, the original ones. This evolution has been occasionally accidental – developing new mechanisms in response to new crises or demands – and sometimes deliberate, as one 'argument' has pressed for one, rather than another, kind of structure. The net result, however, is a complex and often contradictory set of mechanisms that can be confusing, comprehensive or comforting, depending on the time, the circumstance and the purpose, and can easily become (as they did in the late 1970s) the breeding ground for entrenched bureaucracies and islands of privilege. The point is, however, that these mechanisms have become so multifarious and multifaceted that they have created countless series of 'spaces' in the interstices between them, in which less committed Cubans can hide or, more commonly, in which ordinary Cubans can work out a *modus vivendi* with the demands and tensions of the whole system. While large number of Cubans may use these 'spaces' for negative purposes, especially at times of tension or crisis, as one recent study identified (seeing them as essentially 'negative' or 'conflictive' spaces where Cubans can hide, drag their feet or trade informally) (Eckstein 1994), it is in fact more useful to see the 'spaces' more positively from the point of view of political participation.

The reason is that the same 'negative spaces' are also, in practice, 'creative spaces'. While they may exist for individual Cubans to survive, find a niche, deal economically and resolve the contradictions of their relationship with an always challenging system, they also exist as 'creative spaces' for the system itself, which, otherwise potentially controlling, centralizing and instinctively absolutist, must allow everyone their own 'space' in which they can interpret the global demands in their own particular contexts, of themselves, their families, their jobs and their neighbourhoods. These, after all, are the 'spaces' where the codes of the underlying ideology are interpreted daily, where the myths are 'customized', where the demand for commitment is filtered into something adaptable, manageable and yet still loyal, and where Cubans can be both part of the system yet also part of the 'sub-system', a two-way relationship that all Cubans need to accommodate the demands of a genuine, if not always articulated, commitment and loyalty to the basic goals or ethos of the system, and the daily demands of economic survival. They are a critical part of the 'overlap'. Both the leadership and the average Cuban have therefore effectively sought and used 'spaces' within the complexities and the contradictions of the system, to hide, to exist, to develop, to wait, to debate, to challenge, to sound off and to 'store' alternatives.

Finally, the fourth key characteristic is that the system is still essentially 'revolutionary'. For it is still more useful to understand the Cuban system, and its survival, by seeing it in terms of a process of 'revolution' rather than as a 'communist state', given the political baggage of the latter term. How, though, can it still, even in the late 1990s, be 'revolutionary'?

Firstly, it can be considered so because it is always in a process of continual change – of structure, policy, alliance, direction, and so on (although not, until the mid-1990s, of personnel). This process has been sometimes deliberate – for example, to militate against a bureaucratizing institutionalization or to react to a crisis – but sometimes simply reactive, for the reality of Cuba's history of subordination and marginalization, and its present dilemma of essentially Third World economic vulnerability, has meant that the Cuban revolutionary leadership has been obliged – whatever its long-term or immediate programme or political preferences – to react to events beyond its control: the world price of sugar, the superpower conflicts, monoculture, dependency, and so on. If any revolution is by definition a maelstrom of unforeseen developments and crises, how much more so is a process of revolution in a small, underdeveloped, monocultural island, in the sphere of influence of one superpower at a time of challenge and tension with another? In such circumstances, any path will be erratic, problematic and traumatic. There has thus been a natural tendency for the Cuban Revolution not just to change continually, in order to adapt to each new situation, each new challenge, but also to revolutionize itself continually.

This tendency to react has given rise to the second reason for the claim to a 'revolutionary' nature – the fact that the system is constantly in a process of redefinition, as the Revolution reacts to different world circumstances, economic pressures and crises or internal tensions. As we have seen, this process invariably involves the generation of internal debates and a greater fluidity of the 'layers' and the 'spaces'.

The third reason why the system can still be considered 'revolutionary' is that it is in constant mobilization, through the various mass organizations, the rallies, the campaigns, the military alerts, the 'direct democracy', the electoral process and so on. While such a feature could easily be dismissed as mere populism or manipulation by a controlling vanguard, and while it may by no means always be synonymous with empowerment, the evidence is that the whole mobilization experience has in practice always created a sense of belonging and of meaningful participation. While this is not equally true of all organizations and while it does not stop the system being centralizing and 'top-down' in its decision-making, participation in the mobilization system has meant, for example, the recognition of each Cuban's right to defend the country, each Cuban's personal contribution, and each Cuban's right to express a *criterio* within the structure. In the same way that the collective experience of the 1960s radicalized thousands of Cubans, the continuing access to such mechanisms should not be dismissed as mere corporatism or blind loyalty.

Finally, by definition, it is 'revolutionary' as it is still visibly driven by an ideology whose basic premises are revolutionary in implication, with their emphasis on renewal, action and redefinition. Indeed, one of the remarkable aspects of this process of what is often referred to as 'continuous revolution' (despite, or perhaps even because of, its associations with Trotsky) has been the determination of the leadership – and a large number of the led too – not to lose sight of the 'essence' of the goals, of the basic direction that was sought at the start. Such a task can never be easy at the best of times, unless there exists a clear *canon* to which those involved in the process can refer, a clear point of reference.

This all raises the question of the levels and scope of political support for the Revolution. In 1994, following the crisis of the *balseros*, it was possible to draw up a balance sheet of active and passive support, such a reading coming out of public opinion surveys (however unreliable these might have been then), judgements made by internal dissidents, extrapolations from the evidence of electoral arithmetic and observations based on long contact with the subject (Kapcia 1995: 22).

The conclusions then were that the Cuban population could be divided into three groups, in terms of its attitude to the system. We have already seen the nature of one of these groups, the 'dissenting' sector, amounting to roughly one-fifth to one-third (based, not least, on the numbers of those in 1993 – 19 per cent – choosing not to vote for the full official slate, a number confirmed by some dissidents as accurate). The second group, also perhaps of the same size (depending on the moment), could be defined as those Cubans who, largely unquestioningly, were then committed actively to the Revolution. Such a group included especially the older generation (who had gained most, personally and tangibly, from the three and a half decades of reform and who still bore memories of either the pre-1959 hardships and inequalities, or the stresses of the 1960s), the million or so members of the party or the UJC, the CDR activists, the 'core' workers in the education and public service sectors, and, above all, rural Cubans, or, at least, those who lived elsewhere than in Havana.

That left the third sector, the critical one in 1994, ranging between one-third and two-thirds (depending on the size of the other two groups at any one time). These Cubans were those who, although largely if passively committed to the system in some or all respects, were prone to express the greatest criticisms and complaints, but were as yet sufficiently unsure of, opposed to, or frightened by possible alternatives to ensure their continuing loyalty. The judgement in 1994 was that this sector was still largely in favour of the existing system, probably still considered itself 'revolutionary' and was sufficiently loyal to something that it identified as 'the Revolution' (and to Castro as its leader) to provide the material for the demonstrations, mobilizations and consultations of the period.

If that was the situation in 1994, in the depths of the crisis but also at the start of a long period of exhausting and painfully slow recovery, what then might the balance sheet be today? Any such judgements can only be partly informed speculation, partly subjective impression and partly measured assessment, not least since any Cuba-watcher must be well aware of the problems of accurately assessing Cuban responses to an outsider who, however familiar with the system and linguistically able to communicate, is nonetheless still a foreigner. However, as in 1994, it is still possible to make some reasonably accurate assessment – based again on sources such as dissident views, official voting returns, interviews, close observation, and factors such as the size of the various rallies – the May Day parade in Havana in 1999, for example, accounting for about one-third of the population of the province.

It seems reasonable to suggest that the size of that sector of the population more or less defined as unquestioningly in favour of the system – the supporters – has probably remained largely stable, while the other end of the spectrum – the opposition – may even have decreased marginally, leaving the passive support of the 'middle' sector slightly larger. However true that assessment may be, those facts almost certainly disguise a wealth of complex shifts within each sector and between sectors.

One way of arriving at this judgement, and to explain it, is to assess the known impact of the various developments and events that have acted on the average Cuban's political consciousness – and therefore commitment or disenchantment – since that original judgement was made in 1994. Such developments would most obviously include the significant economic improvement that Cuba has seen since 1994, with five years of often impressive growth (from an admittedly appallingly low 1993 level) and the effects of the reforms and of much greater access to the increasingly ubiquitous dollar. This steady improvement, with all its implications, has almost certainly had a variety of often contradictory effects on political attitudes.

The most predictable would be that improving access to material satisfaction, food supplies, energy (especially petrol and electricity – the lack of which caused the most crippling daily effects of the crisis for most Cubans) and the dollar would all help reduce dissatisfaction and political discontent and increase again the degree of public and popular toleration of an obviously crisis-struck and flawed system, restoring, for some, a degree of lost faith in the Revolution's ability to deliver goods and services and to provide its citizens with the basics of a decent existence. This gradual reduction in the corrosive daily frustrations of life, of the street-level economy, should not be ignored in a Cuba whose greatest threat in 1992 may well have been the disappearance of the characteristic optimism and hope. There is a point during a crisis when even the slightest improvement in conditions or opportunities can be grasped eagerly by a population that, having not yet been driven to total disillusion, is desperately seeking some psychological life-raft to which to cling. Given that 1992 did not produce evidence of total breakdown of popular support for, and current identification with, the system, it seems reasonable to surmise that identification with the system on the part of the average Cuban is more likely to be still at that point, rather than being beyond political salvation.

However, set against that natural effect of the economic amelioration since 1994 are three negative political effects. The first is that improvement can all too easily engender expectation, especially after such a deep crisis in the economy, in political legitimacy and in hope, and, although the improvement is impressive (given the earlier catastrophic collapse and the earlier predictions), it may well not be fast enough for many. Indeed, the slowdown in that growth in 1998 (as a result of a range of factors beyond Cuba's control), and the deliberate decision to consolidate reforms, rather than risk further destabilization of the system, expectations, control and the balance between reflation and stagnation, not to mention a political structure whose reform has been not so much rapid or radical, as controlled and measured, has led to a noticeable increase in complaint – especially amongst those either supportive, or tolerant, of the Revolution. Thus, in 1998, it was common to hear genuine complaints about conditions' being worse than in the preceding year, whereas the evidence of macroeconomic statistics, fuller food markets, greater access to *cuenta propia* work and generally healthier and more materially satisfied Cubans directly countered that perception. The conclusion must be, then, that, apart from complaints arising from specific cases of marginalization or disappointment, the discontent arose from the familiar problem of rising expectations (following depression and gloom) being frustrated by economic growth's not having been maintained at the same level.

A second negative effect has been that those Cubans trapped in the still peso-bound sectors of employment – especially those in health, education and the civil service, long hailed as the standard-bearers of the Revolution's social achievements and generally far better qualified than the average – have become steadily frustrated by seeing other sectors improve visibly while their own sectors and their pay and purchasing power stagnate. Resentment is, indeed, rife among these public servants

– a political problem of enormous significance, which was addressed in 1999 by sweeping pay increases.

That leads on to a third negative effect of the improvement – the impact of greater access to the dollar, perhaps the most far-reaching economic reform, but with a clear potential to be double-edged, allowing a greater and much-needed ability for Cubans to assuage their material needs at last, after years of hardship and market sterility, and perhaps reducing political tensions, but also creating a greater awareness of the inadequacies of the non-dollar peso-based system, and thus increasing expectations. Furthermore, there is evidence of the dollar's corrosive effect on a sense of communal solidarity, creating a more individualistic and materialistic mentality in more and more Cubans.

A second event that contributed to changes in the political equation since 1994 was the Pope's visit in 1998, once again a double-edged sword. On the one hand, as we have seen, through its very taking place and with the Pope's criticisms of the embargo it clearly helped increase the 'feel-good' factor in a pressurized society, now sensing a world recognition impossible to contemplate in 1992. The visit also helped strengthen nationalism, as the fostered welcome achieved extensive success among the thousands who flocked to greet the Pope with their national flags and banners and a general carnival atmosphere. As this was accompanied by a brief, but significant, welcoming hand extended to those émigrés who wished to visit the island, the 'feel-good' factor was reinforced.

The visit also created more opportunities for those associated with the Catholic Church to become more integrated into the 'Cuban family', to be heard, to parade their faith publicly and even to enjoy some new prestige. For those Catholics who had long struggled with their consciences between two mutually hostile entities to which they were equally loyal – the Church and the Revolution – that welcome meant a new sense of belonging. As such, this largely beneficial event almost certainly shifted many Cubans from the 'middle' to the 'supporters' camp, and perhaps even from the 'opposition' camp to the 'middle'. Nonetheless, that same event had its negative consequences. Firstly, the greater freedom, respect and power given to the Church encouraged some erstwhile passive Cubans to become more confident 'dissidents', believing perhaps that this first sign of a new pluralism, with a possible alternative 'pole' of political belief, gave them a degree of safety in voicing long-silent opposition views. Certainly, one can imagine that the passive 'middle' group of Cubans has always included those who, having perceived the system as essentially, and irrevocably, unipolar, hitherto decided to resign them-selves to a perhaps unarticulated tolerance.

One further event since 1994 with the capacity to have changed the balance of support was the *avionetas* incident of February 1996, an episode that certainly frightened enough Cubans into believing that an unconstrained Washington was about to unleash its military, as well as economic, power against Castro and the revolution. As such, the incident seems mostly to have enhanced further the 'siege mentality' which, after years of decline, had been recreated during the post-1989 isolation and crisis, only to decline during the gradual trade opening in 1993–5. Certainly the official mobilizations and the alert connected with it all fostered, as ever, a sense of heightened nationalism and defensive unity, especially after Clinton signed the Helms–Burton Act he had previously opposed. However, the episode did not work entirely in favour of the leadership, for many Cubans also reacted with dismay that the gradually improving relations and expectations from 1993 had been dashed by what might just have been Cuban intransigence. As such, it demoralized many, and, even for those seeking refuge in nationalism and mobilization, the corrosive effect of any level of demoralization cannot be ignored. Thus, on balance, the whole episode may well have strengthened the ranks of the 'middle'. Interestingly, the spectre of an unconstrained NATO bombing Serbia in 1999 frightened not a few Cubans into imagining that an unprotected Cuba could easily be a similar 'victim' should Clinton and NATO so decide.

Simultaneously there evolved a further factor with a significant effect on the political balance-sheet – the apparent clampdown on intellectual freedom and activity seemingly signalled by Raúl Castro's speech on the eve of the *avionetas* incident, which became the *caso CEA* ('the CEA affair'), as the highly respected Centro de Estudios sobre América (CEA) was subjected to a long process of investigation, criticism and eventually change. Although this coincided with the *avionetas* incident, it seemed to presage to many, inside and outside Cuba, a political retrenchment and a return to the 1960s 'siege' (Giuliani 1998). Certainly, although the affair ended with little overall damage, no major purge and a degree of compromise, the effect on some intellectuals – either among the 'supporters' or the 'middle' – was to increase fear and caution, and even, in some, disillusion (after a period of encouraged debate). While the numbers involved may have been insignificant, the wider effect on a vociferous group cannot be ignored.

Having said that, however, the adverse effects of this incident may have been partly offset by the general welcome for the visible rejuvenation of the political and administrative structure of Cuba – from Buró Político to local party cell, from ministry to university faculty, a long overdue changing of the guard has been seen, with much younger personnel replacing an ageing and less responsive generation, too long in a bureaucracy and power structure already prone to inertia. The sense of relief, renewal and future opportunity that this much-discussed change has brought have helped restore some legitimacy to, and faith in, the system.

Three further incidents in recent years have helped reinforce the Revolution's active and passive support – the terrorist bombings of summer 1997, the return of Guevara's body to Cuba in 1997 and the 1999 Elián González affair. The first episode was almost universally condemned by Cubans, focusing attention again on the perhaps forgotten extremism of the more hard-line elements in Miami, and even persuading some previously dubious Cubans that Castro was not after all the guilty party in the previous year's confrontation with the United States. The sense of anger perhaps outweighed any potential climate of fear (which never fully materialized), and certainly rallied many to a more supportive position than in the preceding months. The second episode was, as we have seen, a curious moment of national unification, curious because the focus of attention was on someone who, as one of the 1960s rebel generation, was associated directly with those in the vanguard who were, in some eyes, discredited for failure and conservatism; Guevara was also, of course, even more linked to images of ideological firmness than many of his erstwhile *compañeros*. However, the whole phenomenon – the search for his body in Bolivia, the construction of the Santa Clara mausoleum and the return of the body – revealed a depth of loyalty to, and affection for, the figure of the fallen hero. This feeling significantly transcended classes, generations, and political attitudes, with many otherwise cynical young Cubans responding with genuine interest, emotion and support. The episode also inevitably recalled the heroism and sacrifice of the 1960s in a more productive and meaningful way than all manner of official speeches or slogans could do, either reviving memories nostalgically for those who had lived through the decade, or reviving interest in the writings of, and on, those years for those who were too young to remember.

The Elián González incident astonished many outsiders by the vehemence of the official discourse on, and campaigns about, the issue – filling the media daily, but also by the genuine sense of anger and solidarity felt, and expressed, by most Cubans. Demonstrations may have been officially organized, but they clearly reflected a deep sense of outrage, community and, importantly, alienation from the thoroughly discredited 'hard-liners' in the émigré community.

In 2000, we thus see a picture of a six-year period full of incidents, episodes and developments of considerable significance in terms of maintaining, on balance, the active and passive support for the system. Whatever the predictions of collapse, demoralization and disintegration in 1990, or even 1994, there is as yet little evidence that the political system (and its support) is any more fundamentally threatened now than in 1990. The explanations, as we have seen, are many and complex; but so too are the aspects, and contradictions, of the system itself, and the ideological network that sustains it.

This study opened by arguing that much of the literature on Cuba over the four decades of the Revolution's existence has tended to miss certain critical features of the process and the system that has evolved, a failing due either to *a priori* positions adopted or a willingness to be beguiled by individuals, bewildered by changes, or puzzled by the contradictions. None of that should surprise us, given the academic's desire for neat categorization, the politician's preference for simple answers and the polemics that have always surrounded the Revolution. Also, it should not surprise us given the evidently beguiling nature of those key individuals, the bewildering nature of those changes and the puzzling nature of those contradictions.

In the trajectory traced here, what has become evident is that the forty-one years of change and adaptation have corresponded to a very peculiar political context and worked through a process that the Revolution has rarely controlled but that has demanded subtlety, flexibility and contradiction as the only viable ways forward. Thus it is clear that any attempt at straight linear historiography must run the risks of a simplification that misses those subtleties and essential contradictions. It has been the argument here, therefore, that only a focus on the Revolution through a particular prism can shed useful light.

That prism has been the question of ideology, not least because it has been the question most ignored by the literature and least understood. This study has, however, endeavoured to demonstrate that ideology – meaning the particular manifestation of radical nationalism that took the evolving form of *cubanía* – played a fundamental role in creating the conditions and motivation for, and the direction and nature of, the Revolution in 1959, and then proceeded to contribute fundamentally to the shape, direction and outcome of the whole process thereafter.

Certainly, the evidence seems to be that the process of revolutionary transformation since 1959 has not been as chaotic, haphazard and undirected, or capricious, as it has often been made out to be, but, rather, has been guided by a parallel (or, more precisely, an interior) process of ideological development, taking the original *canon* that helped to focus, inspire and direct the early insurrection and radicalization and preserving it through various methods. Those methods have been many, varied and effective – for example, the toleration of competing discourses, the mechanisms of participation, and the evolution of myths. Thus, on the basis of the 'ideological reservoir' evident by the 1950s (created out of the preceding decades of political, economic and social development and conserved through the existence of certain *canonical* myths and codes), came a newer version of the evolving *cubanía*, gradually replacing the hitherto oppositional and dissident *cubanía rebelde* manifestation by the newly hegemonic *cubanía revolucionaria*, replacing in the process the search for an identity of *nación* by a search for an identity of *Revolución*.

A further conclusion, therefore, must be that the post-1959 process has demonstrated a remarkable capacity for the evolving system (meaning both leaders and led) to use ideology creatively as a critical force for radicalization, adaptation and identification. Within that, as we have seen, vanguard and population alike have shown a great willingness and ability to internalize this ideology, 'customizing' it according to individual circumstances, changing situations, and new challenges. In short, ideology – through myth – has been a means for individual Cubans to keep their identification with the process, their place in the system and their motivational sanity, as well as a means for the system to evolve, adapt and debate, without losing an underlying sense of direction or the basic support, or tolerance, of the majority of Cubans.

This is precisely, therefore, where the real role of ideology fits also in the Cuba of 2000, for all of this system – an essentially revolutionary, mobilizing, multi-layered and overlapping, argumentative and space-creating system – has the potential to lack the necessary cohesion, but, in fact, finds that cohesion in the centralizing structures that exist (the party, the OPP system and so on), in the continuities already identified, in the system's perceived efficacy, and, lastly, in its ideological cement. Ideology, and, within that, the myths on which it depends and that are at the individual level the comprehensible distillation of that ideology, are the necessary elements to fill the spaces, bridge the gaps and provide the material for the diverse interpretations necessary at every level.

These mechanisms are also more mundane than that, for – as conscious and unconscious ideology, as coherent old or new myths, and as daily language – it is evident that they play a vitally cohesive, reinforcing and redefining role for the average Cuban. If it is possible to talk of 'banal nationalism' – effective internalization through 'routinization' of the symbols of nationalism – then it must be equally possible to talk of 'banal ideology', working in similar ways, although, given the connotations of 'banal' (intentional in the original use of the term), it is perhaps better to use the term 'mundane ideology'.

In the Cuba of the late 1990s and the year 2000, the examples have abounded. There are the many, changing slogans; but there is also the 'core' of perennial and ubiquitous slogans on hoardings since 1989 – *un eterno Baraguá* ('an eternal Baraguá' – referring to Maceo's refusal to surrender in 1878), *hasta la victoria siempre* ('ever onward to victory'), *socialismo o muerte* ('socialism or death'). There was the linguistic comfort of the common phrase of the 'dark days' of 1993–4 – *estamos pasando por el Período Especial* ('we are going through the Special Period') – with its talismanic implication of hope alongside the double meaning of 'suffering', since, in Spanish, one also 'suffers from hunger', for instance, with the verb *pasar.* Then there are the short-term mythifications – the new emphasis on Maceo (with all that that figure implies for defiance, heroism and also an essentially Cuban black or *mulato* definition), the revivals of Martí and Che, as we have seen, and also, intriguingly, the confident and relieved mythification, in 1999, of the 1993–4 period – admitted more readily by most Cubans as having been a terrible period, repeated both to reaffirm the end of that awfulness, and to stress the shared suffering of those days.

So it is that the critical mechanisms that this study has identified, traced and examined have not only played a fundamental role at the systemic level, but have also been equally fundamental in the daily, personal, individual internalization of the Revolution and the process by which the average Cuban – with all his or her

Figure 9 Tee-shirts now figure prominently as mechanisms of what we might call 'banal ideology'

Figure 10 The mundane and the 'high': two posters on a neighbourhood wall, one calling for water-saving and the other declaring Cuba's determination 'to be erased from the face of the earth rather than to be intimidated or made to yield'

Figure 11 The mundane propaganda of daily life: the word 'Cuba', without elaboration, simply painted on a street wall

Figure 12 Two defiant posters from the 1990s – one declaring simply 'Socialism' and the other asserting 'Here we want no masters'

contradictory attitudes to and involvement in the Revolution – has maintained a basic level of commitment to, identification with, and hope for, the whole enigmatic, bewildering and challenging process of transformation since 1959. If one wishes to understand why the system has survived so much, since 1959, since 1989 and since 1994, one need look no further than these mechanisms for a starting-point of an answer. These mechanisms have, after all, allowed ordinary Cubans to take heart and meaning from the more elevated 'dreams' of the overall ideology of *cubanía*, by making them mundane without losing their quality as 'dreams'.

Mundane, however, does not mean trivial, but, rather, 'customizing' the sophisticated to the daily, grass-roots and individual level (either by the system or by the individual), and it should be remembered that the 'sophisticated' in the case of any ideology means much, for the implicit 'world-view' that we know ideology to be encapsulates what we might rightly call 'dreams' – dreams of a past (real or imagined) that provides either the base of the 'present' or an alternative 'present', and also dreams of an ideal, but organic, future. This is a vital element in understanding Cuba today and at any point in the last four decades, for the dogged survival of commitment, hope and a depth of identification has much to do with the shared 'dream', and the processes of 'customization' (of the myth) – which have been examined here – and of 'mundanization' (of the ideology and its codes) are essentially interpreting the 'high' beliefs, and dreams, at a manageable, 'lower' – but no less powerful or important – level. Thus, the average Cuban is still (often to the surprise and puzzlement of the outsider) remarkably committed to many of the basic ideals and precepts of *la Revolución* and understandably defensive about outside criticisms, about threats to the familiar 'canon' of the ideology – of *cubanía* – and about the possibility that the structure of the ideology might unravel and, with it, destroy the 'dreams' that are a fundamental part of the 'global' existence in which they all live, and also the daily identification with that existence. In this sense, every Cuban who remains more or less a part of the whole project of *cubanía revolucionaria* daily echoes the sentiments of W. B. Yeats – 'Tread softly, because you tread on my dreams' (Yeats 1962: 35).

Bibliography

Abreu, B. and Cabrera, O. (1988), *Guerra y Nación. Diego Vicente Tejera*, Havana: Editorial de Ciencias Sociales.

Ackerman, H. (1996), 'The *Balsero* Phenomenon, 1991–1994', *Cuban Studies*, 26:169–200.

Alvarez Estévez, R. (1986), *La Emigración Cubana en Estados Unidos, 1868–1878*, Havana: Editorial de Ciencias Sociales.

—— (1988), *Azúcar e Inmigración, 1900–1940*, Havana: Editorial de Ciencias Sociales, Historia de Cuba.

Ameringuer, C. D. (1985), 'The Auténtico Party and the Political Opposition in Cuba, 1952–1957', *Hispanic American Historical Review*, 65 (2: May): 327–52.

Anderle, A. (1975), *Algunos Problemas de la Evolución del Pensamiento Antimperialista en Cuba entre las dos Guerras Mundiales: Comunistas y Apristas*, Szeged: Acta Universitatis Szegediensis de Atila Jozsef Nominatae, Acta Historica LII.

Anderson, B. (1991), *Imagined Communities. Reflection on the Origin and Spread of Nationalism*, London and New York: Verso.

Anderson, J. L. (1997), *Che Guevara. A Revolutionary Life*, London, New York, Toronto, Sydney, Auckland: Bantam Press.

Aranda, S. (1968), *La Revolución Agraria en Cuba*, Mexico City: Siglo XXI Editora.

Azicri, M. (1988), *Cuba. Politics, Economics, Society*, London and New York: Pinter Publishers.

Baloyra, E. (1991), 'The Cuban-American Community and US Domestic Politics', in J. Tulchin and R. Hernández (eds), *Will the Cold War in the Caribbean End?*, pp. 129–34, Boulder, CO: Lynne Rienner Publishers.

Baloyra, E. and Morris, J. (eds) (1993), *Conflict and Change in Cuba*, Albuquerque, NM: University of New Mexico Press.

Barnet, M. (1983), *Biografía de un Cimarrón*, Havana: Letras Cubanas.

Bengelsdorf, C. (1994), *The Problem of Democracy in Cuba. Between Vision and Reality*, New York and Oxford: Oxford University Press.

Benítez Rojo, A. (1986), 'Power/Sugar/Literature: Towards a Reinterpretation of Cubanness', *Cuban Studies*, 16: 9–31.

—— (1996), *The Repeating Island: the Caribbean and the Postmodern Perspective*, Durham, NC and London: Duke University Press.

Benjamin, J. R. (1975), 'The Machadato and Cuban Nationalism, 1928–1932', *Hispanic American Historical Review*, 55 (1: February): 66–91.

—— (1977), *The United States and Cuba. Hegemony and Dependent Development, 1880–1934*, Pittsburgh, PA: University of Pittsburgh Press.

Berenguer y Sed, A. (1926), *General Gerardo Machado y Morales: sus Discursos y su Obra de Gobierno* (Vol. 1 1925–1926), Havana: Bouza y Co.

Bergad, L.W. (1990), *Cuban Rural Society in the Nineteenth Century: The Social and Economic History of Monoculture in Matanzas,* Princeton, NJ: Princeton University Press.

—— (1995), *The Cuban Slave Market, 1790–1880,* Cambridge, New York, Melbourne: Cambridge University Press.

Bernardo, R. M. (1971), *The Theory of Moral Incentives in Cuba*, University, AL: Alabama University Press.

Billig, M. (1995), *Banal Nationalism*, London, Thousand Oaks, CA, New Delhi: Sage Publications.

Blackburn, R. (1963), 'Prologue to the Cuban Revolution', *New Left Review*, 21 (October): 52–91.

Blasier, C. and Mesa-Lago, C. (eds) (1979), *Cuba in the World*, Pittsburgh, PA: University of Pittsburgh Press.

Blight, J. G. and Kornbluh, P. (eds) (1998), *Politics of Illusion. The Bay of Pigs Invasion Reexamined*, Boulder, CO and London: Lynne Rienner Publishers.

Bonsal, P. W. (1971), *Cuba, Castro and the United States*, Pittsburgh, PA: University of Pittsburgh Press.

Boorstein, E. (1969), *The Economic Transformation of Cuba*, New York: Monthly Review Press (Modern Readers Paperbacks).

Bourne, P. (1986), *Castro. A Biography of Fidel Castro*, London: Macmillan.

Bray, D. and Harding, T. (1974), 'Cuba', in R. L. Chilcote and J. C. Edelstein (eds), *Latin America: the Struggle with Dependency and Beyond*, pp. 583–730, New York, Sydney, London, Toronto: John Wiley & Sons.

Brundenius, C. (1984), *Revolutionary Cuba: The Challenge of Economic Growth with Equity*, Boulder, CO, London, Kingston, Port of Spain: Westview Press.

Brunner, H. (1977), *Cuban Sugar Policy from 1963 to 1970*, Pittsburgh, PA: University of Pittsburgh Press.

Bunck, J. M. (1990), 'The Politics of Sports in Revolutionary Cuba', *Cuban Studies*, 20: 111–32.

—— (1994), *Fidel Castro and the Quest for a Revolutionary Culture in Cuba*, University Park, PA: Pennsylvania State University Press.

Butterworth, D. (1980), *The People of Buenaventura: Relocation of Slum Dwellers in Post-Revolutionary Cuba*, Urbana, IL: Illinois University Press.

Cabrera, O. (1977), *Guiteras. El Programa de la Joven Cuba*, Havana: Editorial de Ciencias Sociales.

Cabrera Infante, G. (1994), *Mea Cuba*, London: Faber and Faber.

Cardosa, E. and Helinger, S. (1992), *Cuba after Communism*, Cambridge, MA: Massachusetts Institute of Technology.

Carr, B. (1998), 'Identity, Class and Nation: Black Immigrant Workers, Cuban Communism, and the Sugar Insurgency, 1925–1934', *Hispanic American Historical Review*, 78 (1: February): 83–116.

Carr, R. (1966), *Spain. 1808–1939*, Oxford: Clarendon Press.

Casal, L. (1971), 'Literature and Society', in C. Mesa-Lago (ed.), *Revolutionary Change in Cuba*, pp. 447–70, Pittsburgh, PA: University of Pittsburgh Press.

—— (1979), 'Cubans in the United States: Their Impact on US–Cuban Relations', in M. Weinstein (ed.), *Revolutionary Cuba in the World Arena*, pp. 109–36, Philadelphia: Institute for the Study of Human Issues.

Casanovas Codina, J. (1995), 'The Cuban Labor Movement of the 1860s and Spain's Search for a New Colonial Policy', *Cuban Studies*, 25: 83–99.

Castro Ruz, F. (1961), *Palabras a Los Intelectuales*, Havana: Imprenta Nacional.

Casuso, T. (1961), *Cuba and Castro*, New York: Random House.

Centro de Estudios Martianos (ed.) (1991), *Textos Martianos Breves*, Havana: Centro de Estudios Martianos.

Cepero Bonilla, R. (1963), *Obra Histórica*, Havana: Instituto de Historia.

Chang Pon, F. (1981), *El Ejército Nacional en la República Neocolonial, 1899–1933,* Havana: Editorial de Ciencias Sociales.

—— (1998), 'Reajustes para la Estabilización del Sistema Neocolonial', in Instituto de Historia de Cuba (ed.), *Historia de Cuba. La Neocolonia: Organización y Crisis desde 1899 hasta 1940* (Vol. II), pp. 336–86, Havana, Instituto de Historia de Cuba.

Colectivo de Autores (1996), *UBPC. Desarrollo Rural y Participación*, Havana: Universidad de La Habana.

Collazo Pérez, E. (1989), *Cuba. Banca y Crédito, 1950–1958*. Havana: Editorial de Ciencias Sociales.

Connell-Smith, G. (1979), 'Castro's Cuba in World Affairs, 1959–1979', *The World Today*, 35 (No. 1, January): 15–23.

Corbitt, D. C. (1954), 'Historical Publications of the Martí Centennial', *Hispanic American Historical Review*, 34 (August): 399–405.

Crahan, M. E. (1989), 'Catholicism in Cuba', *Cuban Studies*, 19: 3–24.

Cruz-Taura, G. (1997), 'Annexation and National Identity: Cuba's Mid-Nineteenth-Century Debate', *Cuban Studies*, 27: 90–109.

Cuban Economic Research Project (1965), *Cuba, Agriculture and Planning, 1963–1964,* Coral Gables, FL: University of Miami.

Dalton, T. C. (1993), *Everything within the Revolution, Cuban Strategies for Social Development since 1960,* Boulder, CO: Westview Press.

Dana Sims, H. (1991), 'Collapse of the House of Labor: Ideological Divisions in the Cuban Labor Movement and the U.S. Role, 1944–1949', *Cuban Studies*, 21: 123–47.

Deere, C. D. (1998), '"Here come the Yankees", The Rise and Decline of United States Colonies in Cuba, 1898–1930', *Hispanic American Historical Review*, 78 (4: November): 727–66.

Del Aguila, J. M. (1994), *Cuba. Dilemmas of a Revolution* (3rd edn), Boulder, CO: Westview Press.

Departamento de Instrucción, MinFAR (1960), *Manual de Capacitación Cívica*, Havana: MinFAR.

Desnoes, E. (1967a), 'El Mundo sobre sus Pies', in E. Desnoes (ed.), *Punto de Vista*, pp. 99–108, Havana: Instituto del Libro.

—— (1967b), 'Martí en Fidel', in E. Desnoes (ed.), *Punto de Vista*, pp. 21–36, Havana: Instituto del Libro.

—— (1971), *Memories of Underdevelopment*, Harmondsworth: Penguin Books.

Díaz-Briquets, Sergio (1983), *The Health Revolution in Cuba*, Austin, TX: University of Texas Press.

Domínguez, J. I. (1978a), *Cuba: Order and Revolution*, Cambridge, MA and London: Belknap Press of Harvard University Press.

—— (1978b), 'Cuban Foreign Policy', *Foreign Affairs*, 57 (No 1, Fall): 83–108.

—— (1979), 'The Armed Forces and Foreign Relations', in C. Blasier and C. Mesa-Lago (eds), *Cuba in the World*, pp. 53–86, Pittsburgh, PA: University of Pittsburgh Press.

—— (1989a), 'The Obstacles and Prospects for Improved U.S.–Cuban Relations: A U.S. Perspective', in J. I. Domínguez and R. Hernández (eds), *U.S.–Cuban Relations in the 1990s*, pp. 15–33, Boulder, CO, San Francisco, London: Westview Press.

—— (1989b), 'International and National Aspects of the Catholic Church in Cuba', *Cuban Studies*, 19: 43–60.

—— (1989c), *To Make the World Safe for Revolution: Cuba's Foreign Policy*, Cambridge, MA: Harvard University Press.

—— (1990), 'The Cuban Armed Forces, the Party and Society in Wartime and During Rectification (1986–88)', in R. Gillespie (ed.), *Cuba after Thirty Years. Rectification and the Revolution*, pp. 45–62, London: Frank Cass.

—— (1993), 'The Political Impact on Cuba of the Reform and Collapse of Communist Regimes', in C. Mesa-Lago (ed.), *Cuba after the Cold War*, pp. 99–132, Pittsburgh, PA: University of Pittsburgh Press.

Domínguez, J. I. and Hernández, R. (eds) (1989), *U.S.-Cuban Relations in the 1990s*, Boulder, CO, San Francisco, London: Westview Press.

Domínguez García, M. (1998), 'La Juventud Cubana en una Epoca de Crisis y Reestructuración', in J. Moreno *et al.* (eds), *Cuba: Período Especial. Perspectivas*, pp. 223–49, Havana: Editorial de Ciencias Sociales.

Draper, T. (1962), *Castro's Revolution. Myths and Realities*, New York: Frederick A. Praeger Publishers.

—— (1965), *Castroism. Theory and Practice,* New York, Washington, London: Frederick A. Praeger Publishers.

Dumont, R. (1964), *Cuba, Socialisme et Développement,* Paris: Editions du Seuil.

—— (1970), *Cuba, Socialism and Development,* New York: Grove Press.

—— (1974), *Is Cuba Socialist?,* London: André Deutsch.

Duncan, W. R. (1985), *The Soviet Union and Cuba: Interests and Influences*, New York: Praeger.

Dye, A. (1998), *Cuban Sugar in the Age of Mass Production. Technology and the Economics of the Sugar Central, 1899–1929*, Stanford, CA: Stanford University Press.

Eagleton, T. (1991), *Ideology: An Introduction*, London and New York: Verso Press

Eckstein, S. E. (1994), *Back from the Future. Cuba under Castro,* Princeton, NJ: Princeton University Press.

Erisman, H. M. (1985), *Cuba's International Relations. The Anatomy of a Nationalistic Foreign Policy*, Boulder, CO and London: Westview Press.

—— (1991), 'Cuban Development Aid, South–South Diversification and Counterdependency Politics', in H. M. Erisman and J. M. Kirk (eds), *Cuban Foreign Policy Confronts a New International Order*, pp.119–38, Boulder, CO and London: Lynne Rienner Publishers.

—— and Kirk, J. M. (eds) (1991), *Cuban Foreign Policy Confronts a New International Order*, Boulder, CO and London: Lynne Rienner Publishers.

Espina Prieto, M. and Núñez Moreno, L. (1990), 'The Changing Class Structure in the Development of Socialism in Cuba', in S. Halebsky and J. M. Kirk (eds), *Transformation and Struggle. Cuba Faces the 1990s*, pp. 205–18, New York, Westport, CT, London: Praeger.

Fagen, R. R. (1969), *The Transformation of Political Culture in Cuba*, Stanford, CA: Stanford University Press.

Farber, S. (1976), *Revolution and Reaction in Cuba, 1933–1960. A Political Sociology from Machado to Castro*, Middletown, CT: Wesleyan University Press.

Fauriol, G. and Loser, E. (eds) (1980), *Cuba, the International Dimension,* New Brunswick, NJ and London: Transaction Publishers.

Feinsilver, J. M. (1993), *Healing the Masses. Cuban Health Politics at Home and Abroad,* Berkeley, CA, Los Angeles, London: University of California Press.

Fernández, P. A. (1963), *Libro de los Héroes*, Havana: Ediciones Revolución.

Fernández Retamar, R. (1967a), 'Hacia una Intelectualidad Revolucionaria en Cuba', in R. Fernández Retamar, *Ensayo de Otro Mundo*, pp. 159–88, Havana: Instituto del Libro.

—— (1967b), 'Martí en (su) Tercer Mundo', in R. Fernández Retamar, *Ensayo de Otro Mundo*, pp. 19–60, Havana: Instituto del Libro.

Ferrer, A. (1995), *'To Make a Free Nation': Race and the Struggle for Independence in Cuba, 1868–1898*, Doctoral Thesis, Ann Arbor, MI: University of Michigan.

—— (1999), *Insurgent Cuba. Race, Nation, and Revolution, 1868–1898*, Chapel Hill, NC and London: University of North Carolina Press.

Figarola, J .J. (1974), *Cuba 1900–1928, La República Dividida contra Sí Misma*, Havana: Instituto de Libro, Editorial Arte y Literatura (Concurso 28 de Mayo 'Combate de Uvero', Universidad de Oriente).

Fitzgerald, F. T. (1978), 'A Critique of the "Sovietization of Cuba" Thesis', *Science and Society,* 62 (No. 1): 1–32.

—— (1990), 'Cuba's New Professionals', in S. Halebsky and J. M. Kirk (eds), *Transformation and Struggle. Cuba Faces the 1990s*, pp. 189–204, New York, Westport, CT, London: Praeger.

—— (1994), *The Cuban Revolution in Crisis. From Managing Socialism to Managing Survival*, New York: Monthly Review Press.

Foner, P. S. (1977), *Antonio Maceo: The 'Bronze Titan' of Cuba's Struggle for Independence,* New York, London: Monthly Review Press.

Frank, W. (1961), *Cuba. Prophetic Island*, New York: Marzani & Munsell Inc. Publishers.

Free, L. A. (1960), *Attitudes of the Cuban People Toward the Castro Regime.* Princeton, NJ: Institute for International Social Research.

Freire, P. (1972), *Pedagogy of the Oppressed,* Harmondsworth: Penguin Books.

Fuller, L. (1992), *Work and Democracy in Socialist Cuba*, Philadelphia, PA: Temple University Press.

García Olivares, J. (1988), *José Antonio.* Havana: Editora Abril.

García-Pérez, Gladys Marel (1998), *Insurrection and Revolution. Armed Struggle in Cuba, 1952–1959,* Boulder, CO and London: Lynne Rienner Publishers.

Gellner, E. (1988), *Nations and Nationalism* (4th edn), Oxford: Basil Blackwell.

Gillespie, R. (ed.) (1990), *Cuba after Thirty Years. Rectification and the Revolution,* London: Frank Cass.

Giuliano, M. (1998), *El Caso CEA. Intelectuales e Inquisidores en Cuba. ¿Perestroika en la Isla?*, Miami: Ediciones Universal.

Goldenberg, B. (1965), *The Cuban Revolution and Latin America,* New York: Praeger.

González, E. (1974), *Cuba under Castro, The Limits of Charisma,* Boston, MA: Houghton Mifflin Company.

—— (1977), 'Complexities of Cuban Foreign Policy', *Problems of Communism,* XXVI (November–December): 1–15.

Gouré, L. and Weinkle, J. (1972), 'Cuba's New Dependency', *Problems of Communism,* XXI (2: March–April): 68–79.

Gramsci, A. (1986a), 'The Intellectuals', in Q. Hoare and G. Nowell Smith (eds), *Selections from the Prison Notebooks of Antonio Gramsci* (6th edn), pp. 3–23, London: Lawrence and Wishart.

—— (1986b), 'State and Civil Society', in Q. Hoare and G. Nowell Smith (eds), *Selections from the Prison Notebooks of Antonio Gramsci* (6th edn), pp. 206–76, London: Lawrence and Wishart.

Grau San Martín, R. (1936), *La Revolución Cubana ante América*, Mexico City: Ediciones del Partido Revolucionario Cubano (Auténtico).

Greene Walker, P. (1996), 'Cuba's Revolutionary Armed Forces: Adapting in the New Environment', *Cuban Studies*, 26: 61–74.

Griffiths, John (1979), 'Sport: the People's Right', in J. Griffiths and P. Griffiths (eds), *Cuba. The Second Decade*, London: Writers and Readers Publishing Cooperative.

Guadarrama, P. and Tussel Oropeza, E. (1987), *El Pensamiento Filosófico de Enrique José Varona*, Havana: Editorial de Ciencias Sociales.

Guerra y Sánchez, R. (1970), *Azúcar y Población en las Antillas*, Havana: Editorial de Ciencias Sociales.

—— (1974), *En el Camino de la Independencia*, Havana: Editorial de Ciencias Sociales.

Guevara, E. (1968), *Reminiscences of the Cuban Revolutionary War*, London, New York: George Allen & Unwin/Monthly Review Press.

—— (1987), 'Socialism and Man in Cuba', in D. Deutschmann (ed.), *Che Guevara and the Cuban Revolution. Writings and Speeches of Ernesto Che Guevara*, pp. 246–64, Sydney: Pathfinder/Pacific and Asia.

Gunn, G. (1980), 'Cuba in Angola', in G. Fauriol and E. Loser (eds), *Cuba, the International Dimension*, pp. 153–204, New Brunswick, NJ: Transaction Publishers.

Gusdorf, G. (1980), 'Conditions and Limits of Autobiography', in J. Olney (ed.), *Autobiography: Essays Theoretical and Critical*, pp. 28–48, Princeton, NJ: Princeton University Press.

Gutelman, M. (1972), 'The Socialization of the Means of Production in Cuba', in R. E. Bonachea and N. P. Valdés (eds), *Cuba in Revolution*, pp. 238–60, Garden City, NY: Anchor Books, Doubleday & Company Inc.

Habel, J. (1991), *Cuba. The Revolution in Peril*, London and New York: Verso.

Halebsky, S. and Kirk, J. M. (eds) (1985), *Cuba: Twenty-five Years of Revolution, 1959–1984*, New York: Praeger.

—— and —— (1990), *Transformation and Struggle. Cuba Faces the 1990s*, New York, Westport, CT and London: Praeger.

Halperin, M. (1972), *The Rise and Decline of Fidel Castro*, Berkeley, CA and London: University of California Press.

Hamburg, J. (1990), 'Cuban Housing Policy', in S. Halebsky and J. M. Kirk (eds), *Transformation and Struggle. Cuba Faces the 1990s*, pp. 235–50, New York; Westport, CT, London: Praeger.

Harnecker, M. (1979), *Cuba, Dictatorship or Democracy?*, Westport, CT: Lawrence Hill & Co.

Hart Phillips, R. (1959), *Cuba, Island of Paradox*, New York: McDowell Obolensky.

Helg, A. (1991), 'Afro-Cuban Protest: The Partido Independiente de Color', *Cuban Studies*, 21: 101–21.

—— (1995), *Our Rightful Share, The Afro-Cuban Struggle for Equality, 1886–1912*, Chapel Hill, NC: University of North Carolina Press.

Hennessy, C. A. M. (1963), 'Roots of Cuban Nationalism', *International Affairs*, 39 (No 3): 345–59.

Hernández Martínez, J. (1998), 'La Comunidad Cubana, Poder Político y Proyecciones de Estados Unidos hacia Cuba', in J. Moreno, *et al.* (eds), *Cuba: Período Especial. Perspectivas*, pp. 56–71, Havana: Editorial de Ciencias Sociales.

Heymann, C. D. (1998), *RFK. A Candid Biography*, London: William Heinemann.

Hobsbawm, E. J. (1992), *Nations and Nationalism since 1870. Programme, Myth and Reality*, Cambridge: Cambridge University Press.

Horowitz, I. L. (ed.) (1970), *Cuban Communism*, New Brunswick, NJ: Transaction Books Inc.

Huberman, L. and Sweezy, P. (1961), *Cuba – Anatomy of a Revolution*, New York: Monthly Review Press.

—— (1969), *Socialism in Cuba*, New York: Monthly Review Press.

Ibarra Cuesta, Jorge (1967), *Ideología Mambisa*, Havana: Instituto del Libro.

—— (1979), *Aproximaciones a Clio*, Havana: Editorial de Ciencias Sociales.

—— (1980), *José Martí. Dirigente Político e Ideólogo Revolucionario*, Havana: Editorial de Ciencias Sociales.

—— (1992), *Cuba, 1898–1921. Partidos Políticos y Clases Sociales*, Havana: Editorial de Ciencias Sociales.

—— (1994), *Un Análisis Psicosocial del Cubano, 1898–1925*, Havana: Editorial de Ciencias Sociales.

—— (1995a), *Cuba, 1898–1958. Estructura y Procesos Sociales*, Havana: Editorial de Ciencias Sociales.

—— (1995b), 'Historiografía y Revolución', *Temas*, 1 (enero–marzo): 5–17.

Index On Censorship (1972), 'Cuba, Revolution and the Intellectual – The Strange Case of Heberto Padilla', *Index on Censorship*, 1 (No. 2, Summer): 65–134.

James, D. (1961), *Cuba. The First Soviet Satellite in the Americas*, New York: Avon Books.

Jover Marimón, M. (1971), 'The Church', in C. Mesa-Lago (ed.), *Revolutionary Change in Cuba*, pp. 399–425, Pittsburgh, PA: University of Pittsburgh Press.

Judson, C. Fred (1984), *Cuba and the Revolutionary Myth. The Political Education of the Cuban Rebel Army, 1953–1963*, Boulder, CO and London: Westview.

Kahl, J. A. (1970), 'The Moral Economy of a New Society', in I. L. Horowitz (ed.), *Cuban Communism*, pp. 95–115, New Brunswick, NJ: Transaction Books Inc.

Kapcia, A. (1979), 'Cuba's African Involvement, a New Perspective', *Survey. A Journal of East and West Studies*, 24 (No 2, Spring): 142–59.

—— (1983), 'Culture and Ideology in Post-Revolutionary Cuba', *Red Letters*, 15 (Summer–Autumn): 11–23.

—— (1985), 'Cuban Populism and the Birth of the Myth of Martí', in C. Abel and N. Torrents (eds), *José Martí. Revolutionary Democrat*, pp. 32–64, London: The Athlone Press.

—— (1986), 'The Third Congress of the Cuban Communist Party: Continuity and Change', *Journal of Communist Studies*, 2 (No. 2): 196–200.

—— (1987), 'Back to Basics, the Deferred Session of the Third Congress of the Cuban Communist Party', *Journal of Communist Studies*, 3 (No. 3): 311–13.

—— (1993), 'Western European Influences on Cuban Revolutionary Thought', in A. Hennessy and G. Lambie (eds), *The Fractured Blockade. West European–Cuban Relations During the Revolution*, pp. 64–99, London and Basingstoke: Macmillan Caribbean.

—— (1995), *Political Change in Cuba: Before and After the Exodus*, Occasional Papers No. 9, London: Institute of Latin American Studies.

—— (1996a), 'Fulgencio Batista, 1933–44: From Revolutionary to Populist', in W. Fowler (ed.), *Authoritarianism in Latin America since Independence*, pp. 73–92, Westport, CT and London: Greenwood Press.

—— (1996b), 'Cuba after the Crisis. Revolutionising the Revolution', *Conflict Studies*, 289 (April): 1–30.

—— (1997a), 'Political and Economic Reform in Cuba: the Significance of Che Guevara', in M.Rosendahl (ed.), *La Situación Actual en Cuba: Desafíos y Alternativas/The Current Situation in Cuba: Challenges and Alternatives*, pp. 17–48, Stockholm: Institute of Latin American Studies, Stockholm University.

—— (1997b), 'Ideology and the Cuban Revolution: Myth, Icon and Identity', in W. Fowler (ed.), *Ideologues and Ideologies in Latin America*, pp. 83–104, Westport, CT: Greenwood.

Karol, K. S. (1970), *Guerrillas in Power: The Course of the Cuban Revolution*, New York: Hill & Wang.

King, J. (1990), 'Cuban Cinema, a Reel Revolution?', in R. Gillespie (ed.), *Cuba after Thirty Years. Rectification and the Revolution*, pp. 140–60, London: Frank Cass.

Kirk, J. M. (1983), *José Martí. Mentor of the Cuban Nation*, Tampa, FL: University of South Florida Press.

—— (1989a), *Between God and the Party. Religion and Politics in Revolutionary Cuba*, Tampa, FL: University of South Florida Press.

—— (1989b), 'Towards an Understanding of the Church–State Rapprochement in Revolutionary Cuba', *Cuban Studies*, 19: 25–42.

Knight, F. W. (1970), *Slave Society in Cuba during the Nineteenth Century*, Madison, WI: University of Wisconsin Press.

Leach, E. (1974), *Lévi-Strauss*, (2nd edn), Glasgow: Fontana/Collins.

Lenin, V. I. (1966a), 'What is to be Done?', in H. M. Christman (ed.), *Essential Works of Lenin*, pp. 53–176, New York, Toronto, London: Bantam Books.

—— (1966b), 'Imperialism, the Highest Stage of Capitalism', in H. M. Christman (ed.), *Essential Works of Lenin*, pp. 177–270, New York, Toronto, London: Bantam Books.

LeoGrande, W. (1978), 'Civil-Military Relations in Cuba, Party Control and Political Socialization', *Studies in Comparative Communism*, 11 (No. 3, Autumn): 278–91.

—— (1979), 'Theory and Practice of Socialist Democracy in Cuba', *Studies in Comparative Communism*, 12 (No. 1, Spring): 39–62.

—— (1980), *Cuba's Policy in Africa, 1959–1980,* Policy Papers in International Affairs, Berkeley, CA: Institute of International Studies, University of California.

Le Riverend, J. (1971), *La República. Dependencia y Revolución*, Havana: Editorial de Ciencias Sociales.

Levine, B. B. (ed.) (1983), *The New Cuban Presence in the Caribbean*, Boulder, CO: Westview Press.

Lévi-Strauss, C. (1972), *Structural Anthropology*, Harmondsworth: Penguin University Books.

Leyva, R. (1972), 'Health and Revolution in Cuba', in R. E. Bonachea and N. P. Valdés (eds), *Cuba in Revolution*, Garden City, pp. 456–96, NY: Anchor Books, Doubleday and Company Inc.

Liss, S.B. (1987), *Roots of Revolution. Radical Thought in Cuba*, Lincoln, NB and London: University of Nebraska Press.

Little, W. and Posada-Carbó, E. (eds) (1996), *Political Corruption in Europe and Latin America.* London: Institute of Latin American Studies and Macmillan.

Llerena, M. (1978), *The Unsuspected Revolution. The Birth and Rise of Castroism,* Ithaca, NY and London: Cornell University Press.

Lockwood, L. (1969), *Castro's Cuba, Cuba's Fidel,* New York: Vintage.

López Civeira, F., Loyola Vega, O. and Silva León, A. (eds) (1998*), Cuba y su Historia,* Havana: Editorial Gente Nueva.

López Segrera, F. (1981), *Cuba, Capitalismo Dependiente y Subdesarrollo* (Vol. 2), Havana: Editorial de Ciencias Sociales.

Lowy, M. (1973), *The Marxism of Che Guevara. Philosophy, Economics and Revolutionary Warfare,* New York and London: Monthly Review Press.

Lumsden, I. (1996), *Machos, Maricones and Gays. Cuba and Homosexuality,* Philadelphia, PA. and London: Temple University Press/Latin America Bureau.

Luzón, J. L. (1988), 'Housing in Socialist Cuba: An Analysis Using Cuban Censuses of Population and Housing', *Cuban Studies,* 18: 65–83.

Lynch, J. (1973), *The Spanish American Revolutions, 1808–1826*, London: Weidenfeld & Nicolson.

MacEwan, A. (1981), *Revolution and Economic Development in Cuba*, London: Macmillan.

MacFarlane, A. (1996), 'Corruption and Reform in Bourbon Spanish America', in W. Little and E. Posada-Carbó (eds), *Political Corruption in Europe and Latin America*, pp. 41–64, London: Institute of Latin American Studies and Macmillan.

Martí, J. (1975), *Antología*, Madrid: Editora Nacional.

—— (1991a), *Obras Completas* (Vol. 8), Havana: Editorial de Ciencias Sociales.

—— (1991b), *Obras Completas* (Vol. 12), Havana: Editorial de Ciencias Sociales.

Martínez Heredia, F. (1989), *El Che y el Socialismo*, Mexico City: Editorial Nuestro Tiempo, S.A.

Matas, J. (1971), 'Theater and Cinematography', in C. Mesa-Lago (ed.), *Revolutionary Change in Cuba*, pp. 427–46, Pittsburgh, PA: University of Pittsburgh Press.

Matthews, H. (1970), *Castro. A Political Biography*. Harmondsworth: Penguin Books.

Mazarr, M. J. (1988), *Semper Fidel. America and Cuba, 1776–1988*, Baltimore, MD: The Nautical and Aviation Publishing Company of America.

Medin, T. (1990), *Cuba. The Shaping of Revolutionary Consciousness*, Boulder, CO and London: Lynne Rienner Publishers.

Mella, J. A. (1941), *Glosando los Pensamientos de José Martí*, Havana: Editorial Páginas.

Mencía, M. (1986), *El Grito del Moncada* (Vol. 1), Havana: Editora Política.

Meneses, E. (1966), *Fidel Castro*, London: Faber & Faber.

Mesa-Lago, C. (ed.) (1971), *Revolutionary Change in Cuba*, Pittsburgh, PA: University of Pittsburgh Press.

—— (1978), *Cuba in the 1970s. Pragmatism and Institutionalization* (2nd edn), Albuquerque, NM: University of New Mexico Press.

—— (1981), *The Economy of Socialist Cuba: A Two-Decade Appraisal*, Albuquerque, NM: University of New Mexico Press.

—— (1988), 'The Cuban Economy in the 1980s: The Return of "Ideology"', in S. G. Roca (ed.), *Socialist Cuba: Past Interpretations and Future Challenges*, pp. 59–100, Boulder, CO and London: Westview Press.

—— (1990), 'Cuba's Economic Counter-Reform (Rectification): Causes, Policies and Effects', in R. Gillespie (ed.), *Cuba after Thirty Years. Rectification and the Revolution*, pp. 98–139, London: Frank Cass.

—— (ed.) (1993), *Cuba after the Cold War*, Pittsburgh, PA and London: University of Pittsburgh Press.

Metz, A. (1993), 'Cuban-Israel Relations: From the Cuban Revolution to the New World Order', *Cuban Studies*, 23: 113–34.

Miller, R. (1996), 'Foreign Capital, the State and Political Corruption in Latin America between Independence and Depression', in W. Little and E. Posada-Carbó (eds), *Political Corruption in Europe and Latin America*, pp. 65–96, London: Institute of Latin American Studies and Macmillan.

Mills, C. W. (1960), *Listen Yankee*, New York: McGraw Hill.

Moore, C. (1988), *Castro, The Blacks and Africa*, Los Angeles, CA: Center for Afro-American Studies, University of California.

Moreno Fraginals, M. (1977), *El Ingenio* (Vol. 1.), Havana: no publisher.

—— (1983), *La Historia Como Arma y Otros Estudios sobre Esclavos, Ingenios y Plantaciones*, Barcelona, Spain: Editorial Crítica.

Moreno, J. *et al.* (1998), *Cuba: Período Especial. Perspectivas*, Havana: Editorial de Ciencias Sociales.

Morley, M. H. (1987), *Imperial State and Revolution. The United States and Cuba, 1952–1986*, Cambridge, London, New York, New Rochelle, Sydney, Melbourne: Cambridge University Press.

Nelson, L. (1972), *Cuba. The Measure of a Revolution*, Minneapolis, MN: University of Minnesota Press.

Núñez Jiménez, A. (1959), *La Liberación de las Islas*, Havana: Editorial Lex.

O'Connor, J. (1970), *The Origins of Socialism in Cuba*, Ithaca, NY and London: Cornell University Press.

Olney, J. (1980), 'Versions of Memory/Some Versions of *Bios*: The Ontology of Autobiography', in J. Olney (ed.), *Autobiography: Essays Theoretical and Critical*, pp. 236–67, Princeton, NJ: Princeton University Press.

Olson, J. S. and Olson, J. E. (1995), *Cuban Americans. From Trauma to Triumph*, New York: Twayne Publishers.

Opatrný, J. (1993), *Historical Pre-Conditions of the Origins of the Cuban Nation*, Lewiston, Queenston and Lampeter: The Edwin Mellon Press.

—— (1994), 'José Antonio Saco's Path Towards the Idea of Cubanidad', *Cuban Studies*, 24: 39–56.

Paquette, R. J. (1988), *Sugar is Made with Blood: The Conspiarcy of La Escalera and the Conflict between Empires over Slavery in Cuba*, Middleton, CT: Wesleyan University Press.

Paterson, T. G. (1994), *Contesting Castro. The United States and the Triumph of the Cuban Revolution*, New York and Oxford: Oxford University Press.

Paulston, R. (1971), 'Education', in C. Mesa-Lago (ed.), *Revolutionary Change in Cuba*, pp. 375–98, Pittsburgh, PA: University of Pittsburgh Press:

Pérez Jr., L. A. (1982), 'The Collapse of the Cuban Planter Class, 1868–1898', *Inter-American Economic Affairs*, 36, (3, Winter): 3–22.

—— (1983), *Cuba Between Empires, 1878–1902*, Pittsburgh, PA: University of Pittsburgh Press.

—— (1986a), *Cuba Under the Platt Amendment, 1902–1934*, Pittsburgh, PA: University of Pittsburgh Press.

—— (1986b), 'Labor, State and Capital in Plattist Cuba', *Cuban Studies*, 16: 49–69.

—— (1988), *Cuba. Between Reform and Revolution*, New York and Oxford: Oxford University Press.

—— (1995), 'Army Politics in Cuba, 1959–69', in L. Pérez, *Essays on Cuban History: Historiography and Research*, pp. 82–103, Gainesville, FL: University Press of Florida.

—— (1999), *On Becoming Cuban. Identity, Nationality and Culture*, Chapel Hill, NC and London: University of North Carolina Press.

Pérez-López, J. F. (1986), 'The Economics of Cuban Joint-Ventures', *Cuban Studies,* 16: 181–207.

—— (1987), *Measuring Cuban Economic Performance*, Austin, TX: University of Texas Press.

Pérez Rojas, N. (1975), *El Movimiento Estudiantil Universitario de 1934 a 1940*, Havana: Editorial de Ciencias Sociales.

—— and Torres Vila, C. (1998), 'Las Unidades Básicas de Producción Cooperativa (UBPC): Hacia un Nuevo Proyecto de Participación', in J. Moreno, *et al.* (eds), *Cuba: Período Especial. Perspectivas,* pp. 83–110, Havana: Editorial de Ciencias Sociales.

Pérez Sarduy, P. and Stubbs, J. (eds) (1993), *Afrocuba. An Anthology of Cuban Writing on Race, Politics and Culture*, Melbourne: Latin America Bureau/Ocean Press.

Pérez-Stable, M. (1993), *The Cuban Revolution. Origins, Course and Legacy*, New York and Oxford: Oxford University Press.

Pichardo Viñas, H. (1983), *La Actitud Estudiantil en Cuba durante el Siglo XIX*, Havana: Editorial de Ciencias Sociales.

—— (1986), *Documentos para la Historia de Cuba II*, Havana: Editorial Pueblo y Educación.

Pino Santos, O. (1973), *El Imperialismo Norteamericano en la Economía de Cuba.* Havana: Editorial de Ciencias Sociales.

—— (1983), *Cuba. Historia y Economía*, Havana: Editorial de Ciencias Sociales.

Pollitt, B. H. (1984), 'The Cuban Sugar Economy and the "Great Depression"', *Bulletin of Latin American Research,* 3 (No. 2): 3–28.

Poyo, G. E. (1985), 'José Martí, Architect of Social Unity in the Emigré Communities of the United States', in C. Abel and N. Torrents (eds), *José Martí: Revolutionary Democrat*, pp. 16–31, London: Athlone Press.

—— (1989), *'With All, and for the Good of All': The Emergence of Popular Nationalism in the Cuban Communities of the United States, 1848–1898*, Durham, NC and London: Duke University Press.

—— (1991), 'The Cuban Experience in the United States, 1865–1940', *Cuban Studies,* 21: 19–36.

'Program Manifesto of the 26th of July Movement', in R. E. Bonachea and N. P. Valdés (eds) (1972), *Cuba in Revolution*, Garden City, NY: Anchor Books, Doubleday & Company Inc.

Quiroz, A. (1998), 'Loyalist Overkill: The Socio-Economic Costs of "Repressing" the Separatist Insurrection in Cuba, 1868-1878', *Hispanic American Historical Review,* 78 (2: May): 261–305.

Rabkin, R. (1988), 'Cuba: The Aging of a Revolution', in S. G. Roca. (ed.), *Socialist Cuba: Past Interpretations and Future Challenges,* pp. 33–58, Boulder, CO and London: Westview Press.

—— (1991), *Cuban Politics and the Revolutionary Experiment,* New York, Westport, CT and London: Praeger.

Raby, D. L. (1975), *The Cuban Pre-Revolution of 1933. An Analysis*, Occasional Papers, No. 18, Glasgow: University of Glasgow, Institute of Latin American Studies.

Richmond, M. (1991), 'Exporting the Educational Revolution: The Cuban Project to Become a World Educational Power', in H. M. Erisman and J. M. Kirk, *Cuban Foreign Policy Confronts a New International Order*, pp. 167–81, Boulder, CO: Lynne Rienner Publishers.

Ritter, A. R. M. (1974), *The Economic Development of Revolutionary Cuba: Strategy and Economic Performance*, New York: Praeger.

Roa, R. (1964), *Retorno a la Alborada* (Vol. 1.), Santa Clara: Universidad Central de Las Villas.

Roca, S. G. (1976), *Cuban Economic Policy and Ideology: The Ten Million Ton Sugar Harvest*, Beverly Hills, CA: Sage.

—— (1986), 'State Enterprises in Cuba under the New System of Planning and Management (SDPE)', *Cuban Studies,* 16: 153–79.

—— (ed.) (1988), *Socialist Cuba: Past Interpretations and Future Challenges,* Boulder, CO and London: Westview Press.

Roig de Leuchsenring, E. (1937), 'El Movimiento Anexionista. Actitud de los Estados Unidos', *Cuadernos de la Historia Habanera,* 12 (June): 229–37.

Rojas, M. (1973), *La Generación del Centenario en el Juicio del Moncada* (3rd edn), Havana: Editorial de Ciencias Sociales.

Ruffin, P. (1990), *Capitalism and Socialism in Cuba. A Study of Dependency, Development and Underdevelopment*, London: Macmillan.

Ruiz, R. (1968), *Cuba: the Making of a Revolution*, Amherst, MA: University of Massachusetts Press.

Santí, E. M. (1996), *Pensar a José Martí. Notas para un Centenario.* Boulder, CO: Society of Spanish and Spanish-American Studies.

Santos, M. (1979), *The Shared Space: The Two Circuits of the Urban Economy in Underdeveloped Countries*, London and New York: Methuen.

Scheer, R. and Zeitlin, M. (1964), *Cuba. An American Tragedy*, Harmondsworth: Penguin Books.

Schmidt-Nowara, C. (1995a), '"Spanish" Cuba, Race and Class in Spanish and Cuban Anti-Slavery Ideology, 1861–1868', *Cuban Studies,* 25: 101–12.

—— (1995b), *The Problem of Slavery in the Age of Capital: Abolitionism, Liberalism, and Counter-Hegemony in Spain, Cuba and Puerto Rico, 1833–1886*, Ph.D. (UMI Dissertation Services), Ann Arbor, MI.: University of Michigan.

Schons, D. (1926), 'Some Obscure Points in the Life of Sor Juana Inés de la Cruz', *Modern Philology*, 24 (2, November): 158.

Schwartz, R. (1989), *Lawless Liberators: Political Banditry and Cuban Independence*, Durham, NC: Duke University Press.

Scott, R. J. (1985), *Slave Emancipation in Cuba: The Transition to Free Labor 1860–1899*, Princeton, NJ: Princeton University Press.

Seers, D. (ed.) (1964), *Cuba, the Economic and Social Revolution*, Chapel Hill, NC: University of North Carolina Press.

Segré, R., Coyula, M. and Scarpaci, J. L. (1997), *Havana. Two Faces of the Antillean Metropolis*, Chichester, New York, Weinheim, Brisbane, Singapore, Toronto: John Wiley & Sons.

Shearman, P. (1987), *The Soviet Union and Cuba*, London, New York and Andover: The Royal Institute of International Affairs/Routledge & Kegan Paul.

—— (1990), 'Gorbachev and the Restructuring of Soviet–Cuban Relations', in R. Gillespie (ed.), *Cuba after Thirty Years: Rectification and the Revolution*, pp. 63–83, London: Frank Cass.

Silverman, B. (1971), *Man and Socialism in Cuba*, New York: Atheneum Press.

Simpson, R. (1984), *La Educación Superior en Cuba bajo el Colonialismo Español*, Havana: Editorial de Ciencias Sociales.

Skocpol, T. (1988), *States and Social Revolutions*, Cambridge and London: Cambridge University Press.

Smith, W. (1987), *The Closest of Enemies*, New York: Norton.

Sorel, G. (1969), *The Illusions of Progress* (reprint), Berkeley, CA: University of California Press.

Soto, L. (1985a), *La Revolución del 33* (Vol. 1), Havana: Editorial Pueblo y Educación.

—— (1985b), *La Revolución del 33* (Vol. 3), Havana: Editorial Pueblo y Educación.

Stein, E. C. (1962), *Cuba, Castro and Communism*, New York: MacFadden Books.

Stokes, W. S. (1951), 'The "Cuban Revolution" and the Presidential Elections of 1948', *Hispanic American Historical Review*, 31 (1: February): 37–79.

Stubbs, J. (1985), *Tobacco in the Periphery. A Case Study in Cuban Labour History, 1860–1958*, Cambridge, New York, Melbourne: Cambridge University Press.

—— (1989), *Cuba: The Test of Time*, London: Latin America Bureau.

Suárez, A. (1967), *Cuba, Castroism and Communism, 1959–1966*, Cambridge, MA & London: The MIT Press.

Suárez, N. (ed.) (1996), *Fernando Ortiz y la Cubanidad*, Havana: Fundación Fernando Ortiz, Ediciones Unión.

Suchlicki, J. (ed.) (1972), *Cuba, Castro and Revolution*, Coral Gables, FL: University of Miami Press.

—— (1988), *Historical Dictionary of Cuba*, Latin American Historical Dictionaries, No. 22, Metuchen, NJ and London: The Scarecrow Press, Inc.

Szulc, T. (1986), *Fidel. A Critical Portrait*, London, Melbourne, Auckland, Johannesburg: Hutchinson.

Tabares del Real, J. (1973), *La Revolución del 30: Sus Dos Ultimos Años*, Havana: Editorial de Ciencias Sociales.

—— (1998), 'Proceso Revolucionario: Ascenso y Reflujo (1930–1935)', in Instituto de Historia de Cuba (ed.), *Historia de Cuba (Vol. II – La Neocolonia. Organización y Crisis desde 1899 hasta 1940)*, pp. 282–335, Havana: Instituto de Historia de Cuba.

Taber, R. (1974), *The War of the Flea. A Study of Guerrilla Warfare – Theory and Practice*, St Albans: Paladin.

Thomas, H. (1971), *Cuba, or the Pursuit of Freedom*, London: Eyre & Spottiswoode.

—— (1977–8), 'Cuba in Africa', *Survey*, 23 (No. 4): 181–88.

Toroella, G. (1963), *Estudio de la Juventud Cubana*, Havana: Comisión Nacional Cubana de la UNESCO.

Torres-Cuevas, E. (1995a), 'En Busca de la Cubanidad', *Debates Americanos*, 1: 2–17.

—— (1995b), *Antonio Maceo. Las Ideas que Sostienen el Arma*, Havana: Editorial de Ciencias Sociales.

—— (1997), *Felix Varela. Los Orígenes de la Ciencia y Con-ciencia Cubanas*, Havana: Editorial de Ciencias Sociales.

Torres Vila, C. and Pérez-Rojas, N. (1998), 'La Apertura de los Mercados Agropecuarios en Cuba: Impacto y Valoraciones', in J. Moreno, *et al.* (eds), *Cuba: Período Especial. Perspectivas* pp. 148–86, Havana: Editorial de Ciencias Sociales.

Treverton, G. F. (1977), 'Cuba after Angola', *The World Today*, 33 (No. 1, January): 17–27.

Tsokhas, K. (1980), 'The Political Economy of Cuban Dependence on the Soviet Union' *Theory and Society*, 9 (No. 2, March): 319–62.

Tulchin, J. B. and Hernández, R. (eds) (1991), *Will the Cold War in the Caribbean End?*, Woodrow Wilson Center, Current Studies on Latin America, Boulder, CO and London: Lynne Rienner Publishers.

Turton, P. (1986), *José Martí. Architect of Cuba's Freedom*, London: Zed Press Ltd.

Ubieta Gómez, E. (1993), *Ensayos de Identidad*, Havana: Editorial Letras Cubanas.

Urrutia, M. (1964), *Fidel Castro and Company Inc: Communist Tyranny in Cuba*, New York: Frederick A. Praeger.

Valdés, N. P. (1971), 'Health and Revolution in Cuba', *Science and Society*, 35 (Part 3, Fall): 311–35.

—— (1972), 'The Radical Transformation of Cuban Education', in R. E. Bonachea and N. P. Valdés (eds), *Cuba in Revolution*, pp. 422–55, Garden City, NY: Anchor Books, Doubleday & Company Inc.

—— (1975), *Ideological Roots of the Cuban Revolutionary Movement*, Occasional Papers No. 15, Glasgow: University of Glasgow, Institute of Latin American Studies.

—— (1992), 'Cuban Political Culture – Between Betrayal and Death', in S. Halebsky, and J. M. Kirk (eds), *Cuba in Transition. Crisis and Transformation*, pp. 207–28, Boulder, CO, San Francisco, Oxford: Westview.

Valenta, J. (1978), 'The Soviet–Cuban Intervention in Angola', *Studies in Comparative Communism*, 11 (1–2, Spring–Summer): 3–34.

Vignier, E. and Alonso, G. (eds) (1973), *La Corrupción Política Administrativa en Cuba, 1944–1952*, Havana: Editorial de Ciencias Sociales.

Weinstein, M. (ed.) (1979), *Revolutionary Cuba in the World Arena*, Philadelphia, PA: Institute for the Study of Human Issues.

Weyl, N. (1960), *Red Star over Cuba: Russian Assault on the Western Hemisphere*, New York: Devin-Adair.

Williams, W. A. (1962), *The United States, Cuba and Castro*, New York: Monthly Review Press.

Wright, A. (1988), 'Intellectuals of an Unheroic Period of Cuban History, 1913–1923: The "Cuba Contemporánea" Group', *Bulletin of Latin American Research*, 7 (No. 1): 109–22.

Yeats, W. B. (1974), 'He Wishes for the Cloths of Heaven', in A. N. Jeffares, *W. B. Yeats. Selected Poetry*, p. 35, London: Pan Books Ltd.

Yglesias, J. (1970), *In the Fist of the Revolution*, Harmondsworth: Penguin Books.

Zanetti, O. and García, A. (1987), *Sugar and Railroads. A Cuban History, 1837–1959*, Chapel Hill, NC and London: University of North Carolina Press.

Zeitlin, M. (1970a), *Revolutionary Politics and the Cuban Working Class*, New York, Evanston and London: Harper & Row Publishers.

—— (1970b), 'Cuba – Revolution without a Blueprint,' in I. L. Horowitz (ed.), *Cuban Communism*, pp. 117–29, New Brunswick, NJ: Transaction Books Inc.

Zimbalist, A. (ed.) (1987), *Cuba's Socialist Economy Towards the 1990s*, Boulder, CO: Lynne Rienner.

Zimbalist, A. and Brundenius, C. (1989), *The Cuban Economy: Measurement and Analysis of Socialist Performance*, Baltimore, MD: Johns Hopkins University Press.

Index

Index

Printed in the United Kingdom
by Lightning Source UK Ltd.
108396UKS00002BA/1-12